OPIc의 정석! IH공략

OPIc의 정석! IH공략 (개정판)

초　 판　1쇄 발행　2012년 5월 31일
개 정 판　1쇄 인쇄　2014년 4월 17일
　　　　 2쇄 인쇄　2014년 12월 16일
개정2판　1쇄 인쇄　2016년 7월 12일

저자　멀티캠퍼스 외국어연구소
기획　멀티캠퍼스 외국어연구소

펴낸이　박민우
기획팀　송인성, 김선명, 박민하, 박종인
편집팀　박우진, 김영주, 김정아, 최미라
관리팀　임선희, 정철호, 김성언, 권주련
펴낸곳　멀티캠퍼스 하우
주소　서울시 중랑구 망우로68길 48
전화　(02)922-7090
팩스　(02)922-7092
홈페이지　http://www.hawoo.co.kr
e-mail　hawoo@hawoo.co.kr
등록번호　제2014-18호

값　18,000원
ISBN 979-11-955278-8-5 13740

Copyright ⓒ 2016 by Multicampus Co., Ltd.

All rights reserved.
No part of this publication may be reproduced, stored in a retrieval system,
or transmitted in any form or by any means, electronic, mechanical, photocopying, recording,
or otherwise, without the prior permission of the publisher.

이 책은 저작권법에 따라 보호받는 저작물이므로 무단전재와 무단복제를 금지하며,
이 책 내용의 전부 또는 일부를 이용하려면 반드시 저작권자와 출판권자의 서면 동의를 받아야 합니다.

 모범답변 MP3 다운로드 www.opic.co.kr 접속 후 '북&앱북'에서 다운로드

멀티캠퍼스 외국어연구소 저

머리말

OPIc 시험에서 IH, AL과 같은 고득점을 받기 위해서 여러분들은 어떤 노력을 하고 계신가요? 주요 빈출 어휘와 패턴을 암기하고 계신가요? 아니면 모범 답안을 토시 하나 틀리지 않고 주야장천 외우고 있나요? 이 두 방법 모두 틀렸습니다. 단순히 많은 문장을 암기하는 것으로는 OPIc에서 고득점을 받기란 불가능합니다. 그렇다면, 어떻게 학습을 해야 할까요? 바로 핵심은 '스토리텔링'과 '응용'입니다.

스토리텔링이라고 하는 것은 말 그대로 이야기를 만드는 것입니다. 그렇다고 이야기를 허무맹랑하고 두서없이 만들어서는 안 되죠. 스토리텔링에서 중요한 점은 기-승-전-결, 서론-본론-결론으로 이어지는 이야기의 흐름입니다. OPIc 시험은 단순히 여러분의 발음, 문법을 평가하는 것이 아니라 여러분들이 자신, 또는 주변의 이야기를 얼마나 논리적으로 자연스럽고 풍부하게 할 수 있는지를 평가합니다. 그러므로 단순히 모범 답변을 외우는 것이 아니라, 여러분의 이야기를 해당 질문에 맞게끔 구성하여 말하는 연습이 필요합니다.

두 번째로 OPIc 시험에서 고득점을 받기 위한 전략으로 '응용'이 중요하다고 했습니다. 하나의 문장 구조를 한 가지 주제, 한 가지 답변에만 적용하는 것이 아니라 여러 주제에서 다양하게 활용하여 풍부한 답변을 만드는 전략이 필요합니다. 또한, 하나의 주제에 대해 제한된 표현으로 답변을 하게 되면 전체적으로 진부해질 수 있고 채점자들로 하여금 영어 사용 능력이 제한적이라는 인상을 줄 수 있기 때문에 특정 어휘, 구문을 다양한 표현으로 구사할 수 있는 연습도 이 '응용'에 포함됩니다.

이 책은 '스토리텔링'과 '응용' 전략을 통해 여러분들이 단순히 답변을 암기하던 습관에서 벗어나 실제로 여러분들만의 답변을 구성하는 방법을 가르쳐주기 위해 쓰여졌으며 다음과 같이 구성되어 있습니다.

1. 최신 OPIc 트렌드를 반영한 주제 구성

OPIc 시험은 Background Survey를 기반으로 한 개인 맞춤형 시험입니다. 시험 전 본인이 선택한 관심사를 중점으로 질문이 출제되나, OPIc 시험에서 고득점을 받기 위해서는 본인이 선택하지 않은 주제에 대해서도 답변을 할 줄 알아야 합니다. 시험의 난이도가 높아질수록 이 돌발 주제들이 더 많이 나오는 경향이 있습니다. 우리 책은 기본 Background Survey 주제와 돌발 주제를 나누어 구성하여, 자주 출제되는 돌발 주제에도 답변을 할 수 있도록 구성되었습니다. 더불어, 최근 시험이 콤보 문제로 출제되고 있는 경향에 따라 모든 주제를 콤보 유형으로 구성하여, 실제 시험에 대비할 수 있도록 하였습니다.

2. IDEA FLOW를 통한 답변 구성 전략

이 책에 수록된 모범 답변들은 서론-본론-결론의 논리적인 연계성을 가지며, 각 항목에는 구체적으로 어떤 내용이 포함되어 있는지 도표로 정리되어 있습니다. IDEA FLOW를 활용해 답변을 구성하는 연습을 통해 암기식의 학습에서 벗어나, 해당 주제에 대해 논리적인 답변을 구사하기 위해서는 어떠한 내용이 들어가야 하는지에 대해 주체적으로 학습할 수 있습니다. 뿐만 아니라 시험을 앞두고 있다면, IDEA FLOW만 보고 답변 구상의 아이디어를 얻어갈 수도 있습니다.

3. 연습 문제를 통한 자주적 학습 독려

이 책은 3개의 콤보 문제로 이루어진 20개의 주제와 두 개의 모의고사 세트로 구성되어 있습니다. 20개의 레슨에 해당하는 총 60개의 문제에는 여러분들이 직접 IDEA FLOW를 구성하고 답변을 할 수 있는 연습 활동이 있고, 책의 부록으로 각각의 문제의 주요 구문과 답변을 복습해 볼 수 있는 연습 활동도 있습니다. 이를 통해, 여러분들은 하나의 질문에 대해 여러 번 복습, 예습하여 진정한 여러분의 답변을 만들 수 있을 것입니다.

이 책을 통해, OPIc 시험에서 좋은 등급을 획득하는 것을 넘어 여러분들이 영어로 대화를 하거나 업무를 할 때, 영어로 논리적으로 사고하는 법을 배워 실질적인 영어 말하기 실력을 높일 수 있기를 희망합니다.

저자 드림

목차

- 머리말 — 4
- 목차 — 6
- 이 책의 구성과 특징 — 8
- OPIc 시험 소개 — 10
- Background Survey — 12
- OPIc FAQ — 14
- OPIc 고득점 전략 — 16

Lesson 1 직장 1 – 회사 소개 — 18

Lesson 2 직장 2 – 사내 업무 및 연수 — 30

Lesson 3 학생 생활 소개하기 — 42

Lesson 4 뉴스를 보거나 듣기 NEW — 54

Lesson 5 콘서트보기 — 66

Lesson 6 체스하기 NEW — 78

Lesson 7 시험 대비 과정 수강하기 NEW — 90

Lesson 8 카페/커피전문점 가기 NEW — 102

Lesson 9 악기 연주하기 — 114

Lesson 10 신문 읽기 NEW — 126

Lesson 11 주식투자하기 NEW	138
Lesson 12 사진 촬영하기 NEW	150
Lesson 13 재활용 돌발	162
Lesson 14 전화 통화 돌발	174
Lesson 15 집안일 거들기 돌발	186
Lesson 16 테크놀로지 돌발	198
Lesson 17 지역 행사 돌발	210
Lesson 18 국내여행	222
Lesson 19 해외출장	234
Lesson 20 해외여행	246
Actual Test 1	258
Actual Test 2	274
본문 해석	290
Actual Test 1 해석	306
Actual Test 2 해석	310
Supplementary Materials	316

이 책의
구성과 특징

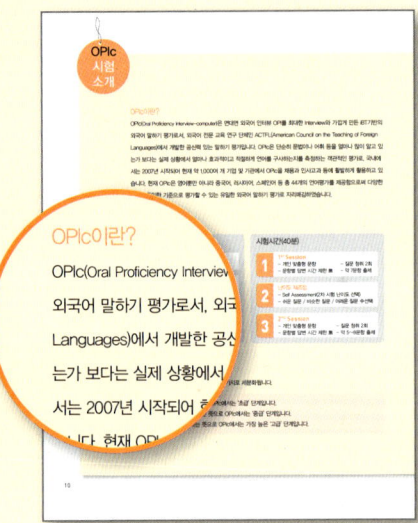

◀ OPIc 소개
본 학습에 들어가기 앞서, OPIc 시험에 대해 알 수 있습니다. Background Survey를 미리 확인하여 시험에 대비하기 용이합니다. 또한, OPIc에서 고득점을 획득할 수 있는 전략을 알려드립니다.

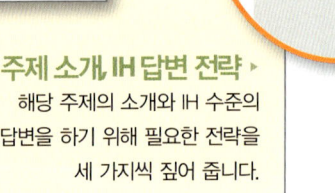

주제 소개, IH 답변 전략 ▶
해당 주제의 소개와 IH 수준의 답변을 하기 위해 필요한 전략을 세 가지씩 짚어 줍니다.

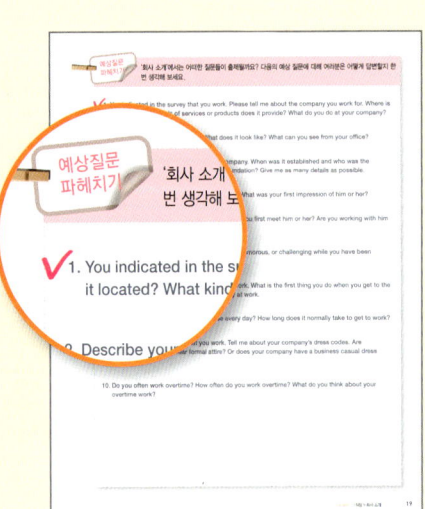

◀ 예상질문 파헤치기
해당 주제에서 빈번하게 출제될 수 있는 예상 질문을 보여줍니다. 예상 질문에 대해 답변을 스스로 만들어보는 연습을 할 수 있습니다.

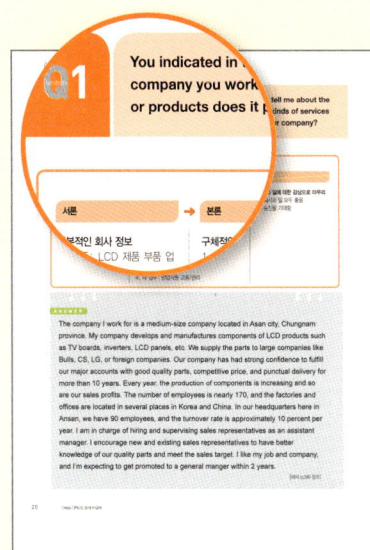

◀ Question

해당 주제의 대표 문제 3개를 골라, 답변을 구성하는 방법을 IDEA FLOW와 모범 답변을 통해 알아볼 수 있습니다.

IH 답변 파헤치기 ▶

모범 답변에서 나온 다양한 문장 구조나 어휘를 설명과 예시를 통해 학습할 수 있습니다. 더불어, 답변을 구성할 때 사용할 수 있는 다양한 응용 문장들도 제시하여 풍부한 답변을 할 수 있습니다.

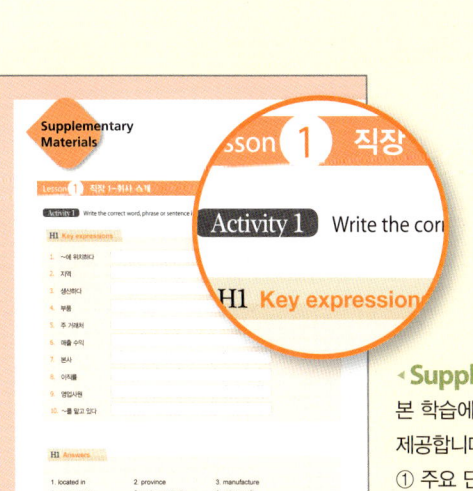

◀ Supplementary materials

본 학습에서 다룬 3개의 대표 문제에 대해 복습해볼 수 있는 부가 학습 자료를 제공합니다. 3가지 형태로 제시됩니다.
① 주요 단어 및 구문 작문해보기
② 문장 내 주요 구문 빈칸 채우기
③ 5개의 질문에 한 문장으로 답변한 내용을 조합하여 하나의 이야기를 만들기

이 복습 활동을 통해 주요 패턴을 익히고 OPIc 답변을 구성해보는 연습을 할 수 있습니다.

OPIc란?

OPIc(Oral Proficiency Interview-computer)은 면대면 외국어 인터뷰 OPI를 최대한 Interview와 가깝게 만든 iBT기반의 외국어 말하기 평가로서, 외국어 전문 교육 연구 단체인 ACTFL(American Council on the Teaching of Foreign Languages)에서 개발한 공신력 있는 말하기 평가입니다. OPIc은 단순히 문법이나 어휘 등을 얼마나 많이 알고 있는가 보다는 실제 상황에서 얼마나 효과적이고 적절하게 언어를 구사하는지를 측정하는 객관적인 평가로, 국내에서는 2007년 시작되어 현재 약 1,000여 개 기업 및 기관에서 OPIc을 채용과 인사고과 등에 활발하게 활용하고 있습니다. 현재 OPIc은 영어뿐만 아니라 중국어, 러시아어, 스페인어 등 총 44개의 언어평가를 제공함으로써 다양한 언어를 동일한 기준으로 평가할 수 있는 유일한 외국어 말하기 평가로 자리매김하였습니다.

OPIc 진행과정

ORIENTATION(약 15분)

1. **Background Survey**
   인터뷰 문항을 위한 사전 설문
2. **Self Assessment**
   시험의 난이도 결정을 위한 자가 평가
3. **Overview of OPIc**
   화면 구성, 문항 청취 및 답변 방법 안내
4. **Sample Question**
   실제 답변 방법 연습

시험시간(40분)

1. **1st Session**
   - 개인 맞춤형 문항
   - 질문 청취 2회
   - 문항별 답변 시간 제한 無
   - 약 7문항 출제
2. **난이도 재조정**
   - Self Assessment(2차 시험 난이도 선택)
   - 쉬운 질문 / 비슷한 질문 / 어려운 질문 中선택
3. **2nd Session**
   - 개인 맞춤형 문항
   - 질문 청취 2회
   - 문항별 답변 시간 제한 無
   - 약 5~8문항 출제

OPIc 등급

OPIc의 등급은 크게 세 가지, 작게는 일곱 가지로 세분화됩니다.

- Novice: '초보자'라는 뜻으로 OPIc에서는 '초급' 단계입니다.
- Intermediate: '중간'이라는 뜻으로 OPIc에서는 '중급' 단계입니다.
- Advanced: '고급의'라는 뜻으로 OPIc에서는 가장 높은 '고급' 단계입니다.

이 세 가지의 등급을 세분화해서 다음과 같이 구분하게 됩니다.

- Novice Low, Novice Mid, Novice High
- Intermediate Low, Intermediate Mid(1~3), Intermediate High
- Advanced Low

OPIc의 모체인 OPI에서는 Advanced도 Low, Mid, High로 구분되지만, 컴퓨터로 시험을 보는 OPIc에서는 Advanced Low라는 등급 하나만 부여됩니다.

사건을 서술할 때 일괄적으로 동사 시제를 관리하고, 사람과 사물을 묘사할 때 다양한 형용사를 사용한다. 적절한 위치에서 접속사를 사용하기 때문에 문장 간의 결속력도 높고 문단의 구조를 능숙하게 구성할 수 있다.
익숙하지 않은 복잡한 상황에서도 문제를 설명하고 해결할 수 있는 수준의 능숙도이다.

개인에게 익숙하지 않거나 예측하지 못한 복잡한 상황을 만날 때, 대부분의 상황에서 사건을 설명하고 문제를 효과적으로 해결한다. 발화량이 많고, 다양한 어휘를 사용한다.

일상적인 소재뿐 아니라 개인적으로 익숙한 상황에서는 문장을 나열하며 자연스럽게 말할 수 있다. 다양한 문장 형식이나 어휘를 실험적으로 사용하려고 하며 상대방이 조금만 배려해 주면 오랜 시간 대화가 가능하다.

일상적인 소재에서는 문장으로 말할 수 있다. 대화에 참여하고 선호하는 소재에서는 자신감을 가지고 말할 수 있다.

일상적인 대부분의 소재에 대해서 문장으로 말할 수 있다.
개인 정보라면 질문을 하고 응답을 할 수 있다.

이미 암기한 단어나 문장으로 말하기를 할 수 있다.

제한적인 수준이지만 영어 단어를 나열하며 말할 수 있다.

＊ Intermediate Mid의 경우 Mid 1, Mid 2, Mid 3로 세분화하여 제공합니다.

Background Survey
배경설문

OPIc의 개인 맞춤형 문제는 Background Survey에 대한 응답을 기초로 출제됩니다. 나에게는 어떤 맞춤형 문제가 출제될지 미리 생각해 보세요.

1 현재 귀하는 어느 분야에 종사하고 계십니까?
☐ 사업/회사   ☐ 재택근무/재택사업   ☐ 교사/교육자   ☐ 군 복무   ☐ 일 경험 없음

1.1. 현재 귀하는 직업이 있으십니까?
☐ 네   ☐ 아니오

1.1.1. 귀하의 근무 기간은 얼마나 되십니까?
☐ 첫 직장 – 2개월 미만   ☐ 첫 직장 – 2개월 이상   ☐ 첫 직장 아님 – 경험 많음

1.1.1.1. 당신은 부하 직원을 관리하는 관리직을 맡고 있습니까?
☐ 네   ☐ 아니오

문항 1에서 교사/교육자로 답변했을 경우

1.1. 당신은 어디에서 학생을 가르치십니까?
☐ 대학 이상   ☐ 초등/중/고등학교   ☐ 평생교육

1.1.1. 귀하의 근무 기간은 얼마나 되십니까?
☐ 2개월 미만 – 첫 직장
☐ 2개월 미만 – 교직은 처음이지만 이전에 다른 직업을 가진 적이 있음
☐ 2개월 이상

---

2 현재 귀하는 학생이십니까?
☐ 네   ☐ 아니오

2.1. 현재 어떤 강의를 듣고 있습니까?
☐ 학위 과정 수업   ☐ 전문 기술 향상을 위한 평생 학습   ☐ 어학 수업

2.2. 최근 어떤 강의를 수강했습니까?
☐ 학위 과정 수업
☐ 전문 기술 향상을 위한 평생 학습
☐ 어학 수업
☐ 수업 등록 후 5년 이상 지남

3 현재 귀하는 어디에 살고 계십니까?
☐ 개인주택이나 아파트에 홀로 거주
☐ 친구나 룸메이트와 함께 주택이나 아파트에 거주
☐ 가족(배우자/자녀/기타 가족 일원)과 함께 주택이나 아파트에 거주
☐ 학교 기숙사   ☐ 군대 막사

아래의 4~7번 문항에서 12개 이상을 선택해 주시기 바랍니다.

4 귀하는 여가 활동으로 주로 무엇을 하십니까? (두 개 이상 선택)
☐ 영화 보기   ☐ 클럽/나이트클럽 가기   ☐ 공연 보기   ☐ 콘서트 보기
☐ 박물관 가기   ☐ 공원 가기   ☐ 캠핑하기   ☐ 해변 가기
☐ 스포츠 관람   ☐ 주거 개선   ☐ 술집/바에 가기   ☐ 카페/커피전문점 가기
☐ 게임하기(비디오, 카드, 보드, 휴대폰 등)   ☐ 당구 치기   ☐ 체스하기
☐ SNS에 글 올리기   ☐ 친구들과 문자대화하기   ☐ 시험 대비 과정 수강하기
☐ TV보기   ☐ 리얼리티쇼 시청하기   ☐ 뉴스를 보거나 듣기
☐ 요리 관련 프로그램 시청하기   ☐ 쇼핑하기
☐ 차로 드라이브하기   ☐ 스파/마사지샵 가기   ☐ 구직활동하기   ☐ 자원봉사하기

5 귀하의 취미나 관심사는 무엇입니까? (한 개 이상 선택)
☐ 아이에게 책 읽어주기   ☐ 음악 감상하기   ☐ 악기 연주하기   ☐ 춤추기
☐ 글쓰기(편지, 단문, 시 등)   ☐ 그림그리기   ☐ 요리하기   ☐ 애완동물 기르기
☐ 독서   ☐ 주식 투자하기   ☐ 신문 읽기   ☐ 여행 관련 잡지나 블로그 읽기
☐ 사진 촬영하기   ☐ 혼자 노래 부르거나 합창하기

6 귀하는 주로 어떤 운동을 즐기십니까? (한 개 이상 선택)
☐ 농구   ☐ 야구/소프트볼   ☐ 축구   ☐ 미식축구
☐ 하키   ☐ 크리켓   ☐ 골프   ☐ 배구
☐ 테니스   ☐ 배드민턴   ☐ 탁구   ☐ 수영
☐ 자전거   ☐ 스키/스노우보드   ☐ 아이스 스케이트   ☐ 조깅
☐ 걷기   ☐ 요가   ☐ 하이킹/트레킹   ☐ 낚시
☐ 헬스   ☐ 태권도   ☐ 운동 수업 수강하기   ☐ 운동을 전혀 하지 않음

7 당신은 어떤 휴가나 출장을 다녀온 경험이 있습니까? (한 개 이상 선택)
☐ 국내 출장   ☐ 해외 출장   ☐ 집에서 보내는 휴가   ☐ 국내 여행   ☐ 해외여행

OPIc FAQ

01 OPIc 시험 중 필기구를 사용하여 답변을 준비해도 되나요?

OPIc 응시자는 필기구를 가지고 시험장에 입실할 수 없습니다. 따라서 시험 중에 필기구를 이용하여 메모 등을 하실 수 없으며, 적발 시 부정행위로 처리되어 OPIc 시험 규정에 따라 향후 시험 응시 기회에 제한을 받습니다.

02 무조건 길게 말하는 것이 도움이 되나요?

짜임새 없는 내용으로 길게만 말하는 것보다는 질문이 요구하는 내용에 충실한 답변을 정확한 문법과 표현을 사용하여 논리적으로 표현할 때 좋은 평가를 받을 수 있습니다. 또한 기-승-전-결 혹은 서론-본론-결론의 짜임새 있는 구성으로 답변해야 합니다. 공식적인 수치는 아니지만, 주어진 시간 내 모든 문제에 풍부한 내용으로 답변을 하려면 한 문항당 짧으면 1분, 일반적으로 2분에서 2분 30초 이상 말할 수 있도록 준비하는 것이 좋습니다.

03 Background Survey 응답 내용대로만 출제되나요?

아닙니다. 시험 전에 체크한 Background Survey 결과는 나에게 맞는 맞춤형 문항이 출제되는 데 영향을 주지만, 그 외 시스템으로 선별된 문항도 출제됩니다. 즉, 여러분이 선택하지 않은 내용에서도 문제가 출제됩니다. 일반적으로 여러분의 일상생활에서 일어나는 일들을 위주로 문제가 출제되며 전문적인 내용이 출제되더라도 일상생활과 연결되어 있는 질문들이 출제됩니다. OPIc 등급 향상을 위해서는 Background Survey 항목에 관련된 답변만을 무조건 외우기보다는 평소에 다양한 말하기 연습을 하는 것이 도움이 될 것입니다.

04 OPIc 문제 중 Background Survey 내용과 관련이 없는 내용이 나오면 답변하지 않아도 되나요?

아닙니다. 수험자는 주어진 문항에 대해서 모두 답변을 진행해야 합니다. OPIc은 Background Survey를 통해 수험자의 개인 맞춤형 문항의 출제가 가능하지만 다른 영역의 질문 또한 출제되어 수험자가 예상하지 못한 문제에 대한 상황 대처능력 및 순발력 또한 평가합니다. 따라서, 질문에 대한 답변이 진행되지 않는 경우 감점의 요인이 될 수 있습니다. 그러므로 답변할 때 모르는 문제가 나왔다고 해서 당황해서는 안 됩니다. 설령, 여러분이 Background Survey에서 선택한 내용과 다른 문제가 출제되더라도 최선을 다해 성실하게 답변하는 것이 좋습니다.

05 시험 보는 중간에 Self Assessment로 레벨을 변경하는 것이 성적에 영향이 있나요?

처음에 높은 레벨로 시작했다가 중간에 낮은 레벨로 바꾸거나, 그 반대로 낮은 레벨에서 시작해서 높은 레벨로 바꾸는 그 자체로 성적이 바뀌지는 않습니다. 철저히 주어진 답변에 얼마나 충실하게 답변했는지가 성적을 좌우한다고 보면 됩니다. 그러나, 나의 영어실력과 너무 동떨어진 레벨을 선택하는 것은 바람직하지 않습니다.

06 문제를 반복해서 들으면 성적이 좋지 않게 나오는 것이 사실인가요?

문제 풀기 전략 중 하나로 문제를 습관적으로 반복해서 듣는 사람들이 있습니다. 문제를 반복 청취하는 것이 성적에 직접적으로 영향을 미치는 것은 아니지만, 문제를 반복 청취했을 때 답변 시간이 줄어들 수 밖에 없으므로, 시간 관리에 어려움을 느낄 수도 있습니다. OPIc 문제의 답변 시간은 질문 청취 시간을 제외하고 약 35분 가량입니다. 따라서 주어진 시간 내 모든 문제에 효율적으로 답변할 수 있도록 시간을 활용해야 합니다.

07 발음이 안 좋거나 더듬거리면 성적에 나쁜 영향을 주게 되나요?

발음은 이해가 가능한 수준일 경우 크게 영향을 미치지 않는 것으로 알려져 있습니다. 그러나 메시지 전달이 안 될 정도로 말을 매끄럽지 못하게 할 경우에는 당연히 채점이 어려울 수밖에 없습니다.

08 OPIc 시험은 현장에서 결과를 직접 확인할 수 있나요?

OPIc 정기 시험은 시험 응시일로부터 7일 후 자정부터 OPIc 홈페이지(www.opic.or.kr)에서 성적 확인이 가능합니다. 예) 8월 6일 시험 응시 → 8월 12일에서 8월 13일로 넘어가는 00:00부터 성적 확인 가능
※성적 확인 및 인증서 출력은 회원 전용 서비스이므로 회원 가입 필요

09 OPIc 시험 일정은 1년에 몇 번 정도 있나요?

OPIc 시험은 일반적으로 월 6회(수요일, 일요일) 있으며 채용 시즌에는 매일 정기 시험을 진행 합니다. 또한 강남 오피스퀘어 센터에서는 채용 시즌 외에도 주중에 3일 이상 시험이 시행되고 있습니다. 자세한 내용은 OPIc 홈페이지(www.opic.or.kr)를 확인해주시기 바랍니다.

10 성적이 UR이라고 나오는 것은 무엇을 의미하나요?

"UR"은 unable to rate를 의미합니다. UR이 나오는 경우는 녹음 불량, 녹음 음량이 너무 작은 경우, 수험자가 자신이 없어 답변을 하지 않은 경우입니다. 수험자의 과실인 경우 응시료 환불은 없으며 재시험의 기회도 없습니다. 시스템적인 오류로 UR이 나왔을 경우 한 번의 재시험 기회를 드립니다.

11 시험에 필요한 규정 신분증이 무엇인가요?

OPIc 시험에서 인정되는 규정 신분증은 주민등록증, 운전면허증, 기간만료 전 여권 등이며, 사원증 및 학생증, 기타 자격증은 신분증으로 인정되지 않습니다.

01 예상 문제, 예상 답변 준비하기

OPIc은 서베이에 표시를 한 것만 출제되는 시험은 아니기 때문에 예상 문제를 100% 딱 맞게 준비할 수는 없습니다. 하지만 자기소개, 회사와 학교 생활, 악기, 영화, 여행 등과 같이 출제가능성이 매우 높은 문제들이 많습니다. 예상 문제를 뽑아서 그에 맞는 답변을 미리 준비해 연습한 후 시험에 응하면 자신감 있고 편안하게 말할 수 있을 것입니다.

02 자신이 익숙하지 않거나 경험해보지 않은 항목에도 과감하게 도전하기

OPIc은 물론 서베이에 표시한 항목에 근거하여 질문이 출제되지만 그렇다고 항상 표시한 것만 나오는 것은 아닙니다. 예를 들어 여가활동에서 게임(보드, 카드 등)을 선택했는데 체스가 나올 수도 있고 운동 항목에서 농구를 선택했는데 태권도가 나오는 돌발상황들이 발생합니다. OPIc을 준비하면서 평소 알지 못했던 새로운 분야를 배워본다는 적극적인 마인드로 약간 어렵겠다 싶은 항목을 용감하게 도전해 보세요.

03 새로운 어휘나 표현은 꼭 문장으로 익히기

새로운 어휘와 표현을 많이 익혀두는 것은 좋은데, 실제 그 어휘로 문장을 만들려고 하면 어려움을 느끼시는 분들이 많습니다. 어떤 어휘나 표현을 접하시더라도 꼭 문장에 활용을 해서 실질적으로 사용할 수 있도록 해야 합니다.

04 문단 단위로 연습하기

답변을 준비할 때는 2~3문장의 짧은 문단이라도 좋으니 문단 단위로 연습하는 것이 좋습니다. 우선 주제문이라 할 수 있는 핵심 문장을 만들어 놓고 그 문장을 중심으로 두 세 문장을 추가하여 하나의 문단을 만들어보세요. 단 문장들끼리는 내용적으로 서로 연결이 되어 있어야 합니다.

05 질문에서 주어진 주제에 집중하기

간혹 발화량은 많은데 그 내용을 보면 질문이 요구하는 답변이 아닌 경우가 있습니다. 이는 주제에서 벗어난 답변으로 산만한 느낌과 응집력 부족으로 좋은 점수를 받기 어렵습니다. 질문에서 묻고 있는 바를 정확히 파악하여 그에 적합한 답변을 해야겠습니다.

06 답변은 되도록 구체적으로 하기

간단한 질문이라도 답변은 자세하고 구체적으로 해주는 것이 좋습니다. 예를 들어 회사나 카페, 공연장 등의 장소 묘사는 외부에서 내부로 정돈되게 묘사를 하되, 크고 작다라는 단순묘사나 아름답다라는 추상적인 묘사에 그칠 게 아니라 무대와 객석 사이의 거리, 가구 배치, 내부 장식품 등 그 장소만이 가진 특징을 구체적으로 묘사해주는 것이 바람직합니다. 또한 좋아하는 여행지에 대한 답변을 할 때도 여행지 이름만 밝힐 것이 아니라 언제, 누구와, 어떻게, 왜 갔는지를 간단히 언급한 후 그 여행지에 대한 자세한 외관묘사 및 감상을 포함한 답변을 해야 진정한 말하기 실력을 보여줄 수 있는 것이라 하겠습니다.

07 정확한 문법 구사하기

가끔 말하기에서 유창성(fluency)만을 중요시해 언어의 정확성(accuracy)을 소홀히 하는 경우가 있는데 이것은 정말 잘못된 생각입니다. 실제로 말이나 글 모두에서 감독자나 평가자가 답변자의 글이나 말을 접하면서 가장 힘들어하는 부분이 문법적 실수라고 할 만큼 문법적 중요성은 의사소통의 결정적인 요소입니다. 예상 답변을 준비하는 과정에서 문법적 정확성에 주의를 기울여야 하겠습니다.

08 다양한 시제와 문장 구조 활용하기

OPIc IH 이상의 고득점을 획득하기 위해서는 단순 현재와 과거 시제에서 벗어나 현재완료나 과거완료, 현재완료 진행형 등 상황에 맞는 시제를 자유롭게 구사할 수 있어야 합니다. 특히 취미의 변천사 혹은 테크놀로지나 신문의 변천사와 같이 과거와 현재를 비교하면서 그 변화 과정을 설명해야 하는 경우 과거완료와 현재완료 시제는 제 몫을 톡톡히 할 수 있을 것입니다.

09 자신의 답변을 녹음해서 들어보기

자신이 말한 내용을 녹음해서 들어보면 어떤 점이 부족한지 빨리 깨닫고 보완점을 찾게 됩니다. 처음에는 어색하고 불편할 수 있겠지만 일단 시작해보시면 말하기 향상에 큰 도움이 될 것입니다.

10 무한 연습하기

너무나 당연한 말이겠지만 연습보다 더 좋은 전략은 없습니다. 세계 최고의 운동선수들이나 악기연주가들도 하루의 반 이상을 그것도 일년 내내 연습에 투자하고 있으니 연습의 중요성은 아무리 강조해도 부족함이 없을 듯 합니다. 위에서 말한 내용을 반영하여 여러 답변을 준비하고 그 답변들을 계속해서 말하는 연습을 하면 실제 시험에서 좋은 성적을 거두실 수 있을 것입니다.

Lesson 1 직장 1-회사 소개

Oral Proficiency Interview-computer

INTRO 직장인의 경우 자신의 회사나 업무 소개에 대한 문제들이 자주 출제됩니다. 회사 소개와 관련해서는 회사가 언제 설립되었고 주된 사업이 무엇이며 어떤 제품이나 서비스에 관련된 회사인지를 묻는 것에서부터 회사 건물이나 사무실의 묘사, 본사와 지사의 위치, 그리고 직원 규모 등에 이르기까지 다양한 문제들이 출제되고 있습니다. 특히 최근 OPIc에서 자주 제시되고 있는 변천사 과정, 즉 설립시기부터 현재까지 회사가 어떻게 발전되고 확장되었는지에 대한 질문에도 대비를 해놓아야 합니다.

IH 답변 전략

① 회사관련 정보 알아두기
- 회사의 이름, 설립 년도, 창립자, 사업 분야와 같은 기본적인 정보를 소개할 수 있어야 합니다.
- 회사 건물이나 사무실 모습과 같은 외형적 특징을 묘사할 수 있어야 합니다.
- 본사와 지사의 위치, 지사의 개수와 직원 수, 최근 매출 등과 같은 구체적인 정보를 알아둡니다.

② 회사 매출이나 발전과 관련된 구체적인 사항에 대한 답변 준비하기
- 현재 시장에서 차지하고 있는 회사의 위치나 영향력 등을 알려줄 수 있어야 합니다.
- 사업 분야의 확장이나 업종의 변화 등과 같은 회사의 변천 과정에 대해 서술할 수 있어야 합니다.
- 회사가 현재 계획하고 추진하고 있는 사업이나 매출 전략에 대한 설명을 준비합니다.

③ 직장생활을 하면서 겪었던 힘들었거나 보람 있었던 사건이나 상황을 생각해두기
- 입사 초기 때 겪었던 고충이나 업무 중 저지른 실수 등의 개인적인 경험을 묻는 질문에 대비를 해야 합니다.
- 단순히 발생한 일만을 설명하기 보다는 그런 상황이 오게 된 구체적인 원인을 말해주거나 그 때 느꼈던 심리적 갈등이나 혼란 등에 대해 언급해주면 이야기의 완성도가 더 높아질 수 있습니다.
- 실수나 어려움 등과 관련된 경험담을 이야기 할 때는 그 일을 어떻게 해결했는지도 함께 설명해주는 것이 좋습니다.

 '회사 소개'에서는 어떠한 질문들이 출제될까요? 다음의 예상 질문에 대해 여러분은 어떻게 답변할지 한 번 생각해 보세요.

✓ 1. You indicated in the survey that you work. Please tell me about the company you work for. Where is it located? What kinds of services or products does it provide? What do you do at your company?

2. Describe your company building. What does it look like? What can you see from your office?

✓ 3. Please tell me about the history of your company. When was it established and who was the founder? How has it developed since its foundation? Give me as many details as possible.

4. I'd like to know about your boss or supervisor. What was your first impression of him or her?

5. Tell me about your favorite coworker. When did you first meet him or her? Are you working with him or her? What do you like him or her about?

✓ 6. Tell me about an experience that was special, humorous, or challenging while you have been working at your company.

7. I'd like to know about your typical routine at work. What is the first thing you do when you get to the office? Give me all the details about your day at work.

8. How do you get to work from your house every day? How long does it normally take to get to work?

9. You indicated in the survey that you work. Tell me about your company's dress codes. Are employees required to wear formal attire? Or does your company have a business casual dress code?

10. Do you often work overtime? How often do you work overtime? What do you think about your overtime work?

You indicated in the survey that you work. Please tell me about the company you work for. Where is it located? What kinds of services or products does it provide? What do you do at your company?

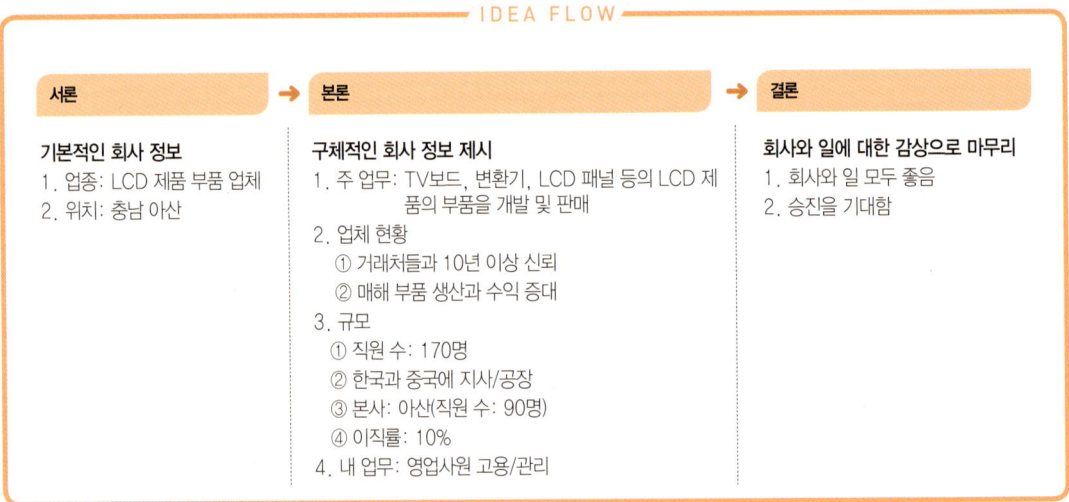

ANSWER

The company I work for is a medium-size company located in Asan city, Chungnam province. My company develops and manufactures components of LCD products such as TV boards, inverters, LCD panels, etc. We supply the parts to large companies like Bulls, CS or foreign companies. Our company has had strong confidence to fulfill our major accounts with good quality parts, competitive price, and punctual delivery for more than 10 years. Every year, the production of components is increasing and so are our sales profits. The number of employees is nearly 170, and the factories and offices are located in several places in Korea and China. In our headquarters here in Asan, we have 90 employees, and the turnover rate is approximately 10 percent per year. I am in charge of hiring and supervising sales representatives as an assistant manager. I encourage new and existing sales representatives to have better knowledge of our quality parts and meet the sales target. I like my job and company, and I'm expecting to get promoted to a general manger within 2 years.

[해석 p.290 참조]

문장 구조 응용하기

so + 동사 도치 + S ~도 마찬가지다
앞 문장의 내용과 일치되는 내용일 때 '~도 역시 마찬가지다'라는 뜻의 so 도치구문입니다. 이럴 때는 앞 문장 동사의 종류와 꼭 일치시켜 주셔야 합니다.

- **본문** Every year the production of components is increasing and so are our sales profits.
- **ex** My branch tries to show the best sales performance in the company and so do other branches.
  우리 지점은 회사에서 가장 좋은 판매 실적을 보이려고 애쓰고 다른 지점들도 마찬가지입니다.

be in charge of ~를 맡고 있다, ~를 담당하다

- **본문** I am in charge of hiring and supervising sales representatives as an assistant manager.
- **ex** I was in charge of advertising and promoting new products in my previous company.
  이전 직장에서는 신상품 광고와 홍보를 담당했습니다.

Word approximately 대략, 약(=about, around), 거의(=nearly, almost)

- **본문** In our headquarters here in Ansan, we have 90 employees and the turnover rate is approximately 10 percent per year.
- **ex** It takes approximately a year to produce a complete product. 하나의 완성된 제품을 생산하려면 거의 1년 걸립니다.
- **ex** I estimate that the sales of my company is about one billion won for this years.
  우리 회사의 올해 매출은 약 10억 정도라고 추정합니다.

업종과 위치를 포함한 기본적인 소개로 서두 열기

- I work for a medium-size manufacturer of leather products, which is located in Chungjongno, Seoul.
  저는 서울 충정로에 위치하고 있는 가죽제품 중소 제조 업체에 근무하고 있습니다.
- I'm working at an insurance company located in Suwon, Gyeonggi Province.
  저는 경기도 수원에 위치한 보험회사에 다니고 있습니다.
- My company is a global electronic company, and my department office is in downtown in Seoul.
  우리 회사는 세계적인 전자회사이고 우리 부서 사무실은 서울 시내에 있습니다.

회사의 주된 제품이나 서비스 또는 업무 제시하기

- Our main job is to make and export cell-phone parts including batteries.
  우리의 주 업무는 건전지를 포함한 휴대전화 부품을 만들고 수출하는 일입니다.
- We develop and publish textbooks and visual materials related to children's English learning.
  우리는 아이들 영어학습과 관련된 교재와 시각 자료들을 개발하고 출판합니다.
- The major products of my company are eco-friendly lunch boxes. 우리 회사의 주요 제품은 환경친화적인 도시락 통입니다.
- We are in the food industry, and our top-selling business is confectionery.
  우리는 식품업계에 있는데 최고 판매 분야는 과자류입니다.

직원 수를 포함한 사업 규모 소개하기

- The total number of employees in my company reaches nearly 10,000, and factories and offices are in several places in my country. 우리 회사의 전 직원 수는 거의 만 명에 이르고 공장과 사무소들은 우리나라 여러 곳에 있습니다.
- We do not have any other branch for now, but plan to open one in a different region after expanding our business. 우리는 아직 어떤 다른 지점도 없지만 사업을 확장하고 나서는 다른 지역에 지사 한 곳을 열 계획입니다.
- There are approximately 50 full time employees and 8 to 10 part-time workers in my branches.
  우리 지점에는 50명 정도의 정규직 직원들과 8명에서 10명의 시간제 직원들이 있습니다.

MAKE YOUR ANSWER

질문에 대한 여러분의 답변을 만들어보세요.

You indicated in the survey that you work. Please tell me about the company you work for. Where is it located? What kinds of services or products does it provide? What do you do at your company?

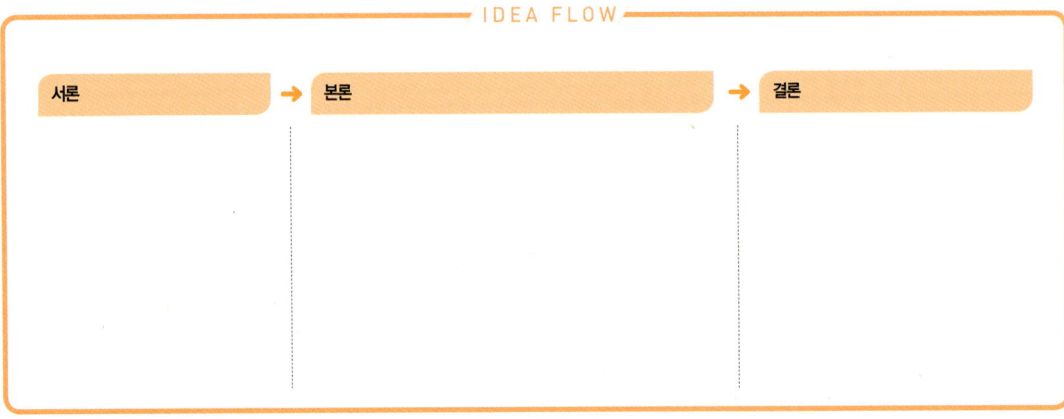

ANSWER

Please tell me about the history of your company. When was it established and who was the founder? How has it developed since its foundation? Give me as many details as possible.

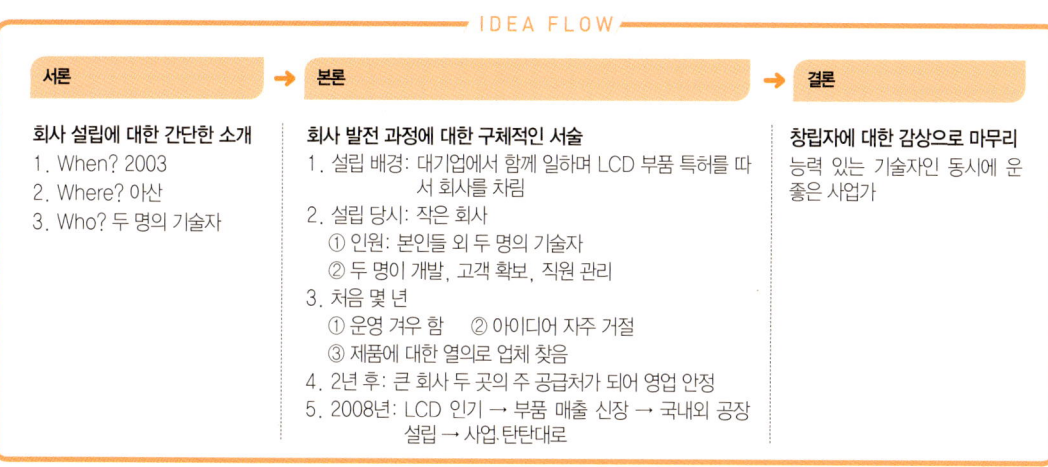

ANSWER

My company was founded by two engineers back in 2003 in Asan. They were working for a large electronics company together, and their jobs were to develop electronic parts. During the period of working, they obtained several patents on LCD products and decided to start their own business. After getting some investment from outside sources and investing all their money, they established a small company in Asan with two more engineers. The two founders did multiple-jobs from developing parts and gaining customers to managing the engineers. For the first few years, they managed to operate their company. Their ideas were frequently rejected by their potential associates, but they persistently sought to find major accounts with enthusiasm for their LCD components. Two years later, they became a major supplier for two large companies, which enabled them to keep their business stable with more employees. As LCDs had a huge popularity in 2008, more companies made LCD products such as LCD TVs and refrigerators with LCD screens. This trend boosted the sales of their components, and they expanded their business. They've built some factories both in Korea and China, and their business has gotten better. I believe they were capable engineers, but also, were lucky in business.

[해석 p.290 참조]

IH 답변 파헤치기

회사 설립 시기와 설립자를 포함한 서두 열기

- My company was founded in the late 1970s. The founder retired, and the company has been operated by CEOs since 2005.
  우리 회사는 1970년대 후반에 설립되었습니다. 창립자께서는 은퇴하셨고 2005년부터는 전문경영인들이 회사를 운영하고 있습니다.

- My company has a long history dating back to the early 1960s. The previous owner of the company passed away, and his first son has been managing the company for 15 years.
  저의 회사는 1960년대 초반으로 거슬러 올라가는 긴 역사를 가지고 있습니다. 선대 회장님은 돌아가셨고 그 아들이 15년째 경영하고 있습니다.

- The company I work for was established 30 years ago. Its founder, who is the current president, is still working in the field.
  제가 일하는 회사는 30년 전에 설립되었습니다. 현 회장이신 창립자께서는 아직도 현장에서 일을 하고 계십니다.

Word manage to 부정사 가까스로~하다, 겨우 ~하다

본문 For the first few years, they managed to operate their company.

ex I heard my current president managed to pay staff and the rent for the office at the beginning of his business.
사업 초반에 현재 사장님은 직원들 월급과 사무실 임대료도 겨우 냈다고 합니다.

Word enthusiasm 열정, 열의

ex I really envy their enthusiasm for working.
저는 정말 그들의 일에 대한 열정이 부럽습니다.

ex As one of the employees, it's good to feel the owner's enthusiasm for her company.
직원의 일원으로 회사 사장의 회사에 대한 열정을 느끼는 건 좋은 일입니다.

회사 변천 과정 관련 아이디어들

- During the financial crisis in 1977, my company was at the risk of bankruptcy, but with dedication and passion of executives and staff, it overcame the crisis.
  1977년 금융 위기 동안 우리 회사는 도산 위기까지 갔었지만 임직원들의 헌신과 열정으로 그 위기를 극복했습니다.

- When my company was established, its business was limited only to dairy products. Through the constant expansion of its business, however, we have sold bread and cookies, and last year, we entered the beverage market.
  우리 회사가 설립되었을 때는 사업이 낙농제품으로만 국한되어 있었습니다. 하지만 부단한 사업 확장을 통해 빵과 쿠키도 판매해 왔고 작년에는 음료시장까지 진출했습니다.

- During the beginning period of my company, the owner experienced serious financial difficulties. He invested all his cash and property for his company and moved around all over the country to get investments from outside sources. His patience and effort have led his company to become one of the most competitive cosmetic companies in my country.
  회사 초기에는 사장님이 심각한 재정난을 겪으셨습니다. 모든 현금과 재산을 회사를 위해 투자했고 밖에서 투자를 얻으려고 전국 방방곡곡을 돌아다니셨습니다. 그분의 끈기와 노력으로 우리 회사는 우리나라에서 가장 경쟁력 있는 화장품 회사들 중 하나가 되었습니다.

질문에 대한 여러분의 답변을 만들어보세요.

Please tell me about the history of your company. When was it established and who was the founder? How has it developed since its foundation? Give me as many details as possible.

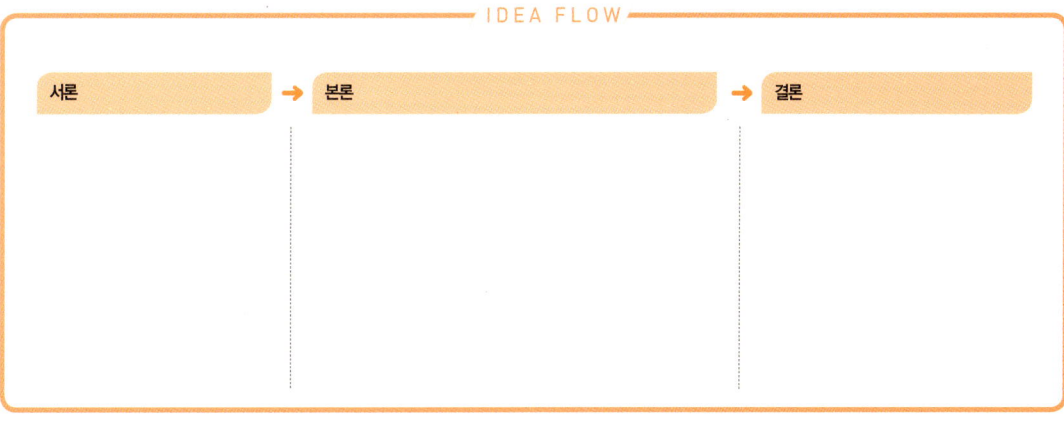

Tell me about an experience that was special, humorous, or challenging while you have been working at your company.

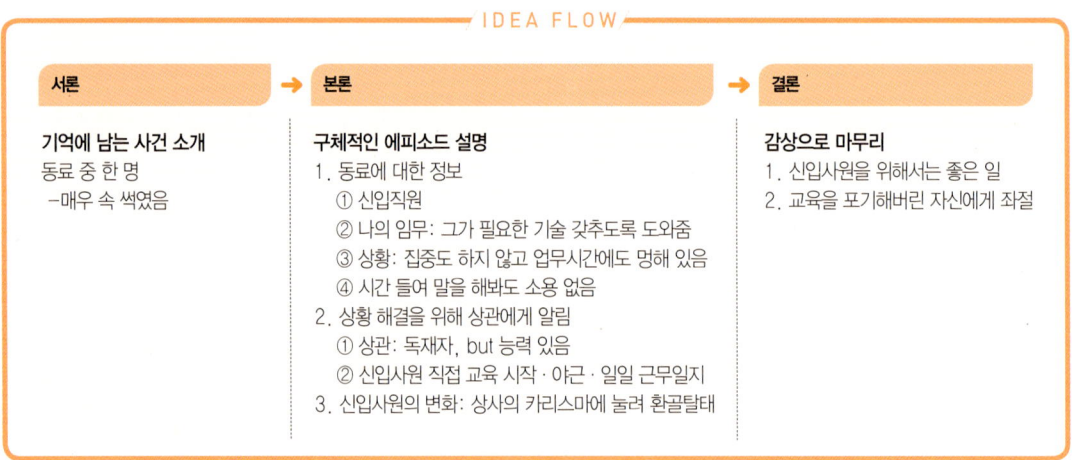

ANSWER

I've gone through various episodes with my coworkers, and I'd like to talk about one of them, who was a real pain in the neck. When I first met him, he was a new employee assigned to my department. My duty was to help him have the necessary skills for his job, but he was so unfocused. He didn't concentrate on listening to me and was often sitting absent-mindedly during working hours. I spent lots of time talking to him to set him on the right track, but his attitude didn't get better. In fact, I had joined only two years earlier than he did, so I wasn't qualified for and experienced in training someone. I eventually asked my boss for help, and my boss had already been aware of his indolence. My boss was sort of a tyrant in our department but also a competent supervisor. He started training the new employee himself, and he was soon overwhelmed by his boss's charisma. He had to work overtime almost every day and submit his daily work report to his boss. In a few weeks, he turned over a new leaf, and I hardly saw him distract from working. It was good for him, but I felt a bit frustrated about myself who gave up training him.

[해석 p.290 참조]

IH 답변 파헤치기

문장 구조 응용하기

help A 동사원형 A가 ~하도록 도와주다

- 본문) My duty was to help him have the necessary skills for his job, but he was so unfocused.
- ex) My boss helped me get familiar with my new working environment.
  제 상관은 제가 새로운 근무환경에 적응하도록 도와주었습니다.

spend 시간/돈 (in)~ing ~하면서 시간을 보내다, ~하느라 돈을 쓰다

- 본문) I spent lots of time talking to him to set him on the right track, but his attitude didn't get better.
- ex) I spend an average of 10 hours a day working for my company.
  저는 하루 평균 10시간씩 회사를 위해 일합니다.

  cf) spend 시간/돈 on + 명사
- ex) I spend more than half of my salary on concert tickets. 저는 콘서트 표 사는데 제 월급의 반 이상을 씁니다.

Word go through = experience = undergo (일, 어려움 등을)경험하다, 겪다

- 본문) I've gone through various episodes with my coworkers.
- ex) I went through very difficult time when I was first transferred to my current department.
  제가 현재 부서로 처음 이동했을 때 무척 힘든 시간을 보냈습니다.

Word concentrate on ~에 집중하다, 전념하다

- 본문) He didn't concentrate on listening to me and was often sitting absent-mindedly during working hours.
- ex) I can't concentrate on the lecture because of the female student sitting next to me.
  저는 제 옆에 앉은 여학생 때문에 강의에 집중할 수 없습니다.

Word on the right/wrong track 올바른(잘못된) 방향으로, 제대로 (안)하는

- ex) When I was working on the term paper, I was worried if I was on the wrong track. So I showed it to my professor, and he said I was on the right track.
  기말 과제를 쓰고 있을 때 제가 제대로 못하고 있는 거면 어쩌나 걱정이 되었습니다. 그래서 그 과제를 교수님께 보여드렸더니 제가 제대로 하고 있다고 하셨습니다.

Idiom a pain in the neck 매우 귀찮은 사람(것), 골칫거리, 눈엣가시(=a headache, a nuisance)

- ex) The new employee kept making errors, so some people said he was a pain in the neck.
  그 신입사원은 계속해서 실수를 했기 때문에 여러 사람들은 그가 민폐덩어리라고 말했습니다.
- ex) The assignment that I took last week was a headache.
  제가 지난 주에 맡은 업무는 골칫거리였습니다.

Idiom turn over a new leaf 새 사람이 되다, 환골탈태하다

- 본문) In a few weeks, he turned over a new leaf, and I hardly saw him distract from working.
- ex) He's turned over a new leaf, and he's never late to work. 그는 새 사람이 되어서 절대 지각을 하지 않습니다.

MAKE YOUR ANSWER

질문에 대한 여러분의 답변을 만들어보세요.

Tell me about an experience that was special, humorous, or challenging while you have been working at your company.

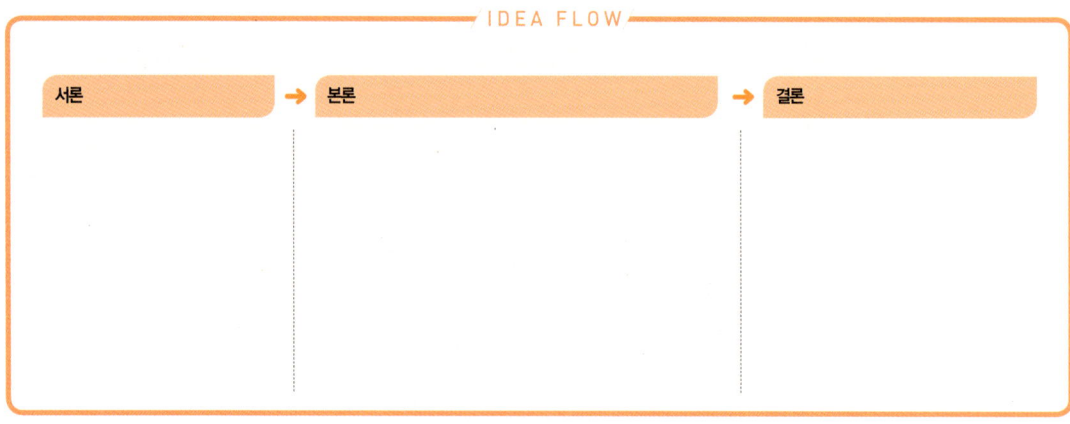

ANSWER

Memo

Oral Proficiency Interview-computer

Lesson 2
직장 2-사내 업무 및 연수

INTRO 직장인의 경우 회사 소개와 사업 분야 외에 개인적인 업무 관련 문제도 자주 출제됩니다. 회사에서 맡았던 프로젝트의 수행 과정은 물론, 프로젝트를 진행하면서 일어났던 에피소드를 소개하라는 문항은 단골로 출제되고 있습니다. 또한 신입사원 연수나 정기적인 회사 워크숍, 특별 교육, 세미나 등 회사가 제공하는 다양한 연수와 교육 관련 문항들도 꾸준히 출제되고 있습니다.

IH 답변 전략

1 자신이 속한 부서 중심의 업무 소개하기
- 부서 내 자신이 책임지고 있는 주요 업무를 정확히 소개합니다.
- 매일 일어나는 일상적인 업무에 대해서 설명할 수 있어야 합니다.
- 회사에서 행하는 daily routine에 해당하는 어휘들을 평소 익혀놓는 것이 좋습니다.

2 자신이 맡았던 프로젝트 소개하기
- 프로젝트 착수 시기, 목적, 내용 등에 대해 꼼꼼히 소개해 줍니다.
- 프로젝트 수행과 관련된 경험을 말할 때는 그 일을 통해 얻은 교훈이나 보람 등을 덧붙여 답변을 마무리해 줍니다.
- 프로젝트 완성을 위해 사용했던 기술적 도구 또는 방법들을 소개해 줍니다.

3 회사에서 제공받은 다양한 교육 프로그램 소개하기
- 교육의 종류, 횟수, 교육 방법 등 회사에서 제공하는 교육의 일반적인 정보를 언급해 줍니다.
- 기억에 남는 교육이나 최근 받았던 교육처럼 특정 교육에 대해 답변할 때는 그 교육의 목적, 시기, 장소, 강사, 내용 등 보다 구체적이고 세밀하게 답변을 해 줌으로써 그 교육 프로그램의 특성이 잘 전달될 수 있도록 합니다.
- 꼭 실제로 받았던 연수 외에도 자신이 받고 싶은 연수 내용을 생각해서 그 내용을 답변으로 사용하는 것도 좋은 방법이 될 수 있습니다.

'사내 업무 및 연수'에서는 어떠한 질문들이 출제될까요? 다음의 예상 질문에 대해 여러분은 어떻게 답변할지 한번 생각해 보세요.

1. You indicated in the survey that you work. Tell me about your first project at work. When did you work on it and what was it about? How did you complete the project? Tell me about the project in as much detail as you can.

2. I'd like to know about any projects or assignments that you recently completed. Did you work in teams or complete it by yourself? Tell me the whole process of working on the project or assignment.

3. What kinds of training do you want to receive from your company? Which training do you need for your job? Why do you want to receive the training?

✓ 4. Let's talk about the training your company offers to its employees. Does your company provide any trainers? Does it use any technological devices? What do you learn from them? What do you think about those training sessions?

✓ 5. I'd like to know about the training sessions that you took when you first started working. They may have been quite different from the ones that you're receiving nowadays. How have the training sessions changed over the years?

6. Tell me about the last training you received at work. When did you take it and what was it about? How did you like it? Give me all the details.

7. How have the trainings you received from your company helped you do your job?

✓ 8. I'd like to know about one of the most memorable training you have received. When did you receive it and what was it about? What made it so memorable to you? Give me all the details.

9. You may have encountered an unexpected, surprising, or challenging situation while working. Tell me one particular experience that you have had.

Let's talk about the training your company offers to its employees. Does your company provide any trainers? Does it use any technological devices? What do you learn from them? What do you think about those training sessions?

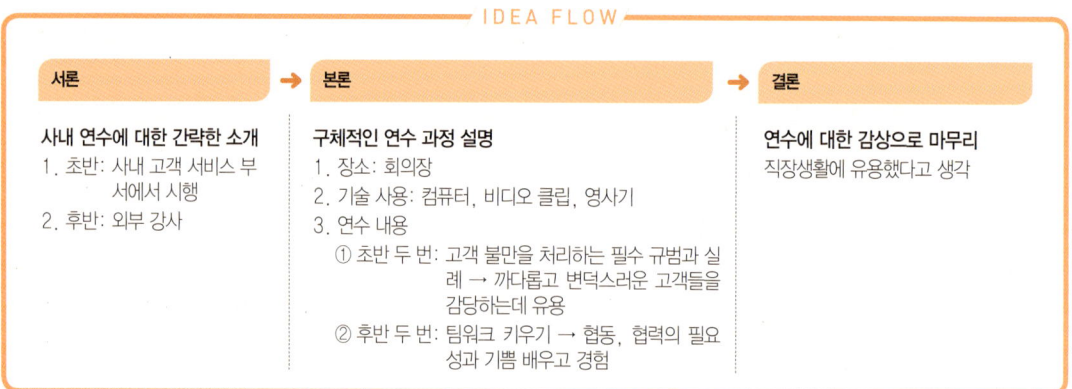

ANSWER

My company is offering its employees four regular trainings on customer service on a quarterly basis. The first two trainings are administered by the supervisors of the customer service department while the other two are conducted by outside trainers. Normally, the trainings are held in the conference hall and all trainers use some technological devices such as a computer, video clips and projector. I'd like to talk about the four trainings I took last year as an example. From the first two training sessions, we learned about the required standards and practices for handling customers' complaints, which practically helped us manage fastidious and unpredictable customers on the spot. The other two trainings aimed to strengthen our teamwork through some activities requiring cooperation and active discussions. From the training sessions, I actually learned how important it is to cooperate with coworkers in order to achieve our sales goals. I also experienced the pleasure of collaboration with them. I think the trainings that I've received from the company were useful for my career.

[해석 p.290 참조]

문장 구조 응용하기

S+V(A) while/whereas S+V(B) B인 반면 A이다

- ex The summer training programs are planned by the Human Resources Department while the winter training ones are devised by the Customer Service Department.
  동계 연수는 고객서비스 부서가 기획하는 반면 하계 연수는 인사부에서 기획합니다.

- ex Some training programs are very constructive and interesting whereas others are boring and impractical.
  어떤 교육 프로그램은 지루하고 비실용적인 반면 어떤 것들은 매우 건설적이고 재미있습니다.

서두에서 회사 교육 소개하기

- I've received only a few trainings from my company. 저는 회사에서 받은 교육이 몇 개밖에 되지 않습니다.
- My school executes regular teacher training in spring. 우리 학교는 봄에 정기 교사 연수를 실시합니다.
- It is mandatory for all new employees to attend an orientation program.
  모든 신입사원들은 신입사원 연수에 참가해야 합니다.
- My company conducts different training sessions for different departments.
  우리 회사는 부서별로 다른 연수 과정을 시행합니다.
- On-the-job training, called OJT is generally served / conducted /provided by a professional trainer.
  OJT라고 불리는 실습훈련은 일반적으로 전문 트레이너가 제공합니다.

교육 목적에 대해 설명하기

- 본문 The other two trainings aim to strengthen our teamwork through some activities requiring cooperation and active discussions.
  나머지 두 연수는 협동과 활발한 토론을 필요로 하는 활동들을 통해 강한 팀워크를 키우는 것을 목표로 하고 있어요.

- ex The main objective of the training is to develop participants' innovative and creative thinking.
  연수의 주 목적은 참가자들의 혁신적이고 창의적인 사고를 개발시키는 것입니다.

- ex My company intends to encourage its employees to build effective communication skills through those training programs.
  우리 회사는 교육 프로그램을 통해 직원들이 효과적인 의사소통 기술을 가질 수 있도록 독려하는 것을 의도하고 있습니다.

Word on a quarterly basis (=quarterly, every three months) 분기별로, 석 달에 한 번

- ex All the employees are taking a regular training session every three months.
  전 직원이 석 달에 한 번 교육을 받고 있습니다.

- ex My department requires its staff members to attend a quarterly job training even if he or she is an experienced employee. 우리 부서는 설사 경력이 있는 직원이라 할지라도 분기별 직무연수에 참가하는 것을 요구합니다.

  cf) Most trainings are given on a yearly basis, but some trainings are also offered monthly.
  대부분의 교육은 1년 단위로 주어지지만 어떤 교육은 매 달 주어지기도 합니다.

사내 교육에 대한 답변 마무리하기

- I'm quite satisfied with the trainings provided by company. 저는 회사에서 제공받는 연수에 상당히 만족합니다.
- I want the training content to be more related to professional expertise.
  저는 연수 내용이 좀 더 직업상의 전문지식과 관계가 있었으면 좋겠습니다.
- I'm expecting my company to further design and develop more practical training programs so that I can put them into a use. 우리 회사가 앞으로 실용적인 교육을 기획하고 개발해서 제가 그것을 실제로 활용할 수 있기를 기대합니다.

MAKE YOUR ANSWER

질문에 대한 여러분의 답변을 만들어보세요.

Let's talk about the training your company offers to its employees. Does your company provide any trainers? Does it use any technological devices? What do you learn from them? What do you think about those training sessions?

IDEA FLOW

| 서론 → | 본론 → | 결론 |

ANSWER

I'd like to know about the training sessions that you took when you first started working. They may have been quite different from the ones that you're receiving nowadays. How have the training sessions changed over the years?

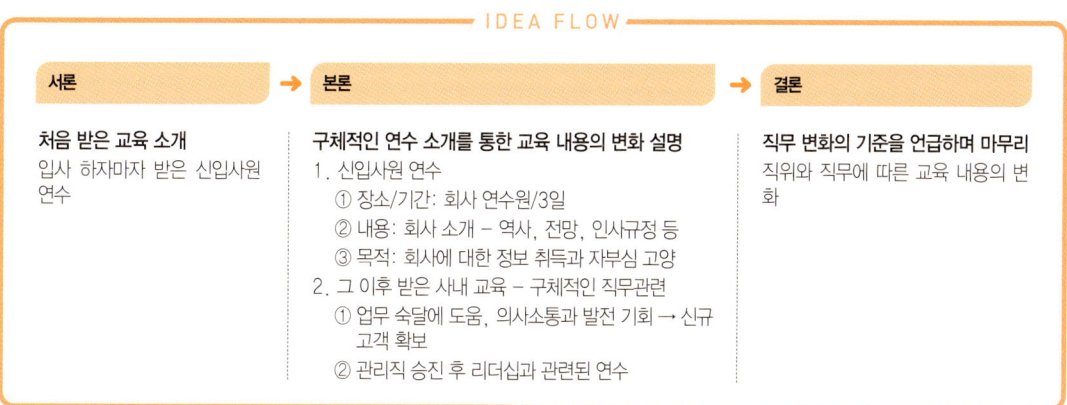

ANSWER

I attended an orientation for new employees as soon as I joined my company. The three-day orientation program was given in the company training center in Gyeonggi-do, and all the new employees including myself had to stay there to receive it. The contents of the program were mostly related to the introduction of the company such as its history, vision, future goals, and personnel policies. I can say that its objective was to motivate the new employees to get the essential information and take pride in their company. In contrast, the trainings that I received after the orientation were related to more specific directions of the job. Those job-related training sessions enabled me to become skilled and qualified for my required tasks more quickly. Some of them also gave me some opportunities to develop communication and presentation skills, which were very useful for me to secure new clients. After my promotion to the managerial position, I got the training regarding leadership, too. As my position and job duties have been changed, the contents of trainings have been changed.

[해석 p.291 참조]

IH 답변 파헤치기

문장 구조 응용하기

S+V(A) as soon as S+V(B) B하자 마자 A하다
A문장과 B문장의 동사 시제는 일치시켜야 합니다.

- 본문) I attended an orientation for new employees as soon as I entered / joined my company.
- ex) As soon as I was transferred to Myeongdong headquarters, I had to receive a special training.
  저는 본사에 발령받자마자 특별 연수에 참석해야 했습니다.

motivate A to 부정사 A가 B하게 동기를 부여하다

- 본문) I can say that its objective is to motivate the new employees to get the essential information and take pride in their company.
- ex) The workshop that I attended as soon as I got promoted motivated me to become a highly effective leader.
  제가 승진이 되자마자 받았던 연수는 저로 하여금 매우 효과적인 지도자가 되도록 동기부여를 했습니다.

enable A to 부정사 A가 B할 수 있게 하다

- 본문) Those job-related training sessions enabled me to become skilled and qualified for my required tasks more quickly.
- ex) The training that I recently received enabled me to improve my presentation skills.
  최근에 받은 교육으로 저는 제 발표 실력을 향상시킬 수 있었습니다.

비교나 대조할 때 쓸 수 있는 표현들

- The first training sessions focus on how to deal with customer complaints while the other ones strengthen how to increase referrals from existing customers.
  첫 번째 교육이 고객 불만을 어떻게 다루냐에 초점을 맞춘다면 나머지 교육은 기존 고객들로부터 어떻게 추천 구매를 받느냐를 강조합니다.
- More various technological equipment is used for the recent training programs compared to the initial ones.
  초기의 연수들과 비교하면 최근의 연수에서는 더 다양한 기술 도구들이 사용됩니다.
- I can't tell a significant difference among trainings that my company has offered to its employees.
  저는 우리 회사가 직원들에게 제공하는 교육들의 중요한 차이를 구별하지 못하겠습니다.

회사에서 받을 수 있는 교육 종류와 예측해볼 수 있는 교육 내용

- A training program for new employees is designed to deliver key knowledge of the company, which enables its new employees to have better understanding of their company.
  신입사원 연수는 회사에 대한 주요 지식을 전달하도록 고안되는데, 그로 인해 신입직원들이 회사를 좀 더 알 수 있게 됩니다.
- Through some executives and management trainings, I've learned about a responsibility for motivating, coaching, inspiring my staff members and consequently contributing to their successful performances.
  간부와 관리자 교육을 통해서 저는 제 부하직원들을 동기유발하고, 이끌고, 독려해서 그 결과 그들이 성공적인 실적을 낼 수 있게 기여하는 책임에 대해 배웠습니다.
- The sales training has helped me better sell the products and manage my customers.
  그 영업 교육은 제가 상품들을 더 잘 팔고 제 고객들을 잘 관리할 수 있도록 도와줬습니다.

 **MAKE YOUR ANSWER**

질문에 대한 여러분의 답변을 만들어보세요.

I'd like to know about the training sessions that you took when you first started working. They may have been quite different from the ones that you're receiving nowadays. How have the training sessions changed over the years?

Q3

I'd like to know about one of the most memorable training you have received. When did you receive it and what was it about? What made it so memorable to you? Give me all the details.

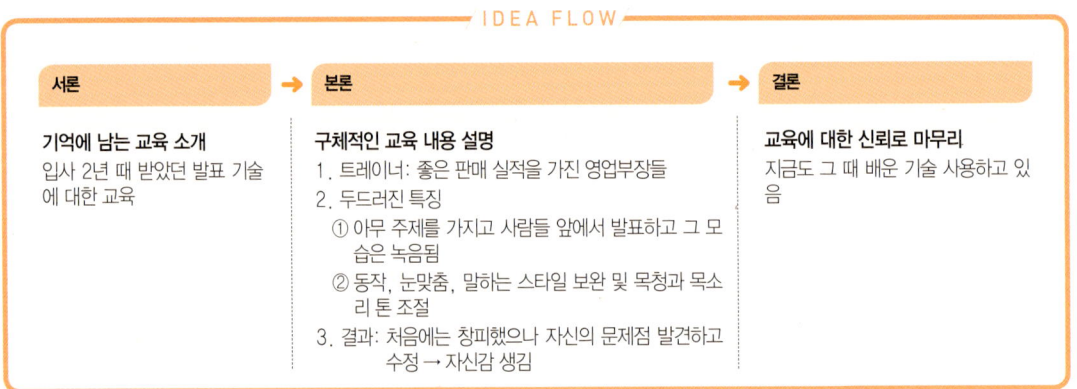

ANSWER

I remember receiving a training program during my second year of working. It was about the presentation skills training, which was a necessary qualification for me to introduce our products to major clients. It was given by some sales managers who had excellent sales performances with good presentation skills. It had one distinctive feature that I hadn't experienced from other presentation skills trainings before. Most training programs for presentation skills showed what key elements for good presentations and demonstrated some examples of them. During that training session, however, the participants were asked to make a presentation about any topics given in public and the presentations were videotaped. Then the sales managers complemented our gestures, eye contact, and speech style. They also taught us how to adjust the pitch and tone of our voice. It was embarrassing to see my speech through video tapes and also have them point out my speech style at first, but I could eventually find out my problems and correct them. I became more confident of standing in public after the training, too. I'm still using the skills that I learned from the training.

[해석 p.291 참조]

IH 답변 파헤치기

문장 구조 응용하기

remember + ~ing (과거에)~했던 걸 기억하다

- 본문: I remember receiving a training program during my second year of working.
- ex: I remember making a huge mistake during my first presentation I gave at my current company.
  현재 회사에서 했었던 첫 번째 발표를 하다가 큰 실수를 했던 기억이 납니다.

  cf) remember + to 부정사 (미래에)~할 것을 기억하다
- ex: I remember to receive a training next week.
  다음 주에 교육을 받아야 할 게 기억나네요.

be asked to 부정사 ~해야 한다(~하도록 요구 받다)

- 본문: During the training session, however, the participants were asked to make a presentation about any topics given in public and the presentations were videotaped.
- ex: We were asked to participate in a group discussion after the lecture.
  우리는 그 강의 후 그룹 토론에 참여해야 했습니다.

인상 깊었던 회사 교육을 언급하면서 서두 열기

- The most memorable training that I took was about effective communication skills.
  제가 받았던 가장 인상적인 교육은 효과적인 의사소통 기술에 관한 것이었습니다.
- I applied for the in-house language training when I worked for the department of overseas trade.
  저는 해외무역 부서에서 일할 때 사내 어학연수를 신청했습니다.
- The 3-day workshop covering the leadership principles and cases was one the best training programs that my company conducted.
  지휘 원칙과 사례들에 대한 사흘짜리 연수는 우리 회사가 실시했던 최고의 연수 중 하나였습니다.

연수 내용 관련 아이디어

- I learned how to use visual aids effectively when I make a presentation.
  저는 발표를 할 때 시각자료를 효과적으로 사용할 수 있는 방법을 배웠습니다.
- I was a little embarrassed to lead a group discussion with no preparation at all.
  저는 아무런 준비 없이 그룹 토론을 이끌게 되어 좀 당황했습니다.
- The trainer was supposed to teach us how to establish special strategies for promoting new products. 그 강사는 우리에게 신제품을 홍보할 때 특별한 전략을 짤 수 있는 방법을 가르쳐주기로 되어있었습니다.
- The training consisted of three parts including beginning, proceeding with, and ending the negotiation. 그 연수는 협상을 시작하고, 진행하고, 마무리하는 세 가지 부분으로 구성되었습니다.

Word complement 보충하다, 보완하다

- The trainer helped me complement my weaknesses in my presentation skills.
  그 강사는 제 발표 기술의 단점을 보완하는 것을 도와줬습니다.
- I could complement my educational background of the marketing with a variety of training programs provided in my company.
  저는 우리 회사에서 제공되는 다양한 연수 프로그램으로 마케팅 교육 배경을 보완할 수 있었습니다.

IH 답변 파헤치기

Word demonstrate/display/show 제시하다, 보여주다

- The trainer demonstrated specific examples of successful marketing projects.
  그 강사는 성공적인 마케팅 프로젝트의 구체적인 예를 보여줬습니다.
- The orientation began by displaying the history of our company.
  그 연수는 우리 회사의 역사를 보여주는 걸로 시작되었습니다.

MAKE YOUR ANSWER

질문에 대한 여러분의 답변을 만들어보세요.

I'd like to know about one of the most memorable training you have received. When did you receive it and what was it about? What made it so memorable to you? Give me all the details.

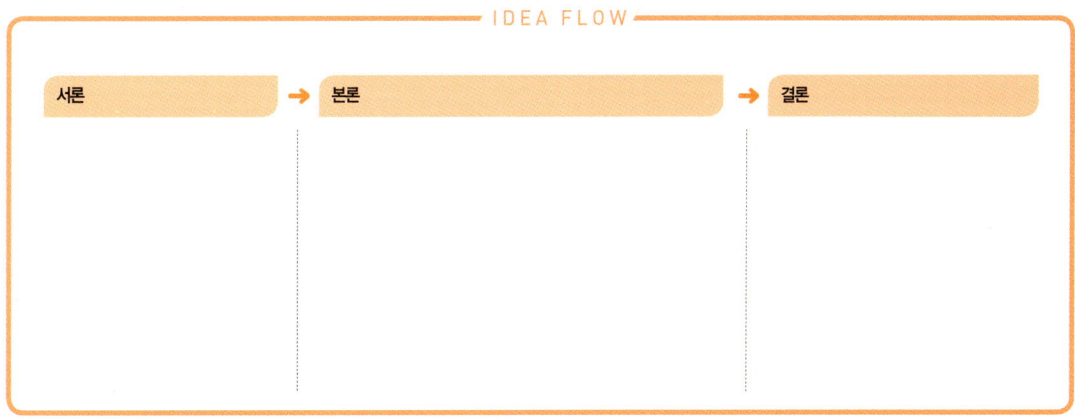

ANSWER

Oral Proficiency Interview-computer

Lesson 3 학생 생활 소개하기

INTRO 사전조사에서 자신의 신분을 학생이라고 선택했거나 학교를 다닌 경험이 있다고 답변한 수검자에게는 학교 생활과 관련된 문항들이 나올 확률이 매우 높습니다. 학교 생활과 관련된 문제로는 단순한 학교의 외관 묘사에서 자신의 전공, 그리고 학위 이수를 위해 수강하고 있는 과목들, 교수님이나 교우들, 그리고 학교 과제에 이르기까지 폭넓게 제시되고 있습니다. 자신이 다니고 있는 학교와 학업에 관련된 다양한 어휘들과 표현들을 숙지하고 학교 생활을 하면서 겪었던 경험담에 대해 비교적 자세하고 구체적인 답변을 준비해놓아야 하겠습니다.

IH 답변 전략

① 학교 캠퍼스나 학교 주위의 정경 묘사를 위한 답변
- 학교의 이름, 위치, 규모 등에 대해 간단히 언급하고, 학교 내 특징적인 건물들을 위주로 캠퍼스 정경을 묘사해 줍니다. 건물의 이름으로는 도서관, 학생회관, 본관 등 모든 학생들이 사용할 수 있는 건물들이나 의대나 인문대관 등 특정 전공과 관련된 건물들을 소개하면 되겠습니다.
- 봄이나 가을 등의 특정 계절을 선택해 그 계절에 볼 수 있는 캠퍼스의 아름다운 풍경이나 특징들을 설명해 봅니다.
- 학교 내 편의시설과 학교 주위에 있는 음식점, 병원, 서점 등을 소개할 때는 그 장소에서 할 수 있는 활동에 대한 간단한 설명을 덧붙여줍니다.

② 학업과 관련된 사항들을 짚어보고 그에 대한 구체적인 답변 준비해두기
- 전공, 전공 관련 이수 과목들, 그리고 이수하고 있는 전체 학점 등의 정보를 언급해 줍니다.
- 학업 관련 과제나 프로젝트는 해당 과목 이름과 프로젝트 제목 등을 언급해주고 완성 과정은 비교적 꼼꼼하고 자세하게 서술해 줍니다.
- 과제나 프로젝트 완성을 위해 사용했던 기술적 도구 또는 방법들을 소개해 줍니다.

③ 학교 생활과 관련된 개인적인 경험이나 느낌, 특정 에피소드 등을 생각해두기
- 학교, 강의실, 혹은 교수님을 묘사할 때는 되도록 구체적으로 답변해야 합니다. 특히 좋거나 싫은 이유를 말할 때 그런 감정을 갖는 계기가 된 자신의 경험담을 추가해주면 훨씬 설득력 있는 답변이 될 수 있습니다.
- 교수님 집무실을 찾아간 일화나 교우 관계를 통한 경험 등은 그 일련의 과정들을 자세하게 서술해 줍니다.
- 과제나 프로젝트 수행 시 잊지 못할 사건, 그 경험을 통해 얻은 교훈 등은 그 느낌이나 의견을 뒷받침할 만한 내용으로 구성하는 것이 좋습니다.

'학생 생활 소개하기'에서는 어떠한 질문들이 출제될까요? 다음의 예상 질문에 대해 여러분은 어떻게 답변할지 한번 생각해 보세요.

1. You indicated in the survey that you are a student. Please tell me about your school. Where is it located? What does it look like? What does the surrounding area look like?

✓ 2. You indicated in the survey that you are a student. Please describe your school campus. What does it look like? Give me as many details as possible.

3. I'd like to know about your first visit to your school. When was it and who did you go with? What was your first impression about the school?

4. Describe one of your professors to me. What kind of person is he or she? What do you like or dislike about him or her?

5. Have you ever visited your professor's office? When was it and why did you go there? Did you achieve your purpose? Please tell me about the situation in as much detail as possible.

✓ 6. What do you study in school? What is your major about? Do you like studying that major? Please tell me about your major in as much detail as possible.

7. Tell me about the courses you have taken. What courses are you currently taking? What is your favorite course and what do you like about it? Give me all the details.

8. What were the last classes you took? Why did you choose them? What did you learn and what did you do in those classes?

9. Please tell me about one of the projects you have successfully completed. What was it about and what did you do for the project? What technology did you use for it? Tell me about the whole story from start to finish.

✓ 10. I'd like to know about any memorable projects or assignments that you have done in school. What was the project about? Did you work alone or work in groups? What did you do to complete it?

11. Tell me about any interesting, unexpected or difficult things that happened while you were working on the project.

You indicated in the survey that you are a student. Please describe your school campus. What does it look like? Give me as many details as possible.

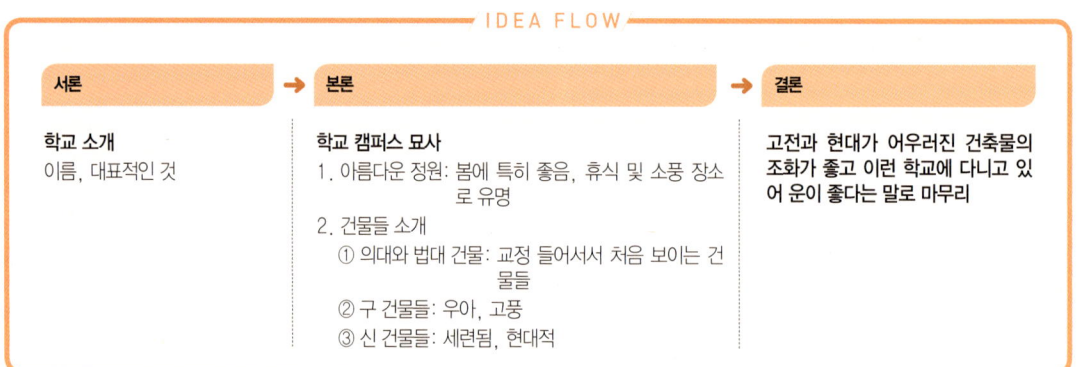

ANSWER

I attend Young Shin University in Seoul, which is famous for its beautiful campus. It has well-groomed gardens with full of flowers, trees, and green lawns. When spring comes, in particular, more than 200 cherry blossom trees are lushly in bloom around the campus. It's a pleasurable experience to stroll around while enjoying the picturesque views. That's why it's a popular picnic place for elementary and middle school students as well as a relaxing site for adults. My university is also fairly big with almost 40 buildings. When you first enter the campus, you'll find the College of Medicine and the College of Law. The two buildings are facing each other across the gigantic fountain, which is well known for the meeting point for students in our university. Some buildings on campus are pretty old, such as the Administration Building and the Central Library. They are stone buildings with an elegant, old-world style look. Other buildings like the Grand Stadium are newly built architectures with refined and modern styles. I like the mixture of classical and modern architectural styles that the campus has. I think I'm lucky to study and have a lot of fun in such a great place.

[해석 p.291 참조]

IH 답변 파헤치기

문장 구조 응용하기

B as well as A (=not only A but (also) B, both A and B) A뿐 아니라 B도

- 본문) That's why it's a popular picnic place for elementary and middle school students as well as a relaxing site for adults.
- ex) The cafeteria is well known for not only its delicious foods but (also) its excellent service.
  그 학교 식당은 맛있는 음식뿐 아니라 훌륭한 서비스로도 잘 알려져 있습니다.
- ex) I can see both historical and modern buildings on campus.
  저는 교정에서 역사적인 건물들과 현대적인 건물들을 볼 수 있습니다.

while ~ing ~하면서, ~하는 동안에

주절의 주어와 종속절인 while 절의 주어가 동일할 때는 종속절의 주어를 생략하고 동사를 ~ing로 만들어줄 수 있습니다.

- 본문) It's a pleasurable experience to stroll around while enjoying the picturesque views.
- ex) I feel my worries and stress melt away while walking hills covered with flowers and trees.
  나무와 꽃으로 뒤덮인 언덕을 오르면서 저는 걱정과 스트레스가 사라짐을 느낍니다.

학교 소재, 규모에 대하여

- I go to the school, which is located in Gyeonggi-do. 저는 경기도에 위치한 학교에 다니고 있습니다.
- My school has a pretty large campus. 우리 학교는 캠퍼스가 꽤 큽니다.
- The campus of my university is small compared to those of some other universities.
  우리 학교 교정은 다른 학교들의 교정에 비하면 작습니다.

교정 또는 학교 내 건물들의 특징

- You can see many artistic sculptures and statues when you pass through the school gate.
  교문을 통과하면 많은 예술적인 조각들과 동상들을 볼 수 있습니다.
- The campus looks most beautiful in fall with plentiful and colorful leaves.
  교정은 풍부하고 다채로운 단풍들로 인해 가을에 가장 아름답게 보입니다.
- The arch has been considered the symbol of my school's campus.
  그 아치형 문은 우리 학교 교정의 상징으로 여겨져 왔습니다.

학교에 대한 만족이나 불만족 표현하기

- I'm not that satisfied with my school facilities. 저는 학교 시설이 그리 만족스럽지 않습니다.
- I wish my school were more spacious. 우리 학교가 좀 더 넓었으면 좋았을 텐데 말이죠.
- I quite enjoy my school life on campus. 저는 교정에서의 생활을 상당히 좋아합니다.

Word 학교 안 건물들 및 시설물들

- student center/student union 학생회관
- administration building/main building 본관
- central library 중앙도서관
- dormitory/residence hall 기숙사
- laboratory 실험실
- cafeteria 학교 식당
- gymnasium 체육관
- athletic field 운동장
- sports center/fitness center 스포츠 클럽
- faculty room 직원실
- register's office/registrar's office 교무처
- administration office 행정실
- College of Liberal Arts 인문대학
- College of Medicine/Medical College 의과대학
- College of Pharmacy/Pharmaceutical College 약학대학

MAKE YOUR ANSWER

질문에 대한 여러분의 답변을 만들어보세요.

You indicated in the survey that you are a student. Please describe your school campus. What does it look like? Give me as many details as possible.

ANSWER

Q2 What do you study in school? What is your major about? Do you like studying that major? Please tell me about your major in as much detail as possible.

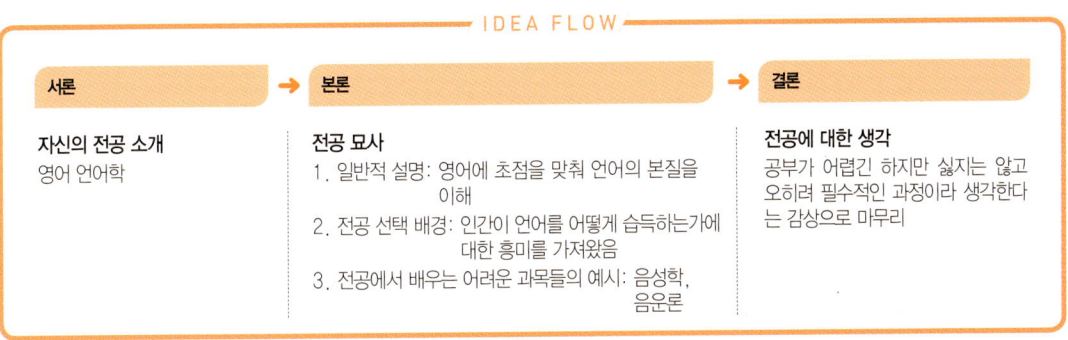

ANSWER

I'm currently majoring in English Language and Linguistics. Linguistics is the so-called scientific study of human language. Like other sciences, it collects data, tests hypotheses, and suggests reliable theories to understand the nature of language. Therefore, English Language and Linguistics, of course, focuses on the study of English. I've been interested in how humans acquire language. It's not a question that I can't answer easily and simply, but I want to have a clear idea of this issue through my courses. I honestly can't say that majoring in English Language and Linguistics is enjoyable. Some subjects, especially phonetics and phonology, are quite difficult to keep up with. They're the study of the sound, and more specifically, how each sound differs from others and how they form systems and patterns. It's very hard for me to identify each sound or group of sounds, and sometimes, I feel discouraged with myself for not understanding them. However, I don't mean that I hate learning those subjects or regret choosing my major. As it is quite clear, all the courses are essential for knowledge of language, and feeling pressure must be one of the mountains I need to climb over to deeply understand the human language.

[해석 p.292 참조]

IH 답변 파헤치기

문장 구조 응용하기

regret + ~ing (과거에)~했던 것을 후회하다

- 본문) But I don't mean that I hate learning those subjects or regret choosing my major.
- ex) I actually regret deciding to study chemistry from time to time.
  나는 사실 가끔씩 화학을 공부하기로 결심한 것을 후회합니다.

  cf) regret to 부정사 ~해서 유감이다
- ex) I regret to major in computer science.
  제가 컴퓨터 공학을 전공해서 유감입니다.

전공이나 수강 현황 설명하기

- My major is Business Administration. 제 전공은 경영학입니다.
- I'm currently studying Education. 저는 현재 교육학을 공부하고 있습니다.
- I majored in Economics. 저는 경제학을 전공했습니다.
- I've taken 6 classes at my school so far. 저는 지금까지 6개 과목을 수강했습니다.
- I take three to four courses per semester. 저는 학기마다 세 과목에서 네 과목을 수강합니다.
- On average, I'm taking 20 credits each semester. 평균적으로 저는 매 학기에 20학점을 이수하고 있습니다.

전공 선택의 배경이나 이유 언급하기

- 본문) I've been interested in how humans acquire language.
- ex) I chose my major to pursue a career in the banking business.
  금융계에서 직업을 찾기 위해 제 전공을 선택했습니다.
- ex) As I've been enjoying dealing with numbers, I decided to major in accounting.
  저는 숫자를 다루는 것을 즐겨왔기 때문에 회계학을 전공하기로 결심했습니다.

전공이나 수업의 어려움 표현

- Most courses that I had taken were physically and mentally demanding.
  제가 수강했던 대부분의 과목들은 신체적으로나 심적으로나 부담이 컸어요.
- I went through a tough year to get familiar with business terms and definitions.
  경영 용어와 정의들에 익숙해지기 위해 힘든 한 해를 겪었습니다.
- It's always challenging to learn a foreign language.
  외국어를 배우는 것은 언제나 어려운 일입니다.

Word as it is clear/obviously/evidently/clearly 분명한 것은, 분명히

- 본문) As it is quite clear, all the courses are essential for knowledge of language.
- ex) Evidently, I want to change my major to Children Education.
  분명한 건 제가 아동학과로 전공을 바꾸고 싶다는 거예요.
- ex) I'm not obviously cut out for law school.
  저는 분명히 법대에 맞지 않습니다.

IH 답변 파헤치기

Word 학업 관련 대학 용어들

- **required/mandatory/compulsory course** 필수과목
- **elective/optional course** 선택과목
- **prerequisite** 선수과목
- **academic advisor** 지도교수
- **academic calendar** 학사일정
- **summer session** 여름 학기
- **drop/add period** 수강신청 변경 기간
- **to register for a course/to sign up for a course/ to enroll for a course** 수강신청을 하다
- **to change the course to another** 수업을 변경하다
- **to apply for a scholarship** 장학금을 신청하다
- **to submit a thesis** 논문을 제출하다
- **to take a class** 수업을 듣다
  (listen to a class가 아님)

MAKE YOUR ANSWER

질문에 대한 여러분의 답변을 만들어보세요.

What do you study in school? What is your major about? Do you like studying that major? Please tell me about your major in as much detail as possible.

ANSWER

Q3 I'd like to know about any memorable projects or assignments that you have done in school. What was the project about? Did you work alone or work in groups? What did you do to complete it?

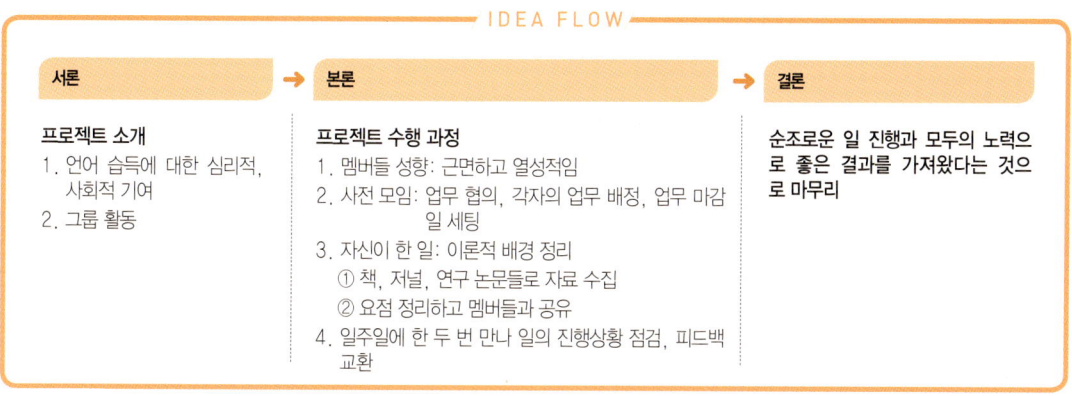

ANSWER

I had worked on an interesting project, which was given to me in the first semester of my sophomore year. The project was about how psychological and social factors contribute to successful language learning. That was a group project, and I had to work with the other four members who were assigned to me. I'm a kind of person who prefers working individually to working in groups, but I tried to collaborate with them to successfully complete the project. Luckily, all of my group members were industrious and enthusiastic for our work. We hit it off immediately and met a couple of times before beginning the project in earnest. We discussed which tasks we need, assigned each member each task, and set the deadline for each task. I was in charge of organizing theoretical background of successful language learning. For my job, I collected a number of materials from books, journals, and research papers. Then I summarized important points and shared them with other members. Condensing a great deal of materials into just a few pages was quite challenging but rewarding. The project was running on all cylinders, and consequently, our efforts paid off. We not only got an excellent grade but were selected as the best team in my class.

[해석 p.292 참조]

IH 답변 파헤치기

문장 구조 응용하기

prefer ~ing(A) to ~ing(B) = prefer to 부정사(A) rather than 동사원형(B) B보다 A를 선호하다

- 본문 I'm a kind of person who prefers working individually to working in groups, but I tried to collaborate with them to successfully complete the project.
- ex I prefer to make a presentation rather than create presentation materials.
발표 자료를 만드는 것보다 발표를 하는 것이 더 좋습니다.

과제나 프로젝트 소개하는 서두 열기

- I was assigned to create a web-based education program.
저는 웹 기반의 교육 프로그램을 만드는 일을 맡게 되었습니다.
- I have worked on the project called "Samrtphone Advertising," which was an individual task.
"스마트폰 광고"라고 불렸던 프로젝트를 수행한 적이 있었는데, 그건 독립 과제였지요.
- I had a memorable experience of completing a big project successfully.
큰 프로젝트를 성공리에 완수한 잊지 못할 경험을 했습니다.
- One group project came to my mind, which was carried out last semester.
지난 학기에 진행되었던 한 그룹 프로젝트가 떠오르네요.

프로젝트 진행을 설명할 때 사용될 수 있는 표현들

- I created a survey with both multiple-choice and open-ended question, and distributed them to as many people as possible through emails and blogs.
저는 객관식과 개방형 문항들로 설문조사를 만들어 그것들을 이메일과 블로그를 통해 가능한 많은 사람들에게 배포했습니다.
- I could gather and analyze numerous reviews on the eco-friendly products with the help of my teammate. 팀원의 도움으로 저는 그 환경친화적인 제품들에 대한 수많은 후기들을 모으고 분석할 수 있었습니다.
- We meet regularly to check how things were going and exchange feedback on each task.
우리들은 일이 어떻게 진행되고 있는지 점검하고 각자의 일에 대한 피드백을 교환하기 위해 정기적으로 만났습니다.

프로젝트 결과, 감상, 견해로 마무리하기

- The fatal mistake that he had made eventually led our group to get a poor grade from the professor. 그가 저지른 치명적인 실수로 결국 우리 그룹은 교수님으로부터 안 좋은 점수를 받았습니다.
- The result wasn't great, but I tried not to be discouraged. I just thought I would need thorough preparations for the next project. 결과는 좋지 않았지만, 위축되지 않으려고 애썼어요. 단지 다음 번 프로젝트 때는 철저한 준비를 해야겠다는 생각을 했습니다.

Idiom run(hit) on all cylinders 원활히 진행되다 (=go smoothly, go off without a hitch)

- The project seemed to run on all cylinders under the new leader.
프로젝트는 새 리더 아래서 원활히 진행되는 것 같았어요.
- Everything went off without a hitch, and I submitted my assignment before the deadline.
모든 것이 순조롭게 진행되어 저는 마감시기 전에 과제물을 제출했습니다.
- The irresponsible team member hindered us from hitting on all cylinders.
그 무책임한 팀원이 순조로운 일 진행을 가로막았습니다.

MAKE YOUR ANSWER

질문에 대한 여러분의 답변을 만들어보세요.

I'd like to know about any memorable projects or assignments that you have done in school. What was the project about? Did you work alone or work in groups? What did you do to complete it?

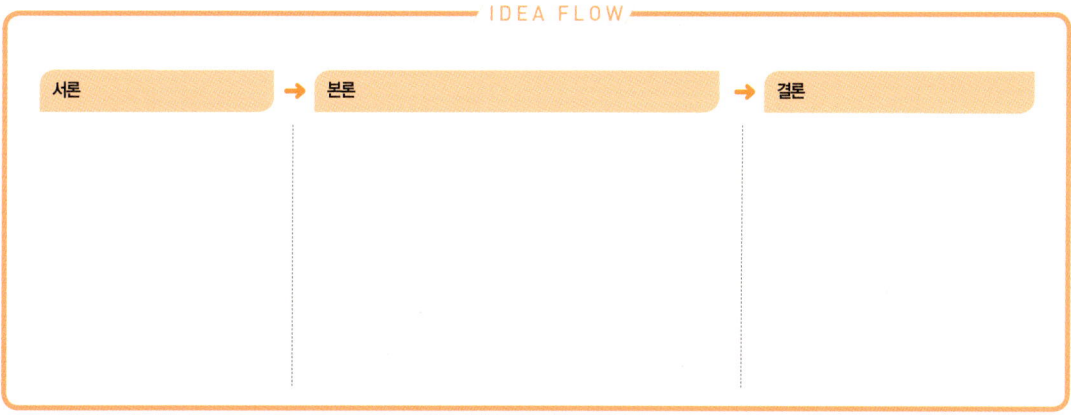

ANSWER

Lesson 4 NEW 뉴스를 보거나 듣기

Oral Proficiency Interview-computer

INTRO 뉴스를 보거나 듣기는 2013년 10월부터 OPIc 서베이 항목에 새롭게 추가된 신경향 문제입니다. 뉴스를 접하는 장비에서부터 좋아하는 뉴스 종류, 과거와 현재의 뉴스 형태 비교 등 다양한 문항들이 출제될 수 있습니다. 기존 OPIc 여가활동 관련한 주제들에 비해 다소 전문적이고 어려운 분야라고 할 수 있겠지만 차근차근 준비해가면 곧 자신감이 생기고 익숙해질 것입니다.

IH 답변 전략

① 뉴스를 얻는 기기나 장비 설정하기
- 요즘 뉴스 기기는 TV나 라디오뿐 아니라 팟 캐스트와 같은 인터넷 라디오를 들을 수 있는 컴퓨터나 스마트폰까지 다양합니다. 그 중 하나를 선택해 그 기기를 통해 뉴스를 보는 이유나 이점 등을 중심으로 답변을 준비하면 되겠습니다.
- 자신이 보는 기기의 이점을 설명할 때는 다른 기기들과 차별화되는 부분을 언급함으로써 내용적인 완성도를 기합니다.

② 뉴스 관련 어휘를 익히고 뉴스의 종류 알아두기
- 좋아하는 뉴스 종류를 정하고 그 뉴스가 다루는 부분을 설명하려면 기본적인 뉴스 어휘들을 알고 있는 것이 유리합니다.
- 좋아하는 뉴스 종류를 말할 때는 좋아하는 이유를 꼭 뒷받침해주도록 합니다.

③ 뉴스 변천사에 대한 답변 준비하기
- OPIc에서 자주 묻는 내용 중 하나가 어렸을 때의 기억이나 경험입니다. 지금과는 차이가 많이 있던 뉴스의 보도 방식, 구성, 앵커의 외모 등 과거의 뉴스가 어떻게 현재의 모습으로 변해왔는지 그 과정을 구체적인 예를 들어 비교, 대조할 수 있어야 합니다.
- 가장 기억에 남는 뉴스나 뉴스 시청/청취와 관련된 개인적인 에피소드도 준비하여 경험을 묻는 문항에 대비합니다.

 **예상질문 파헤치기** '뉴스를 보거나 듣기'에서는 어떠한 질문들이 출제될까요? 다음의 예상 질문에 대해 여러분은 어떻게 답변할지 한번 생각해 보세요.

1. What do you use to watch or listen to the news? Do you watch the news on TV? Do you listen to the news on the radio? Tell me how you watch or listen to the news in detail.

2. How did you first become interested in watching or listening to the news? How has the interest changed over the years?

3. I'd like to know about your favorite news sources. Do you get the news from TV or certain websites? Do you rely on the news sources? Why do you like them?

4. Which topics are you most interested in when you watch or listen to the news? What do you do to watch or listen to the news?

5. What kind of contents or categories do you expect the news to cover? Why do you want to know about them?

6. Is it important for you to watch or listen to the news? How does watching or listening to the news help you in your daily life?

7. Think of the news that was particularly memorable to you. What was the news about and what made it so memorable to you?

8. Tell me about a memorable experience you had while watching or listening to the news. What happened and why was it so special to you?

9. How did you get the news when you were a child? It could have been different from the way you get the news now. How has it changed?

What do you use to watch or listen to the news? Do you watch the news on TV? Do you listen to the news on the radio? Tell me how you watch or listen to the news in detail.

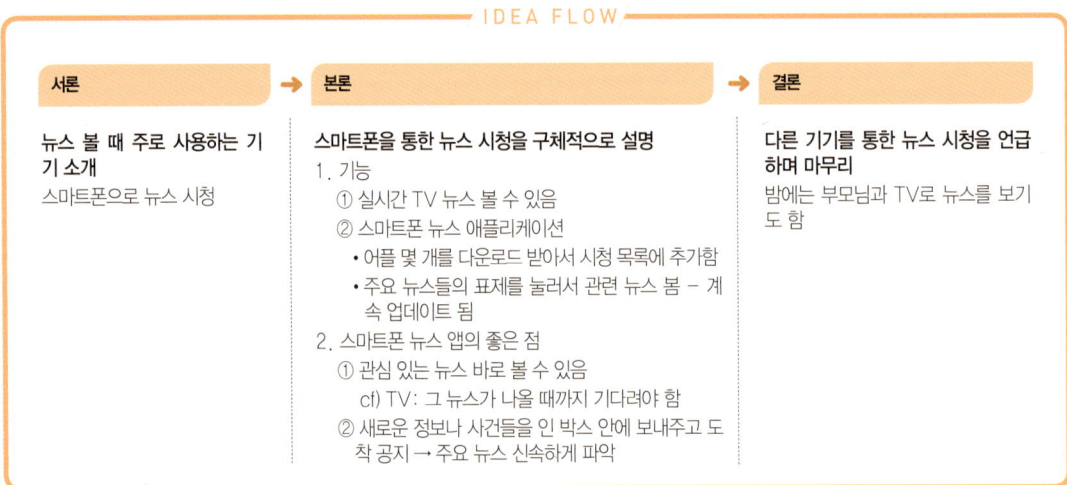

ANSWER

I primarily use my smartphone to watch the news. As long as the Internet connection is fine, I can watch live TV news on my smartphone. There are a number of news applications that can be downloaded for free on smartphones, too. I downloaded and added some of them to my favorite watching lists and check them whenever I want to see the news. The news apps display headlines of important news, which are constantly updated. Then I touch one of the headlines and start watching the relevant news. One of the best parts of watching the news the smartphone apps provide is that I can instantly watch the news I'm interested in; however, I have to wait for the news to be broadcast on TV. Also, some news apps send new information or incidents to my inbox and inform me of their arrival. The service makes it possible for me to check some critical news promptly. I don't mean I never watch the news on TV though. When I am home with my parents at night, I try to watch the news on TV with them.

[해석 p.292 참조]

IH 답변 파헤치기

문장 구조 응용하기

as long as S+V ~하는 한, ~하기만(이기만)하면

- 본문 As long as the Internet connection is fine, I can watch live TV news on my smartphone.
- ex I can work any time in any place as long as I can access the Internet.
  인터넷만 접속할 수 있다면 저는 언제 어디서든 일할 수 있습니다.

whenever S+V ~할 때마다, ~할 때면 언제라도

- 본문 I downloaded and added some of them to my favorite watching lists and check them whenever I want to see the news.
- ex I buy a big bucket of popcorn and Coke whenever I go see a movie.
  저는 영화 보러 갈 때마다 대형 사이즈의 팝콘과 콜라를 삽니다.
- ex Whenever I find some problems with my computer, I ask my brother for help.
  제 컴퓨터에 문제가 생길 때마다 저는 제 남동생에게 도움을 요청합니다.

inform A of B A에게 B를 알리다, 통지하다

- 본문 Also, some news apps send new information or incidents in my inbox and inform me of their arrival.
- ex My boss did not inform me of the conference date.
  제 상관은 저에게 회의 날짜를 알려주지 않았습니다.

뉴스를 접하는 주된 기기 소개하면서 서두 열기

- I mostly watch television to get my news. 저는 대개 텔레비전으로 뉴스를 접합니다.
- I usually listen to the news on radio while commuting to and from work by car.
  저는 승용차로 출퇴근하는 동안 주로 라디오로 뉴스를 듣습니다.
- Mobile applications are my favorite way to watch the news.
  휴대폰 애플리케이션이 제가 가장 좋아하는 뉴스 시청 방법입니다.
- Most of my news sources come from different news websites such as CNN or BBC.
  저의 대부분의 뉴스 근원지는 CNN이나 BBC 같은 각기 다른 뉴스 웹사이트들입니다.

특정 뉴스 청취 기기를 선호하는 이유 설명하기

- I like watching the news on TV because current TV news programs broadcast a diverse range of news. 요즘 TV 뉴스 프로그램들은 다양한 범위의 뉴스를 방송하기 때문에 저는 TV로 뉴스 보는 것이 좋습니다.
- It's easy and convenient to listen to the latest news with a touch of the screen on my smartphone.
  스마트폰을 한 번 터치하는 것으로 최신 뉴스를 들을 수 있는 것이 쉽고 편리합니다.
- Since I'm interested in political news, I stay tuned to a news channel where different political commentators analyze and criticize important political issues.
  저는 정치 뉴스에 관심이 많아서 다양한 정치 평론가들이 중요한 정치 안건을 분석하고 비판하는 TV 뉴스 채널에 채널을 고정해놓습니다.

Word a number of + 복수 명사 많은 (=many)

- 본문 There are a number of news applications that can be downloaded for free on smartphones, too.
- ex A number of people were staying in line to buy the newly released smartphone.
  많은 사람들이 새로 출시된 스마트폰을 사기 위해 줄을 서서 기다리고 있었습니다.
- ex I can give you a number of reasons why I like this application.
  제가 왜 이 응용프로그램을 좋아하는지에 대해 많은 이유를 알려드릴 수 있습니다.

질문에 대한 여러분의 답변을 만들어보세요.

What do you use to watch or listen to the news? Do you watch the news on TV? Do you listen to the news on the radio? Tell me how you watch or listen to the news in detail.

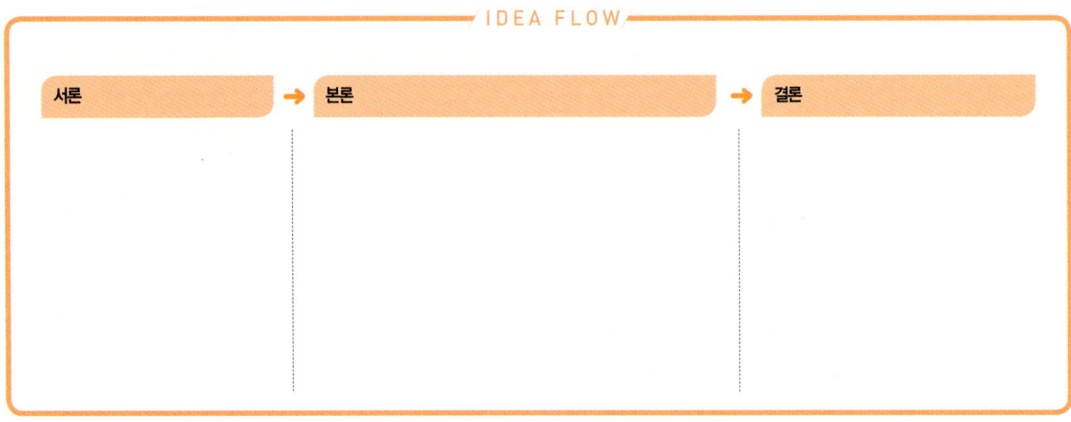

ANSWER

Which topics are you most interested in when you watch or listen to the news? What do you do to watch or listen to the news?

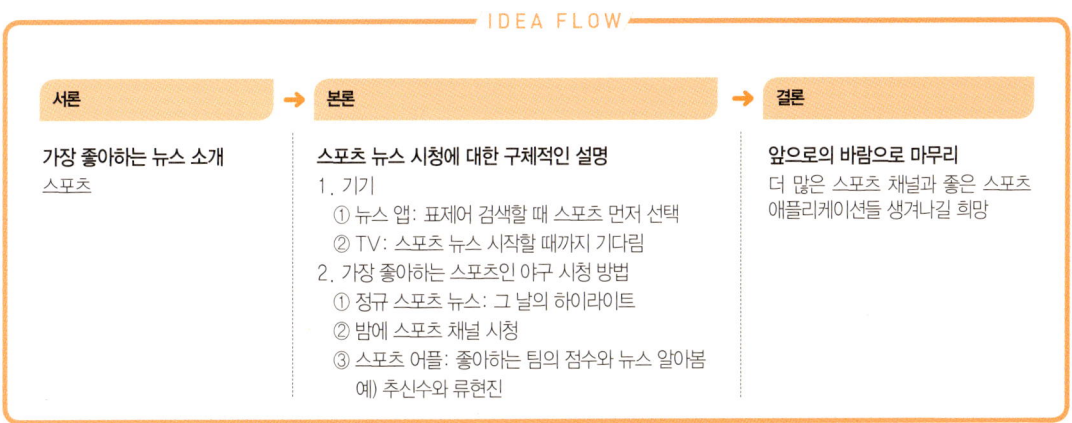

ANSWER

I definitely like the news about sports. Whenever I search headlines on my news applications, I choose the one about sports first. When I watch the news on TV, I also wait for the sports news to start. I'm interested in all kinds of sports, but my favorite is baseball. During the baseball season, I hardly miss the sports news showing the highlights of the games of the day. You know that I can't see all the baseball games played in different regions. Since regular TV news doesn't usually devote much time to sports-related news, I watch it on several sports channels on TV mostly at night. I also download some sports applications and keep track of scores or news of my favorite teams. Some Korean baseball players like Choo Shin Soo and Ryu Hyun Jin are recently playing very well in Major League, so I frequently check the news about them. I hope we get more sports channels and better sports applications available.

[해석 p.292 참조]

문장 구조 응용하기

Since S+V(A), S+V(B) A이기 때문에 B이다
= S+V(B) since S+V(A) = S+V(A), so S+V(B)

- 본문 Since regular TV news doesn't usually devote much time to sports-related news, I watch it on several sports channels on TV mostly at night.
  = Regular TV news doesn't usually devote much time to sports-related news, so I watch it on several sports channels on TV mostly at night.
- ex I mostly watch the short length of a network TV news program at night since I don't have enough time to catch up with the latest news. By doing so, I can get major domestic and international issues.
  저는 최신 뉴스를 따라잡을 시간이 별로 없기 때문에 주로 밤에 짧은 분량의 전국 방송 텔레비전 뉴스를 시청합니다. 그렇게 함으로써 국내외 뉴스를 접할 수 있습니다.

Word hardly 거의 ~아니다, 거의~하지 않다

- 본문 During the baseball season, I hardly miss the sports news showing the highlights of the games of the day.
- ex Although I am interested in celebrities or entertainers, I hardly watch entertainment news on TV.
  저는 유명인이나 연예인들에 관심이 있긴 하지만 TV에서 연예 뉴스는 거의 보지 않습니다.
  cf) I've never been interested in entertainment news.
  저는 연예 뉴스에 한번도 관심을 가져본 적이 없습니다.

Idiom keep track of ~을 계속 파악하다

- 본문 I also download some sports applications and keep track of scores or news of my favorite teams.
- ex Watching some international news on TV helps me keep track of what's happening in different countries. TV로 국제 뉴스를 시청하는 것은 제가 다른 나라에서 무슨 일이 일어나고 있는지 파악하는데 도움이 됩니다.
  cf) I lose track of time when watching political news on TV.
  저는 정치 뉴스를 볼 때는 시간 가는 줄 모릅니다.

좋아하는 주제의 뉴스를 접하는 방법 설명하기

- As a mother of a 3-year-old daughter, I'm particularly interested in the news about parenting. Whenever some good information and knowledge of parenting appear on TV, I try to jot them down and put them into a use.
  세 살 된 딸의 엄마로서 저는 특히 육아에 관한 뉴스에 관심이 갑니다. TV에서 육아에 관련된 좋은 정보와 지식이 나올 때마다 저는 적어놨다가 실제 생활에 적용합니다.
- I am a huge fan of movies and I want to get as much information as possible about any genres of movies. But since television news does not cover the topic frequently, I use mobile applications to check the detailed news of newly-released films and movies playing right now in addition to the recent news about actors and directors.
  저는 영화를 무척 좋아해서 어떤 장르의 영화든 그 정보를 가능한 많이 알고 싶습니다. 하지만 텔레비전 뉴스는 그 주제를 자주 다루지 않기 때문에 배우들과 감독에 대한 최신 뉴스와 더불어 최신작과 지금 상영중인 영화에 대한 뉴스를 확인하려 휴대폰 애플리케이션을 사용합니다.
- I enjoy watching the political news broadcast by cable TV network because it reports some sensitive political issues that the main stream media hardly covers.
  저는 케이블 방송사들이 방송하는 정치 뉴스를 잘 보는데 그건 정규 매체들이 잘 다루지 않는 민감한 정치적 현안들을 보도하기 때문입니다.

MAKE YOUR ANSWER

질문에 대한 여러분의 답변을 만들어보세요.

Which topics are you most interested in when you watch or listen to the news? What do you do to watch or listen to the news?

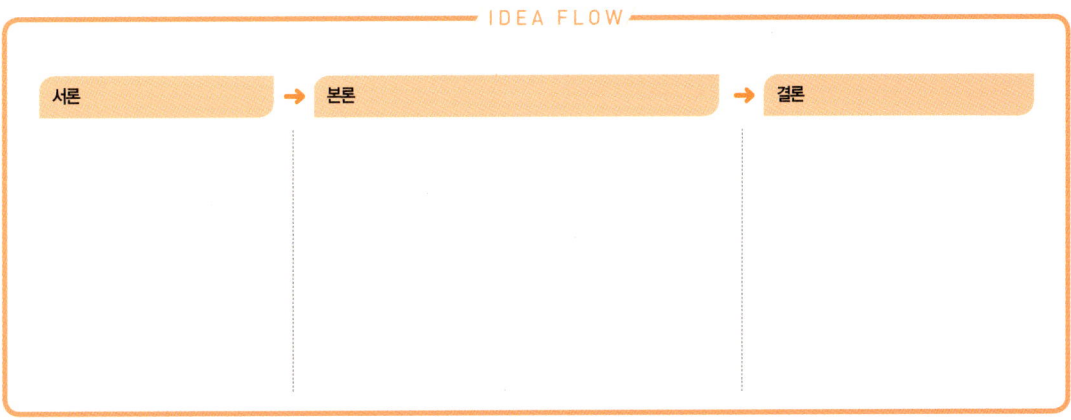

IDEA FLOW

| 서론 → | 본론 → | 결론 |

ANSWER

Q3 How did you get the news when you were a child? It could have been different from the way you get the news now. How has it changed?

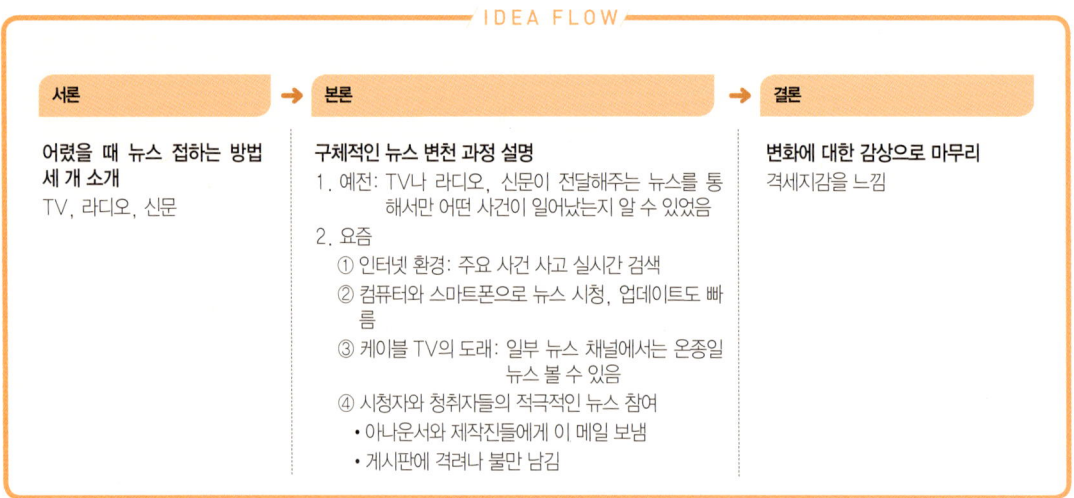

ANSWER

When I was a child, people had only three ways to get the news. They watched the TV news, listened to the radio news, or read a newspaper. People didn't know which events had taken place until the TV or radio broadcast the news or the newspaper was delivered, and they didn't know the news that wasn't covered. It may seem absurd or ridiculous to those who grew up in the internet environment where major accidents and incidents can be searched in real time. Today, we can also get the news from computers and smartphones, and the news is updated very quickly. Since the cable TV became available, we can even watch the news all day long on several news channels. I also want to mention another big change, which is viewers' and listeners' active participation in the news programs. They send their opinions of the news directly to the anchors' or producers' emails without hesitation. They also post comments with encouragement or complaint on the bulletin board of the program homepage. We didn't even dream of this sort of thing when I was little.

[해석 p.293 참조]

IH 답변 파헤치기

문장 구조 응용하기

not A until B B하고(되고)서야 A하다(이다)

- 본문) People didn't know which events had taken place until the TV or radio broadcast the news or the newspaper was delivered.
- ex) I wasn't interested in business news until I started working.
  저는 직장 생활을 시작하고서야 경제 뉴스에 관심을 가졌습니다.
- ex) The sports news doesn't start until 9:30. 스포츠 뉴스는 9시 30분이 되야 시작합니다.

Word mention ~을 말하다, 언급하다

- 본문) I want to mention another big change, which is viewers' and listeners' active participation in the news programs.
- ex) I am going to mention some advantages of using mobile news applications.
  휴대폰 뉴스 애플리케이션을 사용하는 장점을 언급하겠습니다.
  (mention ~~about~~ something)

Word without hesitation 망설이지 않고, 서슴지 않고

- 본문) They send their opinions of the news directly to the anchors' or producers' emails without hesitation.
- ex) I discontinued my subscription of newspaper without any hesitation.
  저는 아무 망설임 없이 신문 구독을 중지했습니다.

뉴스 관련 변화에 대해 설명하기

- The viewers' expectations of news have become much higher than those in the past, so broadcasters try to report more prompt, accurate, and reliable information.
  뉴스에 대한 시청자들의 기대치가 과거보다 훨씬 높아졌기 때문에 방송사들이 보다 신속하고, 정확하며 믿을 수 있는 정보를 보도하려 애씁니다.
- With the help of smartphones, people can watch or listen to the news while on the move today whereas they had to stay in a certain place to watch it on TV when I was young.
  제가 어렸을 때는 사람들이 TV를 보려면 특정 장소에 있어야 한 반면 요즘은 스마트폰 덕분에 이동 중에도 뉴스를 시청하고 청취할 수 있습니다.
- There has been a huge change in the newscasters' clothes especially the anchorwomen. They used to dress up modestly in a plain dark or grey suit several years ago, but nowadays, they wear clothes that look stylish in bold colors and designs.
  뉴스 진행자, 특히 여성 진행자들의 복장에 커다란 변화가 있었습니다. 몇 년 전만해도 검정이나 회색처럼 단색의 수수한 옷차림을 하였으나 요즘은 대담한 색깔과 디자인의 멋스럽게 보이는 옷을 입습니다.

Word 뉴스 관련 어휘들

- **watch the news on TV** TV로 뉴스를 시청하다
- **listen to the news on the radio** 라디오로 뉴스를 듣다
- **broadcast** 보도하다
- **report/announce the news** 뉴스를 보도하다(알리다)
- **cover the news** 뉴스를 다루다
- **news sources** 뉴스근원지
- **regular news** 정규 뉴스
- **breaking news** 뉴스 속보
- **scoop** 특종
- **in-depth coverage** 심층보도
- **anchor/newscaster** 앵커, 뉴스 진행자
- **reporter** 기자, 리포터
- **cable TV network** 케이블 방송사
- **broadcaster/broadcasting company** 방송사
- **website of broadcasting station** 방송사 웹사이트
- **domestic/international news** 국내/해외 뉴스

MAKE YOUR ANSWER

질문에 대한 여러분의 답변을 만들어보세요.

How did you get the news when you were a child? It could have been different from the way you get the news now. How has it changed?

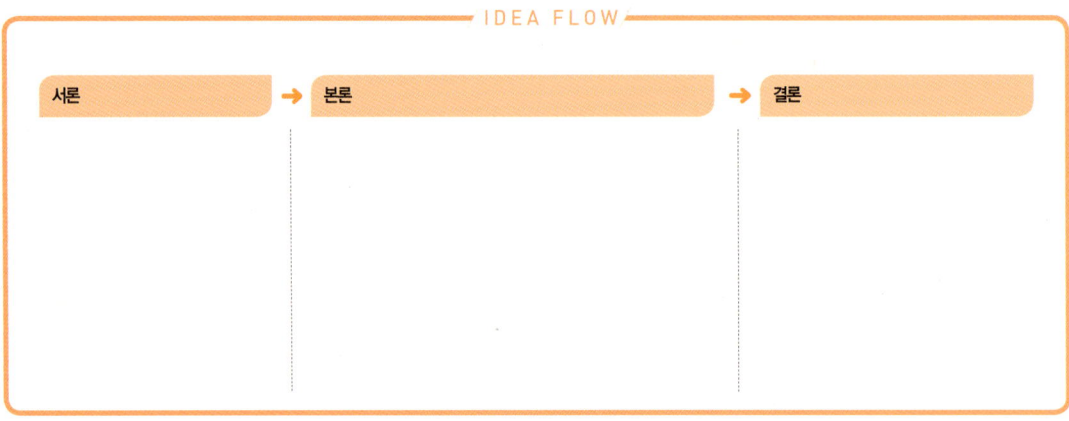

Memo

Oral Proficiency Interview-computer

Lesson 5 콘서트보기

INTRO 콘서트보기 관련 주제를 준비하면 음악 감상, 공연, 노래 부르기 등과 같은 여가활동에 있는 다른 주제들도 한꺼번에 준비할 수 있습니다. 예를 들어 콘서트장 묘사를 준비할 때 사용했던 어휘나 표현들을 공연장 묘사할 때도 사용할 수 있고, 콘서트에서 익힌 음악 관련 소재나 어휘들을 음악 감상 답변에서 활용할 수 있습니다. 하나를 준비하면 다른 여러 개가 이렇게 저절로 따라 오니 콘서트는 정말 기특하고 신통한 주제라고 할 수 있겠죠?

IH 답변 전략

① 장소 묘사하기
- 장소 묘사는 OPIc에서 매우 자주 나오는 유형입니다. 해변이나 공원 등의 자연적인 장소의 묘사뿐 아니라 콘서트장, 공연장, 극장 등 인위적인 건물의 외관 묘사 또한 빈번히 출제됩니다.
- 건물의 외관 묘사를 할 때는 주로 밖에서 안으로, 즉 콘서트장을 둘러싸고 있는 자연경관이나 다른 높은 빌딩들과 같은 주변 환경 → 콘서트장의 규모, 좌석 수, 층수 → 콘서트장 내부(조명, 무대, 내부 분위기 등)의 순서대로 묘사해주는 것이 깔끔하고 조리 있는 답변이 되겠습니다.

② 콘서트에 대한 관심 변천사
- 처음 콘서트에 가게 된 계기와 그때 느꼈던 흥미와 관심이 시간이 흐르면서 어떻게 확장 내지는 변화되었는지 그 발달 과정에 대한 답변을 꼭 준비해두어야 합니다.
- 관심 변천사에 대해 답변을 할 때는 변화의 계기를 준 콘서트를 예로 언급해주는 것이 좋습니다.

③ 콘서트 관련 경험 말하기
- 인상 깊었던 콘서트를 설명할 때는 서두에 콘서트에 대한 일반적 정보, 즉 콘서트 종류, 관람시기와 장소, 동행인 등을 간단하게 언급해 줍니다.
- 콘서트 관련 에피소드인 만큼 콘서트가 중심이 되는 답변이 좋습니다. 장소만 콘서트장이고 그 내용은 콘서트와 별로 상관 없는 답변은 되도록 피하시는 것이 좋습니다.

예상질문 파헤치기 '콘서트보기'에서는 어떠한 질문들이 출제될까요? 다음의 예상 질문에 대해 여러분은 어떻게 답변할지 한번 생각해 보세요.

✓ 1. You indicated in the survey you go to concerts. What kinds of concerts do you like to go to and who do you often go with? What's the main purpose of going to concerts? Give me in as much detail as possible.

2. Do you remember the first time you went to the concert? What concert did you go to and where did you watch it? What did you like or dislike about it?

3. You indicated in the survey that you like to go to concerts. What do you usually do before you go to concerts? What do you do after you go to concerts? Tell me about how you spend your day when you go to concerts.

4. How did you first become interested in going to concerts? How has the interest changed over time?

✓ 5. Which concert have you been to most recently? When and where was the concert held? Did you like the concert hall? Please describe the concert hall in as much detail as you can.

6. You indicated in the survey that you like to go to concerts. What do you like to do in concerts?

✓ 7. What was the most memorable experience you had while watching a concert? What made you think it's the most memorable to you? Please tell me the whole story of that.

8. Eva also likes going to concerts. Ask her three to four questions about going to concerts.

9. How often do you go to concerts? What do you think of the ticket prices for concerts?

10. Tell me about your unexpected, surprising, or embarrassing experience you had in concerts.

11. How do you usually get concert tickets? Do you buy them online or do you buy them at the ticket booth? If they are sold out, what do you do?

Q1 You indicated in the survey you go to concerts. What kinds of concerts do you like to go to and who do you often go with? What's the main purpose of going to concerts? Give me in as much detail as possible.

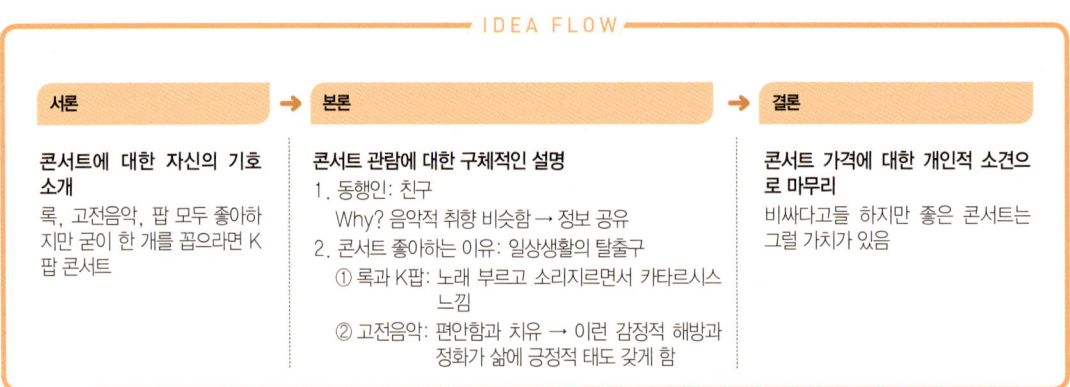

ANSWER

I enjoy going to any kinds of concerts including rock, classical, and pop concerts. But if you ask me to choose what I like the most, I'd say Korean pop concerts. I like many good Korean pop songs, and I can feel the heat and passion of music at the concerts. I normally go to K-pop concerts with my friend. We have the similar taste in music, so we share lots of information of K-pop stars like their songs and their concerts. Concerts are like my escape from daily life full of stress and tension. I can experience some sense of catharsis while I'm singing along and screaming out with other audience especially at the rock and K-pop concerts. Classical music concerts make me feel relaxed and healed, too. Through the emotional freedom or emotional purification, I get to have more positive attitude toward my life. Some people say that tickets for the concerts are too expensive, but I think good concerts are really worth the money spent for the ticket.

[해석 p.293 참조]

IH 답변 파헤치기

좋아하는 콘서트의 소개로 서두 열기

- I'm a huge fan of jazz and go to jazz concerts every other month usually with my friend.
  저는 재즈를 무척 좋아해서 두 달에 한 번씩 대개는 친구와 함께 재즈 콘서트에 갑니다.
- I like any kinds of concerts except rock concerts playing loud music.
  저는 시끄러운 음악을 연주하는 록 콘서트를 제외한 어떤 종류의 콘서트도 다 좋아합니다.
- I attend pop concerts more than five times a year if my favorite pop singers perform.
  제가 제일 좋아하는 팝 가수들이 공연한다면 저는 일 년에 다섯 번 이상 팝 콘서트에 갑니다.
- I never miss classical music concerts where I can listen to world-renowned artists performing.
  저는 세계적으로 유명한 예술가들이 공연하는 클래식 콘서트는 놓치지 않습니다.

콘서트를 즐기는 이유와 관련한 아이디어

- I like going to concerts because I can see my favorite singers and bands perform my favorite songs live. 저는 제가 가장 좋아하는 가수와 밴드가 제가 가장 좋아하는 노래들을 라이브로 부르는 것을 볼 수 있어 콘서트에 가는 것을 좋아합니다.
- Most idol groups play dance music in quick rhythm in their concerts, which gives me energy and vitality. 대부분의 아이돌 그룹은 콘서트에서 빠른 리듬의 댄스곡들을 연주하는데, 그 음악은 제게 에너지와 활력을 줍니다.
- Concerts provide a perfect opportunity for people to share their enthusiasm for particular music or musicians.
  콘서트는 사람들이 특정 음악이나 음악가에 대한 열정을 공유할 수 있는 완벽한 기회를 제공해줍니다.
- A concert is the best place to stay away from my stress of everyday living.
  콘서트는 내가 매일 겪는 스트레스를 멀리 할 수 있는 최고의 장소입니다.

콘서트 관람을 하기 위해 할 수 있는 활동들

- To enjoy the concert, I download the singer's songs and memorize the lyrics before the concert begins. 콘서트를 즐기기 위해 콘서트 시작 전 가수들의 노래를 다운로드 받아서 가사를 외웁니다.
- I have some time to find some background knowledge about the music that I will listen to before going to classical concerts.
  클래식 콘서트에 가기 전에는 제가 들을 음악에 대한 배경지식을 찾아보는 시간을 갖습니다.

콘서트장에서 할 수 있는 활동들

- I normally sit quietly and just clap my hands while my girl friend sing along and dance to the music with a fast, rhythmic beat.
  제 여자 친구는 노래를 따라 부르고 빠르고 리드미컬한 박자의 음악에 맞춰 춤도 추는 반면 저는 대개 얌전히 앉아서 그냥 박수만 칩니다.
- Many girls waved fluorescent green batons and cheered as the five members came on the stage.
  다섯 명이 무대 위로 올라오자 많은 소녀 팬들은 형광 녹색 빛의 막대기를 흔들며 환호성을 질렀습니다.
- During the classical music concerts, I try to appreciate the melody and understand the musician's interpretation of the music. 클래식 음악 콘서트에서는 멜로디를 음미하고 음악가의 곡 해석을 이해하려고 노력합니다.

Word taste 취향, 기호

- Jazz doesn't suit my taste although I know it's wonderful music.
  재즈가 훌륭한 음악이라는 걸 알긴 하지만 제 취향에 맞지 않습니다.
- It's a blessing to meet someone who has a similar taste in music.
  음악에 대한 취향이 비슷한 사람을 만난다는 건 축복입니다.

MAKE YOUR ANSWER

질문에 대한 여러분의 답변을 만들어보세요.

You indicated in the survey you go to concerts. What kinds of concerts do you like to go to and who do you often go with? What's the main purpose of going to concerts? Give me in as much detail as possible.

ANSWER

Which concert have you been to most recently? When and where was the concert held? Did you like the concert hall? Please describe the concert hall in as much detail as you can.

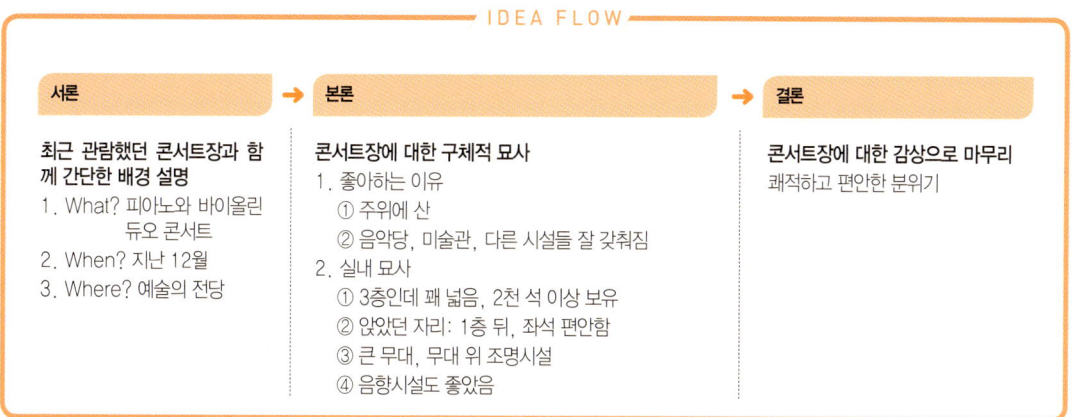

ANSWER

Last December, I went to the piano and violin duo concert played by the two promising Korean musicians, Son Yeol-eum and Clara-Jumi Kang. The concert was performed at the Concert Hall of Seoul Arts Center, which is located in Yangjae-dong in Seoul. I like to go to Seoul Arts Center because it is surrounded by mountains and is well equipped with some art museums and other facilities as well as music halls. The concert hall was pretty large with three stories. I'm not sure about the exact number of seats, but I guess it has more than 2,000 seats. I sat in the back of the first floor and the seat was comfortable enough for me to sit through the two-and-a-half-hour concert. I saw a large stage in the front, and above the stage, there was lighting equipment to give a spotlight on the performers. I remember the acoustics of the hall was also good. To conclude, the concert hall provided a pleasant and comfortable atmosphere for its audience.

[해석 p.293 참조]

IH 답변 파헤치기

콘서트장의 간단한 배경 설명으로 서두 열기

- The concert that I last attended was performed in Olympic Park located in Songpagu, Seoul.
  제가 마지막으로 가서 본 콘서트는 서울 송파구에 있는 올림픽 공원에서 공연되었습니다.
- I went to Exco in Daegu to watch the nationwide tour concert of Cho Young Pil last December.
  저는 지난 12월 조용필의 전국 투어 콘서트를 보기 위해 대구에 있는 엑스코에 갔습니다.
- Two weeks ago I enjoyed the piano concert that was played at the Korea Art Center in Seoul.
  저는 2주 전에 서울에 있는 한국 아트 센터에서 연주된 피아노 콘서트를 즐겁게 관람했습니다.

콘서트홀의 외관 설명하기

- The concert hall is quite spacious with light brownish walls and highly polished floors.
  콘서트장은 꽤 넓었고 벽은 밝은 갈색이 돌았고 바닥은 매끈매끈 윤이 났습니다.
- Two aisles divided the seating area into three sections on both the ground and second floor.
  1, 2층 모두 두 개의 통로가 좌석 구간을 세 구역으로 나누었습니다.
- The half-dome shape of the concert hall can accommodate more than 1,500 people.
  반 돔 형태로 되어 있는 그 콘서트홀은 1,500명 이상을 수용할 수 있습니다.
- It was well equipped with facilities like storage lockers, cafés, a gift shop, etc.
  거긴 보관함, 카페, 선물가게 등의 편의시설들이 잘 갖춰져 있었습니다.
- In the front, there was a large stage on which a grand piano was placed.
  앞에는 큰 무대가 있었고, 그 위에는 그랜드 피아노 한 대가 놓여있었습니다.

콘서트홀에 대한 호불호와 그 이유 설명하기

- It is located within a 5-minute walking distance from Line 5 Gwanghwamun Station, which is very convenient to go to.
  그곳은 5호선 광화문역에서 도보로 겨우 5분 거리에 위치하고 있어서 가기가 무척 편했습니다.
- Since it was surrounded by parks and mountains, I could get some fresh air while walking around there before the concert.
  산과 공원으로 둘러싸여 있어서 저는 콘서트 시작 전 그곳을 걸어 다니면서 좋은 공기를 마실 수 있었습니다.
- I liked the art center that had several art galleries. I saw impressive photo exhibitions at one of the galleries before the concert started.
  저는 예술 전시관들이 있는 그 예술 센터가 좋았습니다. 콘서트가 시작하기 전 그 중 한 전시실에서 인상적인 사진 전시회를 봤습니다.
- It was or maybe due to old sound equipment, the music played by the orchestra didn't sound beautiful at all.
  오래된 음향 장비 때문인지는 잘 모르겠지만 그 오케스트라가 연주했던 곡은 전혀 아름답게 들리지 않았습니다.
- The seats are too hard and close together to fully enjoy the concert.
  좌석들이 너무 딱딱하고 붙어있어서 콘서트를 충분히 즐기지 못했습니다.

콘서트장에 대한 감상으로 마무리하기

- I won't visit the concert hall again even if there are good performances that I want to see.
  내가 보고 싶어하는 좋은 공연을 한다 해도 저는 그 콘서트홀에는 다시 가고 싶지 않습니다.
- I hope the concert that I'll watch next will be held in the music hall.
  저는 제가 다음에 볼 콘서트가 그 음악당에서 열리기를 희망합니다.

MAKE YOUR ANSWER

질문에 대한 여러분의 답변을 만들어보세요.

Which concert have you been to most recently? When and where was the concert held? Did you like the concert hall? Please describe the concert hall in as much detail as you can.

What was the most memorable experience you had while watching a concert? What made you think it's the most memorable to you? Please tell me the whole story of that.

---- IDEA FLOW ----

서론 →	본론 →	결론
인상 깊었던 콘서트 소개 1. What? 싸이의 콘서트 2. When? 그가 세계적인 유명 가수 되기 몇 년 전 연말 3. With whom? 남자친구 4. Why? 새해 전날 밤을 기념하기 위해	콘서트에 대한 구체적 묘사 1. 공연 전: 기대 많이 안 했음 　Why? 노래보다는 공연, 가수보다는 예능인이라는 인식 2. 공연 중 ① 노래 매우 잘하고 춤도 좋음 ② 관객들과 같이 춤추면서 노래도 따라 부름 ③ 교묘한 조명장치로 인상적 무대 연출 → 더욱 신남 ④ 과거~현재 노래, 미국 팝송 부름 ⑤ 8시에 시작한 공연 자정 다 되어 끝남	콘서트와 싸이에 대한 감상으로 마무리 1. 즐거운 콘서트 2. 눈부신 무대매너와 가창력 지닌 좋은 가수

ANSWER

I went to Psy's concert a few years ago, not long before he has become a world-famous singer through his song, Gangnam Style. I watched the concert at the end of December with my boyfriend to celebrate New Year's Eve. It was my first time to attend his concert, but honestly, I didn't expect much about it. To me, he was more like an entertainer than a singer, who made the audience feel excited with his ornate performances but not with his songs. As the show went by, however, I found I was totally wrong. He sang much better than I'd expected, and his energetic dances captured my eyes and mind. I was getting excited and couldn't help but sing along and dance to his fast beat songs with other audience. He incorporated lighting tricks in his performances to create a visually impressive stage, which made us feel more thrilled. He sang all of his old and recent songs and American pop songs throughout the concert. The concert that had began at 8 ended at almost midnight. It was a really enjoyable concert, and I found him a good singer with singing ability as well as dazzling stage presence.

[해석 p.293 참조]

IH 답변 파헤치기

문장 구조 응용하기

long before S+V ~하기 훨씬 이전에
- 본문) I went to Psy's concert a few years ago, not long before he has become a world-famous singer through his song, Gangnam Style.
- ex) I had seen Rain's concert once long before he entered the military service.
  저는 비가 군대 가기 훨씬 전에 한 번 그의 콘서트를 보러 간 적이 있습니다.

cf) long after S+V ~하고 한참 후에
- ex) Long after he was discharged from the army, he held a small concert for his long time fans.
  군대에서 제대한 지 한참 후에 그는 그의 오래된 팬을 위해 작은 콘서트를 열었습니다.

more like A than B B라기 보다는 A
- 본문) To me, he was more like an entertainer than a singer, who made the audience feel excited with his ornate performances but not with his songs.
- ex) Her delicate and sensitive voice felt much more like a musical instrument than a song.
  그녀의 섬세하고 감성적인 목소리는 노래라기보다는 악기처럼 느껴졌습니다.

기억에 남는 콘서트 소개하기
- It was my first time to see an outdoor concert, which made me very excited.
  저는 처음으로 야외 콘서트를 보는 것이었고, 그래서 무척 흥분했습니다.
- During a visit to Busan, I witnessed the rock concerts of its local bands and was fascinated by their intense music. 부산 방문 때 저는 그 지역 밴드들의 록 콘서트를 목격했고 그들의 강렬한 음악에 매료되었습니다.
- One of the most memorable concerts I went to was JYJ's concert held in Olympic Gymnastics Stadium a few years ago. 제가 갔던 가장 기억에 남는 콘서트 중의 하나는 몇 년 전 잠실 체조경기장에서 열린 JYJ의 콘서트입니다.

기억에 남는 콘서트에 관련한 아이디어
- I was a bit embarrassed that so many girls in a frenzy were screaming out his name around me.
  저는 그렇게 많은 소녀들이 열광한 채 제 주위에서 그의 이름을 소리쳐 부르는 것에 좀 당황했습니다.
- The pianist played ten encores in return for our rousing cheer.
  그 피아니스트는 우리의 열렬한 환호에 대한 보답으로 10곡의 앙고르 곡을 쳤습니다.
- I finally got an autograph after a two-hour wait, and even more amazingly, I took a picture with him.
  저는 두 시간의 기다림 후에 드디어 그의 사인을 받았고, 더 굉장한 건, 그와 함께 사진을 찍었다는 것입니다.

Word) incorporate A in/into B A에 B를 포함하다, 혼합시키다
- 본문) He incorporated lighting tricks in his performances to create a visually impressive stage, which made us feel more thrilled.
- ex) He is well known for incorporating interesting performances with an ingenious, creative idea into his music concerts. 그는 기발하고 창의적인 아이디어가 담긴 재미있는 공연들을 음악 콘서트에 포함시키는 걸로 잘 알려져 있습니다.

콘서트에 대한 소회로 마무리하기
- Still, I miss the atmosphere that reminded me of my 20s. 제 20대를 상기시켜준 그 분위기가 아직도 그립습니다.
- I will never forget the concert where I could meet my boyfriend. 제 남자친구를 만나게 해준 그 콘서트를 절대로 잊지 않을 것입니다.

질문에 대한 여러분의 답변을 만들어보세요.

What was the most memorable experience you had while watching a concert? What made you think it's the most memorable to you? Please tell me the whole story of that.

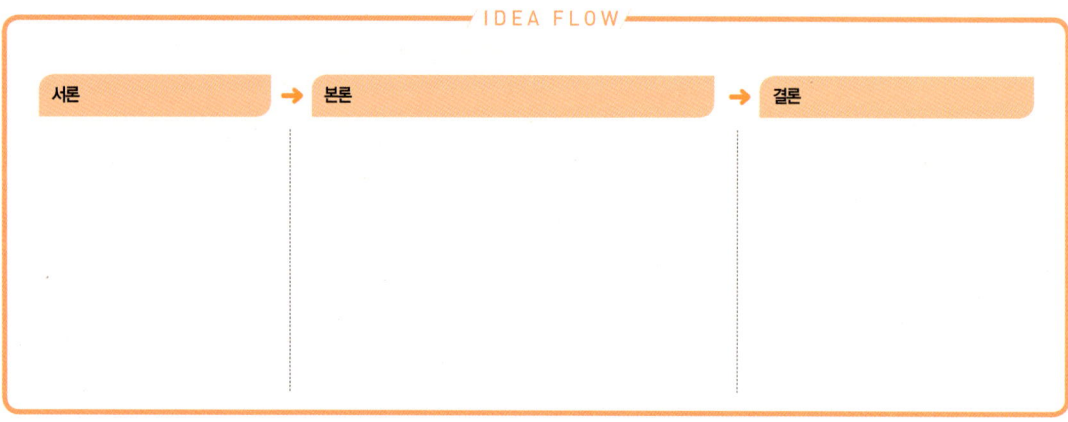

ANSWER

Memo

Oral Proficiency Interview-computer

Lesson 6

체스하기

INTRO

체스하기 역시 최근에 추가된 신경향 주제에 해당합니다. 동양권 문화에서는 그렇게 대중화되어 있지 않는 게임이라 좀 낯설게 여겨질 수도 있겠지만 새로운 여가 문화를 배운다는 적극적인 마인드로 도전을 해 보시는 것도 좋겠습니다. 설령 사전조사에서 체스하기를 표시하지 않는다고 해도 돌발 문제로 얼마든지 등장할 수 있기 때문에 게임의 기본적인 룰과 방식 등을 중심으로 체스하기 답변을 준비해보도록 하겠습니다.

IH 답변 전략

① 체스의 기본적인 룰과 방식 알아두기
- 기존의 게임 항목과 마찬가지로 체스 또한 간단한 게임 방법과 규칙 등을 설명할 수 있어야 합니다. 체스 게임에서만 사용되는 용어를 정리하여 익힌 다음 실제 답변에 활용합니다.
- 체스를 설명하는 답변의 결론부는 체스에 대한 개인적 감상이나 의견으로 마무리해줍니다.

② 체스를 두는 상대, 시간, 목적 등 설정하기
- 체스의 규칙과 체스를 두는 방식 등을 제외한 다른 질문들은 기존의 게임하기나 그 외 여가생활 주제들을 준비하는 과정과 비슷하게 준비하면 됩니다.
- 체스를 언제, 어디서, 누구와, 왜 두는지를 설명하고 아울러 체스만이 가지고 있는 장점까지 포함시켜 주면 훌륭한 답변이 될 수 있습니다.

③ 체스에 대한 관심의 변천사와 체스와 연관된 개인적 경험 소개하기
- 처음 체스에 관심을 갖게 된 계기와 이 관심이 체스를 계속 두면서 어떻게 발전되었는지에 대한 관심의 변천사를 설명할 수 있어야 합니다.
- 체스를 배우면서 있었던 에피소드나 또는 체스 게임의 승패와 관련된 사건 등을 주제로 답변을 준비합니다.

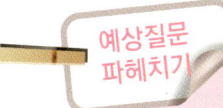

'체스하기'에서는 어떠한 질문들이 출제될까요? 다음의 예상 질문에 대해 여러분은 어떻게 답변할지 한 번 생각해 보세요.

1. You indicated in the survey that you play chess. Tell me briefly about what the chess is. Who do you usually play it with? How often do you play it?

✓ 2. You indicated in the survey that you play chess. What is chess and how do you play it? When and where do you usually play chess? Why do you like it? Tell me about chess in as much detail as possible.

3. How did you first become interested in playing chess? How has the interest developed over the years?

4. Think back to the time when you first play chess. When did you play it and who did you play it with? How did you feel when you first played it?

5. Who taught you how to play chess? Did you learn it by yourself? How long have you played chess? When do you normally play it?

✓ 6. Eva also likes playing chess. Ask her three or four questions that you want to know about chess.

7. What are the benefits of playing chess? Explain the benefits including some specific examples.

8. What were the most difficult things for you to learn to play chess? How did you deal with the difficulties?

✓ 9. I'd like to hear about the memorable experience you have had while playing chess. What was it about and when did it happen? Give me all the details.

You indicated in the survey that you play chess. What is chess and how do you play it? When and where do you usually play chess? Why do you like it? Tell me about chess in as much detail as possible.

--- IDEA FLOW ---

서론	→ 본론	→ 결론

체스를 간략히 소개
64개의 사각무늬 체스 판에서 두 명이 겨루는 게임
	체스에 대한 구체적인 설명
	1. 게임의 규칙 소개
	  ① 체스 말 종류: 왕, 여왕, 루크, 비숍, 기사, 졸 – 총 16개의 말
	  ② 목표: 상대 왕을 부르는 것
	2. 여가 생활로서의 체스
	  ① 상대: 아버지 – 체스를 가르쳐주심
	  ② 때/장소: 집/주로 저녁식사 후
	3. 체스가 좋은 이유
	  ① 재미 있음
	  ② 두뇌 혜택(연구들 인용)
	    • 기억력 향상, 문제해결 능력 증가
	    • 알츠하이머 예방
		체스의 장점을 자신이 체스를 두는 이유와 결부시켜 마무리
		어르신들의 알츠하이머 예방이 아버지와 체스를 두는 가장 큰 이유

ANSWER

Chess is a game that is played between two opponents on a chessboard with 64 squares. Each player has 16 pieces including one king, one queen, two rooks, two bishops, two knights, and eight pawns. To win at chess, I need to checkmate the opponent's king. It means that I should place it in a position where it cannot escape from capture. I often play chess with my dad at home mostly after dinner. My father who taught me how to play chess is my best opponent in chess. I like chess because it's a lot of fun. I've lost track of time playing it. Playing chess gives us benefits to our brains, too. Many studies say that chess makes both sides of the brain exercise that helps us improve our memory and increase problem-solving skills. They also say that it would help the elderly prevent Alzheimer's. In fact, that's one of the biggest reasons I often play chess with my father.

[해석 p.294 참조]

IH 답변 파헤치기

체스에 대한 간단한 소개로 서두 열기

본문 Chess is a game that is played between two opponents on a chessboard with 64 squares.

ex Chess is a kind of board game where two players play with 16 chess pieces each.
체스는 두 사람이 각각 16개의 체스 말을 가지고 겨루는 일종의 보드 게임입니다.

ex Chess is a board game that requires well-calculated strategies for two players.
체스는 두 경기자의 치밀한 전략을 필요로 하는 보드 게임입니다.

간단한 게임 방법 설명하기

본문 Each player has 16 pieces including one king, one queen, two rooks, two bishops, two knights, and eight pawns.

ex The chess pieces are arranged the same way every time I start the game.
체스 말은 제가 게임을 시작할 때마다 똑같은 방식으로 배열됩니다.

ex The white piece always moves first followed by the black one.
흰색 말이 항상 먼저 움직이고 그 후에 검정 말이 그 말을 따라갑니다.

ex Each piece should be placed in its own position at the beginning of the game but moves differently depending on its kinds. For example, the knights move in a very complicated way from the other pieces. 시작할 때는 각각의 말이 자기 자리에 위치해야 하지만, 움직일 때는 종류에 따라 다르게 움직입니다. 예를 들어, 기사는 다른 말들보다 매우 복잡한 방식으로 움직입니다.

체스의 장점이나 체스를 좋아하는 이유 말하기

- I think that chess is very helpful for people of all ages to develop their intellectual and mental abilities because they play with their thought and mind.
저는 체스는 생각과 마음으로 두는 것이어서 남녀노소를 불문하고 그들의 지적, 그리고 정신적 능력을 발달시킬 수 있다고 생각합니다.

- What attracts me about chess is that I can have a battle of wits with my opponent.
체스가 절 매료시키는 것은 제가 상대와 두뇌싸움을 할 수 있다는 것입니다.

- Chess can be played and enjoyed by all my family members together, which enhances my family bond. 체스는 우리 가족 전부가 함께 즐길 수 있고, 그런 점은 가족 유대감을 강화시켜줍니다.

Idiom lose track of time 시간 가는 줄 모르다

- It's easy to lose track of time when I play chess. 체스를 둘 때는 시간 가는 걸 모르기 십상입니다.
  = When I play chess, time just gets away from me.
  = I don't know how time flies playing chess.

Word 체스 관련 어휘 및 표현

- **a chess board** 체스 판
- **64 squares with an eight-by-eight grid** 가로 세로 8개씩의 64개 칸
- **chess piece** 장기 말
- **checkmate** 외통으로 만들다. 도망갈 곳 없이 만들다
- **check** 상대편의 왕(king)을 직접적으로 공격함
- **move one square in any direction** 어느 방향이건 한 칸을 움직일 수 있다
- **blockade** 상대방의 길을 봉쇄하는 것
- **move forward, backward, sideways, or diagonally** 앞, 뒤, 옆, 또는 대각선으로 움직인다
- **castling** 두 칸을 움직이고 루크(rook)를 바깥쪽으로 오게 하여 왕(king)을 보호하는 것
- **sacrifice** 공격 등의 다른 이익을 얻기 위해 스스로 버리는 것
- **promotion** 졸(pawn)이 끝까지 가서 다른 종류의 말로 바뀌는 것
- **fork** 하나의 말로 두 개의 말을 동시에 공격하거나 여러 방향의 공격을 동시에 하는 것

MAKE YOUR ANSWER

질문에 대한 여러분의 답변을 만들어보세요.

You indicated in the survey that you play chess. What is chess and how do you play it? When and where do you usually play chess? Why do you like it? Tell me about chess in as much detail as possible.

ANSWER

Q2 Eva also likes playing chess. Ask her three or four questions that you want to know about chess.

IDEA FLOW

서론

체스에 대해 묻고자 하는 배경 언급
1. 당신도 좋아한다고 들었다
2. 우리 나라에서는 대중적이지 않는 게임이라 아는 사람들이 거의 없다

→

본론

체스에 대한 질문하기
1. 기본적인 규칙
   ① 어떤 말을 가진 사람이 먼저 움직이는지
   ② 모든 말들이 위, 아래, 옆, 대각선으로 다 움직일 수 있는지
2. 체스의 역사
   ① 인도: 6세기 전 체스의 초기 형태의 게임
   ② 중국: 장기가 중국의 초기 문학에 등장
3. 체스가 좋은 이유
   ① 시간 보내기 위해?
   ② 두뇌 훈련이 되어서?

→

결론

에바에게 제안을 하면서 마무리
가까운 장래에 함께 체스를 두길 희망

ANSWER

I heard that you enjoy playing chess. It isn't a popular game in my country, and few people know how to play it. Could you explain some basic rules of chess? Who should move first, the player with the white pieces or the one with the black pieces? How should each of the different kinds of pieces move? Can all of them move up, down, sideways, and diagonally? I'd also like to know about the history of chess. Some people say it evolved from the earlier chess-like game played in India before the 6th century AD. Others suggest Xianggi, which is the world's oldest board game, appeared in the very early Chinese literature. And here is my last question. Why do you like playing chess? Do you play it to simply spend your time? Or do you like it because chess trains your brain? I also like playing chess a lot, so I hope that we'll play it in the near future, Eva.

[해석 p.294 참조]

IH 답변 파헤치기

문장 구조 응용하기

know how to 부정사 어떻게 ~하는 지 안다, ~에 능숙하다

- 본문 It isn't a popular game in my country, and few people know how to play it.
- ex I didn't even know how to lay out my chess pieces on the chess board back then.
  그 당시에는 체스 판에 체스 말을 어떻게 배열해야 하는 지조차 몰랐어요.
- ex Please let me know how to move bishops and knights first.
  우선 비숍과 기사를 어떻게 움직여야 하는지 알려주세요.
- ex I learned how to play chess from my uncle.
  저는 삼촌에게서 체스 두는 법을 배웠습니다.
- ex Who taught you how to play chess?
  누가 당신에게 체스 두는 법을 가르쳐주었습니까?

※ how to 부정사는 know 외에 learn, teach, ask 등의 동사와도 자주 같이 사용됩니다.

질문의 배경이나 경위를 말하면서 서두 열기

- Eva, I need your help because I'm supposed to play chess with my Russian clients next week.
  에바, 다음 주에 러시아 고객과 체스를 둬야 해서 당신의 도움이 필요합니다.
- I've heard you have won several world chess championships, and I'm wondering how you are so good at chess. 당신이 몇몇의 세계 월드 선수권대회에서 우승했다고 들었는데 어떻게 그렇게 체스를 잘 하는지 궁금합니다.
- The rules and terms of chess seem too complicated for me to become familiar with them. Could you explain some of them? 체스 규칙과 용어는 너무 복잡해서 익숙해질 수가 없습니다. 몇 개를 좀 설명해주겠어요?
- I've never won a game at chess. I want to get some tips to winning it.
  저는 체스 경기에서 한 번도 이겨본 적이 없습니다. 이길 수 있는 정보를 좀 얻고 싶습니다.

체스에 대해 물어볼 수 있는 질문들

- How frequently do you play chess? 얼마나 자주 체스를 둡니까?
- Who did you learn to play chess from? Did you study by yourself through reading books or browsing websites? 체스를 누구에게 배웠습니까? 책을 보고 인터넷을 검색하면서 독학했습니까?
- How long did it take you to master all the rules of chess?
  체스의 모든 규칙을 통달하는데 얼마나 걸렸나요?
- Could you give some ideas to popularize chess in your country?
  체스를 당신의 나라에서 대중시킬 수 있는 묘안을 좀 주시겠습니까?
- How do you feel when you lose at chess? Do you think that wins and losses are more important than others? 체스에 지면 기분이 어떻습니까? 이기고 지는 것이 당신에게 중요합니까?
- Could you give me some information about the world chess champions like their genders, ages, and nationalities? 세계 체스 우승자들에 대한 정보, 즉 그들의 성별, 연령, 국적 같은 정보를 알려주시겠습니까?

질문 자연스럽게 마무리하기

- Thank you so much for letting me know about chess. Talk to you later.
  체스를 알게 해 줘서 너무 고맙고 나중에 또 이야기해요.
- You made me have better understanding of chess. I appreciate it.
  당신 덕분에 체스를 잘 알게 되었어요. 감사합니다.
- You know everything about chess! I hope we will have another chance to talk about it.
  당신은 체스에 대해 모르는 게 없군요! 다시 한 번 체스에 대해 이야기 나누게 되길 바랍니다.

MAKE YOUR ANSWER

질문에 대한 여러분의 답변을 만들어보세요.

Eva also likes playing chess. Ask her three or four questions that you want to know about chess.

ANSWER

I'd like to hear about the memorable experience you have had while playing chess. What was it about and when did it happen? Give me all the details.

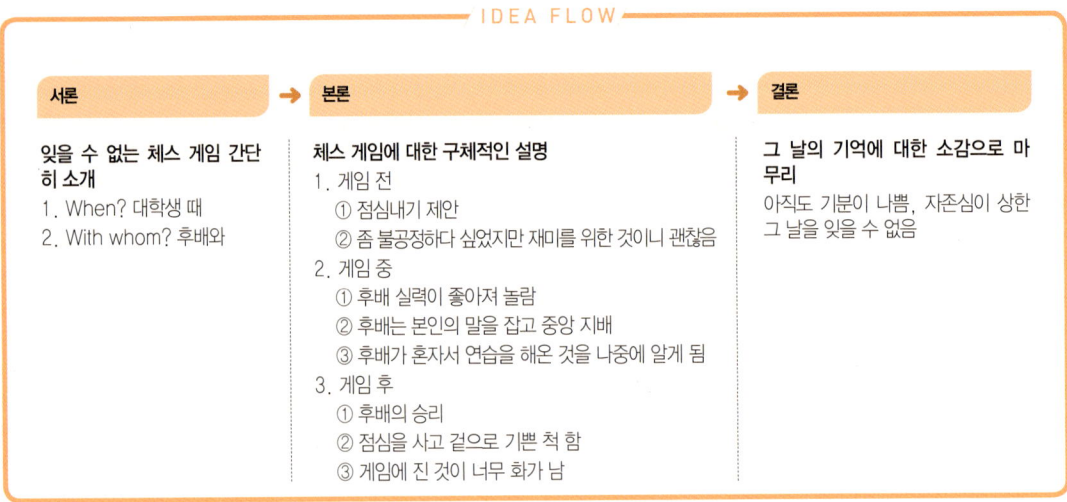

ANSWER

I remember the game of chess that I played with my junior in college. We played it at his place about two years ago. We had a bet on who would win the game. The loser was supposed to buy lunch for the winner. It seemed a bit unfair because he learned how to play chess from me and had never beaten me before. Because it was just for fun, we agreed we would have the lunch in an inexpensive restaurant after the game. Surprisingly, his chess had improved a lot against my expectations. I captured some of his pieces, and he captured more of mine and controlled the center of the board throughout the game. As it turned out, he had constantly practiced by himself and got so much better at it. Eventually, he won the game and I treated him to lunch. I pretended to be glad that he surpassed his teacher, but I was actually so upset about losing the game. I'm a very competitive person who hates to lose. I think he could notice I didn't feel good because I went red in the face. Oh, the memory makes me feel bad again. I don't think I can forget the day when my pride was hurt.

[해석 p.294 참조]

문장 구조 응용하기

be supposed to 부정사 ~하기로 하다, ~하기로 돼있다
- 본문 The loser was supposed to buy lunch for the winner.
- ex I was supposed to participate in a local chess tournament. 저는 지역 체스 토너먼트에 참가하기로 되어 있었습니다.

Word bet v. 내기를 하다 n. 내기
- 본문 We had a bet on who would win the game.
- ex We bet 10,000 won on the game. 우리는 그 게임에 만원 내기를 했습니다.
- ex Only a few of them bet their money that I would win.
  그 중 아주 극소수만 제가 이길 거라는 내기에 돈을 걸었습니다.

Word treat someone to 식사 ~에게 식사를 사다
- I treated him to dinner. = I bought him dinner. = Dinner was on me. = I picked up the bill for dinner.
  저는 그에게 저녁을 샀습니다.

Word against one's expectation(s)/contrary to one's expectation(s) ~의 예상과 달리
- My boyfriend wasn't able to take the lead in the game against my expectation.
  제 남자친구는 제 예상과 달리 그 게임을 주도하지 못했습니다.
- His king escaped from checkmate contrary to my expectations.
  그가 가진 왕은 내 예상과 달리 외통수에서 벗어났습니다.

기억에 남는 체스 일화 관련 아이디어

- I was so absorbed in playing the game that I totally forgot the soup boiling in a pot on the stove.
  저는 그 시합에 너무 열중한 나머지 가스레인지 위에서 수프를 끓이고 있었던 것을 까맣게 잊고 말았습니다.
- Since I was beaten in two straight games in front of my girlfriend, my pride was absolutely broken.
  제 여자친구 앞에서 두 게임 연속해서 졌기 때문에 제 자존심은 완전히 무너지고 말았습니다.
- He kept asking me to allow his rook to move forward again. When I didn't do his favor, he got very angry at me. 그는 저에게 그의 루크를 다시 앞으로 움직이게 해달라고 계속 부탁했습니다. 제가 그 부탁을 들어주지 않자 저에게 막 화를 냈습니다.
- My dad seemed to enjoy learning something new although he found it difficult to memorize the rules of chess. 우리 아버지께서는 비록 체스 규칙을 외우기는 힘들어하셨지만 새로운 것을 배우는 것이 즐거운 눈치셨습니다.

Word pretend to 부정사 ~하는 척 하다
- 본문 I pretended to be glad that he surpassed his teacher, but I was actually so upset about losing the game.
- ex I pretended not to be obsessed with my wins. 저는 승부에 연연하지 않는 척 했습니다.

개인적 소회로 체스 일화를 마무리

- I was glad to teach chess and promote the game to students.
  저는 학생들에게 체스를 가르치고 게임을 알릴 수 있어서 좋았습니다.
- I don't know how I could play such a worst game even now I come to think of it.
  지금 생각해도 어떻게 그렇게 최악의 게임을 했는지 모르겠습니다.
- I would have won the game if we played chess now. 지금 우리가 체스를 뒀다면 제가 이겼을 것인데요.

질문에 대한 여러분의 답변을 만들어보세요.

I'd like to hear about the memorable experience you have had while playing chess. What was it about and when did it happen? Give me all the details.

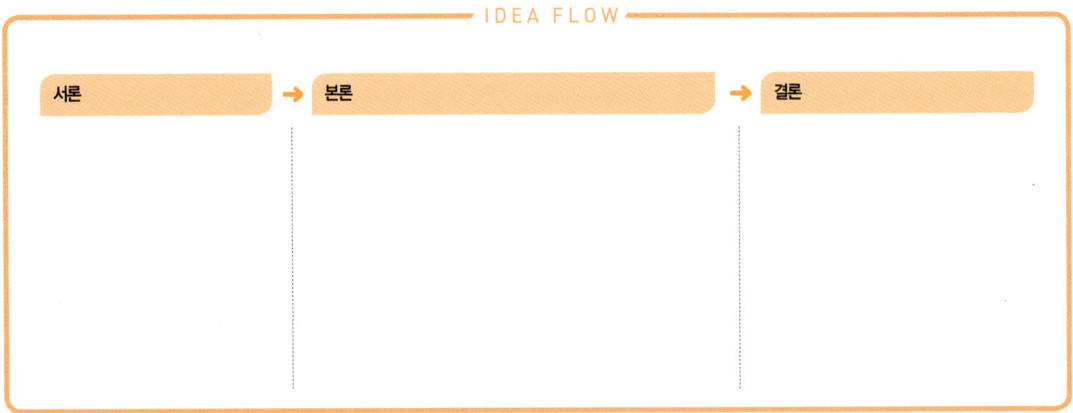

ANSWER

Memo

Lesson 7

시험 대비 과정 수강하기

INTRO 시험 대비 과정 수강하기 역시 최근 새로 추가된 신경향 문제입니다. 대비하는 시험의 종류, 수강 방법, 수강 시기 등에 대한 일반적인 정보는 물론 수강하면서 겪었던 일화 등에 관한 질문까지 다양하게 출제되고 있습니다. 이번 과에서는 대비할 수 있는 각종 시험에 대해 알아보고, 구체적인 시험 대비 과정 수강과 관련하여 강좌 소개, 강좌 수강 방법, 시험 준비를 하면서 겪었던 일화 등에 대한 답변을 준비해보도록 하겠습니다.

IH 답변 전략

① 시험 대비 과정을 수강하는 목적, 방법, 시기 등을 설정하기
- 시험의 종류, 시험 대비 과정 수강의 목적을 정확하게 언급합니다.
- 그 과정을 선택한 이유와 수강 방법, 수강 신청한 과목들을 구체적으로 답변에 포함시킵니다.

② 시험 대비 과정을 수강하면서 실질적으로 배운 내용들 설명하기
- 시험 대비 과정에서 배운 수업 내용들을 이해하기 쉽게 설명할 수 있어야 합니다.
- 전문적인 지식을 포함한 답변을 준비하려 애쓰기보다는 수업의 핵심이 되는 내용 한 두 가지를 소개하고 그 과정을 통해서 자신이 어떻게 시험 준비를 했는지에 초점을 맞춥니다.

③ 시험 대비 과정을 수강하면서, 또는 시험 준비를 하면서 겪었던 에피소드 소개하기
- 시험 대비 과정을 수강하면서 벌어졌던 일화, 또는 시험 준비를 하면서 겪었던 예기치 않은 사건, 사고 등을 소재로 특별한 이야기를 만들어봅니다.
- 단순히 사건 자체만 서술하기보다는, 그 사건으로 인해 느꼈던 감정, 갈등 등의 긴박한 요소를 포함시켜 이야기를 전개해 나가면 더 설득력 있는 답변이 될 수 있습니다.

'시험 대비 과정 수강하기'에서는 어떠한 질문들이 출제될까요? 다음의 예상 질문에 대해 여러분은 어떻게 답변할지 한번 생각해 보세요.

  1. You indicated in the survey you have taken test-preparation courses. When and where did you take the course? Why did you take the courses and why did you choose the institute to take them? Do you think the courses help you prepare for the test? Give me all the details.

2. Tell me about your favorite test-preparation course. When did you enroll in the course and what did you like it most?

3. What was the most disappointing test-preparation course that you took? What did you learn and why do you think it was so disappointing?

4. I'd like to know about the first test-preparation course that you took. What did the course cover and what did you take it for? Give me all the details.

  5. Which classes did you take? What did you learn about test preparation? How did you prepare for the tests?

  6. I'd like to know about interesting, surprising, or unexpected things that happened while you were preparing for the tests. What happened and when did it happen? Tell me the whole story about it.

7. You indicated in the survey you have enrolled in test-preparation courses. Tell me some advantages of taking test-preparation courses.

8. I'll give you a situation and ask you to act it out. You and your friend are planning to take a test-preparation course from a private institute. Call the receptionist and ask three to four questions about its courses.

9. I'm sorry, but there is a problem I need you to resolve. The test-preparation course you and your friend wanted to take is not currently offered. Call your friend and explain the situation including three alternatives to solve it.

Q1 You indicated in the survey you have taken test-preparation courses. When and where did you take the course? Why did you take the courses and why did you choose the institute to take them? Do you think the courses help you prepare for the test? Give me all the details.

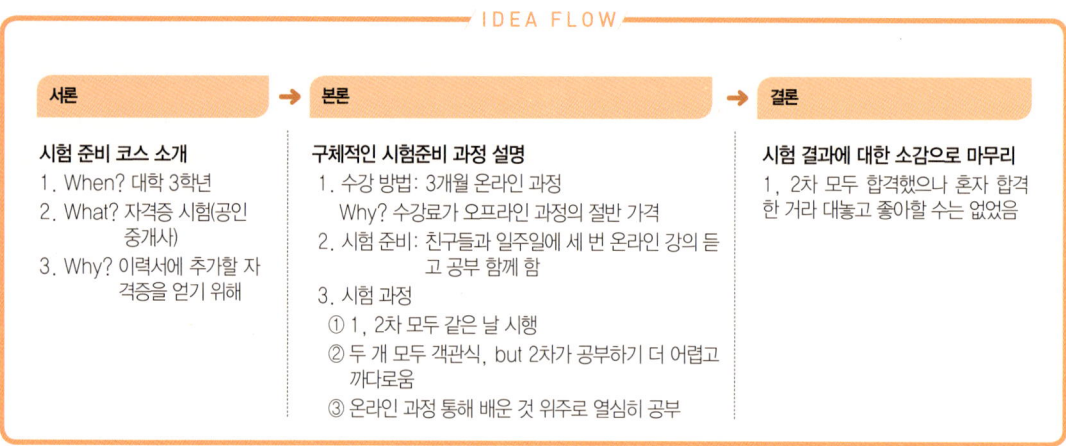

ANSWER

During my third year of college, I prepared for the real estate license examination. The license was necessary for those who want to get a job in the real estate industry. Since many students had hard time getting a job, they tried to obtain as many certificates as possible to include them on their resume. I was no exception and prepared for the exam with my two other friends. We registered for a three-month online course. We chose the course because the tuition was about half the cost of other offline courses. We met three times a week to listen to the lectures and studied together. The exam had two parts including the primary and the second test, and we had to take both tests on the same day. Both were composed of multiple choice questions, but I found it more demanding and tough to study the second test. I studied harder based on what I had learned through the online course, and three months after completing the course, I eventually passed both tests. However, I couldn't feel free to show my joy because the other two friends failed the second test.

[해석 p.295 참조]

IH 답변 파헤치기

수강했던 학원이나 강사, 과정에 대한 아이디어

- The instructor I learned from was licensed in accounting and gave us some strategies for the exam. 제가 배운 강사는 회계사 자격증이 있었고 시험에 대한 전략을 우리에게 알려줬습니다.
- I chose the institute that was well known for producing more successful candidates than any other institute.
  저는 합격자를 가장 많이 배출하는 걸로 잘 알려진 학원을 선택했습니다.
- I was actually reluctant to take the online lectures, but my friend persuaded me to sign up for them.
  저는 사실 그 온라인 강좌를 듣는 것이 탐탁지 않았지만 제 친구의 설득에 등록했습니다.

Idiom land/get/find a job 직장을 구하다

- 본문 The license was necessary for those who want to get a job in the real estate industry.
- ex I thought many licenses would help me find a job after graduation.
  자격증이 많으면 졸업 후에 직업을 구하는 데 도움이 될 거라고 생각했습니다.

Word based on ~에 근거하여

- 본문 I studied harder based on what we had learned through the online course.
- ex The school divided students into five levels based on their placement test results.
  학원은 학생들을 배치 고사 결과에 근거해 다섯 레벨로 나눴습니다.

Word feel free to 부정사 마음 놓고 ~하다

- 본문 However, I couldn't feel free to show my joy because the other two friends failed the second test.
- ex I could feel free to hang out with my friend after the test.
  시험이 끝나고 저는 친구들과 마음대로 놀 수 있었습니다.

Word 시험이나 자격증 관련 어휘들

- prepare for an exam/a test 시험 준비를 하다
- register for/sign up for/enroll in ~을 등록하다
- take an exam/a test 시험을 보다
- pass/fail the exam 시험에 합격/불합격 하다
- earn/get/obtain a certificate(license) 자격증을 취득하다
  - ex I earned a teachers' certificate. = I became certified as a teacher. = I got licensed in teaching.
    저는 교사 자격증을 취득했습니다.
  - ex I enrolled in an OPIc preparation course.
    저는 오픽 준비 과정을 등록했습니다.

Word 준비할 수 있는 시험이나 자격증 종류

- certified public accountant test 공인회계사 시험
  - ex I took a CPA test two years ago.
    저는 2년 전에 공인회계사 시험을 봤습니다.
- tax accountant examination 세무사 시험
- civil-service examination 공무원 시험
- bar examination 사법고시
- teacher recruitment examination 교원임용고사
- national nurse examination 간호사 국가시험
- public administration examination 행정고시
- Level 1 test for Word processing 워드프로세서 1급
- examination for special admission 편입시험
- driver's license 운전면허증

질문에 대한 여러분의 답변을 만들어보세요.

You indicated in the survey you have taken test-preparation courses. When and where did you take the course? Why did you take the courses and why did you choose the institute to take them? Do you think the courses help you prepare for the test? Give me all the details.

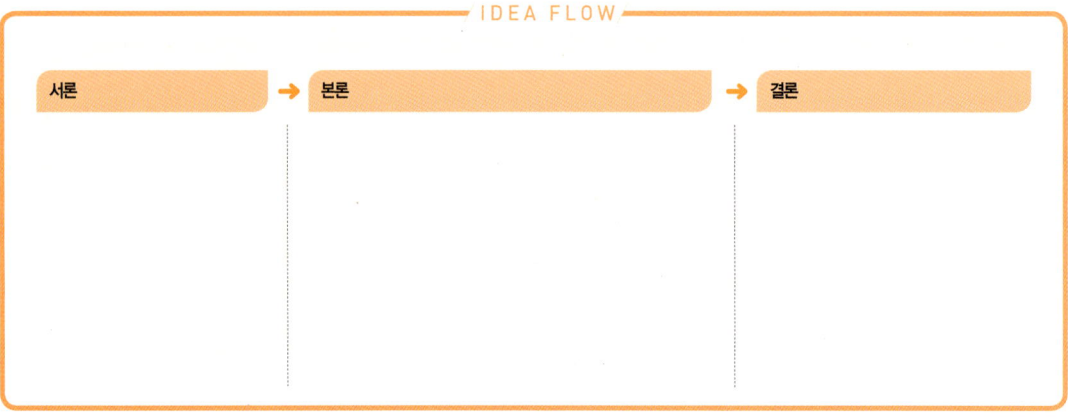

ANSWER

Question Q2: Which classes did you take? What did you learn about test preparation? How did you prepare for the tests?

IDEA FLOW

서론 → **본론** → **결론**

서론
수강한 과목에 대한 간단한 소개
총 다섯 개의 수업을 통해 부동산 이론과 규제, 세금 제도, 부동산공법, 공인중개사 실무를 배움

본론
구체적인 수업 내용 설명
1. 수업 내용
   ① 부동산의 법령과 이론에 대한 강의: 모두 암기
   ② 구체적 내용 및 실제 적용
   ③ 10세트의 모의고사 → 실제 시험을 잘 준비하는데 도움
2. 수업 태도: 강의를 충실히 따름
   ① 주어진 과제들은 모두 완수
   ② 수업 후 복습
   ③ 친구들과 어려운 문제들 혹은 개념을 논의하거나 질문게시판에 게재

결론
시험 준비에 대한 소회로 마무리
한 번에 시험을 통과하면서 노력이 보상을 받아서 운이 좋음

ANSWER

The online course I took consisted of five classes. Two classes were about real estate principles and regulations, two covered tax systems and real estate public law, and the other was about real estate practices. During the first month, the instructor gave us lectures on basic laws and principles on real estate, and we had to memorize all of them. Then he moved to more specific contents and showed some examples for the practical application of the contents. At the final step, he gave us 10 sets of practice tests to answer. Particularly, the practice tests helped me review what I had learned and get well prepared for the real examination. I followed his instructions faithfully. I completed all the assignments given from the instructors and had a review after class. I discussed some difficult questions or concepts with my friends and also posted on the message board that the online institute operated. I'm lucky that my efforts paid off by enabling me to pass the tests on the first try.

[해석 p.295 참조]

문장 구조 응용하기

by ~ing ~함으로써, ~하는 것으로

- 본문 I'm lucky that my efforts paid off by enabling me to pass the tests on the first try.
- ex The instructor normally began by reviewing some important points from the previous class.
  그 강사는 대개 지난 시간에 배운 중요한 몇 가지들을 복습하면서 수업을 시작했습니다.

과목 수강에 대한 서두 열기

- I needed to take four different classes, and finance and business were most challenging among them.
  저는 네 개의 수업을 들어야 했는데 그 중에서 금융과 경영이 가장 어려웠습니다.
- I learned a grammar course online while taking a reading course at the institute.
  저는 읽기 강좌는 학원에서 들었던 반면 문법 강좌는 온라인으로 배웠습니다.
- I registered for an English course at a language school but studied other major-related subjects by myself.
  저는 영어 강좌만 어학원에 등록했고 나머지 전공 과목들은 혼자 공부했습니다.

Word consist of (=include, be composed of, be made up of) ~로 구성되어 있다

- 본문 The online course I took consisted of five classes.
- ex The test included reading, listening, speaking, and writing.
  그 시험은 읽기, 듣기, 말하기, 쓰기를 포함하고 있었습니다.
- Most certificate exams are made up of written examination and practical tests.
  대부분의 자격증 시험은 필기시험과 실기시험으로 구성되어 있습니다.

시험 준비 과정에 대해 설명하기

- She enabled us to understand principles through various practical examples.
  그녀는 다양한 실례들을 통해 우리가 원리를 이해할 수 있게 해줬습니다.
- I had spent six months studying for the exam but was not sure to pass it.
  저는 6개월 동안 시험 공부를 했지만 합격할 자신이 없었습니다.
- Right before the exam, he summarized essential points that were likely to appear on the real test, which was very helpful for me.
  시험 바로 전에는 시험에 나올 만한 것들을 요약해주셨는데, 저에게 매우 도움이 되었습니다.
- I solved almost all types of questions from the tests of the previous two years.
  저는 지난 2년 동안의 모든 유형의 기출 문제들을 풀어봤습니다.

시험 준비에 대한 소회로 마무리하기

- I was able to prepare for the test thoroughly through the online lectures.
  그 온라인 강좌로 저는 시험 준비를 철저히 할 수 있었습니다.
- I could get a high GRE score with the help of the intensive course despite my short period of preparation.
  그 집중 강좌 덕분에 제 짧은 준비에도 불구하고 높은 GRE 점수를 받을 수 있었습니다.
- When I passed the exam, I felt like I was floating on air.
  시험에 합격했을 때는 하늘을 날 것 같은 기분이었습니다.
- The successful result of the test boosted my self-confidence.
  성공적인 시험 결과로 저는 자신감을 얻었습니다.

MAKE YOUR ANSWER

질문에 대한 여러분의 답변을 만들어보세요.

Which classes did you take? What did you learn about test preparation? How did you prepare for the tests?

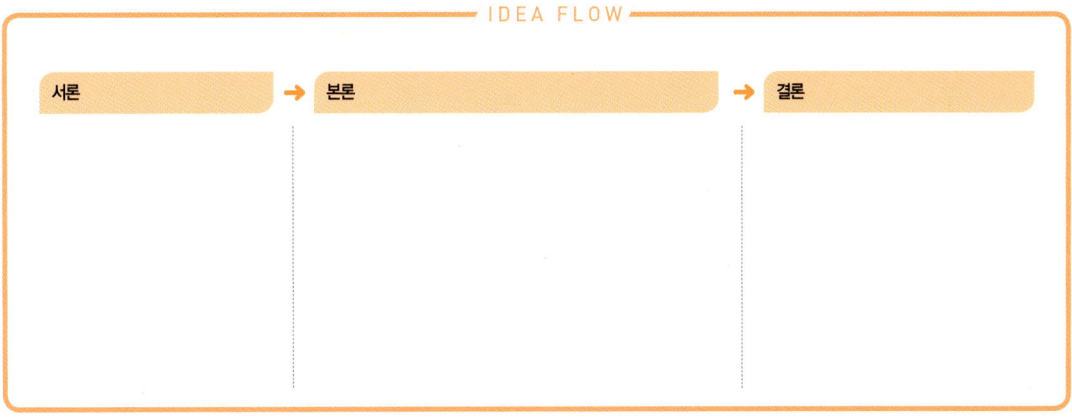

ANSWER

I'd like to know about interesting, surprising, or unexpected things that happened while you were preparing for the tests. What happened and when did it happen? Tell me the whole story about it.

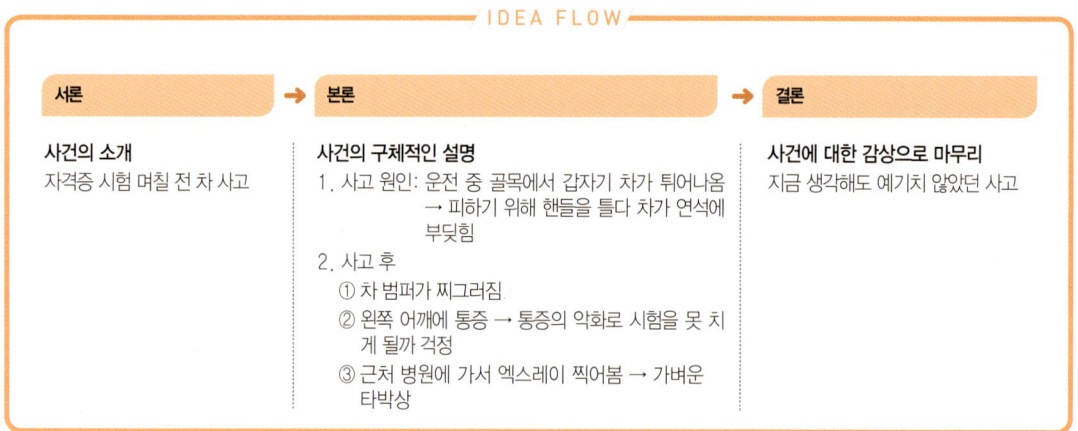

ANSWER

A few days before my licensing examination day, I had a car accident. I was driving home, and a car came suddenly around the corner without slowing down. I had no choice but to swerve quickly to the left to avoid hitting the car, which caused my car to hit the curb. I was really lucky that cars weren't coming on the opposite lane, but the front of my car was dented due to the impact. Although I didn't have any external injuries, I was worried about possible after effects from the traffic accident. My left shoulder was hurt because it hit the window when my car bumped into the curb. The most horrifying thing that I thought back then was that I wouldn't be able to take the exam because of further pain. I immediately went to a nearby orthopedic hospital, and the doctor got my shoulder X-rayed. I was really nervous while I was waiting for the result to come out. Fortunately, there were no serious problems like fractures with my shoulder. I was slightly bruised but didn't have any trouble taking the exam. The accident was quite unexpected to come to think of it.

[해석 p.295 참조]

문장 구조 응용하기

avoid ~ing ~하는 것을 피하다

- 본문 I had no choice but to swerve quickly to the left to avoid hitting the car, which caused my car to hit the curb.
- ex I transferred from the taxi to the subway to avoid being late for class.
  저는 수업에 늦는 걸 피하기 위해서 택시에서 지하철로 갈아탔습니다.

It+be+형용사(A) ~ that S+V(B) B하는 것은 A하다

- 본문 It was really lucky that cars weren't coming on the opposite lane, but the front of my car was dented due to the impact.
- ex It was obvious that I couldn't complete all the courses before exams.
  제가 시험 전에 전 과정을 끝낼 수 없을 거라는 것은 분명했습니다.
  ※ It ~ that 구문으로 여기서의 It는 아무 뜻이 없는 가주어입니다.

have trouble(=difficulty) ~ing ~하는 걸 어려워하다, ~하는 것에 곤란함을 겪다

- 본문 I was slightly bruised, but didn't have any trouble taking the exam.
- ex He knew I had difficulty taking notes and listening at his lectures at the same time during class.
  그는 제가 강의를 들으면서 동시에 필기하는 걸 어려워하고 있다는 걸 알고 있었습니다.

Word bump into ~에 부딪치다

- 본문 My left shoulder was hurt because it hit the window when my car bumped into the curb.
- ex I felt dizzy and nearly bumped into a wall. 저는 어지러워서 하마터면 벽에 부딪칠 뻔 했습니다.

Idiom come to think of it 생각해보니

- 본문 The accident was quite unexpected to come to think of it.
- ex Now I come to think of it, I was overreacting to her attitude since I was so stressed out about the exam.
  지금 생각해보면, 제가 시험 때문에 너무 스트레스를 받아서 그녀의 태도에 과민반응을 보였던 것 같습니다.

시험 준비 관련 에피소드

- I had never imagined that I would take the test with my leg in a cast.
  다리에 깁스를 한 채 시험을 보게 될 줄은 정말 몰랐습니다.
- I sensed that the man sitting next to me was watching me. I turned my head to check him out, and he looked very familiar. Then he told me that we were in the same class.
  저는 제 옆에 앉은 남자가 저를 쳐다보고 있다는 걸 알았습니다. 고개를 돌려 그를 확인해보니 굉장히 낯이 익은 사람이었습니다. 그러자 그는 우리가 같은 수업을 듣고 있다고 말하는 것이었습니다.
- I came down with the flu and couldn't go to the institute for a week. It was too bad that I wasn't able to take the special lecture series.
  저는 독감에 걸려서 일주일 동안 학원에 못 나갔습니다. 특강을 들을 수 없다는 것이 너무 안타까웠습니다.
- The test anxiety kept me up at night before the day of the exam. I tried to sleep even for a few hours by meditating but couldn't. Next morning, I went to the exam center, and fortunately, did a good job. 시험 전날 저는 시험 걱정으로 잠을 자지 못했습니다. 몇 시간이라도 자 보려고 애썼지만 소용이 없었죠. 다음 날 고사장에 갔고 다행히 잘 봤습니다.

MAKE YOUR ANSWER

질문에 대한 여러분의 답변을 만들어보세요.

I'd like to know about interesting, surprising, or unexpected things that happened while you were preparing for the tests. What happened and when did it happen? Tell me the whole story about it.

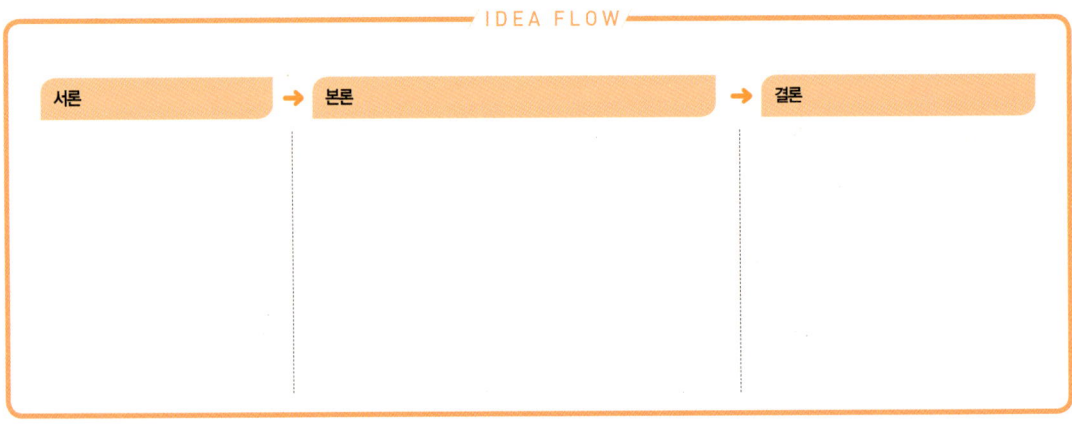

ANSWER

Memo

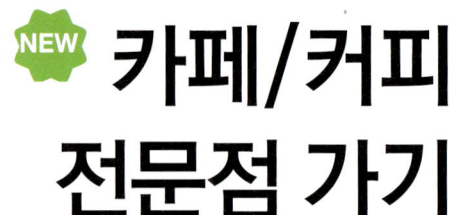

Oral Proficiency Interview-computer

Lesson 8 | NEW 카페/커피 전문점 가기

INTRO

카페/커피전문점 가기 역시 2013년 10월부터 OPIc 서베이 여가활동(4번)항목에 새롭게 추가된 신경향 주제입니다. 최근 몇 년 커피체인점의 증가로 카페 가기가 하나의 문화나 추세로 자리잡은 결과일 텐데요, 그런 만큼 카페/커피 전문점 가기는 여러분께 친숙한 주제가 될 수 있고 답변을 준비하는 과정도 즐겁고 재미있을 것입니다. 다만 한국의 카페 문화나 자주 가는 카페의 외관 묘사 등의 답변 구성은 생각보다 까다로울 수도 있으니 철저히 준비를 해 놓아야 하겠습니다.

IH 답변 전략

① 자주 가는 카페/커피전문점 묘사하기

- 다른 장소 묘사와 마찬가지로 자주 가는 카페의 묘사도 주위 환경이나 위치(층수 포함) 등의 외부 묘사와 함께 인테리어, 조명, 가구 배치 등의 내부 묘사를 자세하게 설명할 수 있어야 합니다. 다만 카페의 특성상 내부 묘사, 즉 분쇄기, 커피 잔, 벽에 걸린 그림, 편안한 의자 등 카페 분위기를 표현할 수 있는 내부 묘사에 더 많은 설명을 할애하는 것이 바람직합니다.
- 자신이 자주 가거나 좋아하는 카페의 경우 그 이유도 꼭 언급해주어야 합니다.

② 카페/커피전문점에서 주로 하는 활동들 설명하기

- 현대인에게 있어 카페는 하나의 휴식 공간이자 활동 공간입니다. 과거에 비해 카페에서 할 수 있는 활동들이 많아졌는데요, 컴퓨터 작업이나 스마트폰으로 영화 보기에서 식사를 하는 활동에 이르기까지 다양한 활동들에 대해 설명할 수 있어야 하겠습니다.
- 사람들의 일반적인 카페 활동과 더불어 자신의 카페 활동들도 살짝 언급하고, 마무리로 카페 문화에 대한 자신의 생각을 제시해주면 깔끔하고 논리적인 답변이 될 수 있습니다.

③ 카페/커피전문점에서 있었던 경험 소개하기

- 카페에서 겪을 수 있는 황당한 일이나 기분 좋은 체험 등을 이야기로 구성해봅니다.
- 음식 메뉴, 사람, 또는 분실 등의 소재를 정리해놓고 각 답변을 준비해봅니다.

✓1. You indicated in the survey that you go to cafés. What cafés or coffee shops are there in your neighborhood? How do they look? Which café do you like to go to? Why do you like the café?

2. When did you first go to a café? How was the café different from the ones you are visiting these days? How have cafés in your country changed over the years?

3. How do you normally choose a café? Do you choose it based on its location or its cleanliness? Tell me about your taste in café.

✓4. What do people in your country do in the café or coffee shop?

✓5. Tell me about the most memorable experience that you had in the café or coffee shop.

6. I'll give you a situation and ask you to act it out. You are going to meet your friend in a café you often go to. Call your friend and make an appointment to see him or her including the direction to the café.

7. I'm sorry, but there is a problem I need you to resolve. You're informed that the café where you are supposed to meet your friend is closed today. Call your friend and explain the situation including three suggestions to solve it.

8. When was the last time that you went to a café? Where was the café located and who did you go there with? Why did you go to the café?

Q1 You indicated in the survey that you go to cafés. What cafés or coffee shops are there in your neighborhood? How do they look? Which café do you like to go to? Why do you like the café?

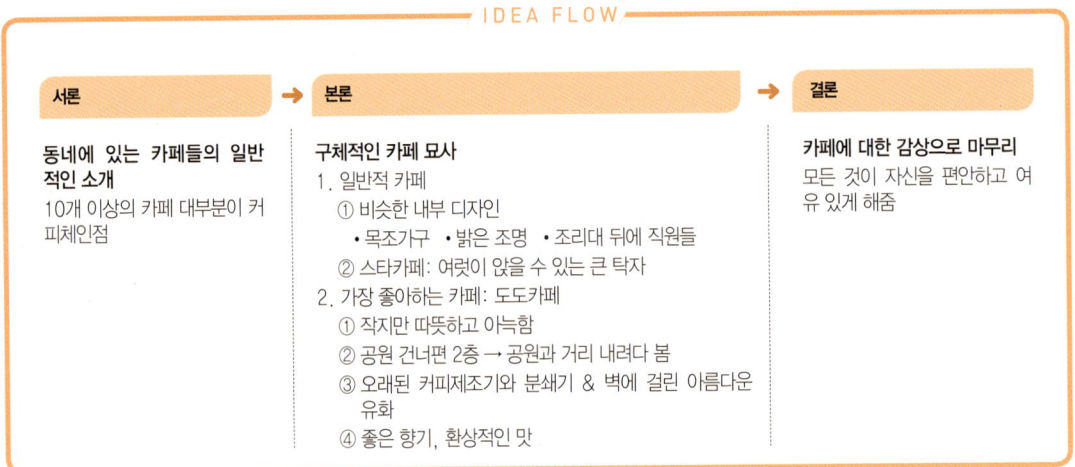

ANSWER

There are more than 10 cafés in my neighborhood. Most of them are coffee chains such as Star Café and Bean Coffee. I think it's kind of trend that such coffee chains have opened everywhere. They all have similar interior designs and sell different types of coffee. I can see wooden furniture and bright lighting, and staff members make coffee behind the countertops. One distinctive feature Star Café has is a large rectangular table that accommodates eight to ten people around it. However, my favorite café is a small café called Dodo Café, which is located a few blocks away from my place. Although it's small, its atmosphere is very warm and cozy. It's on the second floor of the building which is right across from the park, so I can enjoy a good view of the park and streets from the seat by the window. It also has some antique coffee makers and grinders, and a couple of beautiful oil paintings hanging on the wall. I think the owner has a secret of coffee roasting because it smells so good and tastes fantastic. Everything in the café makes me feel comfortable and relaxed.

[해석 p.295 참조]

IH 답변 파헤치기

동네에 있는 일반적인 카페 소개로 서두 열기

- There are only a few cafés in my neighborhood because I'm living in a place remote from the city.
  저는 도시에서 멀리 떨어진 곳에 살고 있기 때문에 우리 동네에는 카페가 몇 개 밖에 없습니다.
- There are two or three coffee shops on every corner in neighborhood.
  우리 동네에는 모든 골목마다 두세 개의 커피숍이 있습니다.
- Since I live in a neighborhood that is one of the most famous tourist attractions in Seoul, I can see many nice cafés.
  저는 서울에서 가장 유명한 관광명소 중의 하나인 동네에 살고 있어서 많은 좋은 카페를 볼 수 있습니다.

Word distinctive 독특한, 눈에 띄는

- **본문** One distinctive feature Star Café has is a large rectangular table that accommodates eight to ten people around it.
- **ex** She enjoys wearing a dress with distinctive flower-patterns.
  그녀는 독특한 꽃무늬가 있는 원피스를 즐겨 입습니다.

Word cozy 아늑한

- **본문** Although it's small, its atmosphere is very warm and cozy.
- **ex** My office was not spacious but is cozy and clean. 제 사무실이 넓지는 않지만 아늑하고 깨끗합니다.

카페 묘사하기

- The coffee shop that I often go to is located in the basement of the finance building in my neighborhood. It has high ceilings and large windows with natural light, making the space look more spacious. 제가 자주 가는 커피숍은 우리 동네에 있는 금융센터 건물 지하에 있습니다. 천장이 높고 자연광이 들어오는 커다란 창문이 있어 커피숍이 더 넓어 보입니다.
- When I step into the café, I find an espresso machine behind the countertop. There are three staff members who are pretty kind. They come by their customers once or twice every hour to check whether they need refills.
  그 카페에 들어서면 조리대 뒤에 에스프레소 커피 기계가 있습니다. 세 명의 종업원들이 있는데 상당히 친절합니다. 그들은 한 시간에 한 두 번 손님들에게 다가가서 리필을 원하는지 확인합니다.
- On the corner of the café is a space for the large collection of LP records. If a customer requests a song or music, the owner plays it.
  카페 한 쪽에는 상당한 수의 레코드가 모아져 있는 공간이 있습니다. 손님이 노래나 음악을 신청하면 주인이 틀어줍니다.

특정 카페 선호하는 이유 설명하기

- The highlights of the café are its waffles. They serve various types of waffles including strawberry, walnut, and blueberry waffles. All of them taste amazing, which make me visit there almost every morning. 그 카페의 최고 장점은 와플입니다. 딸기, 호두, 블루베리 와플 같은 다양한 와플들이 있는데 모두 다 너무 맛있어서 저는 거의 매일 아침 그곳에 갑니다.
- The best part of the coffee shop is that I can see many beautiful flowers in it. Since the owner used to work as a florist, she decorated the coffee shop with flowers herself. It's a pleasant experience to drink coffee, smell the fragrance, and see different types of flowers in one place.
  그 커피숍의 가장 좋은 점은 아름다운 꽃을 많이 볼 수 있다는 것입니다. 주인이 플로리스트로 일을 한 적이 있기 때문에 자신이 직접 커피숍을 꽃으로 장식했습니다. 한 장소에서 커피를 마시고, 향기를 맡으며, 다양한 꽃들을 보는 것은 참 즐거운 경험입니다.

MAKE YOUR ANSWER

질문에 대한 여러분의 답변을 만들어보세요.

You indicated in the survey that you go to cafés. What cafés or coffee shops are there in your neighborhood? How do they look? Which café do you like to go to? Why do you like the café?

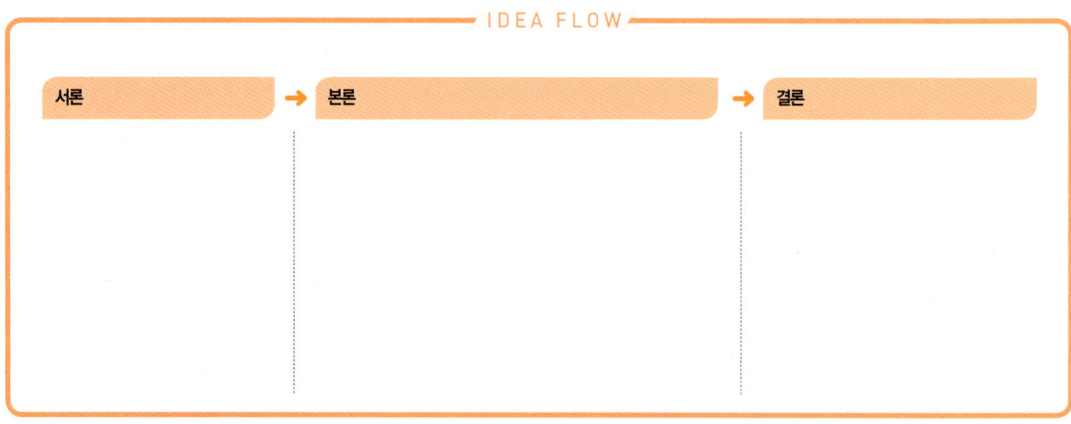

ANSWER

Q2 What do people in your country do in the café or coffee shop?

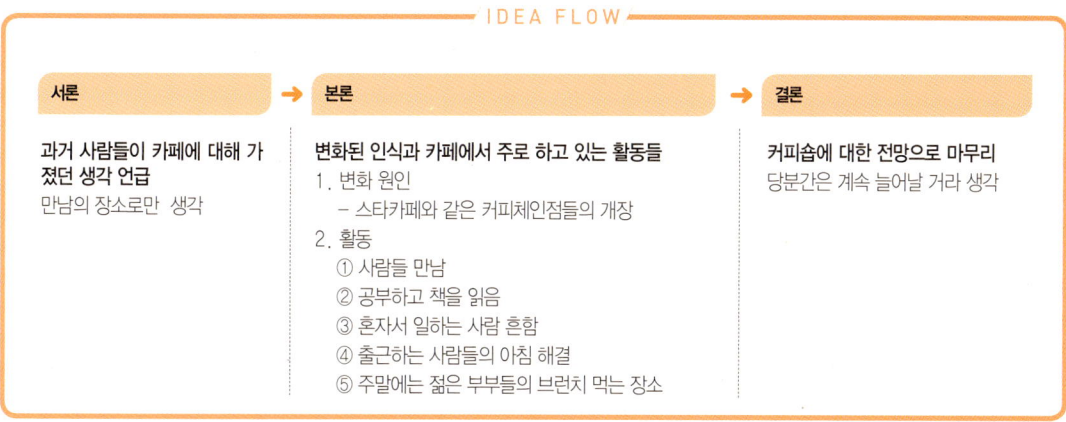

ANSWER

Ten years ago, most people considered a café or a coffee shop simply a meeting place. Few people came in the café alone or worked on their laptops. As more coffee chains like Star Café have opened, however, people have a totally different conception of a café or a coffee shop. It became a place where they study, read books, and work as well as meet people. Now it is very common to see people sitting alone in a coffee shop. In the morning, we can often see some commuters take out some sandwiches and coffee for their breakfast in the coffee shop. Recently, many coffee shops offer brunch at a reasonable price, so young couples have it on weekends. Some freelancers and students spend long hours working on their laptops in the café, too. I sometimes go to Star Café to read a book or do some computer work. I think the number of coffee shops in my country will continuously increase for the time being.

[해석 p.296 참조]

IH 답변 파헤치기

문장 구조 응용하기

consider A (as) B A를 B로 여기다 = **regard A as B** (regard는 as를 생략할 수 없음)

- 본문 Ten years ago, most people considered a café or a coffee shop simply a meeting place.
- ex Some people consider a coffee shop their workspace.
  어떤 사람들은 커피숍을 그들의 작업 공간이라고 여깁니다.
- ex The residents regard the café as one of their best hangouts.
  주민들은 그 카페를 그들이 가장 좋아하는 모임 장소들 중 하나라고 여깁니다.

장소(선행사) + where(관계부사) + S+V
'~하는 장소'라고 해석되지만 사실은 '그 장소 안에서 ~하는 것이다'로 접근하시면 이해하시기 더 편합니다.

- 본문 It became a place where they study, read books, and work as well as meet people.
- ex In this region, there are many nice cafés where students can meet to study.
  이 지역에는 학생들이 만나서 공부할 수 있는 좋은 카페들이 많이 있습니다.
- ex I was supposed to meet him in the coffee shop where we first met each other.
  우리가 처음 만났던 그 커피숍에서 만나기로 되어 있었습니다.

Word on weekends = every weekend 주말마다

- My wife and I go to my parents-in-law's house every weekend. 저와 아내는 주말마다 처가 댁에 갑니다.
- My family goes out for dinner on Saturdays. 우리 가족은 토요일마다 저녁은 외식으로 먹습니다.

Word at a reasonable price 합리적인 가격으로, 적당한 가격으로

- 본문 Recently many coffee shops offer brunch at a reasonable price, so young couples have it on weekends.
- ex My company is trying to provide its consumers with its products at a reasonable price.
  우리 회사는 고객들에게 제품을 합리적인 가격에 제공하려 노력하고 있습니다.
  - cf) The café offers their unsold sandwiches at a reduced price after 8 p.m. each day.
    그 카페는 매일 밤 8시 이후에는 팔리지 않은 샌드위치를 할인 가격으로 제공합니다.

카페에서 특정한 활동을 하지 않는 경우

- I never work in a café because I want to feel relaxed only for myself. I think that a café is a place for pleasure and fun.
  저는 오직 저만을 위한 여유를 즐기고 싶기 때문에 카페에서는 절대로 일하지 않습니다. 카페는 즐거움과 재미를 위한 곳이라고 생각합니다.
- I don't like people who work on a computer in the coffee shop. The sound of someone else typing on a keyboard distracts me from studying or reading.
  저는 커피숍에서 컴퓨터 작업하는 사람을 좋아하지 않습니다. 다른 누군가가 두드리는 자판 소리 때문에 공부를 하거나 책 보는데 집중이 안됩니다.

Word 카페에서 할 수 있는 활동들

- **surf the Internet** 인터넷을 검색하다
- **read a magazine/novel** 잡지/소설을 읽다
- **watch passerby outside** 지나가는 사람들 구경하다
- **watch videos with a smartphone** 스마트폰으로 동영상을 보다
- **work on a computer** 컴퓨터로 작업하다
- **have a chat with friends** 친구들과 수다 떨다

MAKE YOUR ANSWER

질문에 대한 여러분의 답변을 만들어보세요.

What do people in your country do in the café or coffee shop?

Tell me about the most memorable experience that you had in the café or coffee shop.

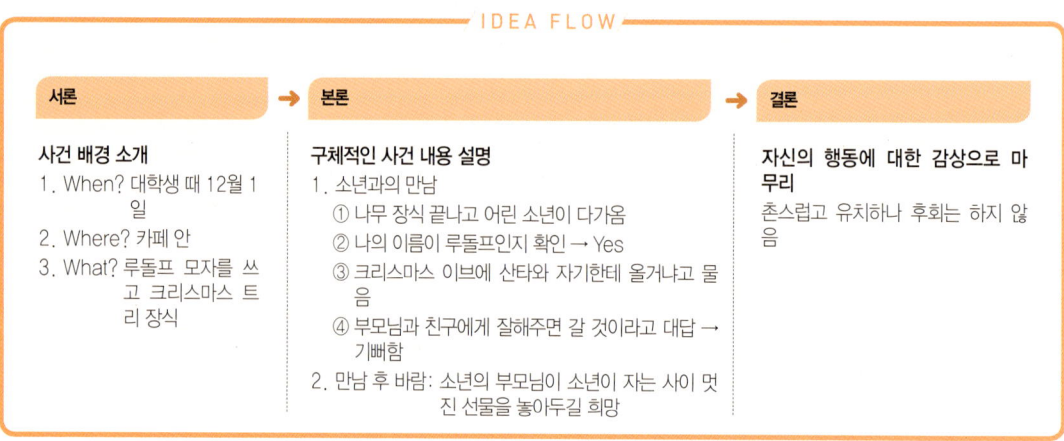

ANSWER

When I was a university student, I worked part time at a café. I was decorating a Christmas tree in the café on December 1st. To make our customers feel the atmosphere of Christmas, I was wearing a Rudolph hat with small cute antlers on it. When I just finished trimming the tree, a little boy who had brunch with his mom approached me. I thought that he was interested in the antlers on my hat. I told him to touch the antlers on my hat, and he asked if my name was Rudolph. He looked so serious that I told him yes. Then he asked if I would visit him with Santa on Christmas Eve. I told him Santa and I would visit him if he was good to his parents and friends. That might sound a little corny, but I didn't want to disappoint him at that time. He seemed to trust me since he looked excited and happy. He was adorable, and I hoped that his parents would leave a nice present on his pillow while he was sleeping. I don't know if I was childish, now I come to think of it, but I don't regret saying so to him.

[해석 p.296 참조]

IH 답변 파헤치기

문장 구조 응용하기

so 형용사/부사 that S+V 너무나 ~해서 ~하다

- 본문 He looked so serious that I told him yes.
- ex His lecture was so long and discursive that I couldn't concentrate on it.
  그의 강의는 너무나 길고 두서가 없어서 저는 도무지 집중할 수 없었습니다.
- ex The café was good but so crowded that we decided to look for a different café.
  그 카페는 좋긴 했지만 너무 붐벼서 우리는 다른 카페를 찾아보기로 했습니다.

seem to 부정사 ~할 것 같다, ~할 모양이다

- 본문 He seemed to trust me since he looked excited and happy.
- ex The customers seemed to care how he looked.
  그 손님은 자기가 어떻게 보이는가에 신경을 쓰는 것 같았습니다.

Word decorate = trim 장식하다, 꾸미다

- 본문 I was decorating a Christmas tree in the café on December 1st.
- 본문 When I just finished trimming the tree, a little boy who had brunch with his mom approached me.
- ex We normally decorate a Christmas tree with jingle bells, colorful ribbons, and tinsels.
  우리는 보통 크리스마스 트리를 딸랑거리는 종, 색깔 있는 리본, 반짝이 조각들로 꾸밉니다.
- ex The girl's dress was trimmed with beads and laces.
  그 소녀의 옷은 구슬과 레이스로 꾸며져 있었습니다.
  cf) trim (조금 잘라내어) 다듬다, 손질하다
- ex I have my hair trimmed every other month.
  저는 두 달에 한 번 머리를 다듬습니다.

Word corny 시시한, 촌스러운, 진부한, 오글거리는

- 본문 That might sound a little corny, but I didn't want to disappoint him at that time.
- ex He told me that he was in love, but I thought it was so corny.
  그는 자기가 사랑에 빠졌다고 말했지만 저는 너무 오글거린다고 생각했습니다.

카페에서 겪은 경험 관련 아이디어

- When I was reading a book in the cafe, a little boy was running around in it. I didn't understand why his parents didn't stop him from running, but I couldn't say anything. Instead, I kept looking unkindly at him, and then he burst into tears standing next to me. I was very embarrassed to make him cry even though I didn't like the boy.
  제가 카페에서 책을 읽고 있는데 어린 소년이 그 안을 뛰어다녔습니다. 저는 그 애의 부모님이 왜 그 애를 못 뛰게 말리지 않는지 이해가 가지 않았지만 아무 말도 할 수 없었습니다. 그대신 저는 그 아이를 계속 째려보았는데 그러자 그 애는 제 옆에 서서 울음을 터뜨리는 것이었습니다. 저는 비록 그 애가 좋지 않았지만 저 때문에 운 것이라 무척 당황했습니다.

- I went to the restroom leaving my laptop on the table in the coffee shop. When I return my seat in just three to five minutes, my laptop was disappeared. I didn't understand how that could happen in the place where many people were sitting around my seat.
  저는 노트북을 커피숍 탁자 위에 놓고 화장실을 갔습니다. 불과 3분에서 5분 사이에 제 노트북이 사라지고 없었습니다. 제 자리 주위에 사람들도 있었는데 어떻게 그런 일이 일어날 수 있는지 이해할 수 없었습니다.

질문에 대한 여러분의 답변을 만들어보세요.

Tell me about the most memorable experience that you had in the café or coffee shop.

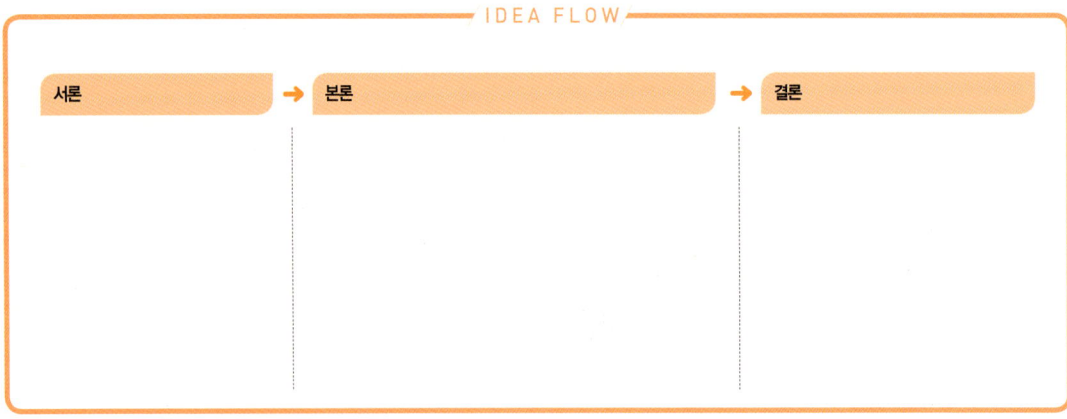

ANSWER

Memo

Lesson 9 악기 연주하기

Oral Proficiency Interview-computer

INTRO 악기 연주를 전문적인 분야로 여겨 어렵다고 느끼시는 분들도 있지만, OPIc에서 요구하는 답변이 전문가 수준의 지식은 결코 아니기 때문에 미리 피하시려고 할 필요는 없습니다. 악기에 대한 기본적인 특징만 파악하면 오히려 준비 과정이 더 수월할 수 있습니다. 악기 연주의 구체적인 방식 보다는 그 악기를 배우게 된 계기나 배울 때 기쁘거나 힘들던 순간, 악기를 연주함으로써 느끼는 즐거움 등을 중심으로 문제가 출제되기 때문에 다른 관심사 및 취미 주제에 대해 준비하는 것과 크게 다를 바 없습니다. 악기 연주, 피하지 말고 자신 있게 도전해보세요.

IH 답변 전략

① 다룰 수 있는 악기를 선정하고 기본적인 특징 파악하기
- 피아노나 바이올린 등 연주할 수 있거나 또는 평소 친숙한 악기를 정하여 그 악기의 특징을 한 두 가지 파악해 둡니다.
- 악기를 주로 연습하는 장소와 시간, 정기적인 연습 시간 등 악기 연주와 관련된 자신의 일상을 소개할 수 있어야 합니다.

② 악기 연주의 관심 변천사 및 배움의 과정 설명하기
- 악기 연주에 흥미를 갖게 된 계기와 그 흥미와 관심이 악기를 계속 배우면서 어떻게 발전되고 변화되었는지 구체적으로 설명할 수 있어야 합니다.
- 악기를 처음 가르쳐준 사람을 간단히 소개하거나, 혹은 독학을 했다면 어떤 방식으로 독학을 했는지도 구체적으로 밝혀줍니다.

③ 악기를 배우거나 연주하면서 일어났던 에피소드 말하기
- 연습하면서 힘들었던 점이나 예기치 않았던 사건들을 정리하고 답변을 만들어 봅니다.
- 실제적으로 사람들 앞에서 연주한 경험을 소재로 이야기를 만들어 보는 것도 좋습니다.

'악기 연주하기'에서는 어떠한 질문들이 출제될까요? 다음의 예상 질문에 대해 여러분은 어떻게 답변할지 한번 생각해 보세요.

1. You indicated in the survey that you play a musical instrument. What was the hardest part in learning or playing the musical instrument? How has the difficulty affected your learning or playing?

✓ 2. You indicated in the survey that you play a musical instrument. What kind of musical instrument can you play? How do you play that instrument? What should you do to play it? Where do you usually practice?

✓ 3. Who did you learn to play the instrument from? How long have you played the instrument? How regularly do you practice?

4. I'd like to know about the most memorable experience you had while learning the musical instrument. What happened and when did you have the experience? What made it so memorable? Please tell me about it in as much detail as you can.

5. Think back to the day when you first played your musical instrument. When and where did you first play it? How did you feel about your playing?

✓ 6. How did you first become interested in learning the instrument? What made you decide to choose the instrument? How have you developed the interest over the years?

7. What are the benefits of playing musical instruments? Please give me a detailed description of it.

8. You indicated in the survey that you play a musical instrument. Do you have any habits when playing the musical instruments? How do they affect your playing?

9. Eva can also play the musical instrument. Ask her three to four questions about her musical instrument.

10. If you learn a different musical instrument, what do you want to choose? What makes you choose it?

Q1 You indicated in the survey that you play a musical instrument. What kind of musical instrument can you play? How do you play that instrument? What should you do to play it? Where do you usually practice?

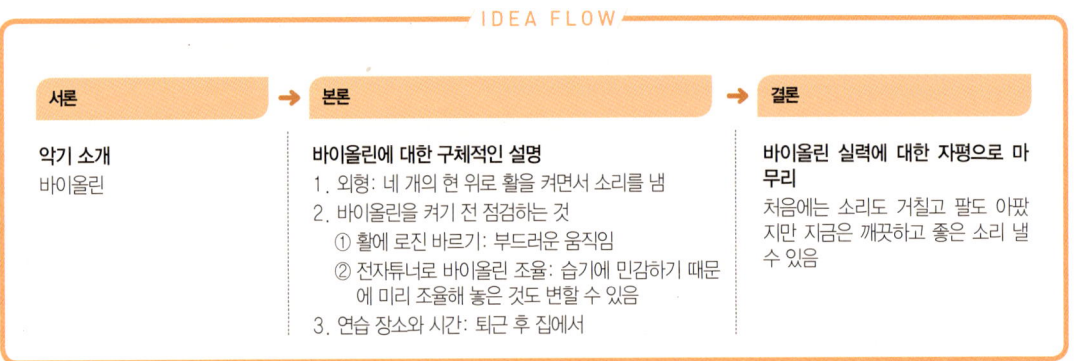

ANSWER

I can play the violin. It has four strings that are sounded by drawing the bow across them. Before playing, I should check two things about my violin. First, I rosin the bow to help it move smoothly on the strings. If not, the sound doesn't come out right. Second, I tune the violin with an electronic tuner. Although I tune the strings, the tuning can be changed depends on the air or weather conditions. Since the violin is very sensitive to humidity, I should tune it new every time I play. I usually practice the violin at home after work with my own violin. I spend more time practicing on weekends. The sound can be noisy to my neighbors, so I use a device that makes the sound smaller. When I first played the violin, the sound was very rough and my muscles of arms ached, but now I can make a good, clean sound.

[해석 p.296 참조]

문장 구조 응용하기

every time S+V ~할 때마다

본문 Since the violin is very sensitive to humidity, I should tune it new every time I play.

ex Every time I play the piano at home my daughter sings a song to the piano.
= Whenever I play the piano at home my daughter sings a song to the piano.
제가 집에서 피아노를 칠 때마다 제 딸은 피아노에 맞춰 노래를 부릅니다.

연주할 수 있는 악기 소개하면 서두 열기

- I've learned to play different musical instruments since I was young.
  저는 어렸을 때부터 여러 가지 악기를 배웠습니다.
- The only musical instrument that I can play is the harmonica. 제가 유일하게 불 수 있는 악기는 하모니카입니다.
- I can play the guitar very well, but I'm not very good at playing the piano.
  저는 기타는 무척 잘 치지만 피아노는 그리 잘 치지 못합니다.

악기 관련 아이디어

- I slide my hand up and down to reach higher notes. To avoid scratchy sounds, I shouldn't put too much pressure when I play the strings.
  저는 고음을 켜기 위해 손을 위 아래로 미끄러뜨립니다. 찢어지는 듯한 소리를 피하기 위해서 현을 켤 때 힘을 너무 많이 주면 안 됩니다.
- The length of the piano keyboard intimidated me, but it was not as complicated as it looked.
  피아노 건반이 너무 많아 겁을 먹었지만 보기만큼 복잡하지는 않았습니다.
- I play the guitar purely for fun of it. I can let go of my worries when playing it.
  기타를 치는 것은 순전히 즐겁기 때문입니다. 기타를 칠 때는 걱정을 털어버릴 수 있습니다.
- I didn't have the patience to learn some instruments like the piano and guitar, but the drums were quite different from them. 피아노나 기타 같은 악기를 배웠을 때는 인내심이 없었는데 드럼은 사뭇 달랐습니다.

악기를 연습하는 장소 언급하기

- Since I don't have a piano at home, I need to go to the academy to practice.
  집에 피아노가 없어서 연습을 하려면 학원에 가야 합니다.
- I normally play the cello in one of the music practice rooms at my school.
  저는 주로 학교에 있는 음악 연습실 중 한 곳에서 첼로를 연습합니다.
- I practice playing the flute either at home or at the academy. 저는 집 혹은 학원에서 플루트 연습을 합니다.

악기에 대한 소견으로 마무리하기

- The more I practice the more I enjoy playing the cello. 연습을 하면 할수록 첼로 켜는 것이 즐겁습니다.
- I think I need to spend more time practicing to improve my piano skills.
  피아노 실력을 향상시키기 위해서 연습을 더 많이 해야 할 것 같습니다.
- Since I've played the guitar for long time, I want to learn a new instrument.
  기타는 오래 쳐왔기 때문에 새로운 악기를 배워보고 싶습니다.
- It was one of my best decisions to learn how to play the drums.
  드럼 치는 걸 배우기로 결심한 것은 제가 한 결정 중에서 가장 잘한 결정 중 하나입니다.
- I was sure to master playing the violin in 2 or 3 years, but it was my huge misjudgment. Now, I think it would take lifetime to master it.
  저는 바이올린을 2, 3년 후에 통달할 거라고 자신했는데 엄청난 판단 착오였습니다. 지금 생각으로는 평생 걸릴 것 같습니다.

MAKE YOUR ANSWER

질문에 대한 여러분의 답변을 만들어보세요.

You indicated in the survey that you play a musical instrument. What kind of musical instrument can you play? How do you play that instrument? What should you do to play it? Where do you usually practice?

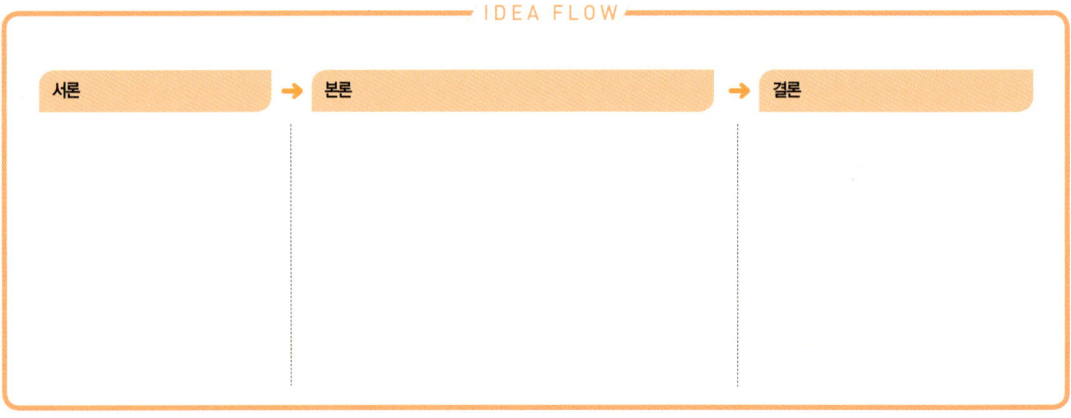

ANSWER

Who did you learn to play the instrument from? How long have you played the instrument? How regularly do you practice?

IDEA FLOW

서론	→	본론	→	결론

바이올린을 배운 장소와 기간, 선택 배경
1. 장소 및 기간: 학원/8년
2. 학원 선택 배경
  ① 집 근처
  ② 성인 수강생이 가장 많은 곳
  ③ 선생님: 바이올린 전공 +5년 이상 강습 경력
		학원에서 배운 과정을 구체적으로 설명
		1. 처음 3년: 개인 교습
		  ① 매 주 토요일 20분씩
		  ② 리듬, 악보 등의 기본적 규칙
		  ③ 바이올린 활 잡는 법
		2. 5년 전부터: 그룹 수업
		  ① 단점: 많은 관심 못 받음, 남 앞에서 켜기 부끄러움
		  ② 장점: 다른 사람 연주 듣는 것이 설레고 흥미로움
				바이올린 켜는 것에 대한 감상으로 마무리
				아주 좋아해서 수업 후에도 30분씩 학원에서 연습

ANSWER

I've been learning to play the violin in an academy called Star Piano for eight years. I searched some academies near my house and chose this academy that had more adult students than any other academy. My teacher majored in violin at university and had over five years of experience teaching students. For three years, I took a one-on-one lesson every Saturday for 20 minutes. She taught me basic rules such as how to follow the rhythm and how to read music and so on. After a while, I learned how to grip the violin and the bow. She always emphasized the importance of bowing practice. I began joining group lessons five years ago. I can't get as much attention as I could in the private lesson, but I found it enjoyable to learn with others. I'm shy to play the violin in front of others, but at the same time, it's quite exciting and interesting to hear others playing. I like playing the violin a lot, and even after class, I practice for 30 minutes or more in the academy.

[해석 p.296 참조]

IH 답변 파헤치기

문장 구조 응용하기

have been ~ing 해 오고 있다 (현재 완료 진행으로 특정 시점을 언급하고자 하면 for 또는 since를 써 줍니다.)
- 본문 I've been learning to play the violin in an academy called Star Piano for eight years.
- ex I've been playing the piano since my childhood.(=since I was a child)
  저는 어렸을 때부터 계속 피아노를 쳐왔습니다.

more ~ than any other+단수명사 = 최상급
- 본문 I searched some academies near my house and chose this academy that had more adult students than any other academy.
  = I searched some academies near my house and chose one that had the most students among academies.
- ex She looked more elegant than any other flutist.
  그녀는 플루트 연주자들 중에서 가장 우아했습니다.

find it + 형용사 + to 부정사 ~라는 걸 알게 되다
여기에서 it는 특정 뜻을 내포하고 있지 않습니다.
- 본문 I can't get as much attention as I could in the private lesson, but I found it enjoyable to learn with others.
- ex But soon I found it much more difficult to play the violin than I had expected.
  하지만 저는 곧 바이올린을 연주하는 것이 내가 예상했던 것보다 훨씬 어렵다는 것을 알아차렸습니다.

악기를 배운 방법 또는 대상에 대해 설명하기

- When I was a middle school student, I started taking private piano lessons from a graduate student whose major instrument was piano. My aunt introduced her to me, and she had a few more students other than me.
  저는 중학생일 때 피아노 전공인 대학원생에게서 개인 교습을 받기 시작했습니다. 우리 숙모가 소개시켜주었고, 그녀는 저 말고도 가르치는 학생이 몇 명 더 있었습니다.

- My cousin who was a member of his school band taught me how to play the guitar. I went to his place to learn it every weekend. 학교 밴드부 회원이었던 사촌 형이 저에게 기타치는 법을 가르쳐주었습니다. 기타를 배우러 주말마다 형의 집에 갔습니다.

악기 연습의 빈도수 또는 시간 언급하기

- I practiced every day for the first few years, but these days, I do only once or twice a week.
  처음 몇 년 간은 매일 연습을 했었지만 요즘은 일주일에 한 두 번만 합니다.
- I've tried to practice at least several times a month. 한 달에 적어도 몇 차례는 연습을 하려고 노력해왔습니다.
- I know I shouldn't miss practices but it's not that easy to act up to my resolution.
  연습을 빼먹으면 안 된다는 걸 알지만, 마음먹은 대로 하기가 그리 쉽지는 않습니다.
- I spend 30 minutes on bowing practice before starting the lesson. After the lesson, I also practice 30 minutes to an hour either in the academy or at home.
  저는 수업 시작 전에 30분 동안 활 켜는 연습을 합니다. 수업이 끝난 후에도 30분에서 1시간 동안 학원이나 집에서 연습을 합니다.

MAKE YOUR ANSWER

질문에 대한 여러분의 답변을 만들어보세요.

Who did you learn to play the instrument from? How long have you played the instrument? How regularly do you practice?

ANSWER

How did you first become interested in learning the instrument? What made you decide to choose the instrument? How have you developed the interest over the years?

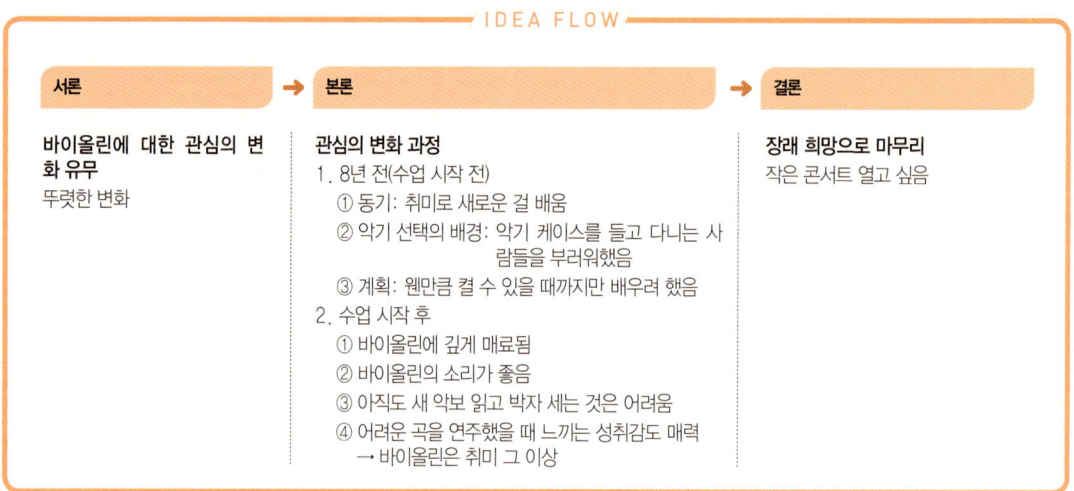

ANSWER

My interest in violin has changed clearly over the years. Eight years ago, I just wanted to learn something new as a hobby. Playing a musical instrument would be a fun and rewarding hobby. I was actually thinking about playing the piano at first. But as you know, piano is too expensive to buy and is not portable either. I might be a little snobbish, but at that time, I envied people who carried the musical instrument case. When I took my first lesson, I never intended to learn it for so long. I planned to quit learning if I could play the violin fairly well enough. But once I started it, I became deeply into violin. I like its sound so much. Still, I feel it's hard to read new music and count rhythm. Sometimes, it takes over one year to finish just one piece. But that's the charm of violin, too. I can feel a sense of accomplishment when I finish very hard pieces and listen to the music that I'm playing. Now playing the violin is much more than a hobby for me. I'm dreaming of holding a small concert at some point in the future.

[해석 p.297 참조]

IH 답변 파헤치기

동기, 취향, 관심 등이 시간의 흐름에 따라 변화됨을 설명할 때 사용되는 표현들

1. 과거(시작 당시)

- At that time, I played the drums just because I wanted to look cool.
  그 당시에는 나는 그저 멋져 보이고 싶어서 드럼을 쳤습니다.
- At the beginning, I didn't enjoy playing the piano at all because I was forced to learn it by my mother.
  초기에는 어머니에 의해 억지로 배우게 된 거라 피아노 치는 것이 전혀 즐겁지 않았습니다.
- I didn't even know how to count rhythm back then.
  그 당시에는 어떻게 박자를 세는지조차 잘 몰랐습니다.

2. 동기나 관심의 변화

- Once I started the lessons, I realized that I had a talent for music.
  막상 수업을 시작하고 보니 제게 음악적 재능이 있다는 걸 깨달았습니다.
- As I spend more time practicing, I came to have a desire for holding my own concert.
  연습을 더 많이 함에 따라 저는 단독 콘서트를 열고 싶다는 욕심을 갖게 되었습니다.
- As time went by, however, I started to get sick and tired of repeated practices.
  하지만 시간이 가면서 저는 반복되는 연습에 싫증이 나기 시작했습니다.

3. 현재의 상태

- Now playing the piano is a very important part of my life.
  이제는 피아노 치는 것이 제 삶의 매우 중요한 한 부분입니다.
- These days, I'm willing to practice every day.
  요즘은 매일매일 기꺼이 연습을 합니다.

Word intend to 부정사 ~할 작정이다, ~할 생각이다

- 본문 When I took my first lesson, I never intended to learn it for so long.
- ex At first, I intended to rent a cello because I couldn't afford to buy it.
  처음에는 첼로를 살 여유가 없어서 빌릴 작정이었습니다.

Word a sense of accomplishment 성취감

- 본문 I can feel a sense of accomplishment when I finish very hard pieces and listen to the music that I'm playing.
- ex I want to suggest my son that he play any kinds of musical instruments to create a sense of accomplishment. 저는 제 아들에게 성취감이 생길 수 있도록 어떤 종류의 악기든 배우라고 하고 싶습니다.

악기를 좋아하는 이유 간단히 소개하기

- I really enjoy working with other musicians in a band while playing the drums.
  저는 드럼을 칠 때 밴드의 다른 음악가들과 함께 연주하는 것이 참 좋습니다.
- I like the cello because it produces a sound that resembles the human voice.
  저는 첼로가 내는 소리가 사람의 목소리와 흡사해서 좋습니다.
- I used to get easily distracted, but the piano helped me build patience.
  저는 쉽게 산만해지곤 했는데 피아노 덕분에 인내심을 길렀습니다.

MAKE YOUR ANSWER

질문에 대한 여러분의 답변을 만들어보세요.

How did you first become interested in learning the instrument? What made you decide to choose the instrument? How have you developed the interest over the years?

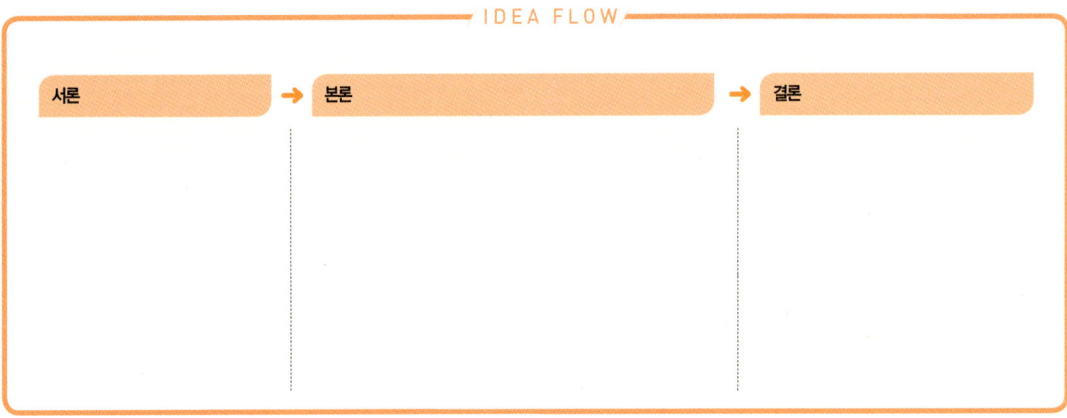

Memo

Lesson 10 신문 읽기

INTRO 앞에서 보여드린 바와 같이 최근 OPIc 서베이에 새롭게 추가된 주제들이 비교적 많습니다. 기존 주제들보다 전문적이고 생각을 더 많이 요하는 주제들이 꽤 있는데요, 이번 과에서 배우는 신문 읽기가 그 대표적인 예가 될 것입니다. 신문 읽기 관련해서 출제되는 문항들을 보면 기대하는 신문의 역할, 신문을 통해 얻을 수 있는 이점, 신문 추세의 변화 과정, 신문의 미래 예측 등 사회 전반적인 상황과 연결시켜 답변을 해야 하는 깊이 있는 문제들이 다루어집니다. 그 어느 주제보다 준비가 많이 필요한 신문 읽기, 이제 도전해볼까요?

IH 답변 전략

1 현재 우리나라의 신문 구독 상황 소개하기
- 일반적인 신문 구독의 방법들(예: 정기 구독, 가판대 구매, 온라인 신문 등)을 소개할 수 있어야 합니다.
- 신문 관련 어휘들을 정리해서 익혀두고 실제 답변에 활용하도록 합시다.

2 과거와 현재의 신문 추세의 변화를 설명하고 앞으로 있을 또 다른 변화 예측하기
- 어렸을 때 구독했던 신문과 지금 접하는 신문은 내용적으로나 시각적으로 분명 차이가 있을 것입니다. 종이신문 내에서도 디자인, 글자 배열, 국한문 혼용 등 변화된 사안들을 구체적으로 언급해주면서 신문 추세에 대한 답변을 준비해봅니다.
- 앞에서 준비한 테크놀로지가 신문에서도 활용될 수 있습니다. 신문 전달 방식의 큰 변화를 가져온 인터넷, 컴퓨터, 스마트폰에 대한 언급으로 신문 추세의 변화를 설명하는 답변도 만들어 봅니다.
- 신문 형태의 변화나 신문에 대한 인식의 변화로 예측될 수 있는 신문의 미래에 대한 답변을 준비해야 합니다.

3 기대하는 신문의 역할, 신문의 장점 등을 설명하기
- 각자가 기대하는 신문의 역할을 생각해보고 그 생각을 조리 있게 말로 전달하는 연습을 꾸준히 해보도록 합시다.
- 다른 매체와 차별되는 신문만의 장점을 정리해보고 그를 토대로 답변을 만들어 봅니다.

'신문 읽기'에서는 어떠한 질문들이 출제될까요? 다음의 예상 질문에 대해 여러분은 어떻게 답변할지 한 번 생각해 보세요.

1. I'd like to know about the newspaper you are currently subscribing to. How long have you read the newspaper and why did you decide to subscribe to it?

2. Think back to the day when you first read the newspaper. How old were you and what did you read about?

3. What are the benefits of reading newspapers? How has reading newspapers affected your life?

4. How do people read newspapers in your country? Do they subscribe to any newspapers or do they buy them when they want to read? What papers do they get at their home or office? Why do you think they read newspapers?

5. Tell me about one of the newspaper articles that you were recently interested in. What was the article about and what made it interesting to you?

6. What section of the newspaper do you read first? What makes you read it first?

7. How have newspapers changed over the past years? How do you see the future of the newspapers? Why do you think so?

8. Some people say that printed newspapers will disappear and be replaced with online news in the future. How do you predict the future of the printed newspapers?

9. What do you expect newspapers to do? What role do you think the newspapers should play? What are the benefits of reading newspapers?

10. Tell me about some advantages of newspapers compared to other media such as TV and radio.

Q1 How do people read newspapers in your country? Do they subscribe to any newspapers or do they buy them when they want to read? What papers do they get at their home or office? Why do you think they read newspapers?

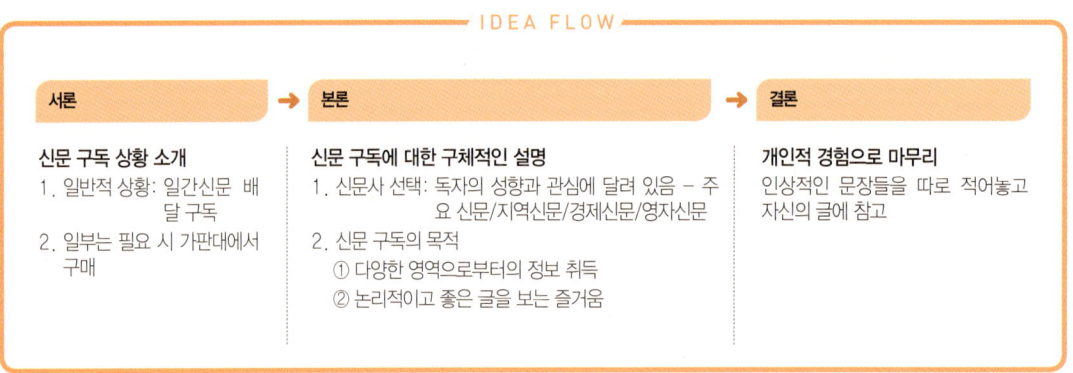

ANSWER

People generally subscribe to daily newspapers in my country. Getting newspapers delivered is more convenient than buying them from vendors, but some people who rarely have time to read it in the morning just buy a copy at the newsstand and read it when they have time. People choose which newspapers to read depending on their inclinations and interests. Some prefer major newspapers and others like local papers. Also, people can choose economic newspapers or English newspapers for their own purpose. I think most people read newspapers to get some information on various categories such as politics, social events, people, business, etc. With in-depth coverage of today's complicated issues, newspapers enable them to better comprehend about some critical incidents. Some people also read them to find joy in reading good, logical writing. I actually write down some impressive sentences in my notebook when I find them from the newspaper. Then, I use them as models when I make up my own sentences in writing.

[해석 p.297 참조]

IH 답변 파헤치기

사람들의 신문 구독 양식을 묘사해보기

- I don't exactly know about other people, but most people around me hardly read the newspaper. They sometimes check a few major issues that some portal sites provide online.
  다른 사람들에 대해서는 정확히 모르겠지만 제 주위 사람들은 신문을 거의 보지 않습니다. 가끔 인터넷 포털 사이트에서 제공하는 중요한 몇 개의 안건들만 체크합니다.
- Some people read only the first page that usually carries the most important stories.
  어떤 사람들은 대개 가장 중요한 내용을 담는 제1면만 읽습니다.
- People normally check all the headlines and then start reading the lead stories carefully.
  사람들은 보통 표제들을 다 점검해보고 나서 머리기사를 자세히 읽기 시작합니다.

신문을 읽는 이유 관련 아이디어들

- Since I'm very interested in politics and politicians, I read the newspaper to get more detailed information of them.
  저는 정치와 정치인들에게 관심이 매우 많기 때문에 그들에 관해 보다 더 자세한 정보를 얻기 위해 신문을 봅니다.
- Honestly, I read the newspaper to look more intelligent and informed at social gatherings.
  솔직히, 저는 사람들하고 만날 때 더 지적이고 아는 게 많은 것처럼 보이기 위해 신문을 읽습니다.
- I don't have any particular reasons why I read the newspaper. I just read it habitually every morning. It's one of my daily routines.
  신문을 읽는 데 뭐 특별한 이유는 없습니다. 그냥 매일 아침 습관적으로 읽습니다. 제 일상 중의 하나인 거죠.
- I always read all of the editorials in the newspaper every day. They suggest solutions as well as analyze critical problems in our society.
  저는 신문에 있는 사설은 매일 빠짐없이 읽습니다. 사설은 우리 사회의 중대한 문제점을 분석할 뿐 아니라 대안도 제시해줍니다.

Word subscribe to 부정사 ~을 구독하다

- 본문 People choose which newspapers to read depending on their inclinations and interests.
- ex My parents started to subscribe to ABC Times before I was born.
  우리 부모님께서는 ABC Times를 제가 태어나기도 전부터 구독하시기 시작했습니다.

Word impressive 인상적인, 감명 깊은

- 본문 I actually write down some impressive sentences in my notebook when I find them from the newspaper.
- ex I read a very impressive article about the Amazon today.
  오늘 아마존에 대한 아주 인상적인 기사를 보았습니다.

Word 신문 관련 어휘들

- **the press** 언론
- **newspaper subscription** 신문 구독
- **morning/evening edition** 조간/석간 신문
- **front page** 제1면
- **article** 기사
- **lead story** 머리기사, 톱뉴스
- **headline** (신문기사의)표제, 제목
- **feature** 특집기사, 대서특필(하다)
- **editorial** 사설, 논설
- **editor/reporter/columnist** 편집장/기자/칼럼니스트
- **correspondent** 특파원
- **an eyewitness report** 목격자 보고
- **comic strip** 시사만화

MAKE YOUR ANSWER

질문에 대한 여러분의 답변을 만들어보세요.

How do people read newspapers in your country? Do they subscribe to any newspapers or do they buy them when they want to read? What papers do they get at their home or office? Why do you think they read newspapers?

ANSWER

How have newspapers changed over the past years? How do you see the future of the newspapers? Why do you think so?

IDEA FLOW

서론	본론	결론
자신의 관점 소개 신문은 지난 수년간 여러 측면에서 변화해 왔음	변화된 측면을 구체적으로 제시 1. 레이아웃 　① 시각적 효과 목적 　② 현재 배열 방식 더 보기 좋음 2. 내용: 문화, 예술에 더 많은 지면 할애 3. 온라인 뉴스의 출현 　① 인터넷/스마트폰 발달에 기인 　② 신문 구독률 감소의 원인 4. 신문의 미래 예측 　① 일반적 의견: 종이 신문 대신 온라인 신문 　② 나의 의견: 반대(근거-오래 누려왔던 방식 쉽게 포기하지 않음)	종이 신문과 온라인 신문의 비교로 마무리 내용을 계속 클릭해야 볼 수 있는 온라인 신문에 비해 종이 신문은 편하게 볼 수 있음

ANSWER

The newspapers have changed over time in many aspects. First, the layout has changed for better visual effects. Thinking of the newspaper my family subscribes to, the way the texts, photos, and advertisements are arranged on the pages looks much better than that of the past. The contents of newspapers have also changed. Newspapers are devoting more space to the articles on culture and art than they did in the past. I think one of the greatest changes is the advent of online newspapers. As the Internet and smartphones have developed, people can read almost all types of newspapers online. The change has led the readership for printed newspapers to decline, especially among young people. Some people predict online newspapers replace all printed newspapers in the near future, but I don't agree with this idea because people do not give up their old ways easily for a long time to come. Besides, reading online news requires us more time and effort than reading the printed version. We have to keep clicking many news headlines displayed online to find what information is in them. In the printed edition, however, we can find any information easily, just flipping through the pages.

[해석 p.297 참조]

IH 답변 파헤치기

문장 구조 응용하기

사람/사물 + ~ing ~하는 사람/사물 (능동의미)
사람/사물 + ~p.p. ~되는 사람/사물 (수동의미)

- **본문** We have to keep clicking many news headlines displayed online to find what information is in them. (→headlines are displayed)
- **ex** The column written by a famous professor was about Korea's aging population problems. (→column was written)
  유명한 교수가 쓴 그 칼럼은 한국의 인구 고령화 문제에 관한 것이었습니다.
- **ex** There are many people reading weekly newspapers in my country. (→people are reading)
  우리 나라에는 주간신문을 읽는 사람이 많습니다.

신문의 변화되는 추세와 관련된 아이디어들

- I can see many color photographs in the newspapers today while most photos were black and white in the past.
  과거에는 대부분의 사진들이 흑백사진들이었던 반면, 요즘은 신문에서 칼라 사진들을 많이 볼 수 있습니다.
- I remember there were some evening papers when I was an elementary school student. But these days, I can hardly find the evening edition, especially among major newspapers.
  제가 초등학생 때는 석간신문들이 좀 있었던 걸로 기억합니다. 하지만 요즘은 특히 주요 신문들 중에서는 석간을 거의 찾을 수가 없습니다.
- I can find few Chinese characters in the newspapers nowadays. But looking back on my teenage years, I had difficulty reading so many Chinese characters written in the articles.
  요즘은 신문에서 한자를 거의 찾아볼 수 없습니다. 하지만 제 십대 시절을 돌이켜보면, 기사에 쓰여진 한자를 읽는데 힘들었습니다.
- Fewer people read conventional newspapers. In particular, young people prefer web or mobile news.
  종이 신문을 읽는 사람들이 점점 줄어듭니다. 특히 젊은 사람들은 웹 뉴스나 모바일 뉴스를 선호합니다.

Word advent 출현, 도래
- **본문** I think one of the greatest changes is the advent of online newspapers.
- **ex** Our life has greatly been changed due to the advent of the Internet.
  우리 삶은 인터넷의 출현으로 엄청나게 변했습니다.

Word replace ~을 대체하다, 대신하다
- **본문** Some people predict online newspapers replace all printed newspapers in the near future.
- **ex** The cartoons are no longer published from next week. Instead advertisements will replace them.
  다음 주부터는 만화가 더 이상 연재되지 않습니다. 대신 광고가 만화를 대신할 것입니다.

Idiom flip through (책장 등을) 획획 넘기다
- **본문** In the printed edition, however, we can find any information easily, just flipping through the pages.
- **ex** My sister flipped through the magazines, looking only at the photos.
  제 여동생은 사진만 보면서 잡지를 획획 넘겨보았습니다.
- **ex** I listened to his explanation, flipping through handouts.
  저는 배포자료를 넘겨보면서 그의 설명을 들었습니다.

MAKE YOUR ANSWER

질문에 대한 여러분의 답변을 만들어보세요.

How have newspapers changed over the past years? How do you see the future of the newspapers? Why do you think so?

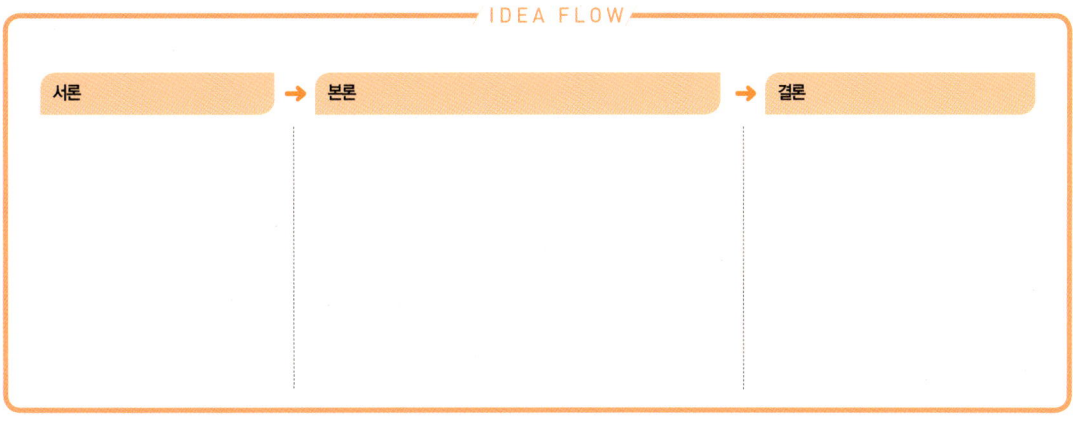

IDEA FLOW

서론 → 본론 → 결론

ANSWER

Q3 What do you expect newspapers to do? What role do you think the newspapers should play? What are the benefits of reading newspapers?

IDEA FLOW

서론 →	본론 →	결론
기대하는 신문의 역할 의사 소통 도구 신문을 통해 우리 주위나 다른 지역 사람들에 대해 알 수 있음	좋은 신문과 신문 구독의 혜택 1. 좋은 신문 ① 정확한 사실에 근거한 공정한 보도 전달 ② 균형잡힌 시각으로 건설적 의견 제시 → 독자들이 다른 사람 이해 2. 신문 구독의 혜택 ① 다양한 주제에 대해 믿을만한 정보 취득 cf) 웹 포탈-사실 확인 없이 성급한 보도 ② 구체적인 지식/정보 제공	신문으로 받은 개인적 혜택으로 마무리 부지런히 신문 읽는 덕에 정보력 많고 아는 게 많다는 말 들음

ANSWER

I expect newspapers to play a role of effective communication tools of our society. They enable us to know what is happening around us or in different parts worldwide. By conveying all sorts of news, they can draw either understanding and good faith or hostility and anger from the readers. I believe that good newspapers should give their readers impartial reporting based on actual facts; therefore, they should present constructive opinions of any issues with a balanced view. One of the benefits of reading newspapers is that we can get reliable information on various subjects. Newspapers are more trustworthy than any other source of information. Web portals often rush to report some stories or cases without ascertaining the truth, but newspapers write articles based on the professional reporters' close coverage of the cases. Besides their reliability, newspapers offer us very specific knowledge and information. In most cases, news portals or TV news do not provide as detailed analysis as newspapers do. I am often told that I am informative and knowledgeable, and the credit should go to my habits of reading newspapers diligently.

[해석 p.297 참조]

IH 답변 파헤치기

신문의 역할 또는 기대하는 바에 관한 아이디어

- I think that newspapers need to play a role of helping their readers know the outside world.
  저는 신문은 독자들이 외부 세계를 알게 해주는 역할을 한다고 생각합니다.
- The articles that I want to see in the newspapers are about human's good will, kind acts, and warm stories rather than crimes or political corruption. I hope that newspapers assign more pages to those positive, bright people.
  제가 신문에서 보고 싶은 기사들은 범죄나 정치 부패보다는 인간의 선의, 선행, 그리고 따뜻한 이야기들에 관한 것입니다. 저는 신문이 그런 긍정적이고 밝은 사람들을 다루는데 더 많은 지면을 할애했으면 합니다.

신문의 혜택 관련 아이디어

- Reading newspapers has obviously helped me with spelling, word spacing, and punctuation. Korean orthography is quite complicated and confusing to write even for Koreans. By reading newspapers, I could reduce such technical errors when writing.
  신문을 읽는 것이 저의 맞춤법, 띄어쓰기, 구두점에는 확실히 도움이 되었습니다. 한국어 맞춤법은 한국인들에게조차 상당히 복잡하고 헷갈립니다. 신문을 읽음으로써 글을 쓸 때 그런 기술적인 실수들을 줄일 수 있었죠.
- Newspapers enable me to know about many things about our world. If it were not for newspapers, I couldn't get such different areas of knowledge.
  신문은 우리 세계에 대해서 많은 것들을 알게 해 줍니다. 신문이 없었다면 그렇게 많은 분야의 지식을 얻을 수 없었을 거예요.
- I read newspapers with my 12-year-old daughter every day. There are certain pages for teens, which are very constructive and educational for her. They have some academic topics that are easy to comprehend, so she is very interested in them.
  저는 12살 된 딸과 함께 매일 신문을 봅니다. 십대를 위한 특정 페이지들이 있는데 딸아이에게 아주 건설적이고 교육적입니다. 학술적인 주제들도 이해하기 쉽게 다뤄서 우리 아이가 무척 관심 있어합니다.

Word hostility 적대감, 적의

- 본문 By conveying all sorts of news, they can draw either understanding and good faith or hostility and anger from the readers.
- ex I was a little uncomfortable to feel his hidden hostility toward my company.
  저는 우리 회사에 갖고 있는 그의 숨겨진 적대감이 느껴져서 좀 불편했습니다.

Word impartial 공정한, 공평한 (= fair, just)

- 본문 I believe that good newspapers should give their readers impartial reporting based on actual facts.
- ex People constantly talked about the impartial judge that came out in today's papers.
  사람들은 오늘 아침 신문에 나왔던 공정한 판사에 대해 계속 이야기했습니다.

Word trustworthy = reliable 신뢰할만한, 믿을만한

- 본문 One of the benefits of reading newspapers is that we can get reliable information on various subjects.
- ex You are so lucky to have a staff member who is so trustworthy.
  그렇게 믿을만한 직원을 두셨으니 정말 행운이시네요.

IH 답변 파헤치기

- **Word** ascertain 알아내다, 확인하다 (=verify)
  - It's not late to complain to her after ascertaining if she really talked badly about you behind your back. 그녀가 정말 뒤에서 당신 험담을 하고 다녔다는 것을 확인한 후에 그녀에게 따져도 늦지 않습니다.

- **Idiom** the credit goes to 부정사 ~의 공이다, ~덕분이다
  - I was finally promoted to a manager, and all the credit goes to my customers. 저는 드디어 지점장으로 승진했는데, 모두 저희 고객들 덕이었습니다.

MAKE YOUR ANSWER

질문에 대한 여러분의 답변을 만들어보세요.

What do you expect newspapers to do? What role do you think the newspapers should play? What are the benefits of reading newspapers?

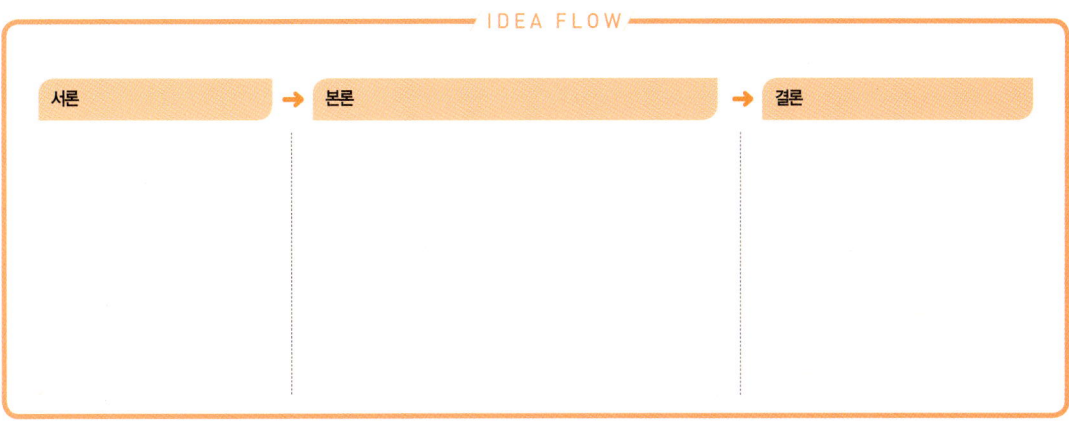

ANSWER

Lesson 11 주식투자하기

Oral Proficiency Interview-computer

INTRO

주식투자하기 역시 신문 보기와 마찬가지로 최근 OPIc 서베이 취미와 관심사(5번) 항목에 새로 추가된 주제입니다. 주식투자를 경험해보지 않은 사람에게는 생소하고 어려울 수 있는 주제기 때문에 각별한 준비가 필요합니다. 다만 전문적인 투자 상식을 답해야 하는 질문보다는 일반적인 주식거래 수단, 주식투자를 시작한 계기, 주식투자를 하면서 겪었던 흥미로운 일 등 개인적 영역의 답변을 요구하는 문항들이 주를 이루기 때문에 미리 너무 걱정하실 필요는 없습니다. 자 그럼 주식투자의 세계로 들어가볼까요?

① 기본적인 주식투자 정보들과 어휘들 파악하기
- 우선 주식거래에 필요한 기본적인 사항들을 파악하고 기억해둡니다.
- 주식투자 및 주식거래와 관련된 어휘들을 익혀두어야 합니다.
- 증권회사 방문, 온라인을 통한 직접거래 등 일반적인 주식거래 방법 및 자신의 거래 수단으로 선택한 주식거래 방식을 소개할 수 있어야 합니다.

② 주식투자를 시작하게 된 계기와 그 이후 변화 과정 설명하기
- 처음 주식투자를 시작하게 된 계기를 매수한 주식 이름, 매수가 등의 구체적인 정보를 포함하여 설명해 줍니다.
- 처음 주식투자를 한 이후 더 공격적이거나 소극적인 투자성향으로 변화된 과정을 설명할 수 있어야 합니다.

③ 주식투자를 하면서 겪었던 흥미롭거나 기억에 남는 에피소드 소개하기
- IMF나 북한 핵 위기, 리만 브라더스 사태 등 주식시장의 크고 작은 사건들을 정리하여 그를 토대로 자신의 경험에 관한 답변을 만들어봅니다.
- 주식시장에서 겪은 경험을 통해 느낀 점이나 그로 인한 주식 성향의 변화 등을 간단히 언급하며 마무리하는 답변을 준비해봅시다.

예상질문 파헤치기

'주식투자하기'에서는 어떠한 질문들이 출제될까요? 다음의 예상 질문에 대해 여러분은 어떻게 답변할지 한번 생각해 보세요.

1. How did you get started investing in stock market? How did you decide which stocks to buy?

✓ 2. How do most people buy and sell stock in your country? Do they go to securities companies to trade stocks or do it online? What should they do to buy and sell stock?

3. Trading stocks may require some time and effort. How has stock trading affected your daily life?

✓ 4. When was the first time you invested in stocks? How much did you invest? Which stocks did you buy? Tell me the whole story from the beginning to the end.

5. What are the benefits of investing in stocks compared to investing in others such as real estate or bonds?

6. What do you think is the most important things when people invest in stock market or trade stocks?

✓ 7. Tell me about your most memorable event concerning the stock market.

8. What advice do you want to give someone who wants to start in stock investment?

Q1 How do most people buy and sell stock in your country? Do they go to securities companies to trade stocks or do it online? What should they do to buy and sell stock?

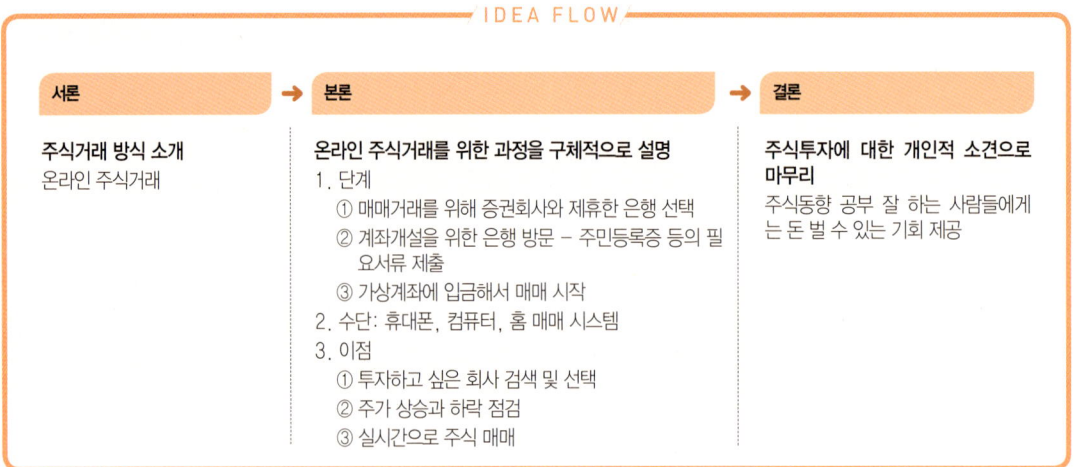

ANSWER

People in my country mostly buy and sell stock online. Some people go to securities firms to directly trade their stocks, but it is much more common to trade online. The very first thing to do for online stock trading is select a bank affiliated with the stock brokerage companies to make transactions. Then you need to visit the bank once to open an account. When visiting, you need to submit several documents, including an ID card. Once you open your account, you can start making transactions by depositing money into a virtual account. You can make trades through your mobile phone, personal computer, and home trading system. On the Internet, you can search and select the companies you wish to invest in and see how their stocks have gone up and down in value. In addition, you can buy and sell stocks in real time. I think that stock investment gives people a chance to make money if they are well informed about the trends in stocks.

[해석 p.298 참조]

IH 답변 파헤치기

주식투자 방법을 소개하는 서두 열기

- In the past, before the Internet and mobile phones were developed, most people went to the securities firms and stayed until the opening of the stock market to buy and sell stock. But nowadays, many people make online transactions at home or in their offices.
  인터넷과 휴대전화가 발전하기 전인 과거에는 대부분의 사람들이 주식을 사고 팔기 위해 증권회사에 가서 주식시장이 개장할 때까지 기다렸습니다. 하지만 지금은 많은 사람들이 집이나 사무실에서 온라인으로 거래를 합니다.
- The average person does not trade stocks through a stockbroker today. It's more common and convenient even for very wealthy people, who transact a large amount of money, to trade online by themselves.
  보통 사람은 증권중개인을 통해서 주식을 거래하지 않습니다. 거액을 거래하는 부자한테도 혼자서 온라인으로 거래하는 게 더 흔하고 편리합니다.

주식에 대한 감상으로 마무리하기

- It is not guaranteed that we will have a good return on our investment, but at least, we can have an opportunity to make a gain on it.
  우리가 한 투자에 좋은 투자수익률을 거둔다는 보장은 없지만, 적어도 수익을 얻을 기회는 가질 수 있습니다.
- If I am not greedy when investing in stocks, I can earn extra pocket money that my wife doesn't know about. 제가 주식투자를 할 때 욕심만 그렇게 부리지 않는다면, 제 아내가 모르는 용돈은 벌 수 있습니다.
- I think that it is so risky to invest all of the money that people have in stocks. I prefer sound conservative investing to active and aggressive investing.
  가진 돈 전부를 주식에 투자하는 것은 너무 위험한 것 같습니다. 저는 적극적이고 공격적인 투자보다는 안전하고 보수적인 투자를 선호합니다.

Word open an account/make transactions 구좌를 개설하다/거래하다

- ex I opened a bank account to start trading stocks this morning.
  저는 주식거래를 시작하기 위해서 은행구좌를 개설했습니다.
- ex There are some rules and procedures to make secure mobile transactions.
  안전한 모바일 거래를 하기 위한 몇 가지 규칙과 절차가 있습니다.

Word affiliate with ~와 제휴하다, 연계하다

- 본문 The very first thing to do for online stock trading is select a bank affiliated with the stock companies to make transactions.
- ex My store plans to affiliate with more credit card companies this year.
  우리 가게는 올해 좀 더 많은 신용카드 회사와 제휴할 계획입니다.

Word 주식투자 관련 어휘들

- share/stock 주식, 주
- shareholder/stockholder 주주
- equities 주식, 보통 주
- blue chip stocks 우량주
- listed stock 상장주식
- unlisted (over-the-counter) stock 비상장주식
- stock exchange 증권거래소
- stock(share) value/stock(share) price 주가
- capital (기업의)자본
- insider(trading) 내부자(내부자 거래)
- mutual fund 뮤추얼 펀드(투자자들의 자금 모아서 운영)
- portfolio(management) 포트폴리오(자산관리)
- return on investment(ROI) 투자수익률
- trading session 개장시간
- invest in ~에 투자하다
- control the risks 위험(요소)를 관리, 조절하다
- limit one's losses 손실을 제한하다

질문에 대한 여러분의 답변을 만들어보세요.

How do most people buy and sell stock in your country? Do they go to securities companies to trade stocks or do it online? What should they do to buy and sell stock?

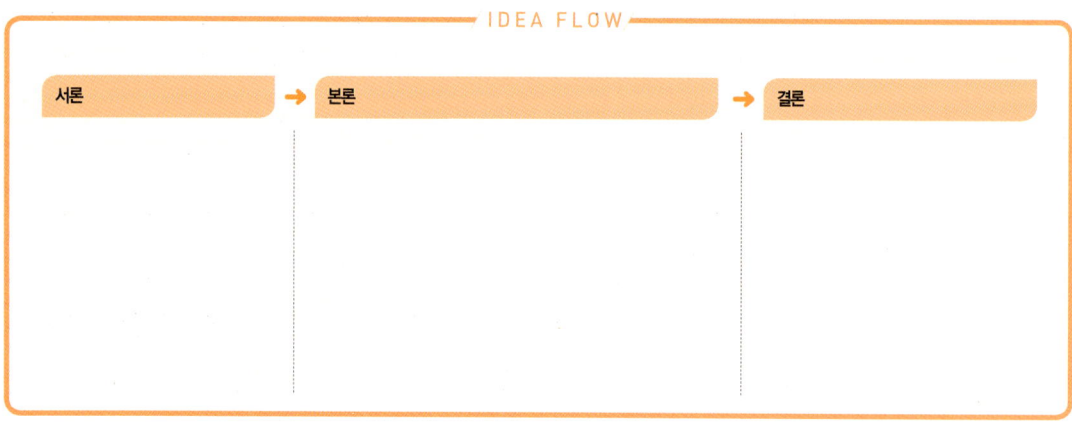

When was the first time you invested in stocks? How much did you invest? Which stocks did you buy? Tell me the whole story from the beginning to the end.

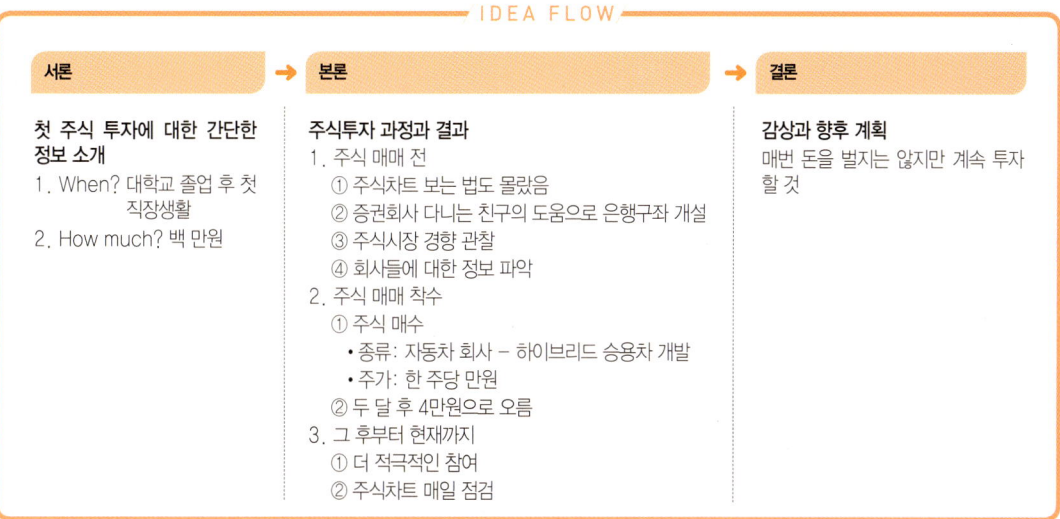

ANSWER

I invested a million won in stocks when I got my first job right after graduating from university. At that time, I didn't know where to buy stocks and how to read flow charts about stocks. With the help of my friend who was working at the securities company, I opened a bank account affiliated with his company. Then, I started to observe the trends in stock market and tried to get news about some companies such as their new products and how the economic situation affected those companies. A month later, I bought some shares of an automobile company. The company was in the middle of developing a new model of hybrid cars, and I predicted that the car would be released soon. Thus, I bought stocks of that company for 10,000 won a share. In two months, the stock price soared to 40,000 won a share, so I earned 4 times of my initial investment. Since then, I've been more actively involved in trading stocks. I check the stock charts that show how the value of companies' stocks has risen and fallen every day. Of course, I don't get a good return from trading stocks all the time, but I will continue investing in stocks to try to make money.

[해석 p.298 참조]

IH 답변 파헤치기

문장 구조 응용하기

의문사 to 부정사

- 본문 At that time, I didn't know where to buy stocks and how to read flow charts about stocks.
  (=where I should buy/how I should read)
- ex Although the stock price dropped to 5,000 won, I couldn't decide whether to sell it or not.
  주가가 5천원 아래로 떨어졌는데도 저는 팔아야 할지 말지 결정을 못했습니다.
- ex It's always difficult for me to decide when to sell my stocks.
  제 주식을 언제 팔아야 할지 결정하는 것은 언제나 어렵습니다.

첫 주식투자에 대한 간단한 정보로 서두 열기

- Last winter, I decided to buy mutual funds since I wasn't confident of trading stocks for myself.
  저는 제 힘으로 주식거래를 할 자신이 없어서 뮤추얼 펀드를 사기로 결정했습니다.
- I bought my first stock when SC Electronics was just over 150,000 won per share.
  저는 SC전자 주식이 한 주에 15만원 좀 넘었을 때 제 첫 주식을 샀습니다.
- I started investing in stocks with 500,000 won that I had when I was a college student.
  저는 대학생일 때 50만원으로 주식에 투자하기 시작했습니다.
- Two years ago, I took the first step into the stock market by buying 1,000 shares of a medical supplier that had a good financial standing.
  저는 재무상태가 좋은 한 의료업체의 주식을 천 주 사는 걸로 주식시장에 발을 들여놓았습니다.

Word in the middle of 한참 ~ 중인

- 본문 The company was in the middle of developing a new model of hybrid car, and I predicted that the car would be released soon.
- ex The computer system was switched off when I was in the middle of buying and selling stocks online.
  제가 한참 인터넷으로 주식 매매를 하고 있을 때 컴퓨터 전원이 꺼져버렸습니다.
- ex When the stockbroker called me, I was in the middle of dinner.
  주식중개인이 전화했을 때 저는 한참 저녁식사 중이었습니다.

Word soar 치솟다, 급등하다

- 본문 In two months, the stock price soared to 40,000 won a share, so I earned 4 times of my initial investment.
- ex I expect profits from our LCD TVs to soar this month.
  우리 LCD TV의 수익이 이번 달에 급등하기를 기대합니다.

Word be/get/become involved in ~에 관계되다, ~에 관여하다, ~에 몰두하다

- 본문 Since then, I've been more actively involved in trading stocks.
- ex I didn't want to get involved in my staff's private lives.
  저는 직원들의 개인적인 일에 관여하고 싶지 않았습니다.
- ex I was a little worried if he would be involved in such an dishonorable act.
  저는 그가 불명예스러운 일에 엮이게 될까 봐 걱정이 되었습니다.

MAKE YOUR ANSWER

질문에 대한 여러분의 답변을 만들어보세요.

When was the first time you invested in stocks? How much did you invest? Which stocks did you buy? Tell me the whole story from the beginning to the end.

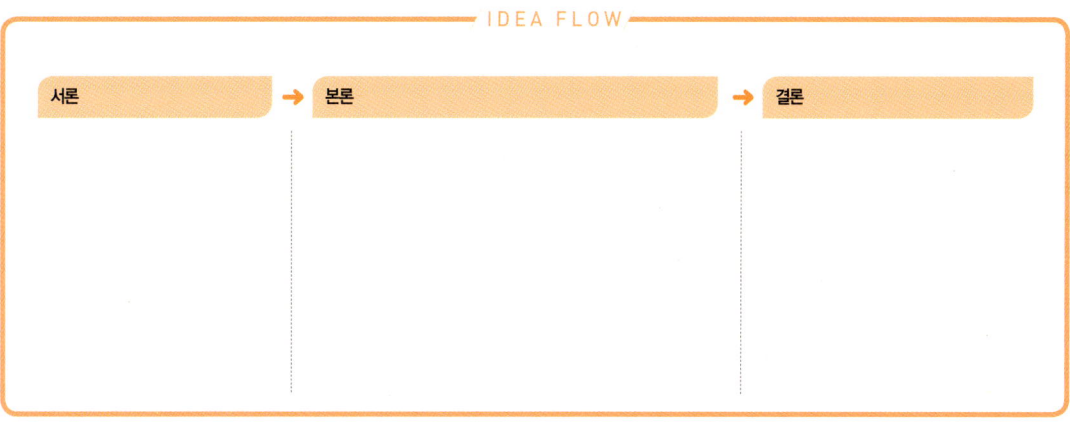

ANSWER

Tell me about your most memorable event concerning the stock market.

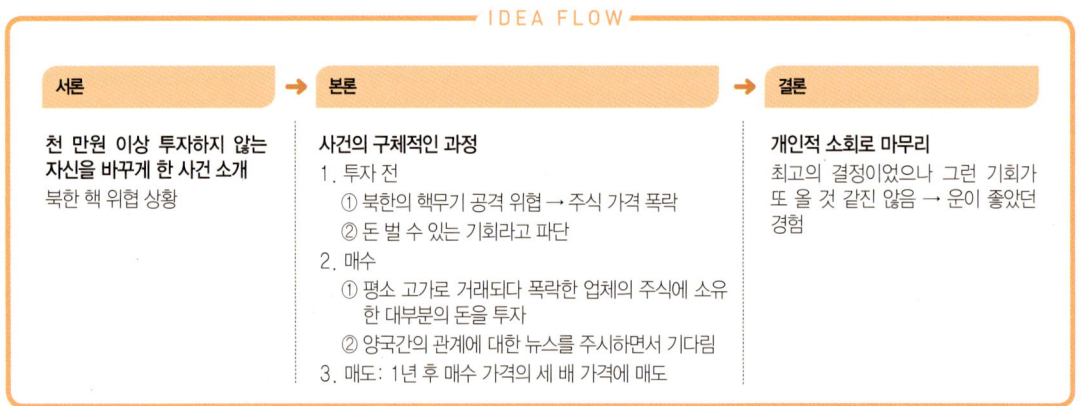

ANSWER

I had never invested more than ten million won in stocks. I thought that the more money I invest, the riskier it becomes; however, there was an incident that made me change my mind last year. You may remember that North Korea threatened to attack South Korea with nuclear weapons. When this happened, the stock market was greatly affected, and the prices of many stocks plummeted deeply. This, I felt instinctively, was a chance to make lots of money. I withdrew most of the money that I had and bought stocks that had greatly declined in value, but which had frequently traded at high prices when the market was better. Then, I waited until the prices went up while observing the news regarding the relationship between North and South Korea. I knew that being patient was as important as making a bold decision. After one year, I sold all of my stocks for three times the price I had bought it at, so I made a lot of money. I had the great timing when I invested, and that was the best decision I have ever made. I don't think this kind of opportunity will ever come again. I was so lucky to have that opportunity.

[해석 p.298 참조]

IH 답변 파헤치기

문장 구조 응용하기

the 비교급, the 비교급 ~하면 할수록 더욱 ~하다

- 본문 I thought that the more money I invest, the riskier it becomes.
- ex Some executives think that the longer employees stay at the office, the harder they work.
  어떤 임원들은 직원들이 사무실에 더 오래 있을수록 일을 더 열심히 한다고 생각합니다.
- ex The more money I lost in the stock market, the more money I invested in stocks.
  주식시장에서 돈을 잃으면 잃을수록 저는 더 많은 돈을 투자했습니다.

주식시장과 관련된 기억에 남는 경험

- The financial crisis caused a slump in the stock market in my country. Most companies' stocks and bonds became almost wholly useless. Then my father advised me to buy as much stock as I could, but I was skeptical about his opinion and didn't buy any stock. A few months later, when the stock prices soared, I really regretted ignoring my father's advice.
  금융 위기는 우리나라의 주식시장의 급락을 야기했습니다. 대부분의 회사주식과 채권은 거의 모두 휴지조각이 되었습니다. 그런데 저희 아버지께서는 살 수 있는 만큼 주식을 많이 사놓으라고 하셨습니다. 하지만 저는 아버지 의견에 회의적이었고, 그래서 사지 않았습니다. 불과 몇 달 후 주식값이 폭등했을 때 저는 아버지의 조언을 무시한 것을 너무나 후회했습니다.

Word threaten to 부정사 ~하겠다고 위협하다, 협박하다

- 본문 You may remember that North Korea threatened to attack South Korea with nuclear weapons.
- ex The criminals threatened to steal the key financial information of our individual customers.
  그 범죄자들은 우리 개인고객들의 주요 금융 정보를 빼가겠다고 위협했습니다.

Word plummet 곤두박질치다, 급락하다

- 본문 When this happened, the stock market was greatly affected, and the prices of many stocks plummeted deeply.
- ex During the foreign exchange crisis in 1997, Korean won plummeted against the US dollars.
  1997년의 외환위기 때 원화 가치가 달러 대비 폭락했습니다.
- ex Seoul's average temperature plummeted 10 degrees this morning.
  오늘 아침 서울의 평균 기온이 10도나 뚝 떨어졌습니다.

Word instinctively 본능적으로

- 본문 This, I felt instinctively, was a chance to make lots of money.
- ex I knew instinctively he was hiding something.
  저는 본능적으로 그 사람이 뭔가 숨기고 있음을 알았습니다.

Word regarding ~에 관하여 (= about = concerning = with respect to = in/with reference to)

- 본문 Then, I waited until the prices went up while observing the news regarding the relationship between North and South Korea.
- ex My wife didn't mention anything concerning the stock I had bought.
  제 아내는 제가 산 주식에 대해서 아무 말도 하지 않았습니다.
- ex He gave me good pieces of advice in reference to the test preparation.
  그는 시험 준비에 관해서 좋은 충고들을 해주었습니다.

IH 답변 파헤치기

Idiom make a (bold) decision (과감한) 결정을 하다

- 본문 I knew that being patient was as important as making a bold decision.
- 본문 I had the great timing when I invested, and that was the best decision I have ever made.
- ex I tend to make a sound investment decision when trading stocks.
  저는 주식거래를 할 때 안전한 투자 결정을 하는 편입니다.

질문에 대한 여러분의 답변을 만들어보세요.

Tell me about your most memorable event concerning the stock market.

ANSWER

Oral Proficiency Interview-computer

Lesson 12 사진 촬영하기

INTRO 사진 촬영 또한 OPIc 서베이 취미나 관심사(5번)항목에 새롭게 추가된 주제입니다. 사진 찍는 대상, 사진 찍기에 대한 관심 변천사, 그리고 사진을 찍으면서 겪었던 개인적 경험 등은 기존의 취미나 관심사 주제들과 비슷하게 준비하면 됩니다. 다만 현재 소유하고 있는 사진기 묘사와 시대에 따른 사진기 변천사와 같은 테크놀로지 영역의 문제들처럼 답변하기 다소 까다로울 수 있는 문제들도 최근 연속 출제되고 있으니 철저한 준비가 필요합니다.

IH 답변 전략

① 사진기 묘사하기
- 사진기 묘사를 위해서는 사진기 관련 어휘들을 알아두어야 합니다. 아주 전문적인 지식까지는 아니더라도 기본적으로 사진기 작동과 사진 촬영을 위한 어휘와 표현들은 반드시 숙지합시다.
- 자신이 소유하고 있는 사진기의 기능 몇 가지는 꼭 기억해 놓았다가 답변에 활용합니다.

② 사진 촬영의 대상 묘사 및 사진기 변천사 설명
- 인물, 동물, 또는 자연, 자연 중에서도 산이나 바다 등 자신이 사진 찍기 좋아하는 대상을 선정해 좋아하는 이유와 그 대상을 촬영하는 장소 등을 포함한 구체적인 답변을 준비합니다.
- 아날로그(필름)카메라에서 디지털 카메라, 전화 카메라 등 카메라의 변천 과정은 그야말로 극적이고 혁명적이라 할 수 있습니다. 그런 만큼 카메라의 변천사를 묻는 문제가 출제될 가능성이 매우 높으니 조리 있는 답변을 준비해두도록 합니다.

③ 사진기나 사진 촬영에 얽힌 개인적 경험 소개하기
- 사진기가 고장 났거나 사진기를 분실한 경험 등 사진기와 관련된 답변을 준비해봅니다.
- 사진을 찍으면서 일어났던 예상치 못했던 사건이나 상황들을 정리해놓고 그를 토대로 이야기를 만들어봅니다.

'사진 촬영하기'에서는 어떠한 질문들이 출제될까요? 다음의 예상 질문에 대해 여러분은 어떻게 답변할지 한번 생각해 보세요.

1. You indicated in the survey that you photograph. What do you usually take pictures of? Do you like to take pictures of people or nature? Describe the subject you take pictures of.

2. You indicated in the survey that you photograph. Which camera do you currently have? Where did you get it? What functions does it have? Are you satisfied with your camera? Tell me everything about your camera.

3. Who did you learn how to take pictures from? Did you learn it by yourself? Tell me the whole process of learning to take pictures.

4. How did you first become interested in taking pictures? How have you developed the interest over the years?

5. Cameras have changed greatly over the years. Do you remember when you first started taking pictures? How were they different from present-day cameras? How has the change affected the way you take pictures?

6. I'll give you a situation and ask you to act it out. You want to borrow a digital camera from your friend for a day trip. Call your friend and ask him or her to lend it to you.

7. I'm sorry, but there is a problem I need you to resolve. The digital camera you borrowed from your friend is broken due to your carelessness. Call your friend and explain the situation including three alternatives to solve it.

8. Please tell me your experience that was unexpected or surprising related to taking a photo.

9. What are some benefits of photography in comparison with other hobbies?

Q1 You indicated in the survey that you photograph. Which camera do you currently have? Where did you get it? What functions does it have? Are you satisfied with your camera? Tell me everything about your camera.

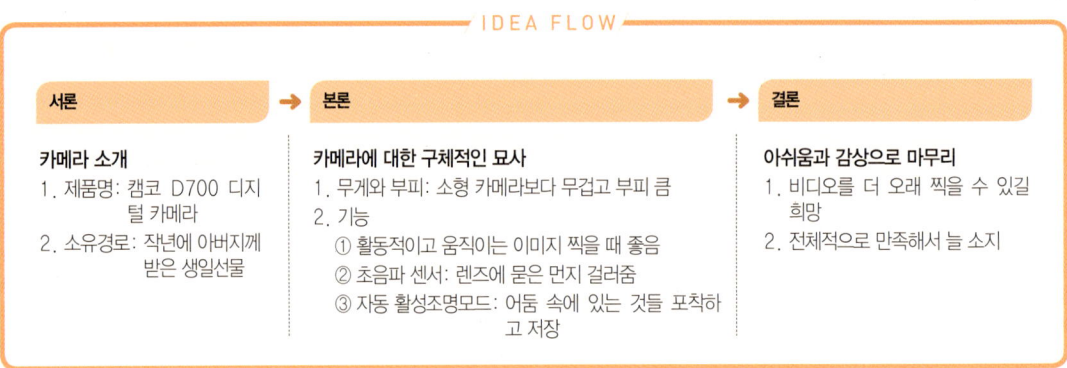

ANSWER

I have a digital camera D700 made by Camco that my father gave me for my birthday last year. It is equipped with a shutter, a three-inch color monitor, auto-focus buttons, and various functional modes. Although it is a bit heavier and bulkier than compact digital cameras, I like my camera. It shows its charm when it shoots active and moving images. It has a special function that takes panorama shots up to 8 frames per second. With this function, I can capture every motion even while the object is moving. Also, an ultrasonic sensor cleans dust particles on the lenses of the camera, which helps me take clean, natural photos. The most amazing feature of this camera is that it automatically adjusts the lighting. Shadows and darkness sometimes cause problems when taking pictures since the subjects may be in shadows. In cases like this, the auto mode of active lighting is able to restore and capture the details in shadows. If it could take longer videos, the camera would have been even better, but overall, I'm satisfied with my camera and always take it out with me.

[해석 p.298 참조]

IH 답변 파헤치기

자신의 카메라를 소개하는 적절한 서두 열기

- **본문** I have a digital camera D700 made by Camco that my father gave me for my birthday last year.
- **ex** The camera that I currently have is a DSLR made by ACE. I bought it with the money that I had earned for stock trading.
  제가 지금 가지고 있는 카메라는 에이스에서 만든 DSLR 카메라입니다. 주식거래 해서 번 돈으로 이 카메라를 샀습니다.
- **ex** I have an Olie digital camera that I purchased three months ago. I bought it at the duty free shop when I went on a business trip, but I don't remember its exact model name.
  저는 석 달 전에 구입한 올리 디지털 카메라를 가지고 있습니다. 저는 이 카메라를 출장 갔을 때 면세점에서 샀는데 정확한 모델명은 기억이 나질 않습니다.

카메라 묘사 관련 아이디어

- My camera is thin and light, but has a pretty big LCD screen.
  제 카메라는 얇고 가벼운데도 꽤 큰 LCD 화면을 가지고 있습니다.
- My camera's zoom extends farther than other common digital cameras, which enables me to zoom in very close on distant objects.
  제 카메라 줌은 다른 디지털 카메라보다 더 멀리까지 나갈 수 있어서 멀리 있는 대상을 매우 가깝게 끌어당겨 찍을 수 있습니다.
- I set my camera to auto-focus modes so that I don't have to check for focus before taking a picture.
  저는 제 카메라를 자동 초점 모드로 맞춰놓아서 사진 찍기 전에 초점을 확인할 필요가 없습니다.

자신의 카메라에 대한 감상으로 마무리하기

- Since my camera is quite old and doesn't have advanced functions, I'll buy a new one soon.
  제 카메라는 좀 오래됐고 고급 기능도 없기 때문에 곧 새로운 것을 하나 장만할 것입니다.
- My camera is fine enough for me to take pictures of people and scenery.
  제 카메라는 사람과 풍경을 찍기에 충분히 괜찮습니다.

Word 사진기와 관련된 어휘들

- **film camera/film-based camera** 필름 카메라 (= analogue camera/traditional camera)
- **digital camera** 디지털 카메라
- **DSLR(digital single lens reflex) camera** 디지털 일반 반사식 카메라
- **digital image** 디지털 화상, 디지털 사진
- **lens** 렌즈
- **pixel** 화소
- **wide-angle** (렌즈가)광각인, 광각 렌즈를 사용하는
- **focal length** 초점 거리
- **zoom** 초점 거리를 조절할 수 있는 렌즈
- **viewfinder** 뷰파인더(피사체를 찍을 때 보는 부분)
- **tripod** 삼각대
- **flash** 플래시

Word 사진 촬영과 관련된 표현들

- **photography** 사진술, 사진 찍기
- **click/press the shutter** (카메라)셔터를 누르다
- **take a shot/photo/picture** 사진을 찍다
- **capture** 담아내다, 포착하다
- **snapshot/snapshoot** 순간촬영/순간촬영을 하다
- **zoom in/out** 피사체를 확대/축소하다
- **darkroom** 암실
- **develop** 현상하다
- **black and white** 흑백사진
- **enlarge a photo** 사진을 확대하다

질문에 대한 여러분의 답변을 만들어보세요.

You indicated in the survey that you photograph. Which camera do you currently have? Where did you get it? What functions does it have? Are you satisfied with your camera? Tell me everything about your camera.

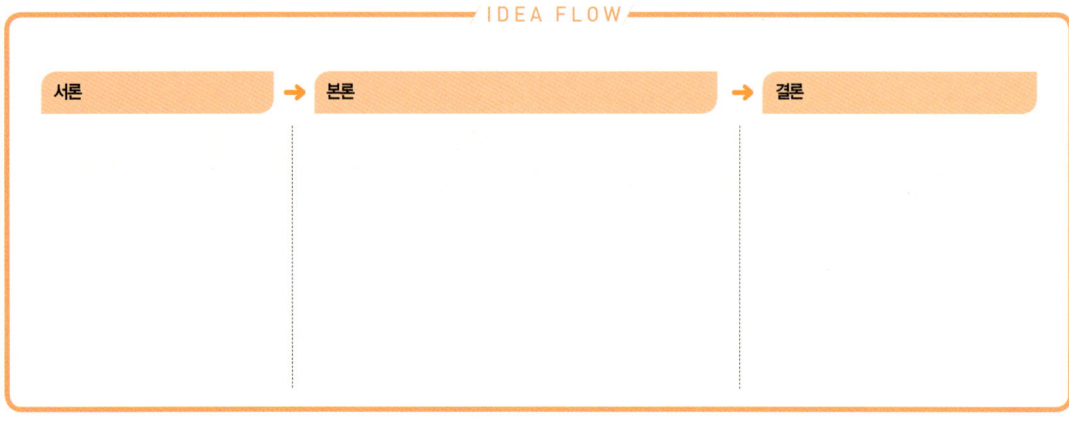

ANSWER

Cameras have changed greatly over the years. Do you remember when you first started taking pictures? How were they different from present-day cameras? How has the change affected the way you take pictures?

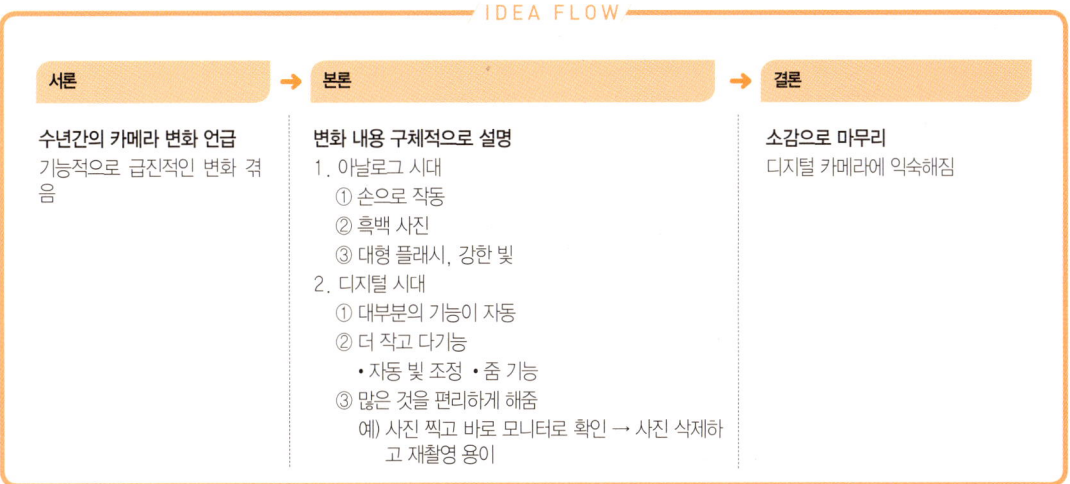

ANSWER

In terms of their functions, cameras have gone through radical changes over the years. In the analogue age, most cameras were operated manually, and the images they shot were black and white. However, nowadays, so many digital cameras are available, and most of their functions are automatic. I was seventeen years old when I used a film camera to take pictures. It had been handed down to me from my grandfather, and whenever I took a picture, I had to wind the film manually and adjust the focus of the lens depending on the picture I was taking. The flash was very big, and the light coming from it was quite strong. Present-day cameras are more compact and multifunctional. They adjust the light automatically, and the zoom function helps me not touch the lens every time I take a picture. Digital cameras make many things convenient. For instance, images on digital cameras can be checked right after taking a picture by looking at the monitor attached to the camera, so it is very easy to delete or retake photos when the pictures don't look nice. Since I got used to digital cameras, I don't think I can operate the analogue cameras anymore.

[해석 p.299 참조]

IH 답변 파헤치기

카메라(사진) 변천사에 대해 적절한 서두 열기

본문 In terms of their functions, cameras have gone through radical changes over the years.

ex The advent of digital cameras brought a huge change in analogue cameras and photography.
디지털 카메라의 출현은 아날로그 카메라와 아날로그 사진술에 커다란 변화를 가져왔습니다.

ex Digital photography has greatly changed the way we take pictures.
디지털 사진술은 우리의 사진 찍는 방법을 크게 변화시켰습니다.

카메라 및 사진 찍기의 변화와 관련한 아이디어

- With the development of digital photography, we need neither film to take pictures nor darkrooms to develop film.
디지털 사진술의 발전으로 우리는 더 이상 사진 찍기 위한 필름도, 필름을 현상할 암실도 필요하지 않습니다.

- Before I got my smartphone, I always had a digital camera with me just in case. But nowadays, I hardly use it and don't even take it when I go on a trip. It's more convenient to take pictures with my smartphone.
스마트폰을 사기 전에는 저는 만일을 대비해서 늘 디지털 카메라를 가지고 다녔습니다. 하지만 요즘은 잘 사용하지도 않고 심지어 여행을 갈 때도 가져가지 않습니다. 스마트폰으로 사진을 찍는 게 훨씬 편리하거든요.

- Smartphone cameras allow us to post the photos stored in it directly on blogs even right after we took the photos.
스마트폰 카메라 덕분에 우리는 그 안에 저장된 사진들을, 심지어 찍고 난 즉시 블로그에 올릴 수 있게 되었습니다.

- I think that creating the camera phone is more revolutionary idea than making the digital camera. I had never imagined that a phone could be used to take pictures.
저는 디지털 카메라를 만든 것보다 카메라폰을 만들었다는 것이 더 혁신적인 아이디어라고 생각합니다. 전화기가 사진을 찍는 용도로 쓰일 수 있다는 걸 전 상상도 한 적이 없었거든요.

- It's easier and more convenient to sort and label the pictures on my computer than to put them in an album one by one.
사진 한 장, 한 장씩 앨범에 끼우는 것보다 컴퓨터에서 분류하고 이름 붙이는 것이 더 쉽고 편리합니다.

변화에 대한 개인적 감상으로 마무리

- I sometimes miss those days I used a film-based camera. For some reasons, I feel it was more classical and artistic.
저는 가끔 필름 카메라를 사용했던 때가 그리울 때가 있습니다. 왠지 더 고전적이고 예술적으로 느껴지거든요.

- Every single shot costs money to develop with a film camera, so I paid more attention to taking a good picture. But now, I can feel free to take pictures with a digital camera without worrying about the cost. It causes me to take too many pictures though.
필름 카메라는 한 방, 한 방에 현상비가 들기 때문에 좋은 사진을 찍기 위해 심혈을 더 기울였습니다. 하지만 이제 디지털 카메라로는 현상비 걱정 없이 마음대로 사진을 찍을 수 있습니다. 하지만 또 너무 많은 사진을 찍게 되기도 하죠.

Idiom hand down to ~(으)로 전하다, 남기다

- This china was handed down to me from my father. I will also hand this down to my son as a family treasure.
이 도자기는 우리 아버지께서 남겨주신 것입니다. 저도 이 도자기를 제 아들에게 가보로 남기고 싶습니다.

질문에 대한 여러분의 답변을 만들어보세요.

Cameras have changed greatly over the years. Do you remember when you first started taking pictures? How were they different from present-day cameras? How has the change affected the way you take pictures?

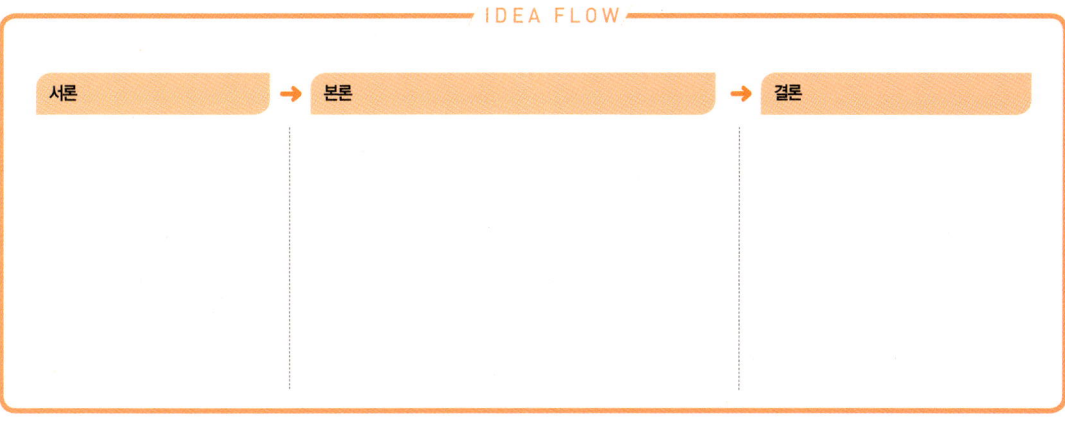

ANSWER

Please tell me your experience that was unexpected or surprising related to taking a photo.

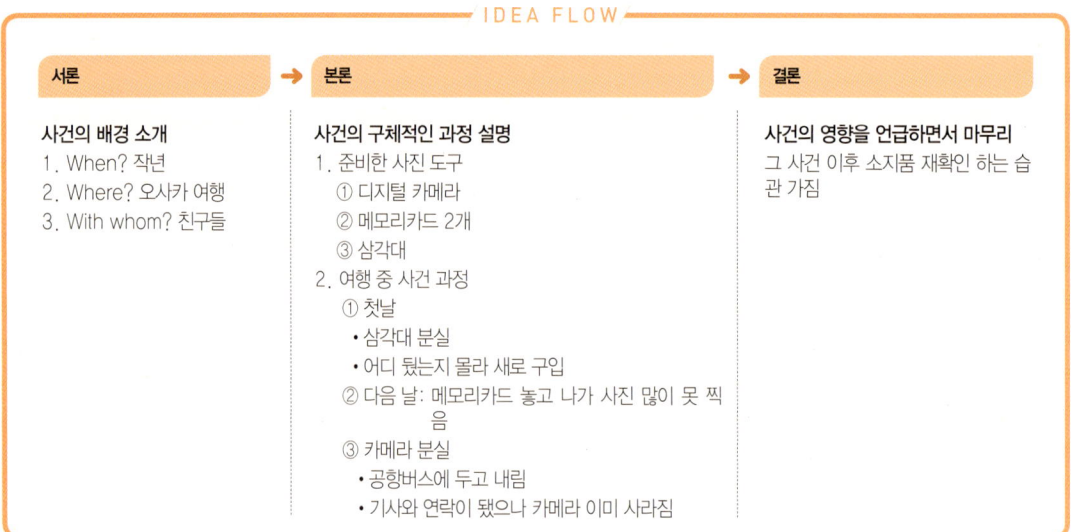

ANSWER

I traveled to Osaka, Japan, with my friends last year. I brought my digital camera with two memory cards and a tripod to take as many photos with my friends as possible. On the first day of the trip, however, I lost my tripod. I couldn't remember where I had put it, so I had to buy another one. Then, the next day, I forgot to bring my memory card from my hotel room, so I was not able to take many pictures. The worst part of the trip was the last day. I packed all of my stuff at the hotel and checked in at the airport. While waiting to board the plane, I realized that I didn't have my camera bag. On my way to the airport, I must have left it on the airport shuttle bus. I contacted the bus driver with the help of the airport staff, but my camera was missing. I was very frustrated but had no choice but to come back home without it. Although my friends sent me some photos of me, I didn't have any pictures of Osaka that I had taken. Since then, I have made a habit of double-checking my belongings.

[해석 p.299 참조]

IH 답변 파헤치기

문장 구조 응용하기

must have + p.p. (과거에) ~했었음이 분명하다

- 본문 On my way to the airport, I must have left it on the airport shuttle bus.
- ex Jerry must have dropped my camera. Its lens didn't have any problem before he borrowed it from me.
  제리가 제 카메라를 떨어뜨린 것이 분명합니다. 그가 빌려가기 전에는 렌즈에 아무런 문제가 없었단 말입니다.
  - cf) Jerry cannot have dropped my camera.
    제리가 제 카메라를 떨어뜨렸을 리 없습니다.

must + 동사원형 (현재) ~함이 분명하다

- ex Her camera can create 3D-images and has many other state-of-the-art functions. It must be very expensive.
  그녀의 사진기는 3D 화상도 만들어낼 수 있고 다른 많은 최첨단 기능들이 있습니다. 비싼 카메라임이 분명합니다.
  - cf) It cannot be expensive. 비싼 카메라일 리 없습니다.

사진에 얽힌 경험 소개하기

- When I copied photos from my camera to my computer, I realized I hadn't used the flash to take pictures in the dark area. I could barely recognize my child's face in the picture.
  카메라에 있는 사진들을 컴퓨터에 옮길 때서야 제가 어두운 데서 플래시를 사용하지 않은 채 사진을 찍었다는 걸 깨달았습니다. 사진 속의 제 아이는 얼굴만 겨우 알아볼 정도였습니다.
- While I took good pictures of her, most pictures that she took of me were blurry from shaking the camera. I was getting angry that she didn't press the shutter steadily.
  저는 그녀의 사진을 잘 찍어준 반면 그녀가 저를 찍은 사진들은 카메라가 흔들려서 거의 다 흐려 보였습니다. 저는 주의 깊게 카메라 셔터를 누르지 않는 그녀에게 약이 올랐습니다.
- I bought a new DSLR camera at a high price, and I took it when I went swimming with my son. When I tried to take a shot of him in the water, however, I dropped it in the swimming pool. I picked it up very quickly, but the screen was just black when I turned it on.
  저는 새 DSLR 카메라를 비싼 가격에 사서 아들과 함께 수영장에 갈 때 가져갔습니다. 그러나 아들이 물 속에 있는 사진을 찍으려다 그만 그걸 수영장 물 속에 빠뜨리고 말았습니다. 재빨리 건져냈지만 전원을 켜보니 화면은 그냥 까맣게만 나왔습니다.

Word double-check 재확인하다 (= check again, check twice)

- 본문 Since then, I have made a habit of double-checking my belongings.
- ex I double checked if the faucet was turned off before leaving home.
  저는 집을 나설 때 수도꼭지가 잠겼는지 재확인했습니다.
- ex You need to double check that you pack your camera battery charger.
  카메라 충전기 챙긴 것을 다시 확인해야 합니다.

Word belongings 소지품

- ex We were asked to leave our personal belongings behind when entering the interview room.
  우리는 면접실에 들어갈 때 개인 소지품은 놔두고 가라는 요청을 받았습니다.
- ex I had few belongings in my bag, so the pickpocket must have been disappointed when checking the inside. 제 가방에 소지품이 거의 없었기 때문에 그 소매치기는 안을 확인하고 틀림없이 실망했을 것입니다.
  ※ 이와 같이 belongings가 소지품, 소유물 등의 의미로 사용될 때는 항상 복수형으로 써주셔야 합니다.

질문에 대한 여러분의 답변을 만들어보세요.

Please tell me your experience that was unexpected or surprising related to taking a photo.

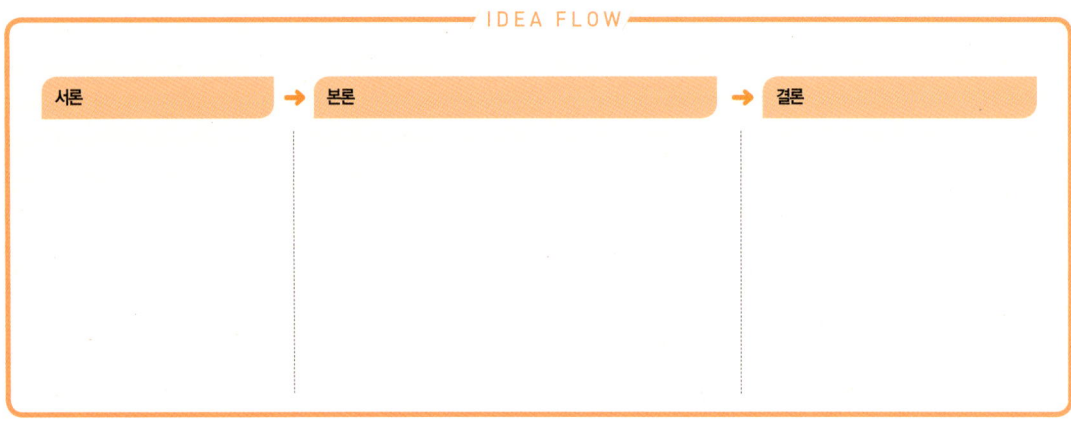

Memo

Lesson 13

Oral Proficiency Interview-computer

돌발 재활용

INTRO

재활용은 최근 OPIc 문제에서 꾸준히 나오고 있는 주제들 중 하나입니다. 재활용은 얼핏 보면 좀 어렵게 느껴질 수도 있는 주제지만 나올 수 있는 유형이 제한적인 편이고 관련된 어휘와 표현을 익혀놓으면 생각보다 그렇게 까다롭지 않게 답변할 수 있습니다. 실제 재활용을 하는 과정에서 일어날 수 있는 사건이나 상황들이 Role-play 문제로 나오기도 하니까 대화하듯이 가볍고 편안한 마음으로 준비해보세요.

IH 답변 전략

① 현재 우리나라에서 시행되고 있는 일반적인 재활용 제도에 대해 알아두기

- 지역마다 다른 재활용 제도를 세세하게 말할 필요는 없지만 공통적인 재활용 정책에 대해서는 간단하게라도 언급할 수 있어야 합니다.
- 재활용이나 쓰레기 분리수거에 관련된 어휘와 표현들을 알아두어 실제 시험에서 수월하게 활용하도록 합시다.
- 일반적인 사항에 대해 답변을 할 때는 결론 부분에 개인적인 소감이나 평가를 간단하게 덧붙여 마무리해주는 것이 좋습니다.

② 재활용의 변천사에 관한 답변 준비하기

- 과거 재활용의 시행과 현재 재활용 제도의 차이나 변천 과정을 설명할 수 있어야 합니다.
- 과거 재활용에 대한 사람들의 인식이 현재에 이르러 어떻게 변했는지를 언급합니다.
- 과거 재활용에 대해 이야기할 때는 자신이 직접 목격했거나 경험했던 일을 구체적인 예로 사용해 주면 더 논리적인 답변이 됩니다.

③ Role-play와 개인적 경험과 소감에 대한 답변 준비하기

- 종이나 페트병 등을 집에서 어떻게 재활용하고 있는지, 재활용하고 있다면 그 과정에 대해 구체적으로 서술해줍니다.
- 실제 재활용 쓰레기 처리 과정에서 발생할 수 있는 상황들을 설정해놓고 질문과 답변을 준비해둠으로써 Role-play 문제에 대비합니다.

'재활용'에서는 어떠한 질문들이 출제될까요? 다음의 예상 질문에 대해 여러분은 어떻게 답변할지 한번 생각해 보세요.

1. Tell me about a recycling system in your country. Is recycling mandatory or optional? What do you think of the current recycling system?

2. How is waste recycling being managed in your country? Do you have specific recycling policies? Explain how people recycle in your country in as much detail as you can.

3. I'd like to know how you recycle at home. Describe the whole process of recycling at your home.

4. Home recycling may require some time and effort. Tell me about your own ways to save time and effort while recycling at home.

5. What effort do you put into reducing the amount of recyclables?

6. How was garbage recycled at home when you were young? Did you have a home recycling area in your neighborhood? Please tell me about your experiences regarding recycling when you were young.

7. How has residents' awareness of recycling changed in your community since they first recycled their garbage?

8. I'll give you a situation and ask you to act it out. You are about to separate your recyclables, but the recycling bins are full. Call a janitor's office and explain the situation.

9. Some trash is too big to put in a recycling bin or place at the recycling area. If so, how do you take care of the trash?

How is waste recycling being managed in your country? Do you have specific recycling policies? Explain how people recycle in your country in as much detail as you can.

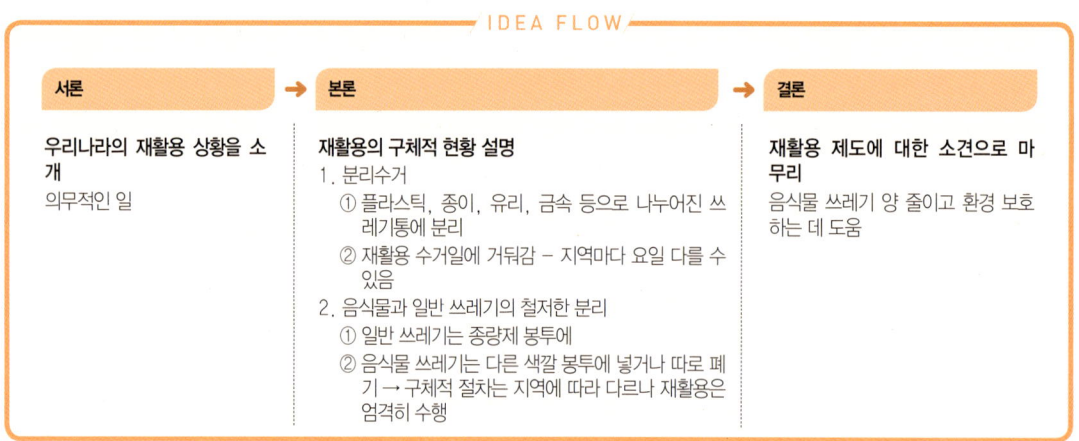

ANSWER

Recycling is mandatory in my country. Recyclable waste must be put in separate trash bins, labeled with Plastic, Paper, Glass, Metal, etc. It is common to see Korean people dispose of their garbage separately on designated areas outside their apartments or houses. The separate garbage is collected on the recycling pick-up day, which can be slightly different depending on the districts. The recyclable garbage in my neighborhood, for example, is collected every Tuesday and Thursday. We also separate general waste from food waste. General wastes should be placed in special garbage bags called jongnyangie bags. We can purchase at our local supermarkets. Garbage collectors don't pick up the garbage that is not placed in the jongnyangie bag. Also, food wastes must be placed in different colored bags or separately disposed outside the residential buildings. The specific procedures such as the prices and colors of bags vary from one district to another, but all the districts are fairly strict with their recycling policies. The recycling systems in my country might seem complicated or bothering, but I think they have helped preserve our environment and reduce the amount of food wastes.

[해석 p.299 참조]

IH 답변 파헤치기

Word mandatory 의무적인 ≠ optional 선택적인

- 본문 Recycling is mandatory in my country.
- ex It is mandatory to separate recyclables from common garbage and food waste in Korea.
  한국에서는 의무적으로 재활용 쓰레기를 일반 쓰레기와 음식물 쓰레기와 분리시켜야 합니다.
- ex Attendance and participation in the upcoming workshop is mandatory.
  다가오는 워크숍의 출석과 참여는 의무입니다.
- ex Working overtime is optional. 야근은 선택사항입니다.

Word designated 지정된, 정해진

- 본문 It is common to see Korean people dispose of their garbage separately on designated areas outside their apartments or houses.
- ex We must put food waste in the designated trash bags. 우리는 지정된 쓰레기 봉투에 음식물 쓰레기를 버려야 합니다.

Word vary from A to B A에서 B까지 다양하다, ~마다 다르다

- 본문 The specific procedures such as the prices and colors of bags vary from one district to another, but all the districts are fairly strict with their recycling policies.
- ex Dress codes considerably vary from company to company.
  복장 규정은 회사마다 상당히 다릅니다. (= Different companies have different dress codes.)

재활용 관련 아이디어들

- We can visit our local recycling center and check what materials they accept for recycling.
  우리는 지역 재활용 센터를 방문해서 어떤 재료들을 재활용품으로 받아주는지 알아볼 수 있습니다.
- People do not really wash or rinse before taking out their PET bottles or plastic containers.
  사람들은 페트병이나 플라스틱 용기들을 버리기 전에 잘 씻거나 헹궈주지를 않습니다.
- Many facilities like government offices, banks, and hospitals set up separate trash bins so that people can separate their garbage properly. In a restaurant or coffee shop, we are also asked to throw out leftover food separately from other trash.
  관공서, 은행, 병원과 같은 많은 시설들은 분리수거 쓰레기통을 준비해놓아서 사람들이 쓰레기를 적절하게 분리수거할 수 있습니다. 식당이나 커피숍에서도 남은 음식물을 버릴 때 분리수거를 해야 합니다.
- Large items such as furniture or electronic goods cannot be put in trash bins or in jongnyangie bags. In that case, we ask some agencies / junk removal services that collect large items to take them away and pay a fee for disposing of them. The fees vary from 1,000 won to 20,000 won. Some local governments offer their residents this service for free.
  가구나 전자 제품과 같은 대형 물품들은 쓰레기통이나 종량제 봉투에 버리면 안됩니다. 그럴 때는 대형 물품들을 수거해가는 업체에게 가져가달라고 부탁하고 폐기해주는 수수료를 지불하면 됩니다. 수수료는 천원에서 2만원까지 다양합니다. 어떤 지방자치단체에서는 주민들을 위해 무료로도 이런 서비스를 제공하고 있습니다.

재활용에 대한 소감으로 마무리 하기

- I sometimes feel bothered to recycle, but I think it's the right thing.
  가끔 재활용이 짜증나기도 하지만 옳은 일이라 생각합니다.
- I think that some people who don't follow the recycling policy have to pay larger fines.
  저는 재활용 정책을 따르지 않는 사람들이 더 많은 벌금을 내야 한다고 생각합니다.
- I'm confused of the current recycling system. I hope we'll have simpler and easier procedures of disposing of garbage. 저는 현재 재활용 제도가 좀 헷갈립니다. 더 단순하고 쉬운 절차로 쓰레기를 버리면 좋겠습니다.

질문에 대한 여러분의 답변을 만들어보세요.

How is waste recycling being managed in your country? Do you have specific recycling policies? Explain how people recycle in your country in as much detail as you can.

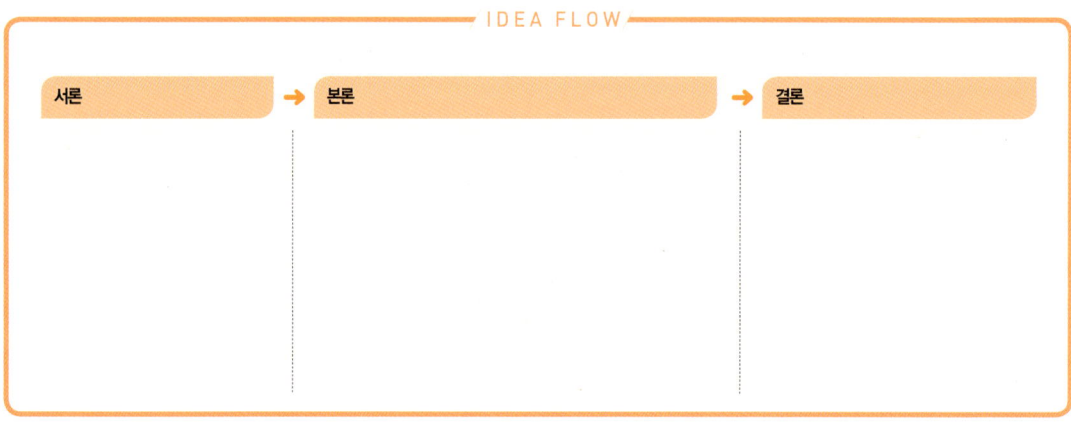

ANSWER

Home recycling may require some time and effort. Tell me about your own ways to save time and effort while recycling at home.

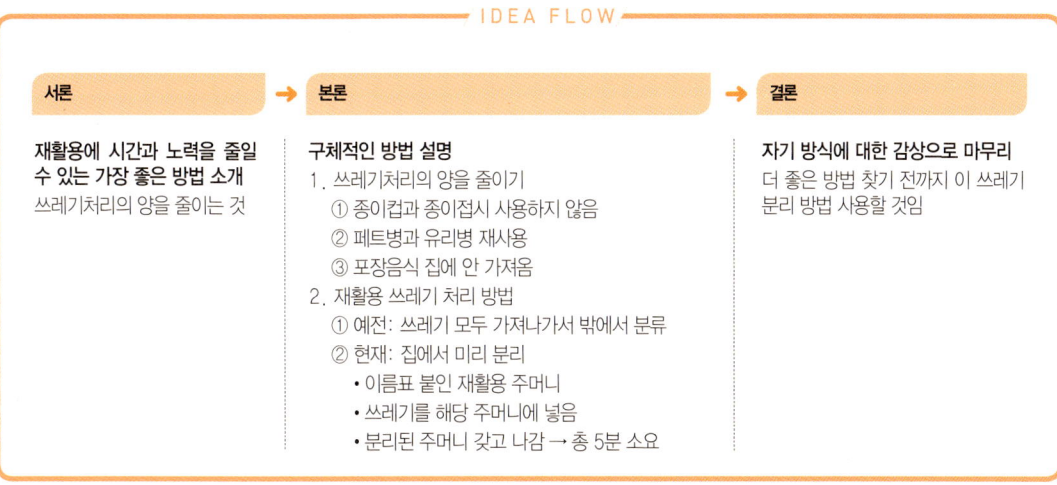

ANSWER

I try to reduce the amount of waste I dispose of, which can save me time and effort when I am separating recyclable items from non-recyclable garbage. I never use paper cups or plates and try to reuse PET and glass bottles. I rinse out the bottles and use them to store some food or seasonings. I hardly bring takeout food home either, which definitely causes plastic and Styrofoam waste. I also have my own way to spend less time and effort separating my recyclables. I used to take all of my trash outside and started to sort it there. It was pretty annoying and time consuming to separate the recyclables from the trash in front of the recycling bins. It was also freezing outside in winter. So, I came up with the idea to separate them at home. I made several recycling bags labeled Plastic, Paper, Metal, etc. Then, I put them on the terrace so that I could place the items into each suitable bag. It took me only five minutes to take the separate recycling bags outside and to empty them. I'll use this way to separate my recyclables until I find a better time-saving idea.

[해석 p.300 참조]

IH 답변 파헤치기

문장 구조 응용하기

S+V so that S + can/could ~하도록 ~하다, ~할 수 있게 ~하다

- 본문 Then, I put them on the terrace *so that* I *could* place the items into each suitable bag.
- ex The owner of the shop has placed the trash bins in a plain view *so that* visitors *can* find them easily when disposing of their trash.
  가게 주인은 방문객들이 쓰레기를 버릴 때 쉽게 발견할 수 있도록 쓰레기통을 잘 보이는 곳에 놓아두었습니다.
- ex I always put trash out for recycling with my 5-year-old son *so that* he *can* build a recycling habit.
  저는 다섯 살짜리 아들이 분리수거 습관을 기를 수 있도록 항상 아들과 함께 쓰레기를 버리러 나갑니다.
  cf) My son is *so* young *that* he *can't* take out the trash. (so 원인 that 결과)
  우리 아들은 너무나 어려서 쓰레기를 버리지 못합니다.

used to 부정사 (과거에)~하곤 했다

- 본문 I *used to* take all of my trash outside and started to sort it there.
- ex It's embarrassing to say, I *used to* throw out the garbage without a permit.
  말하기 부끄럽지만 저는 쓰레기를 무단 투척하곤 했습니다.
  cf) be used to ~ing ~하는 것에 익숙하다
- ex I *am* now *used to* separat*ing* my recyclables.
  저는 이제 재활용 쓰레기를 분리수거하는 데 익숙합니다.

Word come up with (해결될 만한 것을)생각해내다, 고안해내다, 찾아내다

- 본문 So, I *came up with* the idea to separate them at home.
- ex After long argument with my wife, I finally *came up with* our own rules for sharing our household chores.
  아내와의 오랜 논쟁 후에 저는 드디어 가사일을 분담하는 우리만의 규칙을 생각해냈습니다.

집에서 할 수 있는 재활용 관련 아이디어들

- I use newspapers for removing stains from the mirror in my bathroom, cleaning shoes, and wrapping fragile items like china and glasses. I also use them to absorb cooking oil or grease on my cooking counter and kitchen table.
  저는 신문으로 욕실에 있는 거울의 얼룩을 없애고, 구두도 닦고, 도자기나 유리처럼 깨지기 쉬운 물건들을 싸기도 합니다. 또 조리대와 부엌 식탁 위의 식용유나 기름을 흡수하는데 사용합니다.
- My family hardly sends out for food packed with plastic and Styrofoam. But if the restaurant takes their food containers back, we have their food delivered.
  우리 가족은 비닐이나 스티로폼으로 포장된 음식은 배달시키지 않습니다. 하지만 식당에서 음식 그릇을 다시 찾아간다면 그 집 음식은 시켜먹습니다.
- I normally buy recycled copying paper at the stationery and always make copies on both sides.
  저는 문구점에서 주로 재활용된 복사용지를 사고 항상 양면 복사를 합니다.
- I use old towels and blankets as ironing board pads and covers.
  저는 낡은 타월과 담요들을 다리미 받침대 덮개로 씁니다.
- I donate old clothes and shoes to charity centers.
  저는 오래된 옷과 신발들을 자선센터에 기부합니다.

MAKE YOUR ANSWER

질문에 대한 여러분의 답변을 만들어보세요.

Home recycling may require some time and effort. Tell me about your own ways to save time and effort while recycling at home.

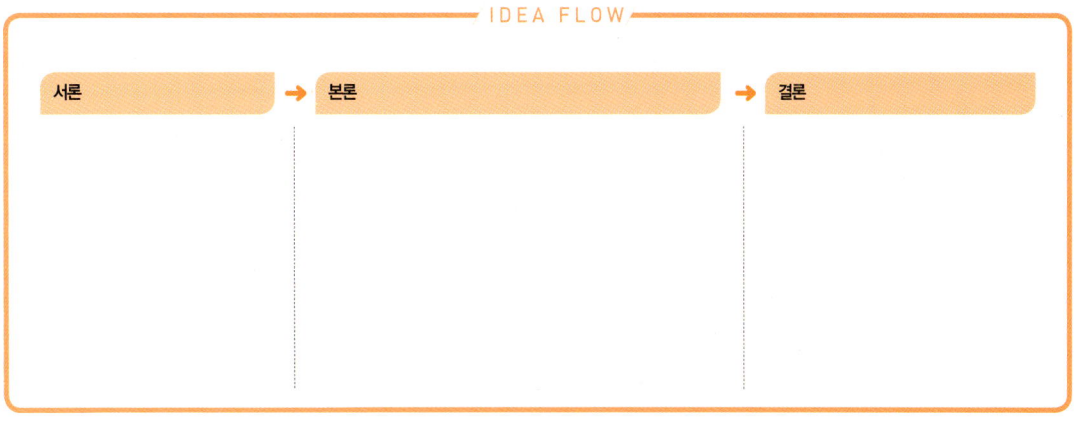

ANSWER

Q3 How was garbage recycled at home when you were young? Did you have a home recycling area in your neighborhood? Please tell me about your experiences regarding recycling when you were young.

IDEA FLOW

서론	본론	결론
어렸을 때 재활용 상황 간단히 언급 사람들 큰 관심 없었고 정부에서도 구체적 정책 없었음	동네에서 이루어졌던 재활용 노력에 대한 구체적 설명 1. 학교 　① 자발적 재활용 날: 매주 수요일 　② 종이와 유리병을 모아서 학교로 가져감 　③ 합쳐진 재활용 쓰레기들은 동네 재활용 센터 사람에 의해 수거됨 2. 동네 슈퍼마켓: 빈 병을 가져가면 한 병당 10원이나 20원 받음	어렸을 때 경험한 재활용에 대한 소감으로 마무리 그 경험으로 인해 현재 재활용 제도를 기꺼이 따르게 된 것이라 생각

ANSWER

When I was a child, not many people were very interested in recycling. As far as I can remember, the government didn't even have specific policies on recycling. The people in my neighborhood made some efforts to recycle garbage though. I lived in Daejeon when I was in elementary school, and some students brought paper and glass bottles that were collected in school every Wednesday. It was a voluntary recycling day, and I participated in that activity. The recyclable items that all of the students collected were combined into several burlap bags and picked up by garbage collectors from the recycling center in my neighborhood. My friends and I also took empty glass bottles to our local supermarkets to get refunds. We used to get 10 won to 20 won for each empty bottle that we brought back to the supermarket in those days. I don't think I was seriously aware of the importance of saving our environment back then, but I think those recycling experiences have led me to readily follow the current recycling system in my country.

[해석 p.300 참조]

IH 답변 파헤치기

문장 구조 응용하기

lead + A + to 부정사 A가 ~하도록 이끌다

- 본문: But I think those recycling experiences have led me to readily follow the current recycling system in my country.
- ex: My parents were very strict with recycling at home, which might lead me to study environmental engineering.
  우리 부모님께서는 집에서 매우 엄격하게 재활용을 하셨는데, 그것이 아마 제가 환경공학과를 전공하게 했는지도 모르겠습니다.

Word be aware of ~를 인식하다, ~을 알다

- 본문: I don't think I was seriously aware of the importance of saving our environment back then.
- ex: No one there was aware of my intention, which made me feel excited.
  거기 있는 누구도 내 의도를 알아차리지 못해서 신이 났습니다.

Word be combined into ~로 결합되다, 합쳐지다

- 본문: The recyclable items that all of the students collected were combined into several burlap bags and picked up by garbage collectors from the recycling center in my neighborhood.
- ex: The three different offices were combined into one community center.
  세 개의 각기 다른 사무소들이 결합하여 하나의 지역 문화회관이 되었습니다.

어렸을 때를 회상하며 서두 열기

- When I was a child, I didn't even know what recycling meant.
  저는 어렸을 때 재활용이 무엇을 의미하는지조차 몰랐습니다.
- My parents emphasized the importance of recycling during my childhood.
  우리 부모님께서는 제 유년시절에 재활용의 중요성에 대해 강조하셨습니다.
- I remember separating glass bottles and paper from other trash at an early age.
  어린 시절 유리병과 종이를 다른 쓰레기와 분리했던 기억이 납니다.
- I didn't separate recyclable things from non-recyclable garbage until I went to university.
  저는 대학에 들어가서야 재활용 분리수거를 했습니다.

어렸을 때 경험한 재활용 관련 아이디어

- I cut the PET bottle to use it as a flower vase. I also put flowers in an empty glass jar wrapped with pretty wrapping paper.
  저는 페트병을 잘라서 꽃병으로 사용했습니다. 빈 유리 병을 예쁜 포장지로 싸서 꽃을 꽂기도 했습니다.
- My family raised two big dogs when I was an elementary school student. My mom always collected our food leftovers to give it to the dogs. We didn't have designated food waste containers in our community and buying dog food was not common at that time. That would probably be my first recycling experience.
  제 가족은 제가 초등학생일 때 큰 개 두 마리를 키웠습니다. 우리 엄마는 항상 우리가 먹다 남은 음식물을 개들에게 주셨지요. 그 당시에는 지역에 지정된 음식물 쓰레기통도 없었고 개의 사료를 사는 일도 흔하지 않았으니까요. 그것이 아마도 제 첫 번째 재활용 경험일 것 같습니다.
- We used to collect branches from our garden to make a Christmas tree when we lived in a house. After moving to an apartment, we just bought a new one and have reused it every Christmas.
  개인주택에 살았을 때는 정원에서 나뭇가지를 주워다가 크리스마스 트리를 만들었죠. 아파트로 이사온 이후에는 새로운 걸 하나 사서 크리스마스 때마다 재사용하고 있습니다.

질문에 대한 여러분의 답변을 만들어보세요.

How was garbage recycled at home when you were young? Did you have a home recycling area in your neighborhood? Please tell me about your experiences regarding recycling when you were young.

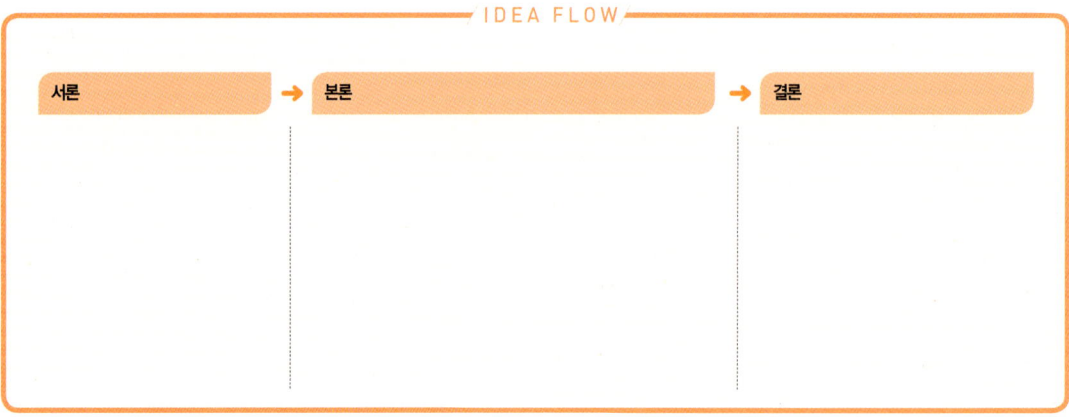

ANSWER

Memo

Oral Proficiency Interview-computer

Lesson 14 — 돌발 전화 통화

INTRO 전화 통화는 일상생활에서 친구와 나누는 전화 담소에서부터 거래처와 하는 업무용 전화 통화까지 모두 답변 대상이 될 수 있습니다. 특히 친구와의 전화 통화는 최근까지 꾸준히 출제되고 있으므로 대화의 주제나 소재, 통화의 중요성 등에 대한 다양한 답변을 준비해 보는 것이 좋겠습니다. 전화 통화는 다른 전문적인 주제에 비해서는 다소 마음이 편하고 수월하게 느껴질 수도 있겠으나 전화를 처음 하게 된 계기라든지 전화 통화의 전개 방식 등 논리적인 답변을 요하는 문제들도 등장을 하기 때문에 방심은 절대 금물입니다.

IH 답변 전략

① 통화 대상에 따른 통화 주제 선정하기
- 통화 대상을 묻는 걸로 시작하는 문항과 처음부터 친구와의 전화를 전제로 한 문항에 각각 대비해야 합니다.
- 통화 대상에 따른 통화 내용의 주제를 선정합니다. 초반에 바로 통화 주제를 언급하는 것도 나쁘진 않겠으나 '친한 정도에 따라 통화 주제가 다르다'라는 말로 서두를 열면 좀 더 신선하고 차별화된 답변으로 들릴 것입니다.

② 전화 통화의 전개 방식과 전화 통화를 처음 하게 된 계기 설명하기
- 가벼운 안부의 교환에서 시작해 점차 진지한 이야기로 발전시키는 전개 방식과 처음부터 용건을 바로 말해버리는 직설적 스타일로 나누어 답변을 준비해 봅니다.
- 처음 전화 통화를 시작하게 된 계기나 처음 친구들과 전화 통화를 한 시기 등에 대한 문제는 사실 답변하기가 까다로울 수 있습니다. '휴대폰의 일상화로 특별한 의식 없이 전화로 의사소통을 하는 것이 생활화 되었다'는 일반적인 답변에서부터 중요한 약속이나 과제의 확인 등을 통한 전화로 친구들과의 통화를 시작하게 되었다는 구체적인 답변까지 모두 생각해 볼 수 있습니다.

③ 전화 통화의 중요성 강조하기
- 전화 통화의 중요성을 강조하기 위해서는 그것이 자신의 일상생활에 어떤 영향을 미치는지에 대해 구체적인 예를 들어 설명해주는 것이 좋습니다.
- 문자메시지나 편지 등과 비교해서 그 중요성을 강조하는 것도 효과적인 방법이 됩니다.

 '전화 통화'에서는 어떠한 질문들이 출제될까요? 다음의 예상 질문에 대해 여러분은 어떻게 답변할지 한 번 생각해 보세요.

 1. Do you often talk on the phone with your friends? When do you normally talk and what do you talk about? Tell me about your phone conversation in detail.

2. When did you first start talking to your friend on the phone? What was the telephone conversation about? Tell me everything that you remember about the telephone conversation.

3. How frequently do you talk to your friend over the phone? How long do you normally talk on the phone once you start a phone conversation with your friend?

4. Please tell me about any interesting, humorous, or funny stories from your recent telephone conversation.

5. When you have a serious issue to talk about to your friend over the phone, how do you start and develop the talk?

6. Who do you usually talk on the phone? When do you call him or her and what do you talk about?

 7. Are phone calls important for your life? Why do you think they are important? How do they affect your life?

8. You may have made an international call. When did you call and what were you talking about? Please explain the international phone call in as much detail as possible.

9. How important are the phone calls for you? How do they help you in your daily life? How have phone calls affected your life?

 10. Have you ever had any memorable phone conversation? Who did you talk with and what was it about? Why was it so memorable to you? Tell me about the conversation in detail.

Do you often talk on the phone with your friends? When do you normally talk and what do you talk about? Tell me about your phone conversation in detail.

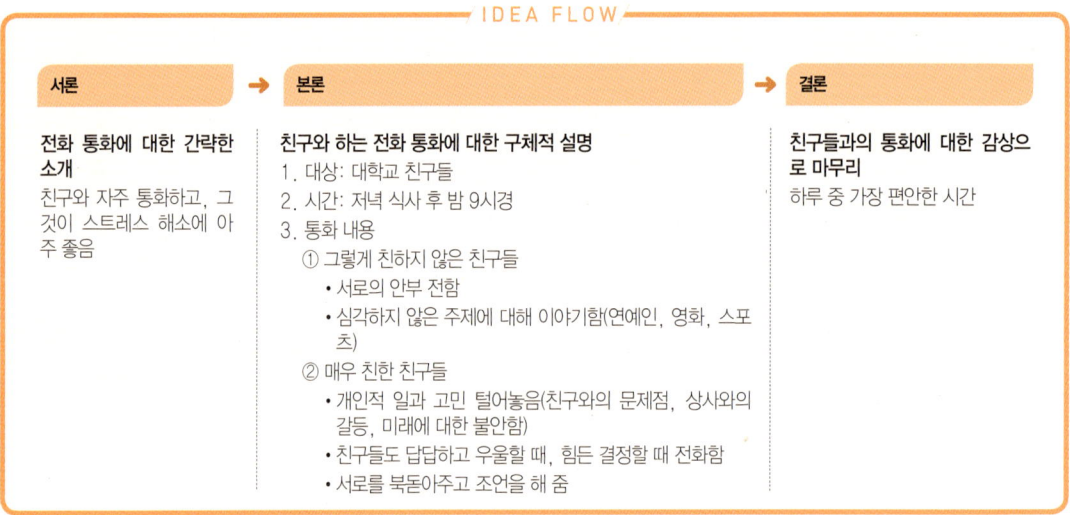

ANSWER

I talk on the phone with my friends quite often. For me, having a chat on the phone is one of the best ways to reduce stress. Since I have few close coworkers, those who I mostly talk with on the phone are my friends from college. I usually talk to them at home at around 9 p.m. after dinner. What we are talking about depends on how intimate we are. If we are friends, but not quite that close, we just ask how we're doing and talk about what's going on in our daily lives. Topics that are not serious, like celebrities, movies, or sports, come up frequently in our conversations. It's funny and pleasant to exchange information or joke around about such common topics. With my best friends, on the other hand, I often talk about personal things and get something off my chest. I talk about some trouble with my boyfriend, conflict with my boss, anxiety about my future, etc. They also call me when feeling dull and gloomy or when having to make a tough decision. We always cheer each other up and give advice to one another. I have the most relaxing time when talking to my friends on the phone.

[해석 p.300 참조]

IH 답변 파헤치기

전화 통화를 나타낼 수 있는 표현들

- I enjoy talking with my friends on the phone. 저는 친구와 전화 통화하는 것을 좋아합니다.
- It is good to shoot the breeze on the phone with my close friends at night.
  밤에 친한 친구들과 전화로 수다를 떠는 것이 좋습니다.
- I can have a long phone conversation on weekends.
  주말에는 전화 통화를 오래 할 수 있습니다.
- I want to spend more time having a chat with my girlfriend on the phone.
  저는 제 여자친구와 전화로 더 오랜 시간 이야기하고 싶습니다.
- I don't usually have a talk on the phone with my coworkers. 저는 직장동료와는 전화로 잘 이야기하지 않습니다.

전화 통화 주제에 대한 아이디어들

- The topics of our phone conversation are mostly about our common interests like sports, jobs, or travels. 우리 전화 통화의 주제들은 대부분 스포츠, 일, 또는 여행과 같은 공통 화제들에 관한 것입니다.
- Asking how her day's been is the first topic I bring up when I talk on the phone to my girlfriend.
  여자친구에게 전화를 걸 때 제가 꺼내는 첫 번째 주제는 하루가 어땠냐는 것입니다.
- We normally talk about current affairs that interest both of us from celebrity gossip to political issues.
  우리는 연예인 가십에서 정치적 사안에 이르기까지 우리가 관심을 갖는 시사에 대해 주로 이야기합니다.
- We talk about all sorts of trivial things such as what I saw on the road, what I had for lunch, or which program I watched on TV.
  우리는 모든 종류의 소소한 것들, 예를 들면 길거리에서 뭘 봤나, 점심으로 뭘 먹었나, TV에서 뭘 봤나 같은 것에 대해 이야기합니다.

전화 통화 목적에 대한 아이디어들

- I can catch up with all the latest news while talking on the phone with my friends.
  저는 친구들과 전화 통화를 하면서 모든 최신 뉴스들을 따라잡을 수 있습니다.
- I'm on the phone simply to pass the time without particular interest.
  별다른 관심 없이 그냥 시간을 때우기 위해 통화를 합니다.
- Phone conversations with my close friends help me relieve my stress.
  친한 친구들과의 전화 통화는 스트레스를 푸는데 도움이 됩니다.

Word few/a few +복수명사 ~이 거의 없다/조금 있다

- I have few friends to talk with on the phone. 저는 전화 통화를 할 친구가 거의 없습니다.
- It's fortunate I have a few close friends to talk about my personal stuff with.
  개인적인 일들에 대해 말할 수 있는 친구가 어느 정도 있다는 게 다행입니다.

Word on the other hand 한편, 반면에
  ※ 화제의 전환이나 두 가지를 대조 비교할 때 쓸 수 있습니다.

- I can't talk long on the phone at work. On the other hand, I can feel free to have a long phone chat with my friends at home. 회사에서는 통화를 오래 할 수 없습니다. 반면 집에서는 친구들과 긴 전화 통화를 마음껏 할 수 있습니다.

Idiom get something off one's chest/ pour out my troubles/ pour one's heart out 고민을 털어놓다

- I can pour out all my troubles to my best friend. 저는 가장 친한 친구에게 제 모든 고민을 털어놓을 수 있습니다.
- I can't pour my heart out to any friends. 아무 친구에게나 마음을 털어놓을 수는 없습니다.

MAKE YOUR ANSWER

질문에 대한 여러분의 답변을 만들어보세요.

Do you often talk on the phone with your friends? When do you normally talk and what do you talk about? Tell me about your phone conversation in detail.

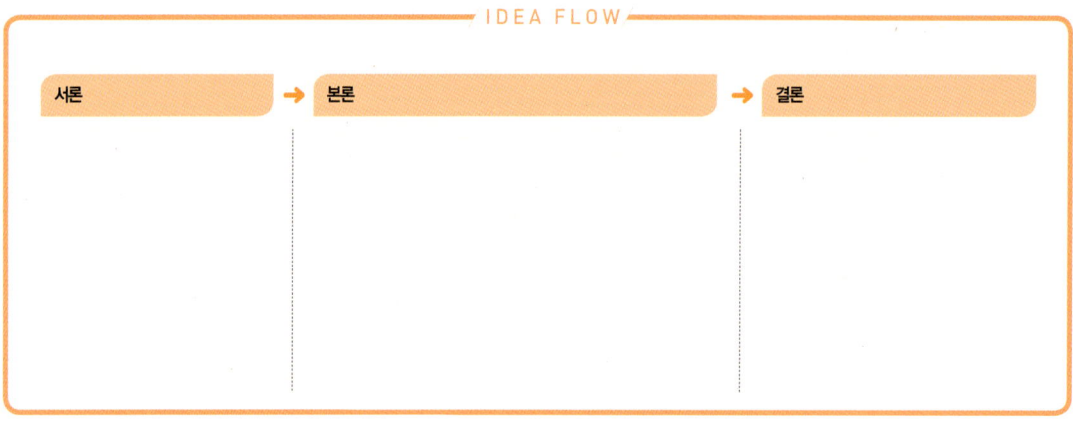

ANSWER

Are phone calls important for your life? Why do you think they are important? How do they affect your life?

IDEA FLOW

서론	본론	결론
전화 통화의 중요성에 대한 답변 물론 중요함	전화 통화가 중요한 이유를 구체적으로 설명 1. 친구들과의 전화 통화 ① 거의 전화로 연락 유지 → 우정 돈독하게 함 ② 멀리 떨어진 시골에 사는 친구는 전화 아니면 연락 쉽게 끊김 ③ 문자보다 전화 선호 2. 업무로써의 전화 통화 ① 거래처 사람들과 거의 모든 일을 전화로 해결 ② 파일 첨부 제외하고는 이메일도 주고 받지 않음 Why? 즉각적인 피드백 필요	전화 통화에 대한 의견으로 마무리 효율적이고 신속한 일 처리를 가능하게 해줌

ANSWER

Yes, phone calls are surely important for my life. I've been keeping in touch with my friends mostly by phone. Since we are too busy to see each other often, we need to promote our friendship by having frequent phone conversations. In case of some friends who are living in the remote country, it'd be easy to lose touch with them without phone calls. I personally prefer talking on the phone to texting when contacting my friends. Phone calls are also essential for me to work. I have few chances to have conversations with my business associates in person unless we have to discuss a very serious issue. We sort most work out on the phone, sometimes even on weekends. We hardly exchange emails except attaching some files because we have to give and receive immediate feedback from each other. Phone calls make it possible for me to deal with large and small incidents efficiently and promptly.

[해석 p.300 참조]

IH 답변 파헤치기

문장 구조 응용하기

too 형용사/부사 to 부정사 너무 ~해서 ~할 수 없다

- 본문 Since we are too busy to see each other often, we need to promote our friendship by having frequent phone conversations.
- ex We all live too far away from each other to meet even once a year.
  우리는 서로 너무 멀리 떨어져 살아서 심지어 1년에 한 번도 만날 수가 없습니다.

unless S+V ~하지 않으면, ~하지 않는 한

- 본문 I have few chances to have conversations with my business associates in person unless we have to discuss a very serious issue.
- ex Unless something urgent comes up, I hardly call my staff members.
  급한 일이 생기지 않는 한 저는 제 직원들에게 전화하지 않습니다.

make it possible (for + A) + to 부정사(B) A가 B하는 것을 가능하게 하다
여기서의 it은 가목적어라서 특정한 의미를 나타내지 않습니다.

- 본문 Phone calls make it possible for me to deal with large and small incidents efficiently and promptly.
- ex Instant feedback from customers through phone calls makes it possible to prevent further damage.
  전화 통화를 통한 고객으로부터의 즉각적인 피드백이 더 큰 피해를 막았습니다.

Idiom keep(stay) in touch = stay(keep) in contact = maintain contact 연락을 유지하다

- Phone conversations make it possible for me to stay in touch with my old friends.
  전화 통화는 제가 옛 친구들과 연락을 유지하는 것을 가능하게 해 줍니다.
- I've been keeping in contact with my high school friends over 10 years.
  저는 고등학교 친구들과 10년 넘게 연락을 해오고 있습니다.
- I can maintain contact with my former coworkers easily by having a chat on the phone.
  저는 전화로 이야기를 하면서 예전 동료들과 연락을 유지할 수 있습니다.
  cf) It's a sad thing to lose contact with someone who I was on intimate terms with.
  친밀한 관계였던 누군가와 연락이 끊기는 것은 슬픈 일입니다.

전화 통화의 중요성과 관련한 아이디어

- I can contact my clients while on the move.
  저는 이동 중에도 고객에게 연락을 할 수 있습니다.
- I could stand someone up unless I make a phone call and let him know I can't make it.
  전화해서 약속을 지킬 수 없다는 걸 알리지 않는다면 누군가를 바람맞힐 수도 있습니다.
- Phone calls enable me to stay in contact with friends who are living in a foreign country.
  전화 통화는 외국에 살고 있는 친구들과 연락을 유지할 수 있게 해 줍니다.

전화 통화의 중요성을 강조하는 마무리

- The life without phone calls can be dry and stressful. 전화 통화가 없는 생활은 건조하고 긴장될 것입니다.
- Living without phones has become impossible. 전화 없이 사는 것은 이제 불가능해졌습니다.
- It is vital to talk on the phone in our daily life. 전화 통화는 우리 일상생활에서 대단히 중요합니다.

질문에 대한 여러분의 답변을 만들어보세요.

Are phone calls important for your life? Why do you think they are important? How do they affect your life?

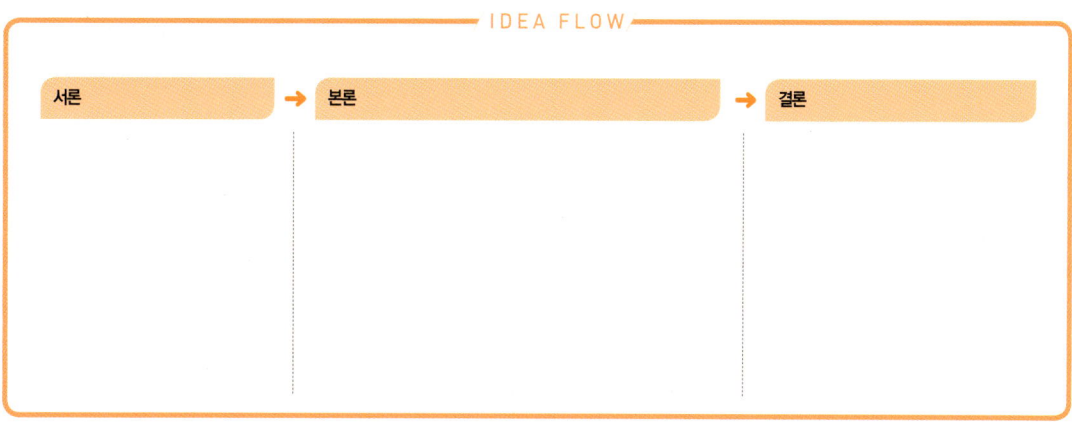

ANSWER

Have you ever had any memorable phone conversation? Who did you talk with and what was it about? Why was it so memorable to you? Tell me about the conversation in detail.

IDEA FLOW

서론 →	본론 →	결론
기억에 남는 전화 통화를 한 배경 소개 미국에 있을 때 매주 토요일에 항상 통화를 했던 엄마가 전화를 안 받으심	전화 통화의 구체적인 내용 설명(언니와의 전화 통화) 1. 힘 없는 목소리 → 불길한 생각 2. 지난 밤 엄마가 넘어지셔서 고관절 부러짐 → 구급차에 실려가심, 수술 중 3. 예상 시간보다 길어지는 수술에 너무 슬프고 두려웠음	수술 결과와 그날의 전화 통화에 대해 언급하며 마무리 1. 수술은 성공적으로 끝나고 어머니 곧 회복하심 2. 지금도 통화했던 순간이 기억남

ANSWER

When I studied in the US, I used to call my mother at 3 p.m. Seoul time every Saturday. My mom always picked up the phone as soon as it rang. But one day, she didn't answer although I kept ringing her up. Then I called my sister, and she answered in a feeble voice. Some dark thoughts occurred to me, and I asked her why I couldn't reach Mom. She hesitated to answer for a moment and told me, "Don't be so surprised of what I'm saying." All kinds of thoughts were running through my head for the brief moment. She finally said Mom fell down last night and broke her hip joint. She was taken to the hospital by ambulance and was under operation. Then she added that the surgery was taking longer than the estimated time. Although she told me that I didn't have to worry too much, I couldn't help but cry in sadness and fear. I was too far away from my mother, which made me feel sad and guilty so much. Fortunately, the operation was successfully finished, and my mother was recovered soon. However, I still remember how astonished I was from the phone call.

[해석 p.301 참조]

IH 답변 파헤치기

문장 구조 응용하기

Although S+V(A), S+V(B) 비록 A 해도 B다

- 본문 Although she told me that I didn't have to worry too much, I couldn't help but cry in sadness and fear.
- ex Although I found him in the lobby, I couldn't break the bad news easily about his bad performance reviews. (=I found him in the lobby but couldn't break the bad news easily about his bad performance reviews.)
그를 로비에서 찾아내긴 했지만, 그의 나쁜 인사고과에 대한 소식을 알릴 수 없었습니다.

can't help but + 동사원형 = can't help ~ing = have no choice but to 부정사 ~하지 않을 수 없다

- I couldn't help but give a shout of joy when I heard of my promotion on the phone.
전화로 제 승진 소식을 들었을 때 환호성을 지르지 않을 수 없었습니다.
- Because my professor suddenly appeared, I couldn't help hanging up the phone before listening to her explanation. 갑자기 교수님이 나타나는 바람에 저는 그녀의 설명을 듣기도 전에 전화를 끊어버리지 않을 수 없었습니다.
- I was so desperate that I had no choice but to call him. 저는 너무나 절박해서 그에게 전화할 수 밖에 없었습니다.

Idiom call(phone) someone/give someone a call/ring someone up/make a (phone) call to ~에게 전화를 걸다

- My wife rang me up one night when I was working overtime.
제가 야근을 하고 있던 어느 날 밤 제 아내가 전화를 했습니다.
- I got a little upset since he didn't call me back. 그가 답신 전화를 하지 않자 좀 화가 났습니다.
- My mom didn't know how to make international calls to the US.
우리 어머니는 미국으로 국제전화를 어떻게 하는지 모르셨습니다.

Idiom get hold of/get through to/complete one's call with/reach someone ~와 통화가 되다

- I ended up failing to reach my boss on that day. 결국 그날은 제 상사와 통화하지 못했습니다.
- I finally got hold of my dad and told him the good news. 마침내 아버지와 통화가 되어 좋은 소식을 알렸습니다.
- She said she tried several times to get through to my department.
그녀는 우리 부서와 통화를 하려고 몇 차례 전화를 걸었다고 했습니다.

Word dark thoughts/gloomy foreboding/ominous presentiment 어두운(불길한) 생각들(예감들)

- 본문 Some dark thoughts occurred to me and I asked her why I couldn't reach Mom.
- ex I was full of dark and gloomy foreboding.
저는 온통 불길한 예감뿐이었습니다.
- ex We tried to get rid of ominous presentiment, but it was no use.
우리는 불길한 예감을 떨쳐버리려 노력했지만 소용이 없었습니다.

잊을 수 없는 전화 통화에 대한 감상으로 마무리하기

- The five minutes of waiting for her answer seemed like 10 years.
그녀의 답변을 기다린 그 5분이 마치 10년처럼 여겨졌습니다.
- I still think that I was lucky to pick up the phone right before leaving my office.
저는 아직도 퇴근하기 직전 그 전화를 받은 것이 행운이었다고 생각합니다.
- I can't forget the moment I heard of the news from his call.
저는 그의 전화를 통해 그 뉴스를 들었던 순간을 잊을 수 없습니다.

질문에 대한 여러분의 답변을 만들어보세요.

Have you ever had any memorable phone conversation? Who did you talk with and what was it about? Why was it so memorable to you? Tell me about the conversation in detail.

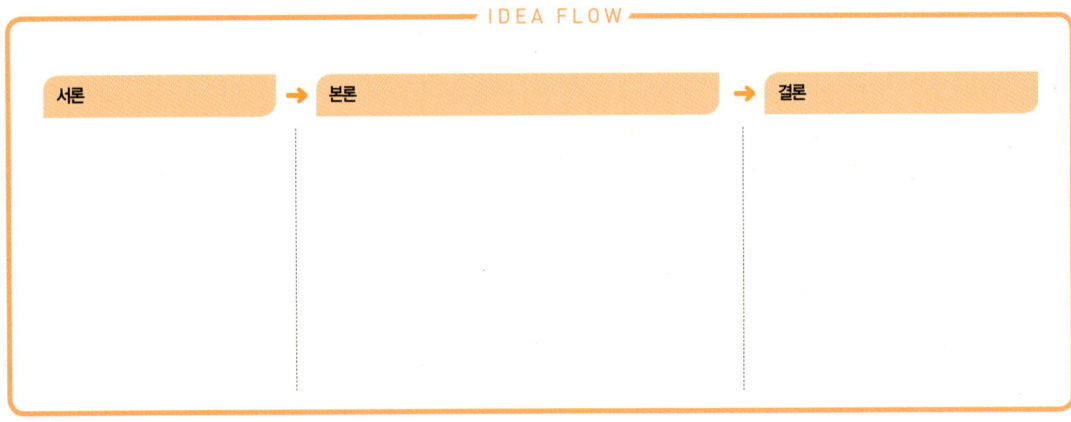

Memo

Lesson 15 · 집안일 거들기

INTRO 집안일 거들기는 OPIc 문항에서 자주, 꾸준히 출제되고 있는 중요한 주제입니다. 특정 취미나 특기와 상관없이 보편적으로 행하는 일이기 때문에 더 그럴 텐데요, 우선 각종 집안일에 대한 어휘와 표현들을 반드시 익혀두고 가족 구성원끼리 어떻게 집안일을 분담하고 있는지 구체적으로 답변 준비를 해야 합니다. 청소나 요리 등의 가사노동과 관련된 집안일 외에도 아이들 숙제 봐주기나 학교 데려다 주기 등의 아이 양육이나 가계지출 등의 책임분담도 함께 다뤄보도록 하겠습니다.

IH 답변 전략

① 가족 구성원마다 맡고 있는 책임과 그 책임을 어떻게 수행하고 있는지 설명하기
- 아이들 숙제 봐주기, 예방 접종시키기, 학교에서 데려오기 등 부모 역할을 중심으로 답변을 준비해 봅니다.
- 동생 공부 도와주기, 동생과 놀아주기 등 어렸을 때 수행했던 형제 역할에 대해서도 준비합니다.

② 집안일 분담 상태와 각자의 집안일 묘사하기
- 정리해놓은 집안일 관련 어휘와 표현으로 각 가족 구성원이 맡고 있는 집안일을 구체적으로 묘사해줍니다.
- 어렸을 때 수행했던 집안일에 대한 질문도 자주 출제되니 먹은 그릇 부엌에 갖다 놓기나 냉장고 문 꼭 닫기 등의 사소한 일들에서부터 방 닦기, 쓰레기 버리기 등의 구체적인 집안일까지 단계적으로 설명해보는 준비를 합니다.

③ 과거나 현재의 집안일과 책임 중에서 특정한 집안일 하나 골라 설명하기
- 어렸을 때 수행했던 집안일이나 책임 중에서 힘들었거나 부담스러웠던 일들을 언급하고 그 이유를 설명해 봅니다.
- 현재 하고 있는 집안일 중에서 수월하거나 하기 싫은 일을 골라 그 이유를 설명해 봅니다.

'집안일 거들기'에서는 어떠한 질문들이 출제될까요? 다음의 예상 질문에 대해 여러분은 어떻게 답변할지 한번 생각해 보세요.

1. I'd like to know about the responsibilities that you and your family members have at home. What are your responsibilities at home? Who is responsible for what? Give me in as much detail as possible.

2. You might have encountered problematic situations while you were doing housework. The toilet may be clogged, things may break, and your kids may mess up the house. Tell me about the situations or problems that you had difficulty dealing with.

3. What were your housework responsibilities at home when you were a child? How did you handle them? How have your responsibilities at home changed as you grew up?

4. What kinds of housework did you find most difficult when you were a child? Why did you find them so difficult? How did you handle them?

5. What housework did you hate to do the most when you were a child? Why did you hate it? How did you handle it?

6. Some household responsibilities that you have had might be easy and others might be difficult. Please tell me about them.

7. I'd like to talk about the household chores that you were supposed to do but could not complete. What were they and why couldn't you finish them? Please tell me about the situation from the beginning to the end.

I'd like to know about the responsibilities that you and your family members have at home. What are your responsibilities at home? Who is responsible for what? Give me in as much detail as possible.

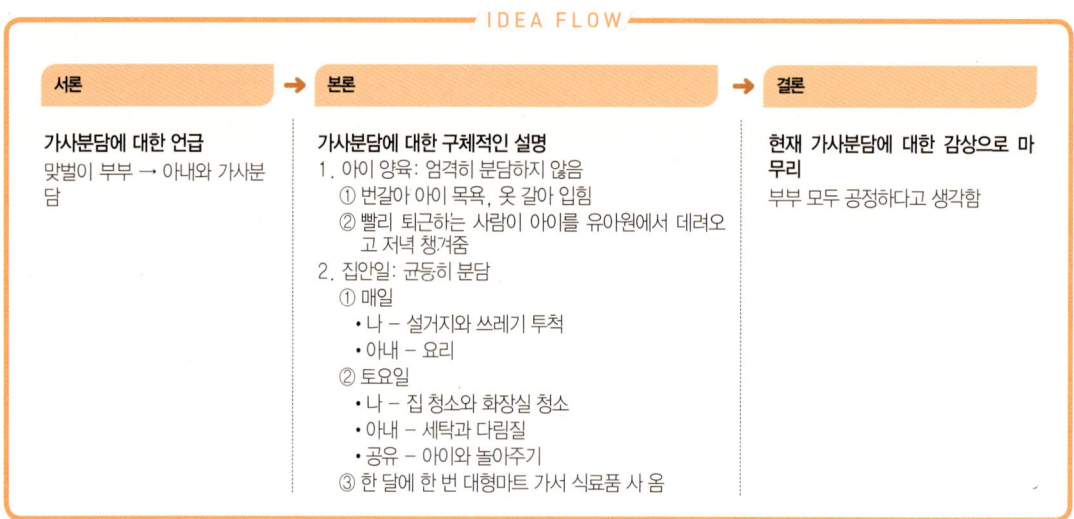

ANSWER

As both my wife and I work, we agreed to share household responsibilities. We don't strictly divide up our own responsibilities for raising our 5-year-old son. We take turns bathing him and changing his clothes. Whoever gets off work earlier picks him up from the nursery school and serves him dinner. My working hours are more flexible than hers, so I usually take him to the hospital when we need to have him vaccinated. We equally divide household chores though. For daily chores, I do the dishes and take out the garbage while my wife cooks. We do most chores on Saturday mornings. I vacuum the house and clean the bathroom, and my wife does the laundry and irons the clothes. We normally spend all Saturday afternoon playing with our son. We read books to him, play with robots with him, and take him to the park. We go grocery shopping together once a month. We go to the major supermarkets such as K-mart and Home Mart to shop for a month's worth of meals at one time. We both think the division of our housework is fair.

[해석 p.301 참조]

IH 답변 파헤치기

문장 구조 응용하기

whoever +V ~하는 사람은 누구든지
- 본문 **Whoever** gets off work earlier picks him up from the nursery school and serves him dinner.
- ex I want to hire **whoever is** honest and reliable as a housekeeper.
  저는 정직하고 믿을만한 사람이면 누구라도 가정부로 고용하고 싶습니다.

Word take turn ~ing 교대로 ~하다, 번갈아 ~하다
- 본문 We **take turns** bath**ing** him and chang**ing** his clothes.
- ex My brother and I **take turns** throw**ing** away trash, depending on which day of the week it is.
  제 남동생과 저는 요일에 따라 돌아가면서 쓰레기를 버립니다.

Word divide(up)/share/split 나누다, 분담하다
- 본문 As both my wife and I work, we agreed to **share** household responsibilities.
- ex My family members discussed how to efficiently **divide up** our household chores.
  우리 가족은 집안일을 어떻게 효율적으로 분배할 지 의논했습니다.
- ex I think it's difficult to **split** household tasks exactly in half with your spouse.
  집안일을 배우자와 정확히 나누는 것은 불가능할 것 같습니다.

가족 구성원들의 집안일 설명하기

- My father sweeps the garden and grows some houseplants while my mother cooks and does the laundry. 우리 어머니는 음식을 만들고 빨래를 하시는 반면 아버지는 정원을 쓸고 분재를 가꾸십니다.
- Since I am responsible for managing household budgets, I pay for all the food expenses. But my husband is in charge of taking care of other family occasions.
  제가 가계 예산을 책임지고 있기 때문에 모든 식비는 제가 냅니다. 하지만 경조사는 남편이 챙깁니다.

현재 가사분담에 대한 개인적 소견 말하기

- I actually feel doubts about the equality of the division of our household chores.
  저는 사실 우리의 집안일 분담의 공정성에 대해 회의를 느낍니다.
- I hope that my parents will have my little sister do more chores.
  저는 부모님께서 제 여동생에게 집안일을 좀 더 시키셨으면 좋겠습니다.
- I feel sorry for my wife, and I try to do as much housework as I can on weekends.
  아내에게 미안해서 주말에는 가능한 많이 집안일을 하려고 노력합니다.

Word 집안일 관련 표현들

- **mop the floor** 바닥을 닦다
- **vacuum the house** 진공청소기로 집 청소하다
- **wipe the window with a damp rag** 젖은 걸레로 창문을 닦다
- **brush away dust** 솔로 먼지를 털다
- **keep the desk clean** 책상을 치우다
- **make the bed** 이불을 개다, 침구를 정리하다
- **separate garbage** 쓰레기 분리수거를 하다
- **do the laundry** 빨래를 하다
- **hang out/spread out the laundry** 빨래를 널다
- **fold the laundry(clothes)** 빨래(옷)를 개다
- **iron out wrinkles (from clothes)** 다리미로 옷의 주름을 펴다
- **set the table** 상을 차리다
- **clear the table** 상을 치우다
- **pay one's utility bills** 공과금을 납부하다

MAKE YOUR ANSWER

질문에 대한 여러분의 답변을 만들어보세요.

I'd like to know about the responsibilities that you and your family members have at home. What are your responsibilities at home? Who is responsible for what? Give me in as much detail as possible.

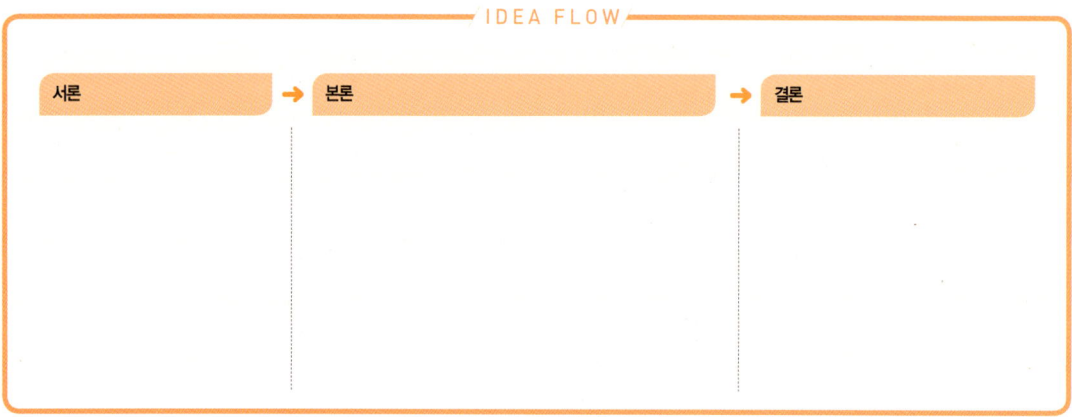

ANSWER

What were your housework responsibilities at home when you were a child? How did you handle them? How have your responsibilities at home changed as you grew up?

IDEA FLOW

서론	본론	결론
학교에 들어가기 전에 했던 집안일에 대한 언급 장난감 치우고 냉장고 문 꼭 닫는 것 외 특정 임무 없었음	나이에 따라 조금씩 복잡해진 집안일의 종류를 구체적으로 설명 1. 초등학교 　① 자리 개고 저녁 식탁 차림 　② 방 청소와 저녁 식탁 치움 　③ 세탁물 접고 옷과 양말 서랍에 넣음 2. 중고등학교 　① 일주일에 두 세 번 마당 쓸고 매주 일요일마다 청소기 돌림 　② 설거지와 교복 다림질 → 지금도 다리미로 바지에 주름 잘 잡음	집안일에 대한 감상으로 마무리 1. 귀찮지 않음 2. 엄마를 도와드리기 위해 기꺼이 했음

ANSWER

My parents didn't have me do specific housework or chores during my preschool years. They just told me to put away my toys or close the refrigerator door all the way. But after I became an elementary school student, they gave me small tasks to handle like making the bed and setting the dining table. As I moved up to higher grades, my housework tasks increased and became more complex. I cleaned my room, cleared the dinner table, and folded a load of laundry. I took my clothes and socks to my dresser drawers too. During my middle and high school years, I swept the garden clean twice or three times a week and vacuumed the floor every Sunday. I sometimes washed the dishes and ironed my school uniforms too. I'm still very good at putting a crease in my trousers with an iron. Doing housework chores was not a big hassle to me. I wanted to help my mom, so I was willing to do all the chores.

[해석 p.301 참조]

IH 답변 파헤치기

문장 구조 응용하기

tell A to 부정사 A에게 ~하라고 말하다

- 본문: They just told me to put away my toys or close the refrigerator door all the way.
- ex: I kept telling him to turn down the TV, but he wasn't even listening to me.
  저는 그에게 TV 볼륨을 낮추라고 계속 말했지만 그는 들은 척도 하지 않았습니다.

Word specific 구체적인, 특정한 (= particular, certain)

- 본문: My parents didn't have me do specific housework or chores during my preschool years.
- ex: My mother gave me quite specific instructions of the household chores I should do.
  우리 어머니께서는 저에게 제가 할 가사일에 대해 상당히 구체적인 설명을 하셨습니다.
- ex: If I choose one particular chore that I cannot do well, that would be keeping my desk clean.
  제가 잘 못하는 일을 하나 고른다면 그건 책상 정리를 하는 것일 겁니다.

Word handle (= deal with, cope with, take care of) ~을(를) 처리하다, 다루다

- 본문: But after I became an elementary school student, they gave me small tasks to handle like making the bed and setting the dining table.
- ex: It was a huge headache for me to deal with a pile of dusty old books.
  먼지투성이의 오래된 책을 처리하는 것은 내게 큰 골칫거리였습니다.

Word crease (옷, 종이 등이 접혀서 생긴) 구겨짐, 주름

- My mom always puts a good crease in my dress pants with an iron.
  어머니께서는 제 정장바지에 다리미로 항상 멋진 주름을 잡아주십니다.
- I found out how to remove creases from my shirt without an iron.
  저는 남방에 남은 구김을 다리미 없이 없앨 수 있는 방법을 찾았습니다.

Word hassle 번거로운(귀찮은) 일

- It's not difficult to dry bowls with a cloth, but just a hassle.
  행주로 그릇의 물기를 닦는 것은 어려운 일은 아니지만 그냥 귀찮을 뿐입니다.
- I don't want my husband to make some food in the kitchen. To me, cleaning up after him is a bigger hassle than doing it myself.
  저는 남편이 부엌에서 음식을 좀 만들지 않았으면 좋겠습니다. 뒷정리를 하는 것이 제가 직접 하는 것보다 더 귀찮습니다.

어렸을 때 할 수 있는 집안일 아이디어

- I started helping my dad mow the lawn when I was 6 years old.
  저는 여섯 살 때부터 아버지께서 잔디 깎으시는 일을 도와드렸습니다.
- My parents gave me allowance when I completed my routine chores such as cleaning their shoes and sweeping floors. Then I put the money in my piggy bank.
  우리 부모님께서는 제가 일상적으로 하는 집안일, 예를 들어 두 분의 구두를 닦거나 마루를 쓰는 일을 끝낼 때마다 용돈을 주셨습니다. 그럼 전 그 돈을 제 돼지 저금통에 넣었습니다.
- I remember I took the letters or postcards out of the mail box when I was a child. I also took out the trash and picked up some food at the grocery store.
  아이였을 때 편지나 엽서를 우편함에서 꺼내왔던 게 기억납니다. 쓰레기를 갖다 버리고 식료품점에서 음식을 사기도 했습니다.

MAKE YOUR ANSWER

질문에 대한 여러분의 답변을 만들어보세요.

What were your housework responsibilities at home when you were a child? How did you handle them? How have your responsibilities at home changed as you grew up?

--- IDEA FLOW ---

| 서론 | → | 본론 | → | 결론 |

ANSWER

Some household responsibilities that you have had might be easy and others might be difficult. Please tell me about them.

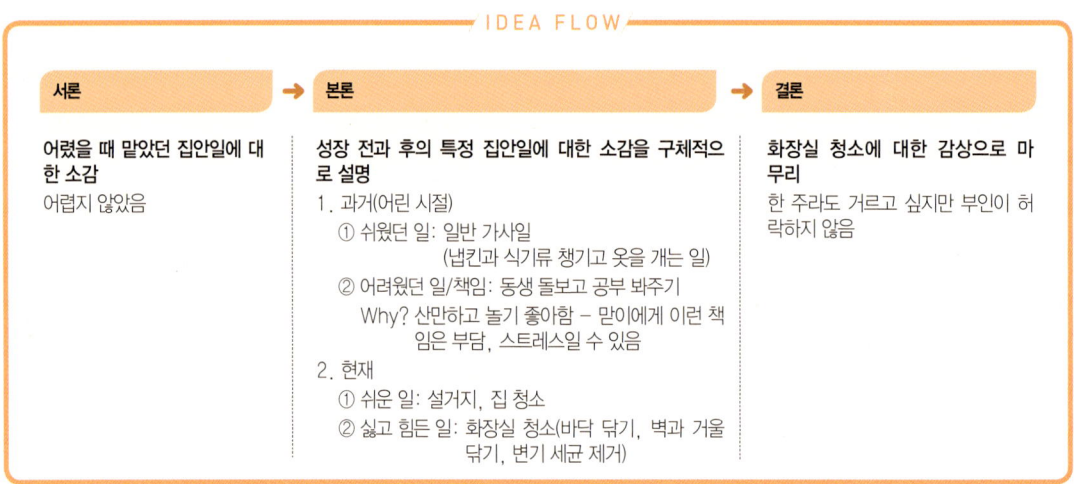

> **ANSWER**
>
> As for my household responsibilities that I had during my childhood, I didn't feel them that challenging. Putting a napkin and silverware on the table or folding some clothes was not a difficult task at all. Since my parents gave me different levels of housework as I grew up, I don't think I did too much hard housework for children or teens. However, I had a responsibility that was tough for me. It was to take care of my little brother and help him with study. I loved my little brother, but he was very distracted and stubborn, which made me feel frustrated. I know most firstborns look after their little siblings, but I think that parents need to know they're also children and may feel it stressful and burdensome. When it comes to my housework that I'm currently doing, I don't mind washing dishes and vacuuming the house. But frankly speaking, I don't like cleaning the bathroom. It is kind of hard work. Mopping the floor, cleaning the walls and a big mirror, and getting rid of germs in the toilet with a brush are just endless work. I sometimes want to skip one week of cleaning the bathroom, but my wife never allows me to do that.
>
> [해석 p.301 참조]

문장 구조 응용하기

allow A to 부정사 A가 ~하는 것을 허락하다

- 본문 I sometimes want to skip one week of cleaning the bathroom, but my wife never allows me to do that.
- ex While my grandmother never allowed my dad to enter the kitchen, my mom had me wash the dishes and set the table.
  우리 할머니께서 아버지가 부엌에 들어오는 걸 절대로 허락하지 않으셨던 것과 달리 우리 어머니는 제가 설거지를 하고 상을 차리게 하셨습니다.

when it comes to = speaking about = as for ~에 관해서라면, ~에 관한 한

- 본문 When it comes to my housework that I'm currently doing, I don't mind washing dishes and vacuum the house.
- ex When it comes to cooking steamed chicken, my wife is an expert.
  닭찜을 요리하는 것에 관한 한, 우리 아내는 전문가입니다.
- ex My husband is the best father when it comes to playing with his kids.
  제 남편은 아이들과 놀아주는 것에 관해서는 최고의 아버지입니다.

mind ~ing = be reluctant to 부정사 ~하는 것을 꺼리다

- I didn't mind feeding and walking my dog but was reluctant to give him a bath for some reasons.
  저는 제 개를 먹이고 산책시키는 건 개의치 않았는데 왠지 목욕을 시키는 건 좀 꺼려했습니다.

Idiom get rid of = remove ~을 제거하다, ~을 없애다, ~하는 것을 꺼리다

- 본문 Mopping the floor, cleaning the walls and a big mirror, and getting rid of germs in the toilet with a brush are just endless work.
- ex It's troublesome to get rid of stains on clothes. Particularly, I can't remove a coffee stain no matter how hard I rub it with liquid laundry detergent.
  옷에 묻은 얼룩을 없애는 건 성가신 일입니다. 특히 커피 얼룩은 액체 세탁 세제로 아무리 세게 비벼 빨아도 지워지지 않습니다.

어렵거나 쉬운 집안일에 대한 아이디어

- I want to help my wife with kitchen work, but I'm so clumsy that I spill water or break dishes so often.   저는 아내의 부엌일을 도와주고 싶은데, 손이 워낙 어둔해서 자주 물을 쏟고 접시를 깨뜨립니다.
- I don't have any complaint about doing the laundry. All I need to do is put the laundry in the washing machine and press the button.
  저는 세탁하는 것에 대해서는 아무 불만이 없습니다. 그냥 세탁기에 빨래를 넣고 버튼을 누르기만 하면 되니까요.
- I felt it difficult to change a light bulb since I was afraid of going up a ladder to reach it.
  저는 전구를 가는 것이 어렵게 느껴졌는데, 거기에 손이 닿으려면 사다리를 타고 올라가야 했기 때문입니다.

집안일에 대한 소감으로 마무리 하기

- When my parents gave me some chores, I felt good because I thought I grew up.
  부모님께서 제게 집안일을 맡기셨을 때 저는 제가 어른이 된 것 같아 기분이 좋았습니다.
- I felt a sense of pride and accomplishment for helping my family when finishing my housework.
  집안일을 끝냈을 때 우리 가족을 도왔다는 자부심과 성취감을 느꼈습니다.
- I don't think I'll never be familiar with any household chores.
  저는 어떤 집안일에도 결코 익숙해질 것 같지 않습니다.

MAKE YOUR ANSWER

질문에 대한 여러분의 답변을 만들어보세요.

Some household responsibilities that you have had might be easy and others might be difficult. Please tell me about them.

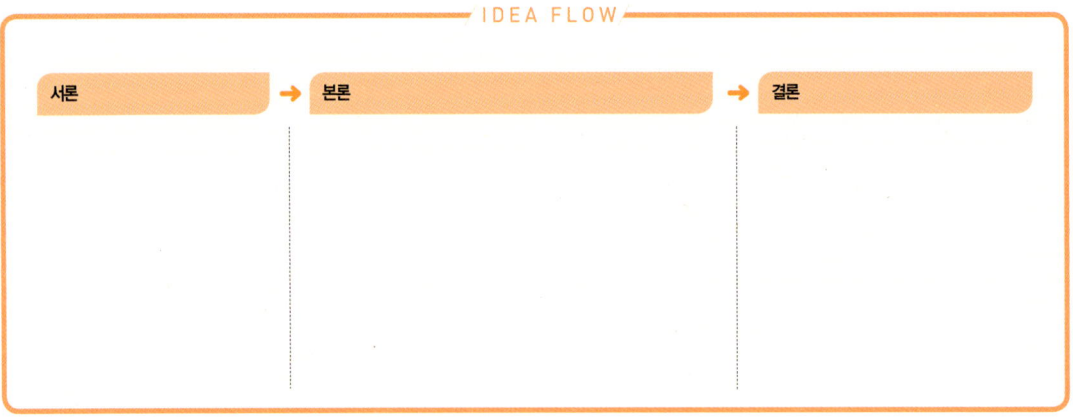

ANSWER

Memo

Lesson 16 돌발 테크놀로지

INTRO 테크놀로지 주제에서는 테크놀로지 자체의 생성과 발전 과정 같은 광의의 개념보다는 실제 회사 업무나 학교 프로젝트 등에 사용되는 구체적인 테크놀로지와 관련된 지엽적인 문제들이 주로 출제됩니다. 평소 사용하고 있는 테크놀로지를 잘 알아두고 그 테크놀로지를 어떻게 활용하여 업무 수행을 했는지에 중점을 두고 준비해봅시다.

IH 답변 전략

① 학교나 직장 등 일상생활에서 사용하는 테크놀로지 소개하기
- 컴퓨터나 휴대폰과 같이 일상생활에서 가장 많이 사용하고 있는 테크놀로지를 소개하고 구체적으로 자신의 업무나 생활에 어떻게 도움이 되고 있는지 설명합니다.
- 서론 부분에서는 컴퓨터나 휴대폰 외에도 일반적으로 사용되고 있는 다른 테크놀로지(예: 인쇄기, 팩스기, 프로젝터 등)도 간단히 언급해주는 것이 좋습니다.

② 테크놀로지 변천사를 자신의 업무나 생활과 연관시켜 설명하기
- 어렸을 때 혹은 입사 초기에 사용했던 테크놀로지와 지금 현재 사용하고 있는 테크놀로지를 비교하며 그 변천 과정을 설명해줍니다.
- 테크놀로지 변천 과정을 설명할 때는 실제 테크놀로지가 사용되었던 업무나 과제를 예로 제시하여 변천 과정 설명과 같이 연관시켜 주어야 더 완성도 있는 답변이 됩니다.

③ 테크놀로지 오작동으로 인해 겪었던 다양한 경험담 소개하기
- 예기치 않는 사건으로 당황했거나 놀랐던 경험은 OPIc 콤보 마지막 문제의 단골 손님이죠. 테크놀로지 오작동으로 과제나 프레젠테이션 수행에 난처함을 겪었던 이야기들을 떠올려 봅니다.
- 테크놀로지 오작동 경험담에는 그 상황을 어떻게 해결했는지에 대한 설명도 추가로 준비하는 것이 좋습니다.

예상질문 파헤치기

'테크놀로지'에서는 어떠한 질문들이 출제될까요? 다음의 예상 질문에 대해 여러분은 어떻게 답변할지 한번 생각해 보세요.

1. Describe technology you frequently use in school these days.

✓2. What kinds of technology do you usually use at work? What tasks do you use them for?

✓3. How has technology changed at work over the years? How has the change affected your life at work?

4. How did you learn to use technological equipment? Did you learn it from someone or did you learn by yourself? Tell me everything you had to do to learn how to use the technology.

5. I'd like to know about technology you use most frequently these days. What is it and why do you use it so often?

6. Tell me about some difficulties you experienced while you learned how to use particular technology or technologically advanced equipment. How did you handle them?

7. I'm going to give you a situation and ask you to act it out. The laptop you recently purchased is not working properly. Call the electronics shop where you bought it and describe the problem your laptop has.

8. I'd like to know about your school project that has successfully been completed. Which technology did you use to complete it? Tell me the whole process from the beginning to the end.

✓9. You might have experienced a time when your technology did not work properly. Tell me about the experience in as much detail as possible.

Q1 What kinds of technology do you usually use at work? What tasks do you use them for?

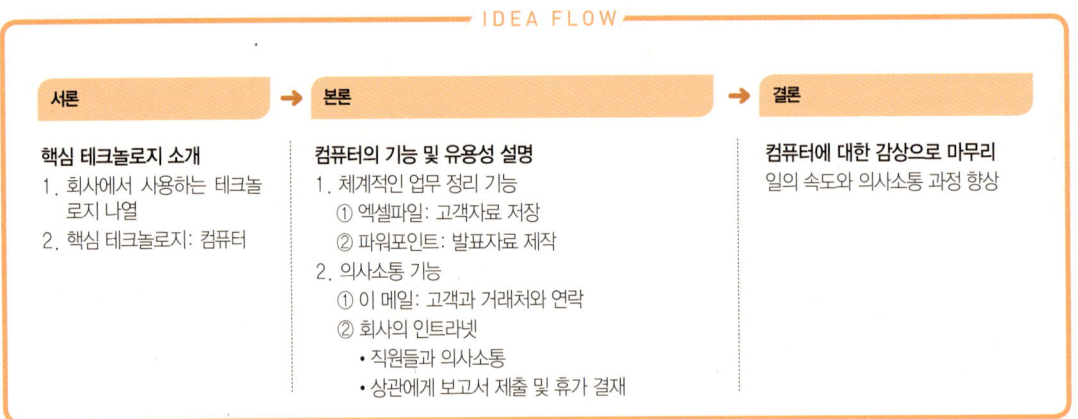

ANSWER

I use many kinds of technological equipment at work, including computers, photocopiers, fax machines, and projectors. The piece of equipment that I use the most is definitely the computers. I start the day by turning on my computer and use it until I finish work. It enables me to organize my work systematically with the help of a lot of useful software. I store all of my information about my clients on Excel files and make PowerPoint presentations with it. I can also contact with my clients and associates by email. If it were not for my computer, I would spend a lot of time calling and meeting them in person. My company recently implemented an intranet system, which makes it possible for all employees to communicate with each other online. The employees submit their reports to their supervisors or get approval to take leave through the intranet system. Like this, computers have increased the speed of my work and improved the process of communication a lot.

[해석 p.302 참조]

IH 답변 파헤치기

문장 구조 응용하기

if it were not for ~, S + 조동사과거 +동사원형 ~이 없다면(아니었다면) ~할 것이다(~했을 것이다)

- 본문) If it were not for my computer, I would spend a lot of time calling and meeting them in person.
- ex) If it were not for computers, my life would be more inconvenient, but simpler.
  컴퓨터가 없다면 내 삶은 더 불편하겠지만, 더 단순하겠지요.
- ex) If it were not for telephones, I couldn't work as a telemarketer.
  전화기가 아니었다면 저는 전화통신판매원으로서 일을 할 수 없었겠지요.

cf) if it had not been for ~, S + 조동사과거 + have p.p. ~이 없었다면(아니었다면) ~했을 것이다

- ex) If it had not been for the Internet, smartphones wouldn't have been created.
  인터넷이 없었다면 스마트폰은 만들어지지 않았을 것입니다.

특정 테크놀로지 소개하면서 서두 열기

- The most important technology at work for me must be computers.
  직장에서 제게 가장 중요한 테크놀로지는 컴퓨터임에 분명합니다.
- Among other things, I'd like to choose tablet PCs as the most useful technological equipment for me. 무엇보다 저는 태블릿 PC를 저에게 가장 유용한 기기로 고르고 싶습니다.
- I use my computer the most at work. I start the day by turning on my computer and use it until I finish work. 저는 직장에서 제 컴퓨터를 가장 자주 씁니다. 컴퓨터를 켜는 걸로 하루를 시작해서 일을 마칠 때까지 사용합니다.

Word implement (정책, 혁신, 변화 등을)시행하다

- 본문) My company recently implemented an intranet system, which makes it possible for all employees to communicate with each other online.
- ex) My company decided to implement changes in the security system as soon as possible.
  우리 회사는 보안 장치의 변화를 최대한 빨리 시행하기로 결정했습니다.

Idiom take leave = take a leave (of absence) 휴가를 내다, 휴직하다, 휴학하다

- 본문) The employees submit their reports to their supervisors or get approval to take leave through the intranet system.
- ex) My boss didn't allow me to take a leave although I had a high fever.
  우리 상관은 제가 고열이 있었는데도 휴가를 내는 것을 허락해주지 않았습니다.
- ex) I managed to persuade my husband to take leave to care for our new baby.
  저는 겨우 남편이 우리 아기를 돌보러 휴직을 하게 설득했습니다.

Word 회사에서 사용할 수 있는 테크놀로지 종류

- **desktop/laptop** 책상용 컴퓨터/노트북 컴퓨터
- **fax machine** 팩스기
- **printer** 인쇄기
- **projector** 영사기
- **shredder** 파쇄기
- **laser pointer** 레이저 포인터

Word 테크놀로지 관련 표현

- **turn on/off the computer** 컴퓨터를 켜다/끄다
- **access the Internet** 인터넷에 접속하다
- **be connected to the Internet** 인터넷에 연결되다
- **communication functions** 의사소통 기능
- **up-to-date technology** 최첨단 테크놀로지
- **user-friendly technology** 사용자 친화적 테크놀로지
- **videoconference** 영상회의
- **webcam** 웹캠

질문에 대한 여러분의 답변을 만들어보세요.

What kinds of technology do you usually use at work? What tasks do you use them for?

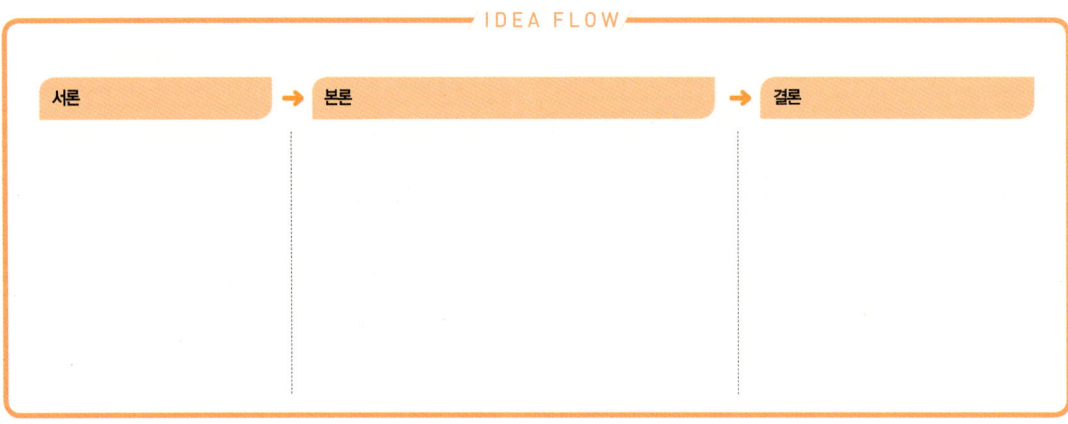

ANSWER

How has technology changed at work over the years? How has the change affected your life at work?

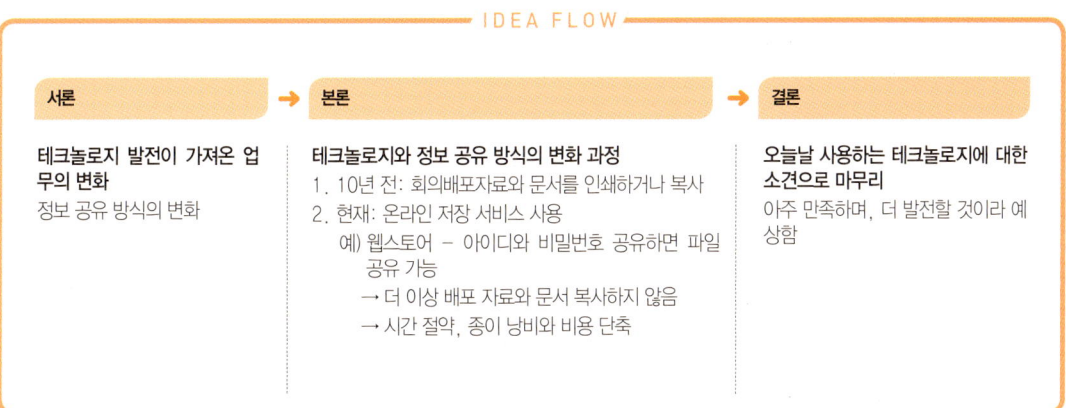

ANSWER

There are many changes that the development of technology has caused in my work life. Among these changes, I'd like to talk about the way we share information with one another. About 10 years ago, when I had to attend a meeting and share documents with other staff members, I printed meeting handouts and the documents or photocopied the original documents. But as useful online storage services have sprung up over the years, we share most of our work online. For example, we actively use Webstore, which allows us to share documents with others as long as we share the ID and password. When one person uploads a file onto Webstore, the others can access the file anytime and download it to look through it. As a result, we no longer print the handouts and documents to give the others. That reduces paper waste and expenses as well as saves time. I'm pretty much satisfied with the technology I use today, but I predict it'll be further developed, which will keep changing the way we do our jobs.

[해석 p.302 참조]

IH 답변 파헤치기

문장 구조 응용하기

the way S+V ~하는 방식, ~하는 방법

본문 Among these changes, I'd like to talk about the way we share information with one another.
= Among these changes, I'd like to talk about how we share information with one another.

본문 I'm pretty much satisfied with the technology I use today, but I predict it'll be further developed, which will keep changing the way we do our jobs.

ex The way we approach our potential customers has been changed.
우리가 잠재 고객에게 접근하는 방식은 변해왔습니다.

Word no longer 더 이상 ~이 아니다

본문 As a result, we no longer print the handouts and documents to give the others.

ex We no longer use a typewriter at work. 우리는 직장에서 더 이상 타자기를 쓰지 않습니다.

Idiom spring up (속속)생겨나다, 나타나다

본문 But as useful online storage services have sprung up over the years, we share most of our work online.

ex Different types of mobile applications are springing up. 다양한 종류의 휴대폰 애플리케이션이 생겨나고 있습니다.

ex A lot of coffee chains have sprung up in Seoul over the past few years.
지난 몇 년 동안 서울에는 많은 커피체인점들이 생겨났습니다.

Idiom look through 검토하다, 죽 훑어보다 (= run through, go through, examine)

본문 When one person uploads a file onto Webstore, the others can access the file anytime and download it to look through it.

ex Before using my new laptop, I read through its instruction manual.
새 노트북을 사용하기 전 사용설명서를 죽 훑어봤습니다.

ex My staff member didn't examine his presentation materials until I told him to do.
제 직원은 제가 그의 발표 자료를 점검해보라고 말하고서야 그렇게 했습니다.

테크놀로지 발전 관련 아이디어

- Laptops have been becoming thinner and lighter. When looking back on my first laptop, it was too heavy to carry it around so often. However, the tablet PC is lighter than the laptop, so I can take it with me when I meet my clients. It's convenient to read or share the screen with them.
  노트북은 점점 얇고 가벼워졌습니다. 제 첫 번째 노트북을 생각해보면 너무 무거워서 자주 들고 다닐 수도 없었거든요. 하지만 태블릿 PC는 노트북보다 더 가벼워서 고객을 만날 때 가져갈 수 있습니다. 고객과 화면을 같이 볼 수 있어서 편리합니다.

- Smartphones have much more functions than the early cell phones. They're equipped with Internet access, electronic dictionary, MP3 player, and daily planner. I can type some memos and store them on my smartphone, too.
  스마트폰은 초기 형태의 휴대폰보다 훨씬 많은 기능들을 가지고 있습니다. 인터넷 접속, 전자사전, MP3 플레이어, 일일 플래너가 갖춰져 있습니다. 저는 제 스마트폰에 메모를 써서 저장할 수도 있습니다.

- Smartphones are becoming literally smarter. Making calls is just one of their basic functions. I like the webcam that my smartphone has. The regional managers arrange conference calls by using the webcam and three-party phone call function.
  스마트폰은 말 그대로 점점 똑똑해집니다. 전화를 거는 건 그저 가장 단순한 기능들 중 하나일 뿐이지요. 저는 제 스마트폰의 웹캠 기능을 좋아합니다. 지점장들은 웹캠과 3자 전화 기능을 이용해서 전화회담을 합니다.

질문에 대한 여러분의 답변을 만들어보세요.

How has technology changed at work over the years? How has the change affected your life at work?

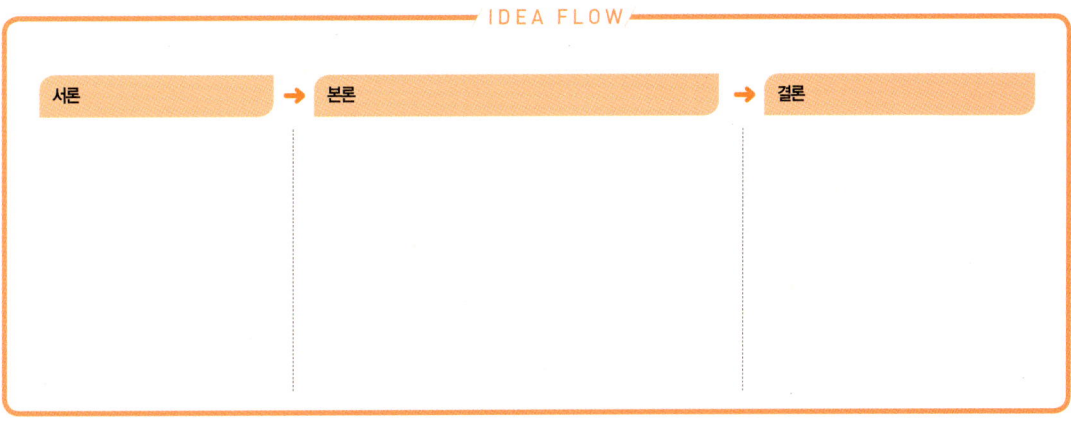

ANSWER

Q3 You might have experienced a time when your technology did not work properly. Tell me about the experience in as much detail as possible.

IDEA FLOW

서론 →	본론 →	결론
사건 소개 1. When? 지난 가을 2. What? 호주 고객들 대상 프레젠테이션 3. How long? 한 달 준비	구체적인 사건 과정 설명 1. PT 시작 15분 전 파일 날라간 것 발견 2. 고객은 기다리고 상관은 화를 내는 상황 3. 패닉 상태에서 사직서 쓸 생각 4. 클라우드 서버(작업파일 실시간 저장) 생각이 나서 바로 접속 → 파일 그대로 저장되어있음 5. 프레젠테이션 제 시간에 시작, 고객들 만족함	감상으로 마무리 다시는 겪고 싶지 않은 끔찍한 사건

ANSWER

I'd like to talk about an incident that took place last fall. I was supposed to make a presentation in front of some clients who came from Australia. I had thoroughly prepared for it for a month since I received the assignment. I turned on my computer to open the files about 15 minutes before the presentation, but I couldn't find the files anywhere on the computer. I didn't know why that had happened, but it was clear that the files were missing. I didn't even know whether they had been erased or if they had not been saved. The clients were waiting outside the conference room, and my boss shouted at me in anger. I got into a panic, thinking that I should submit my resignation. All of sudden, it occurred to me that I had a cloud server. My computer automatically saves the files that I'm working on in the cloud in real time. I logged in with my cloud account, and, thankfully, all of the texts in the file were saved there. Fortunately, I made my presentation on time, and my clients were satisfied with it. It was a terrible experience that I never want to go through again.

[해석 p.302 참조]

문장 구조 응용하기

S+V (절), ~ing ~하면서 ~하다
※ 부대상황(동시동작): 두 개의 동작이나 상황이 동시에 일어날 때, 한 개의 동사 형태를 ~ing로 만들어줄 수 있습니다. 단, 두 동사의 주어가 동일해야 합니다.

- **본문** The clients were waiting outside the conference room, and my boss shouted at me in anger. I got into a panic, thinking that I should submit my resignation.
- **ex** I chatted on the phone with my friend, trying to forget about the conflict with my client.
  저는 고객과 있었던 갈등을 잊어버리려 애쓰면서 친구와 전화로 수다를 떨었습니다.
- **ex** I was listening to the work report from one of my staff members, searching for the files on my laptop.   저는 제 노트북에 있는 자료를 찾으면서 부하 직원의 업무보고를 듣고 있었습니다.

be supposed to 부정사 ~하기로 되어 있다, ~해야 한다
- **본문** I was supposed to make a presentation in front of some clients who came from Australia.
- **ex** I am supposed to attend a meeting at 3 pm.   저는 오후 3시에 회의에 참석해야 합니다.

Idiom take place = happen 일어나다, 발생하다, 벌어지다
- **본문** I'd like to talk about an incident that took place last fall.
- **본문** I didn't know why that had happened, but it was clear that the files were missing.
- **ex** No one predicted such an unexpected accident took place at that moment.
  아무도 그런 예기치 않은 사건이 그 순간 벌어질 줄 예측하지 못했습니다.

Word thoroughly (= closely, carefully) 꼼꼼히, 철저히
- **본문** I had thoroughly prepared for it for a month since I received the assignment.
- **ex** I thoroughly reviewed my term paper before submitting it to my professor.
  저는 교수님께 드리기 전에 제 기말 과제를 꼼꼼하게 살펴봤습니다.

테크놀로지와 관련한 경험 아이디어

- Before the conference, I had to make copies of handouts. As soon as I started making the copies, I heard a beeping noise. There was a paper jam in the photocopier. I tried to fix the paper jam, but I didn't even know where the paper was stuck. As a new employee, I was so frustrated at the situation.
  회의 전에, 저는 배포 자료를 복사해야 했습니다. 하지만 제가 복사를 시작하자 시끄럽게 울리는 소리를 들었지요. 복사기에 종이가 걸린 것이었습니다. 저는 긴 종이를 빼보려고 노력했지만 종이가 어디 걸려있는지조차 몰랐습니다. 신입직원으로서 그 상황에 너무 좌절했습니다.

- My computer screen kept flickering when I turned on my computer. I checked the connection between my computer and its monitor but didn't find any problem. I was very annoyed because I was so busy working on my annual report back then. At the same time, I was worried if my computer had gotten a virus.
  제가 컴퓨터를 켜면 컴퓨터 스크린이 계속 깜박거렸습니다. 컴퓨터와 모니터 연결을 확인해봤지만 아무 이상이 없었습니다. 저는 그 당시 연간 보고서를 작성하느라 너무 바빴을 때라서 아주 짜증이 났습니다. 동시에 제 컴퓨터가 바이러스에 감염 되었을까봐 걱정됐습니다.

- During the presentation, I had a problem with my PowerPoint controller. The arrow buttons that let me move to the previous and next slides didn't work at all. I was very embarrassed because it worked well when I used it during the practice.   프레젠테이션 중, 제 파워포인트 리모콘에 문제가 생겼습니다. 이전 화면과 다음 화면으로 이동할 수 있게 해주는 화살표 버튼이 작동을 하지 않았던 것입니다. 예행연습 때는 멀쩡했기 때문에 무척 당황했습니다.

질문에 대한 여러분의 답변을 만들어보세요.

You might have experienced a time when your technology did not work properly. Tell me about the experience in as much detail as possible.

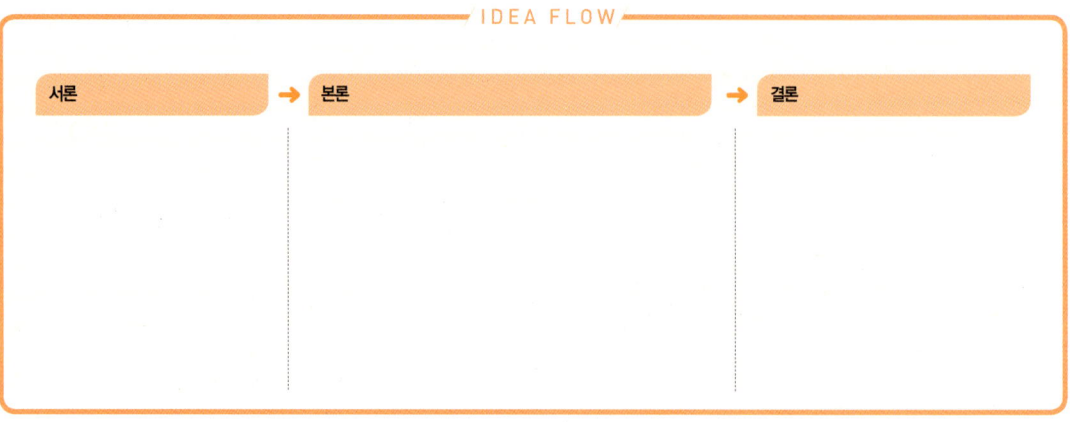

ANSWER

Memo

Lesson 17

돌발 지역 행사

Oral Proficiency Interview-computer

INTRO 지역 행사 주제는 특별히 자신이 참여하고 있는 지역 행사가 없어 낯설 수도 있지만, 바자회나 마라톤, 불우이웃 돕기나 축구대회 등 주위에서 흔히 볼 수 있는 일반 행사나 활동들을 떠올려 보면 쉽게 접근할 수 있을 것입니다. 다양한 행사들을 정리해놓고 자신이 실제로 참여했거나 혹은 참여할 만한 행사를 골라 답변을 준비해보도록 합시다.

IH 답변 전략

① 지역 행사들의 종류와 행사 별 취지, 그리고 참여할 수 있는 활동들을 정리해보기
- 우리 주위에서 흔히 볼 수 있는 지역 행사들의 종류를 살펴보고 아이디어를 얻습니다.
- 행사의 취지는 크게 친목 도모와 지역 홍보, 그리고 기금 모금 등이 있습니다. 이를 중심으로 행사의 목적을 언급해주고 이 목적을 달성하기 위한 참여 활동들을 구체적으로 소개해 줍니다.

② 처음 지역 행사에 참여하게 된 계기와 그 이후 활동 참여도의 변화나 강화 설명하기
- 행사 정보를 스스로 알아낸 경우, 주위의 권유와 소개로 해당 행사에 참여하게 된 경우 등을 고려해서 참여 계기를 설명해 줍니다.
- 첫 행사 참여 이후 어떻게 자신의 인식이 변화되었는지, 얼마나 적극적으로 지역 행사 참여를 하게 되었는지를 구체적으로 설명해 줍니다.

③ 특정 지역 행사에 참여했던 경험을 통해 그 행사의 장단점 설명하기
- 처음 참여한 지역 행사나 최근 참여한 지역 행사, 또는 가장 인상 깊었던 지역 행사 등 개인적 경험을 묻는 질문이 특히 많이 나올 수 있는 것이 지역 행사 주제입니다.
- 경험담을 이야기할 때는 행사 시기, 주최측, 목적 등을 간단히 소개해주고 난 뒤 본격적인 행사 당일 진행 상황을 설명해주는 것이 좋습니다.

'지역 행사'에서는 어떠한 질문들이 출제될까요? 다음의 예상 질문에 대해 여러분은 어떻게 답변할지 한 번 생각해 보세요.

✓ 1. What kinds of special events do you have in your community? What do people do during these events? How do people participate in them?

2. What things do you need to do in order to participate in your community events?

3. What kinds of events do you expect your community to plan and hold? Why do you want to join those events?

✓ 4. What was the most memorable event in your community? When was it held and where did it happen? What made you think it's memorable?

5. Do you remember the community events held when you were a child? How were they different from the ones you are joining now? How have the community events changed over the years?

6. What do you think is the most important thing to draw more attention from residents to the community events? How can the community motivate its residents to actively participate in the events?

✓ 7. I'd like to know about an event in your community that you last participated in. When did you participate in it and what was it about? What did you like or dislike about it?

Q1 What kinds of special events do you have in your community? What do people do during these events? How do people participate in them?

IDEA FLOW

서론	본론	결론
다루고자 하는 지역 행사 선정 고양 꽃 박람회 1. 1997년 시작 2. 전국 규모 행사 3. 지난 4월 7번째 박람회	박람회에 대한 구체적인 설명 1. 전시장 종류 　① 세계 꽃: 35개국의 다양한 꽃 　② 한국 꽃 　③ 고양 꽃 2. 시민 참여 행사들 　① 꽃꽂이 대회 　② 꽃 그리기 　③ 개·폐막식 행사: 라이브 공연, 불꽃놀이	전시회에 대한 감상으로 마무리 1. 다음에도 참여 예정 2. 지역인들과 세계인들 모두를 위한 행사가 되길 희망

ANSWER

My community, Goyang, has held flower exhibitions since 1997. It is not an annual event, but it has become quite famous on a national scale. The 7th world flower exhibition took place for 16 days last April, and it was a great success. At the event, there were three different exhibition halls: the world flower hall, the Korea flower hall, and the Goyang city flower hall. In the world flower hall, people could look at many kinds of flowers from 35 countries, such as the Netherlands, Germany, and Malaysia. The Korean and Goyang flower halls showed gorgeous and spectacular flower arrangements and decorations, which caught our attention well. There were a variety of activities the citizens could take part in, including a flower-arranging contest and a flower-painting event. Some other appealing events were the live performances at the opening and closing of the exhibition and the fireworks show at night. I will attend the exhibition the next time it takes place, and I hope it will be a unique and special event for the people of the world, not just for the people in my community.

[해석 p.302 참조]

IH 답변 파헤치기

Idiom on a national scale 전국적으로 = all over the nation (country)

- 본문 It is not an annual event, but it has become quite famous on a national scale.
- ex The flu virus has rapidly spread on a national scale.
  독감 바이러스가 전국적으로 빠르게 번져갔습니다.
  cf) The environmental campaign has become a nationwide event, and more than 10 million people all over the nation joined this year.
  그 환경캠페인은 전국적인 행사가 되어서, 올해 전국적으로 천만 명 이상의 사람들이 캠페인에 동참했습니다.

Word spectacular 장관인, 극적인, 눈부신

- 본문 The Korean and Goyang flower halls showed gorgeous and spectacular flower arrangements and decorations, which caught our attention well.
- ex I wish I could show you a spectacular view of Niagara Falls.
  당신에게 나이아가라 폭포의 장관을 보여줄 수 있으면 좋을 텐데 말입니다.

Idiom take part in = participate in = join ~에 참여하다, 참가하다

- 본문 There were a variety of activities the citizens could take part in, including a flower-arranging contest and a flower-painting event.
- ex All employees are required to take part in the summer workshop.
  모든 직원들은 여름 워크숍에 참가해야 합니다.
- ex I encouraged introverted students to actively participate in any kinds of classroom activities.
  저는 내향적인 학생들이 어떤 종류의 교실 활동이든 적극적으로 참여하도록 독려했습니다.

Word unique 고유의, (좋은 의미로) 독특한, 유일무이한

- I'm sorry to miss such a unique opportunity to experience Asian tea cultures.
  아시아 차 문화를 경험할 수 있는 독특한 기회를 놓친 것이 유감입니다.
- My twin sons look exactly alike, but each boy has his unique personal trait.
  제 쌍둥이 아들들은 외모는 똑같지만 자기만의 고유한 특성이 있어요.

Word 지역 행사들의 종류

- **bazaar** 바자회
- **flea market** 벼룩시장
- **night market** 야시장
- **five-day market** 5일장
- **firework festival** 불꽃 축제
- **cherry blossom festival** 벚꽃 축제
- **bicycle race** 자전거 경주
- **marathon race** 마라톤 경주
- **mobile library services** 이동도서관 서비스
- **outdoor music concert** 야외 음악회
- **art exhibition** 미술 전시회
- **historical and cultural inquiry** 역사 문화 탐방
- **athletics meeting** 체육대회, 운동회

Word 지역 행사들의 목적

- **raise funds** 기금을 모으다, 모금하다
- **celebrate an anniversary** 기념일을 축하하다
- **promote/develop community networking**
  지역사회를 홍보하다/발전시키다
- **bring residents within a community together**
  지역 주민들을 화합시키다
- **draw attention to the environment** 환경에 주의를 모으다
- **encourage residents to use domestic agricultural products** 우리 농산물 애용을 장려하다

MAKE YOUR ANSWER — 질문에 대한 여러분의 답변을 만들어보세요.

What kinds of special events do you have in your community? What do people do during these events? How do people participate in them?

ANSWER

What was the most memorable event in your community? When was it held and where did it happen? What made you think it's memorable?

― IDEA FLOW ―

서론	→	본론	→	결론
기억에 남는 지역 행사 소개 모금 행사 1. When? 2011년 2. Where? 미국 버지니아 3. What for? 일본의 피해 복구 도와줌		행사 과정 자세히 서술: 지역센터와 초등학교들과의 협력 1. 행사이름: Penny War 2. 형태: 학급간 경쟁 3. 방법 ① 학생들에게 페니 걷음 ② 학교는 수집한 돈을 지역센터에 제출 ③ 지역센터는 우승자 발표 4. 결과 ① 성공적인 목표 달성 ② 학생들에게는 남을 돕는 방법 가르침		행사에 대한 소견으로 마무리 장래에 비슷한 행사를 주관해보고 싶음

ANSWER

It was in 2011 when I found an interesting fundraising event. That year I was staying in Virginia in the US to study for my master's degree. The event aimed to help the Japanese recover from the damage caused by an earthquake and tsunami of the year. Cooperating with local elementary schools, the community center put the notice of the fundraising event on their bulletin boards. The event was called "Penny War," which took the format of a competition among classes. All students could take part in this event, and each class collected pennies from the students for a month. Then the schools submitted it to the community center, which in turn, announced the winner of the contest. Young children actively participated in this event and tried to collect as many pennies as they could. The community center successfully achieved its goals and also taught their students how they could help others in need. Even though that community did not belong to my country, I've kept that event in mind. I want to organize such a fundraiser, maybe under a different name and purpose, in the future.

[해석 p.303 참조]

IH 답변 파헤치기

문장 구조 응용하기

It is(was) ~ that 바로 ~이다

- 본문 It was in 2011 when(=that) I found an interesting fundraising event.
  ※ 일명 It ~that 강조구문이라 불리는 이 형식은 사람, 사물, 시간(시기), 장소 등을 강조하고 싶을 때 요긴하게 사용할 수 있는 문장 구조입니다. It은 아무 의미가 없는 비인칭 주어이고, 이 문장에서 강조하고 싶은 것은 2011년이라는 때(시기)이므로 that 대신 when을 사용해도 무방합니다.
- ex It was a fundraising event that I recently participated in. 제가 최근에 참여했던 것은 바로 기금 모금 행사였습니다.
- ex It was in New York that(=where) I took part in the marathon.
  제가 마라톤에 참가했던 곳은 바로 뉴욕이었습니다.
- ex It was my mother that(=who) organized the music festival.
  그 음악 축제를 주관했던 분은 바로 우리 어머니였습니다.

Word fundraising 모금, 모금활동

- I searched for some fundraising organizations to help some African children.
  저는 아프리카 아이들을 도와주기 위해서 모금단체를 찾아봤습니다.
  cf) My community plans to host a bazaar to raise funds for homeless people.
  우리 지역에서는 노숙자들을 위한 기금을 조성하기 위해 바자회를 열 계획입니다.

Word aim to 부정사 ~을 목표로 하다, ~을 의도하다

- 본문 The event aimed to help the Japanese recover from the damage caused by an earthquake and tsunami of the year.
- ex The upcoming exhibition aims to draw residents' attention to local development.
  다가오는 박람회는 주민들의 관심을 지역 발전에 끌어들이는 목적이 있습니다.

Word cooperate with ~와 협력하다

- 본문 Cooperating with local elementary schools, the community center put the notice of the fundraising event on their bulletin boards.
- ex I was willing to cooperate with other residents to successfully hold our community festival.
  저는 우리 지역 축제를 성공적으로 개최하고자 다른 주민들과 기꺼이 협력했습니다.

Idiom achieve one's goal ~의 목적(목표)을 달성하다

- 본문 The community center successfully achieved its goals, and also taught their students how they could help others in need.
- ex I achieved my goal of earning a Ph.D. degree. 저는 박사학위를 받으려는 목표를 이뤘습니다.

Word belong to ~에 속하다, ~소속이다, ~소유이다

- Since all office equipment that employees are using belongs to the company, I shouldn't take it home.
  직원들이 사용하는 모든 비품들은 회사 소유기 때문에 그걸 집으로 가져가서는 안 됩니다.
- I am proud that I belong to my community. 저는 우리 지역 사회에 속해있는 것이 자랑스럽습니다.

Idiom keep someone/something in mind ~을 명심하다/유념하다/마음에 담아 두다

- 본문 Even though that community did not belong to my country, I've kept that event in mind.
- ex The boy who I met during the volunteer medical service has kept me in mind since I visited his community. 의료봉사 기간에 만났던 그 소년은 제가 그 소년의 지역을 방문한 이후로 저를 기억하고 있었습니다.

MAKE YOUR ANSWER

질문에 대한 여러분의 답변을 만들어보세요.

What was the most memorable event in your community? When was it held and where did it happen? What made you think it's memorable?

Q3 I'd like to know about an event in your community that you last participated in. When did you participate in it and what was it about? What did you like or dislike about it?

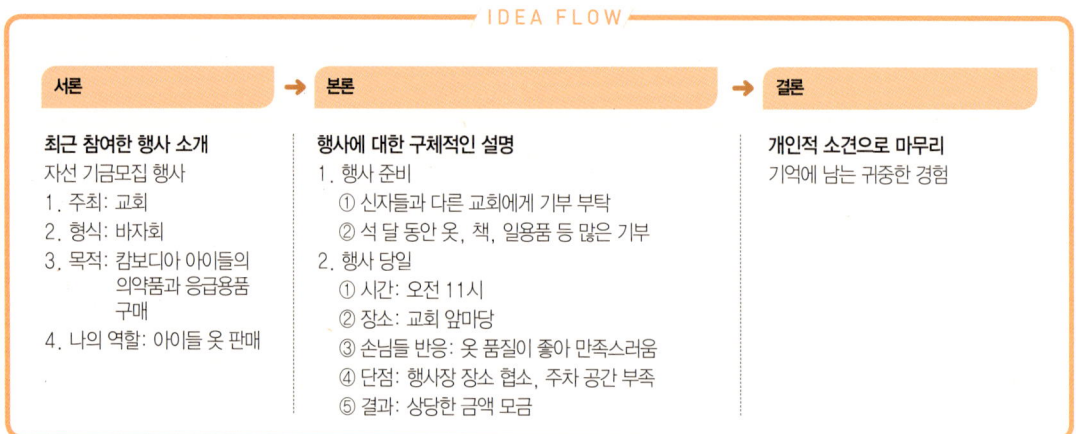

ANSWER

A few months ago, I participated in the charity fundraiser held by my church. It was a type of bazaar, and I took a task of selling children's clothing. All profits from this bazaar went to purchasing some medicine and first aid supplies for children in Cambodia. For the bazaar, the church asked for donations from its devotees and other churches, and collected plenty of items for three months, ranging from clothes and books to daily necessities. The charity event was started at 11 a.m. in the front yard of the church, and many people voluntarily worked for it. Since the items I was selling had quite good quality, the buyers were satisfied with them. But the place for the event was a little small, and there were too many people cramped in there. Furthermore, the number of parking spaces was limited, and the front and back yards were full of people and cars. Even though the place was not spacious enough to accommodate many people, the charity itself was successfully finished. Most items were sold, and we got a substantial amount of money. As a result, that event gave me a memorable and valuable experience.

[해석 p.303 참조]

IH 답변 파헤치기

문장 구조 응용하기

형용사/부사 enough to 부정사 ~할 만큼 충분히 ~하다

- 본문) Even though the place was not spacious enough to accommodate many people, the charity itself was successfully finished.
- ex) My daughter is old enough to make the bed and set the table.
  제 딸은 자리를 개고 상을 차릴 수 있는 충분한 나이가 됐습니다.

Word plenty of 많은, 풍부한 (= sufficient, enough)

- 본문) For the bazaar, the church asked for donations from its devotees and other churches, and collected plenty of items for three months, ranging from clothes and books to daily necessities.
- ex) We had plenty of time left until we started raising funds for the orphanage.
  고아원을 위한 기금 조성이 시작할 때까지 충분한 시간이 있었습니다.
- ex) I now need a sufficient sleep because I stayed up all night studying for three days.
  공부 하느라 사흘 밤을 샜기 때문에 저는 지금 충분한 잠이 필요합니다.

Word substantial (양, 수, 중요성 등이)상당한 (= considerable, significant)

- 본문) Most items were sold and we got a substantial amount of money.
- ex) There was a substantial increase in profits from our food products this year.
  올해 우리 식품에서 나온 수익에 상당한 증가가 있었습니다.
- ex) I found a significant difference between the two classes.
  저는 두 학급간의 상당한 차이를 발견했습니다.

최근에 참여한 지역 행사에 관한 답변 만들어보기

- The community center in my neighborhood hosted an amateur photo exhibition last year. Any residents could submit their photos, but only 25 to 30 of them were selected and exhibited. The center didn't put any limits on the subject of the photos. I took some pictures of nature and sent them to the exhibition. Although my photos were not chosen, I was very impressed by the photos displayed at the exhibition. Most photos looked beautiful and professional.
  우리 동네 문화회관에서는 작년에 사진 전시회를 개최했습니다. 주민이면 누구든지 사진을 출품할 수 있었지만 그 중에서 25~30점만 채택되어서 전시됐습니다. 사진 소재에는 어떤 제한도 두지 않았습니다. 저도 자연 사진을 몇 장 찍어서 보냈습니다. 비록 제 작품이 선택되진 않았지만 전시된 사진들을 보고 무척 감탄했습니다. 대부분의 사진이 아름답고 전문적으로 보였으니까요.

- I participated in the night markets that my community held a few weeks ago. I never missed the night market because it's my favorite event to join in my community. The market was held near our community center at 7 p.m. for three nights straight. I enjoyed trying many kinds of delicious Korean food like meat pancakes, kimchi pancakes, pajeon, and japchae. I could also buy environment-friendly agricultural products from the market.
  저는 몇 주 전 우리 지역에서 열렸던 야시장에 참가했어요. 야시장은 우리 지역에서 제가 참여하길 가장 좋아하는 행사라서 결코 놓친 적이 없습니다. 지역회관 근처에서 3일 밤 내내 저녁 7시에 시장이 섰어요. 저는 고기전, 김치전, 파전, 잡채 등의 맛있는 한국 음식을 즐겼어요. 친환경 농산품들도 살 수 있었습니다.

질문에 대한 여러분의 답변을 만들어보세요.

I'd like to know about an event in your community that you last participated in. When did you participate in it and what was it about? What did you like or dislike about it?

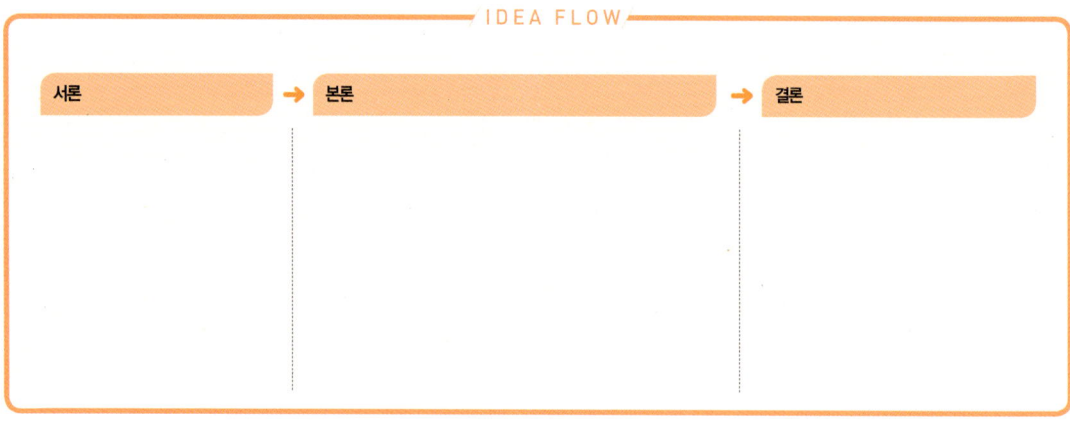

Memo

Lesson 18
국내여행

INTRO

국내여행과 관련해서는 목적지 소개, 교통편의 변화, 어렸을 때 간 여행, 여행에 대한 주요 이슈 등 다양한 문제들이 출제될 수 있습니다. 자주 가는 여행지 중에서 몇 곳을 선택해 그 여행지에 대한 정보를 자세하게 설명하는 연습이 필요합니다. 또한 여행지에서 겪은 기억에 남는 상황이나 즐거웠던 순간들을 이야기하는 답변도 충실히 준비해놓아야 하겠습니다.

IH 답변 전략

① 구체적인 여행지 묘사와 여행 조건 제시
- 국내여행은 해외여행에 비해 여행지에 대한 묘사 문제가 자주 출제되고 있습니다. 자신이 좋아하거나 자주 가는 여행지의 특징, 유명 명소, 특산물 등의 구체적인 여행지 정보를 소개하는 답변을 준비합니다.
- 여행 시기, 목적, 동행인, 여행지 활동 등 또한 명확하고 구체적으로 알려줍니다.

② 여행에 대한 주요 이슈와 여행을 떠나기 전 실질적으로 준비하는 일들 설명하기
- 사람들이 여행할 때 고려하고 신경 쓰는 사안들이 많습니다. 교통편, 교통체증, 비용, 시간, 안전 등 여행과 관련된 이슈들을 생각해보고 그를 토대로 답변을 준비해봅니다.
- 위에 열거한 사안들은 실질적인 여행 전 준비로 이어질 수 있습니다. 여행가기 전 처리해놓아야 하는 여러 가지 일들을 정리해보고, 이 외에도 여행갈 때 꼭 가져가는 것들을 적어놓고 답변에 활용해보도록 합시다.

③ 여행지에서 겪은 일화나 기억에 남는 순간들 소개하기
- OPIc 서베이 7번 항목(국내/해외여행, 국내/해외출장, 휴가) 중에서 어떤 것을 선택하든 인상 깊었던 여행(출장, 휴가)을 소개하는 문제가 나올 확률이 매우 높으니 국내여행에서 준비한 답변을 해외여행 및 출장, 휴가에 모두 활용하시면 됩니다.
- 어렸을 때 갔던 여행, 최근에 갔던 여행, 가장 좋아했던 여행 모두에 답변이 될 수 있는 구체적인 경험이 담긴 답변을 준비합니다.

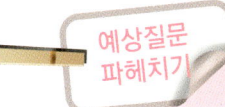

'국내여행'에서는 어떠한 질문들이 출제될까요? 다음의 예상 질문에 대해 여러분은 어떻게 답변할지 한 번 생각해 보세요.

✓ 1. Tell me about your favorite travel destination in your country. When do you go there and who do you go with? Why do you like the place?

2. When and how did you first become interested in traveling? How has the interest developed over the years?

3. I'm going to give you a situation and ask you to act it out. You are planning to rent a car to travel in your country. Call a car rental agency and ask three or four questions about how you rent a car.

4. I'm sorry, but there is a problem I need you to resolve. An urgent circumstance has come up, and you are not able to go on a trip. Call the car rental agency and explain the situation including three alternatives to solve the situation.

5. I also like traveling in my country. Ask me three or four questions about my travel style.

6. Tell me about the place you last traveled to in your country. When did you go and who did you go there with? What did you like and dislike about the trip?

✓ 7. How do you prepare for a trip in your country? What do you do before you go on the trip?

8. Tell me about your most memorable trip that you took in your country when you were young. Where did you go and what did you do there? What made it so memorable?

9. Which transportation did you use when you traveled when you were young? How has it changed as you grew up?

✓ 10. What are people's concerns and considerations regarding traveling? How do these concerns and considerations influence on the effort and expense for their trips?

Q1 Tell me about your favorite travel destination in your country. When do you go there and who do you go with? Why do you like the place?

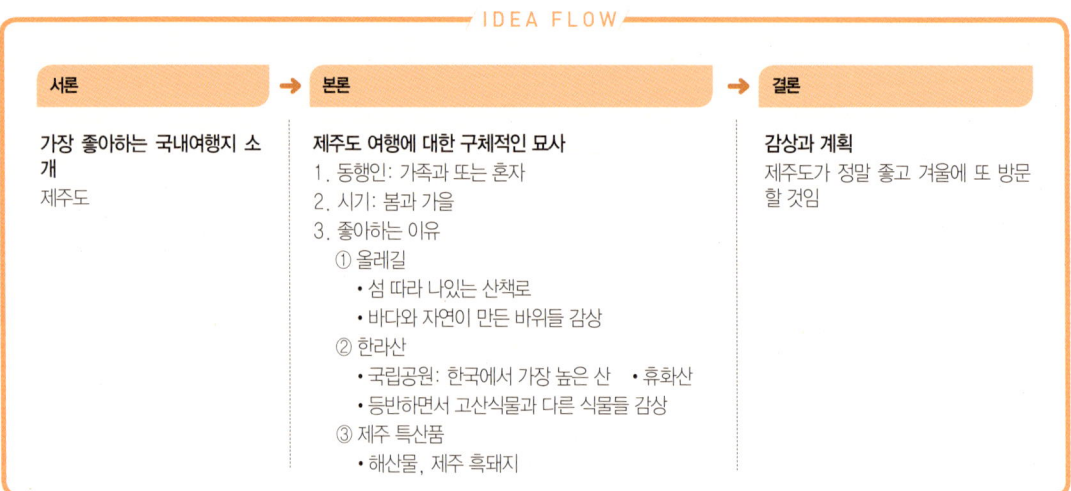

ANSWER

My favorite place is Jeju Island, which is the southern island in my country. Whenever I have some time off, I go there and stay for several days either with my family or by myself. There are many things to enjoy on Jeju Island. Since the views on Jeju are breathtaking, everywhere I look is amazing, especially in spring and autumn. The walking trails, called olle, which wind around the island, are my favorite places. I can hike on the trails while appreciating all of the different views of nature, including the ocean and the marvelous shapes of the rocks the nature has made. In addition to the trails, another favorite hiking place of mine is Halla Mountain, which is in a national park and is the highest mountain in my country. Halla Mountain is a dormant volcano that has a big crater lake at the top, and you can see plenty of alpine plants and other vegetation on your way up the mountain. Jeju's local specialties are another reason to visit there. Besides the fresh raw seafood, the barbecued pork from Jeju's black pigs is very juicy and savory. I really like Jeju Island and plan to visit there the upcoming winter again.

[해석 p.303 참조]

IH 답변 파헤치기

좋아하는 여행지 소개하면서 서두 열기

- My favorite destination is Seoraksan, which is in Gangwon Province. I've been there almost every summer with my family since my sophomore year of university.
  제가 가장 좋아하는 여행지는 강원도에 있는 설악산입니다. 저는 대학교 2학년 때부터 가족과 함께 거의 매 해 여름마다 그곳에 가고 있습니다.
- I often travel to Busan since my close friend has been living there since marriage. I was unfamiliar with the city at first, but after visiting there several times, I became a huge fan of it.
  저는 부산에 자주 가는데, 친한 친구가 결혼한 후에 그곳에서 살고 있기 때문입니다. 처음에는 그 도시가 좀 낯설었지만, 몇 번 방문하다 보니 너무 좋아졌습니다.
- I want to choose Gyeongju as my favorite travel destination in my country. Unlike many other large cities, it conserves a number of archaeological sites and historic remains. I enjoy traveling around the city by myself.
  저는 경주를 우리나라에서 가장 좋아하는 여행지로 꼽고 싶습니다. 많은 대도시들과는 달리, 경주는 고고학적 장소들과 역사적인 유물들이 아주 많습니다. 저는 혼자 그곳을 다니는 것을 좋아합니다.

여행지에서 할 수 있는 것 관련 아이디어

- I appreciate natural views and get fresh air, strolling through the woods.
  저는 산림욕을 하면서 자연의 경관도 감상하고 신선한 공기도 마십니다.
- I enjoy fresh seafood at many restaurants and hangouts and sometimes catch fish with local people.
  저는 많은 식당과 단골집들에서 신선한 해산물을 먹고 가끔은 그 지역 사람들과 고기도 잡습니다.
- I like watching sunset at the vacation place. It reminds me that I'm away from home.
  저는 여행지에서 일몰을 바라보는 것을 좋아합니다. 제가 집에서 떠나 있다는 것을 상기시켜줍니다.
- At the last night of the trip, we always have a bonfire party. We play music, sing, dance, and play Truth or Dare.
  우리는 여행 마지막 날에 항상 모닥불 파티를 합니다. 음악을 틀고, 노래도 부르고, 춤도 추고, 진실게임도 합니다.

해당 여행지를 좋아하는 이유

- The sound of the waves brings a feeling of serenity, and I can completely stay away from stress and tension.
  파도소리는 고요한 느낌을 갖게 해줘서 저는 긴장과 스트레스로부터 완전히 벗어날 수 있습니다.
- The city has traditional and beautiful architecture and I like its upbeat atmosphere.
  그 도시는 전통적이면서 아름다운 건물이 있고 저는 그 도시의 낙관적인 분위기를 좋아합니다.

Word 여행지 관련된 표현들

- **capital city** 수도
- **tourist attraction** 관광명소
- **local food/people** 현지 음식/현지인들
- **local specialties** 지역 특산품들
- **hangout** (자주 가는)장소, 단골집
- **historic/archeological site** 역사적인/고고학적인 장소
- **ruins/remains/relics** 유물
- **souvenir** 기념품

- **physical and mental refreshment** 육체적, 정신적 충전
- **breathtaking/pleasant scenery** 숨이 멎을 듯한/기분 좋은 풍경
- **enjoy spa(treatment)** 스파를 즐기다
- **refresh one's mind** 충전이 되다, 정신이 맑아지다
- **let one's worries float away** 걱정이 날아가버리다
- **forget work for a while** 잠시 일을 잊다
- **look deep into oneself** 내면을 들여다보다

MAKE YOUR ANSWER — 질문에 대한 여러분의 답변을 만들어보세요.

Tell me about your favorite travel destination in your country. When do you go there and who do you go with? Why do you like the place?

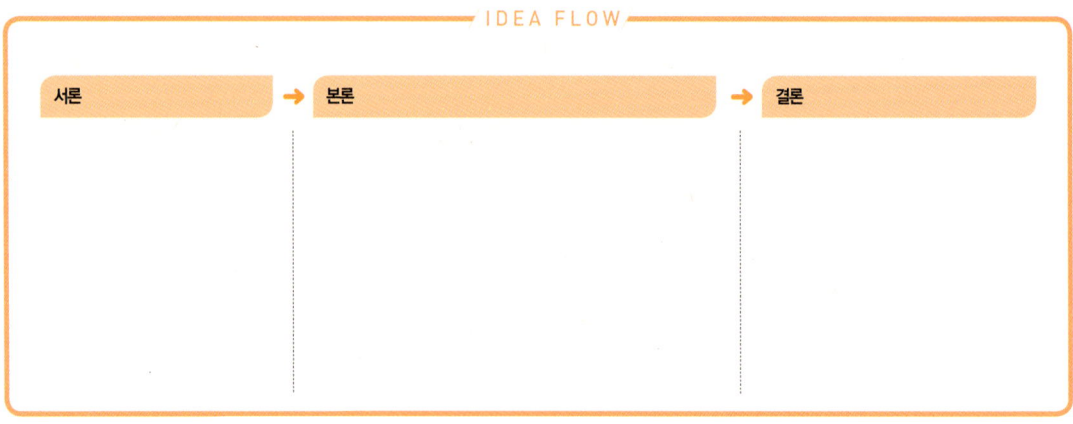

ANSWER

How do you prepare for a trip in your country? What do you do before you go on the trip?

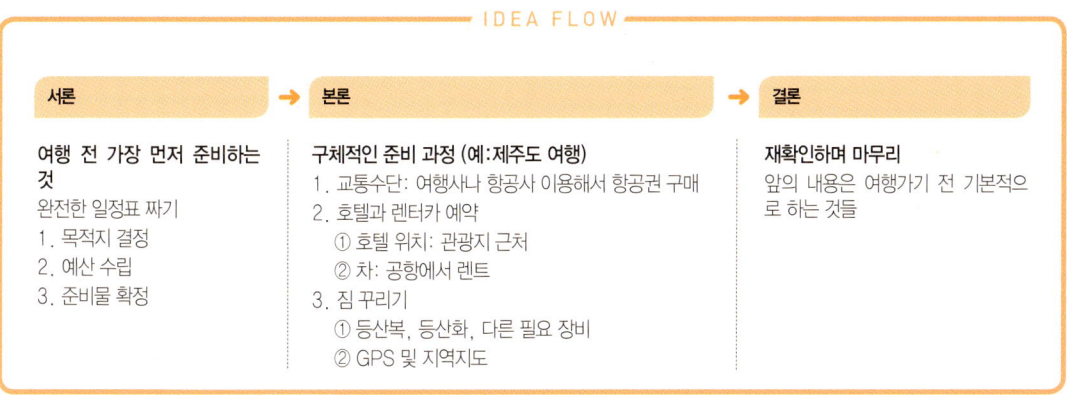

ANSWER

There are many things to consider before going on a trip. Making a complete itinerary from the beginning to the end is the first thing that I do. Determining which places I want to go makes me plan my budget and know what to bring on the trip. Once I set the departure date, I make my travel reservations. To mention my trip to Jeju Island as an example, many travel agencies and airlines offer good deals on airfare, so I can compare the prices to find the most reasonable one. After making my flight arrangements, I book a hotel and rental car next. The location of the hotel is crucial. It should be close to the attractions I am going to visit. I normally rent a car at the airport and drive to the hotel. After deciding on my transportation and accommodations, I start packing. Since I spend most of my time there hiking on Jeju Island, I pack climbing clothes, hiking boots, and other necessary equipment. I also always bring my GPS and a local map since they are essential and useful when driving around. This is what I basically do before going on a trip.

[해석 p.303 참조]

IH 답변 파헤치기

자신만의 여행 준비 스타일로 서두 열기

- I don't put too much effort to prepare for my trip since I enjoy an impromptu trip. When I want to take off to somewhere, I take as few belongings as possible with me and leave. I don't fix any transportation and accommodation in advance.
  저는 즉흥적인 여행을 좋아하기 때문에 여행 준비하는 데 그렇게 애쓰지 않습니다. 어디론가 떠나고 싶을 때 최소한의 소지품만 챙겨서 떠납니다. 교통편과 숙박도 미리 정해놓지 않습니다.

짐 싸는 준비 관련 아이디어

- I pack light because I don't want to bother dragging bulky suitcases. For example, I pack minimum underwear and socks. I can wash them in my hotel room.
  저는 무거운 여행가방을 끌고 가는 수고를 하고 싶지 않기 때문에 짐을 가볍게 쌉니다. 예를 들면 속옷과 양말은 최소한만 가져갑니다. 호텔방에서 세탁이 가능하니까요.
- I always take my own towel to my trip. I suspect the tower the hotel provides is clean.
  저는 여행갈 때 제 수건을 꼭 챙겨갑니다. 호텔에서 주는 수건이 깨끗할지 의심스럽습니다.
- I pack my slippers or flip flops. Some hotels don't offer them.
  저는 슬리퍼나 조리를 챙겨 갑니다. 어떤 호텔들은 안 주더라고요.
- Since I like walking or hiking in most travel places, I need to prepare comfortable shoes.
  저는 대부분의 여행지에서 걷거나 등반하는 것을 좋아하기 때문에 편안한 신발을 준비해야 합니다.
- One of the most important things that I pack is my diary. I write down some important information of the travel destinations on it while traveling.
  제가 여행갈 때 꼭 싸가는 것들 중 하나는 수첩입니다. 여행 다니면서 여행지에 대한 중요한 정보를 적어놓습니다.
- We always pack some snacks and bottled drinks for our kids. If we are stuck in traffic, they may be hungry. 우리는 아이들을 위해 과자와 음료를 꼭 챙깁니다. 차가 막혀 꼼짝 못하게 되면 애들이 배가 고플 수 있으니까요.

Word 여행지에서 이용할 숙박시설
- inn 여관
- motel 모텔
- hotel 호텔
- cabin 오두막
- B&B(=bed and breakfast) 아침을 제공하는 민박집

Word 여행에 이용할 교통편 관련 어휘들
- take a road trip 자동차 여행을 하다
- take a train trip 기차 여행을 하다
- go on a bicycle trip 자전거 여행을 하다
- enjoy a walking tour/travel on foot 도보 여행을 즐기다/도보로 여행하다
- rent a car at the airport 공항에서 차를 렌트하다
- buy a round trip ticket 왕복표를 사다

Word 여행갈 때 챙겨가야 할 물품들
- first aid kit 구급상자
- insect repellant 살충제
- sleeping bag/tent 침낭/텐트
- flashlight/lantern 손전등
- toiletries/cosmetics 세면용품/화장품
- sunscreen/sunblock 자외선 차단제
- razor/aftershave lotion 면도기/애프터셰이브 로션
- toothbrush/toothpaste 칫솔/치약
- beach towels 해변용 수건
- underwear/socks 속옷/양말
- hair dryer 헤어 건조기
- swimming suit/bathing suit/swimsuit 수영복
- sunglasses/cap/hat 선글라스/야구모자/모자
- map 지도
- camera/battery/recharger 카메라/건전지/충전기
- umbrella/parasol 우산/양산

MAKE YOUR ANSWER

질문에 대한 여러분의 답변을 만들어보세요.

How do you prepare for a trip in your country? What do you do before you go on the trip?

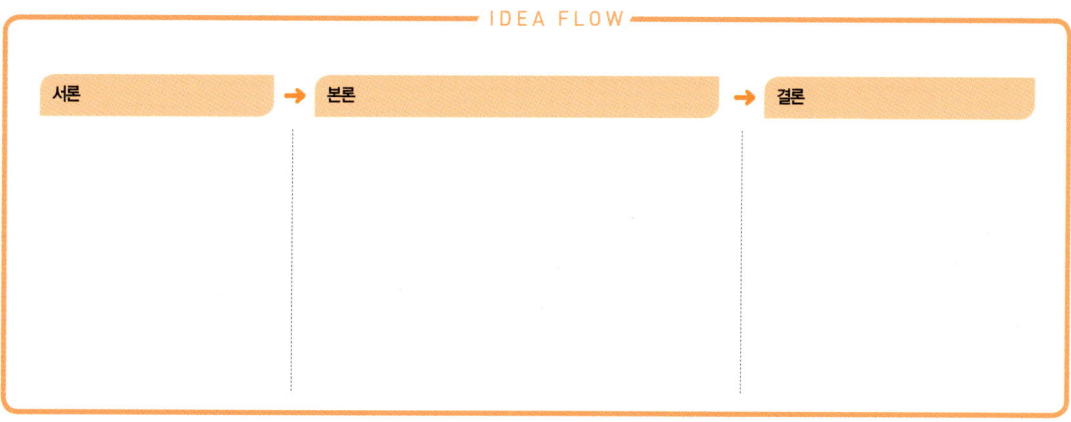

ANSWER

Q3 What are people's concerns and considerations regarding traveling? How do these concerns and considerations influence on the effort and expense for their trips?

― IDEA FLOW ―

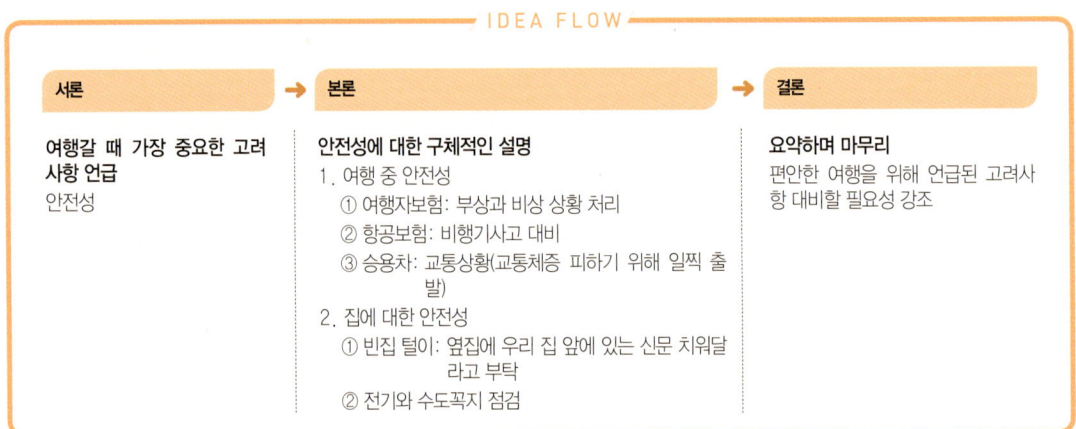

ANSWER

When people go on a trip, they are considering many things, including safety and expenses. The biggest concerns they have may be their safety while on their trip. For a safe and secure trip, they normally buy travel insurance, which can cover injuries and emergency situations for the duration of the trip. If they travel by airplane, the insurance is one of the most important things for them to take care of since its accident can often lead to a tragic disaster. If they drive, the traffic conditions are a critical issue. I usually leave home very early in the morning when driving to avoid heavy traffic, especially during holidays. People can also be concerned that burglars may break into their empty house during their trip. My family is no exception, so we ask our next-door neighbor to pick up our newspapers while we are away. Newspapers piled up in front of my door may indicate that nobody is currently at home. In addition, turning off all of the electrical appliances and faucets is necessary for travelers before they step out their door. All of these activities can be done with just a few minutes' care and effort, and they will make you feel comfortable during your trip.

[해석 p.304 참조]

IH 답변 파헤치기

일반적인 진술로 서두 열기

- There are so many things to consider before taking a trip, especially a long-term travel. So I make a checklist of everything I need to do before leaving home.
  여행을 떠나기 전에는, 특히 장기 여행일 경우 신경 써야 할 것들이 너무 많습니다. 그래서 저는 집을 떠나기 전 해야 할 모든 것을 체크리스트로 만들어놓습니다.
- It's always worrying to leave my house empty even for two or three days, so I ask my parents or younger brother to stay in my house while I am away. When they can't do it, I have to take care of several things before departure.
  집을 비우는 것은 다만 2~3일 동안이라 해도 늘 걱정스럽습니다. 그래서 저는 부모님이나 남동생에게 집을 비우는 동안 집에 와 있어 달라고 부탁합니다. 그게 여의치 않다면 출발 전 여러 가지를 처리해놓아야 합니다.

여행할 때 특별히 고려해야 할 점들 언급하기

- Since we have two kids, my wife and I always arrange our trip around them. We choose the travel destination that is suitable for them to have fun and do activities safely.
  우리는 아이가 둘이라서 여행은 항상 아이들 위주로 계획합니다. 여행지는 아이들이 즐거워하고 안전하게 활동할 수 있는 곳을 선택합니다.
- Since we raise a puppy, I have to ask someone to look after him. He needs food, baths, and regular walks. I usually ask my mother-in-law to take him.
  우리는 강아지 한 마리를 기르기 때문에 누군가에게 강아지를 보살펴 달라고 부탁해야 합니다. 식사, 목욕, 정기적인 산책이 필요하거든요. 저는 주로 시어머니께 강아지를 맡아달라고 부탁 드립니다.

Word pile up 쌓(이)다, 모아놓다, 많아지다

- 본문 Newspapers piled up in front of my door may indicate that nobody is currently at home.
- ex I always pile up documents and reference books on the desk when I work.
  저는 일할 때 꼭 서류들과 참고 도서들을 책상 위에 쌓아놓습니다.
- ex Emails and work have piled up when I got back from vacation.
  휴가에서 돌아와보니 이메일들과 할 일이 쌓여있었습니다.

Word break into(in) ~에 침입하다

- 본문 People can also be concerned that burglars may break into their empty house during their trip.
- ex Someone broke into my car and stole the car navigator.
  누군가가 내 차에 들어와서 자동차 내비게이터를 훔쳐갔어요.
- ex Thieves broke in and stole some money and valuables while the owner was away from the shop.
  주인이 상점을 비운 사이 도둑들이 침입해서 돈과 귀중품들을 가져갔습니다.

Word 여행하기 전 챙겨야 할 것들

- prearrange school absences for children 아이들 결석에 대해 미리 학교와 조정하다
- car maintenance 차 정비
- check due dates for utility bills 공과금 기일을 확인하다
- suspend newspaper/milk delivery service 뉴스/우유 배달을 정지시키다
- check the weather for one's destination 여행지 날씨를 확인하다
- turn off the heat/light/all the electrical equipment 가스 불/전기/전자제품 전원을 끄다

MAKE YOUR ANSWER

질문에 대한 여러분의 답변을 만들어보세요.

What are people's concerns and considerations regarding traveling? How do these concerns and considerations influence on the effort and expense for their trips?

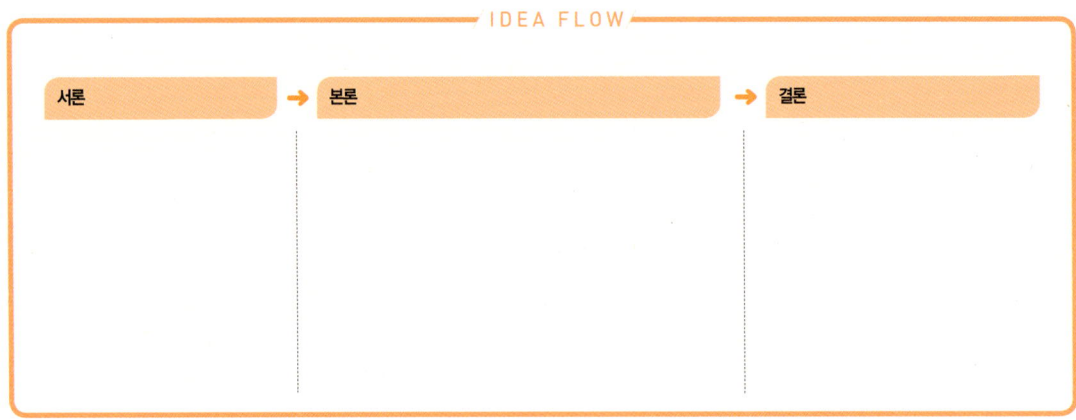

ANSWER

Memo

Lesson 19 해외출장

INTRO 출장은 여행과 휴가와 함께 독립된 OPIc 항목 7번에 자리잡고 있을 만큼 비중 있게 다뤄집니다. 여행과 마찬가지로 국내출장과 해외출장으로 분리 출제되고 있으며 돌발문제와 Role-play문제 등 그 유형도 다양하게 제시되고 있습니다. 이번 과에서는 해외출장지에서 예기치 않은 상황에 부딪쳐 그 상황을 설명하고 문제를 해결하기 위한 방안을 모색해보는 Role-play를 연습해보겠습니다.

IH 답변 전략

❶ 특정 요구 사항이 과제에 주어진 경우 문제에서 주어진 상황을 더 보충해 상황 설명하기
- 가져갔던 물품에 문제가 생겨 새 상품이 필요한 경우처럼 특정 요구 사항을 과제로 부여받는 경우 질문에 주어진 문제만 간단히 언급하지 말고 문제 발생 배경이나 이유 등의 상황 보충을 포함시켜 설명해주는 것이 바람직합니다.
- 요청 사항을 정확하게 전달함은 물론 물건을 받을 주소나 비상 시 연락처 등의 후속 조치도 추가하여 답변을 작성해봅니다.

❷ 예기치 않은 상황 설명하고 적절한 대안 제시하기
- 해외출장을 가다 보면 자료가 담긴 컴퓨터의 분실이나 행사 취소 등의 예기치 않은 일들이 벌어지기 쉽습니다. 업무와 관련한 급작스런 상황들을 적어놓고 그 상황을 설명하는 연습을 해 봅니다.
- 각 상황들에 맞는 대안을 준비해놓아야 합니다.

❸ 출장을 하면서 겪었던 다양한 에피소드 소개하기
- Role-play 상황에 준비해놓았던 각종 사건들은 경험 소개하기 유형의 좋은 소재가 될 수 있습니다.
- 계약, 제품 소개, 공장 견학 등 해외출장지에서 겪은 경험의 소재들을 많이 준비해 놓고 이를 토대로 논리적인 답변을 준비해두어야 합니다.

'해외출장'에서는 어떠한 질문들이 출제될까요? 다음의 예상 질문에 대해 여러분은 어떻게 답변할지 한 번 생각해 보세요.

1. You indicated in the survey that you go on a business trip. How frequently do you go overseas for business? What are the main purposes for the trips? Who do you usually go with? Give me all the details.

2. I'd like to know about your favorite city you have visited on business. Where was it and what did you go there for? Why do you like the city the most?

3. What kinds of things do you typically pack in your suitcase for your business trips? Why do you always take them to your business travel?

4. I'd like to give you a situation and ask you to act it out. You are going to travel abroad for business. Call your business partner and ask him or her three to four questions about the travel destination.

5. I'm sorry, but there is a problem you need to resolve. You are waiting to board at the airport for a business meeting with your client, but your flight has been delayed. Call your client and explain the situation including some alternatives to solve the problem.

✓6. I'll give you a situation and ask you to act it out. You are on a business trip, but the sample you brought has a problem. Call your boss and leave a message explaining the situation and asking for a new sample.

✓7. I'm sorry, but there is a problem you need to resolve. Your boss told you the new sample won't arrive until tonight, but you need to use it when you meet your business associate this afternoon. Call him or her and explain your situation including some alternatives to solve the problem.

✓8. That's the end of the situation. Please tell me about the most unexpected or difficult incident you have had during your business trip. What was the incident about and how did you handle the situation? Tell me the whole story from the beginning to the end.

I'll give you a situation and ask you to act it out. You are on a business trip, but the sample you brought has a problem. Call your boss and leave a message explaining the situation and asking for a new sample.

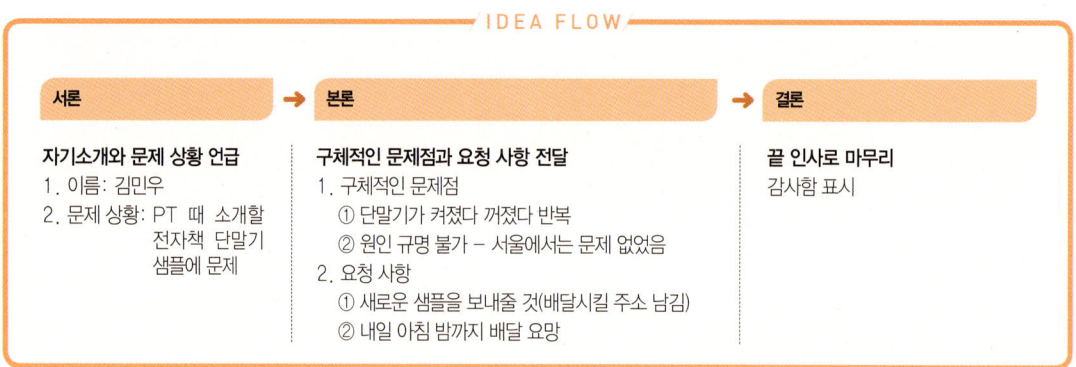

ANSWER

Hello, this is Min Woo Kim. It appears that I'm having a trouble with the sample of an e-book reader that I brought here. It keeps turning on and off. I recharged it and also changed the battery, but the same thing happened. I don't think I brought a defective device because I didn't find any operational problems when I tested it in Seoul. I don't think I can fix it here, so could you send me a new one? You know I brought the Nobo PTR3, don't you? Oh, I think it'd be safer that you send me a few more samples just in case. I'll leave the address you need to get them delivered to. I'm at Diamond Hotel, 220 West Mart Drive, Chicago, Illinois 60632. I'm supposed to introduce the device when I make a presentation tomorrow afternoon, so they should be arrived by tomorrow morning at latest. Thank you and talk to you later!

[해석 p.304 참조]

IH 답변 파헤치기

문장 구조 응용하기
It appears that S+V (분명히/아무래도)~인 것 같다
- 본문 It appears that I'm having a trouble with the sample of an e-book reader that I brought here.
- ex It appears that the meeting hasn't started yet.
  회의는 아직 시작하지 않은 것 같네요.

부가 의문문(tag question)
평서문 뒤에 의문문을 첨가해주는 것으로, 자신이 한 말을 상대방에게 확인 받으려고 할 때 즐겨 사용됩니다.
※ 부가의문문 형태: 긍정 평서문 + 부정 의문문
　　　　　　　　　부정 평서문 + 긍정 의문문 (동사의 시제와 성격은 반드시 일치시켜 줍니다.)
- 본문 You know I brought the Nobo PTR3, don't you?
- ex We are supposed to meet at 5 pm, aren't we?
  우리 오후 5시에 만나기로 되어 있죠, 그렇죠?
- ex You won't attend the seminar, will you? 당신은 세미나에 참석 안 하죠, 그렇죠?
- ex Megan has known Jim for 5 years, hasn't she? 메간은 짐을 5년 동안 알고 지냈죠, 그렇죠?

문제가 발생했음을 알리면서 서두 열기
- I've got a problem here. 이쪽에 문제가 좀 생겼습니다.
- There's a problem with a sample that I brought. 제가 가져온 견본품에 문제가 좀 있어요.
- I'm in big trouble here. 여기 큰 문제가 생겼어요.

주어진 상황과 문제의 원인을 설명하기
- The sample e-book reader has black horizontal lines running across the screen. I think I brought a defective one. 견본 전자책 화면에 검정 선들이 보여요. 아무래도 제가 불량품을 가져온 것 같아요.
- The screen on the sample mobile phone is cracked. I dropped it while taking it out of the package.
  견본 휴대폰 액정에 금이 갔어요. 제가 상자에서 꺼내다가 그만 떨어뜨렸어요.
- I lost my laptop that my presentation materials were stored on. At the airport, I put it on the floor when I was picking up my luggage in the baggage claim. I forgot to take it with me when I left there. I tried to get it back later, but someone already took it.
  프레젠테이션 자료가 저장되어 있는 제 노트북을 잃어버렸어요. 공항에서 짐을 찾을 때 그걸 바닥에 놓아두었거든요. 제가 거길 떠날 때 그만 잊어버리고 가져가질 않은 거예요. 나중에 다시 찾으려고 했지만 누군가 이미 가져가 버렸어요.
- The list of local staff members hasn't fixed yet. I can't conduct market research tomorrow in this situation. I think I have to postpone the research.
  현장요원들이 아직 정해지지도 않았어요. 이런 상황에서는 내일 시장조사를 할 수가 없어요. 아무래도 조사를 연기해야 할 것 같습니다.

Idiom just in case 만약을 대비해서, 혹시 모르니
- 본문 Oh, I think it'd be safer that you send me a few more samples just in case.
- ex I'll arrive at the designated place 30 minutes before the trade show starts just in case.
  혹시 모르니 무역박람회 시작 30분 전에 지정된 장소에 제가 가 있겠습니다.
  cf) in case S+V ~할 걸 대비해서, ~할지 모르니
- ex I'll give you the number for the hotel where I'm staying in case my phone is not working.
  혹시 제 전화기가 작동하지 않을 걸 대비해서 제가 묵고 있는 호텔 전화번호를 알려드리겠습니다.

질문에 대한 여러분의 답변을 만들어보세요.

I'll give you a situation and ask you to act it out. You are on a business trip, but the sample you brought has a problem. Call your boss and leave a message explaining the situation and asking for a new sample.

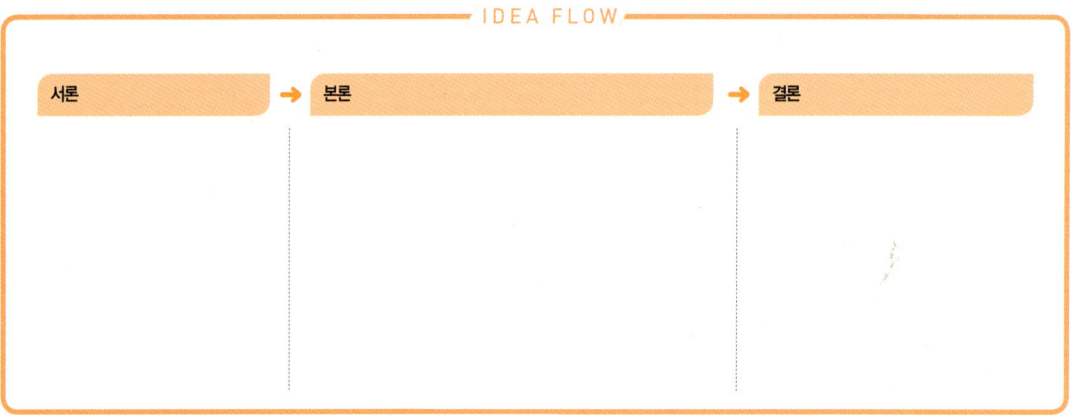

ANSWER

I'm sorry, but there is a problem you need to resolve. Your boss told you the new sample won't arrive until tonight, but you need to use it when you meet your business associate this afternoon. Call him or her and explain your situation including some alternatives to solve the problem.

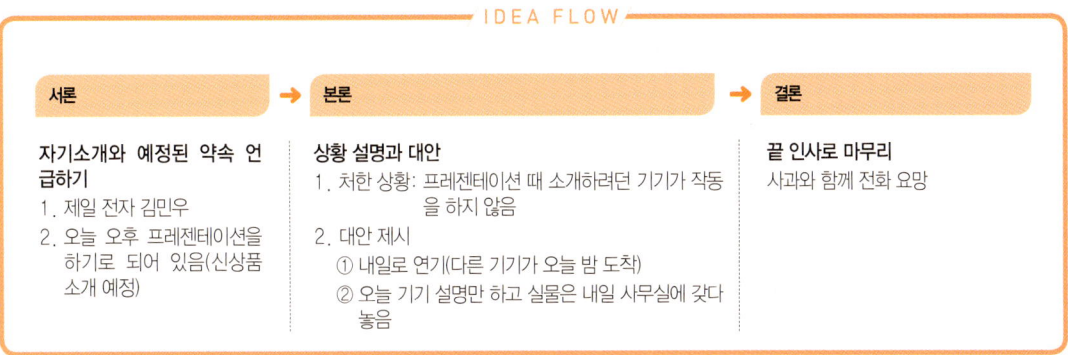

ANSWER

Hello, Mr. Thomson? This is Min Woo Kim from Jaeil Electronics Corporation. I'm supposed to make a presentation to you this afternoon. I am expecting to introduce the Nobo PTR3 that will come into the market next month during the presentation. But unfortunately, the device that I brought is not functioning properly, which makes it impossible to present it to you today. Could we push back the presentation until tomorrow? Another device is in the mail and will arrive here tonight, so I can visit your office anytime tomorrow. If you are only available today, then I'll visit you today as scheduled and give you the general instruction of the product. Then, I'll just leave the sample device at your office tomorrow. You can review it whenever you're free. I really apologize to you for the inconvenience and hope you will understand my situation. Please call me back if you get this message. Thank you.

[해석 p.304 참조]

IH 답변 파헤치기

약속 변경할 때 사용할 수 있는 표현들

1. Could we/I ~? ~할 수 있을까요?, ~해도 될까요?
- Could we postpone the meeting? 미팅을 연기할 수 있을까요?
- Could we put off the meeting until tomorrow? 회의를 내일로 연기해도 될까요?
- Could I reschedule the presentation until tomorrow afternoon?
  프레젠테이션을 내일 오후로 재조정해도 될까요?

2. Do you mind if I/we ~? ~해도 될까요?
- Do you mind if I visit your office tomorrow, not this afternoon?
  제가 오늘 오후 말고 내일 사무실로 찾아가도 괜찮을까요?
- Do you mind if we meet at 4, instead of 3? 3시 대신 4시에 만나도 괜찮을까요?

3. Would it be possible that S+V? ~하는 게 가능할까요?, ~해도 될까요?
- Would it be possible that we meet at 11 a.m. tomorrow instead?
  = Would it be possible for us to meet at 11 a.m. tomorrow instead?
  대신 내일 오전 11시에 만나도 될까요?

Idiom come into(onto) the market 시판되다, 출시되다 (=be released)
- 본문 I am expecting to introduce the Nobo PTR3 that will come into the market next month during the presentation.
- ex Our new refrigerator will come into the market within this month.
  우리의 새로운 냉장고가 이번 달 내로 시판될 것입니다.
- ex The digital camera was released last May. 그 디지털 카메라는 지난 5월 출시되었습니다.

Word in the mail 배달 중 (=on its way)
- 본문 Another device is in the mail and will arrive here tonight.
- ex The electrical parts are on their way, but the earliest we can get them is tomorrow afternoon.
  전자부품들이 배달 중에 있긴 하지만 빨라야 내일 오후에나 받을 수 있습니다.

Word as scheduled 예정대로 (=as planned, as arranged)
- 본문 If you are only available today, then I'll visit you today as scheduled and give you the general instruction of the product.
- ex I was able to make a presentation as arranged. 저는 예정대로 프레젠테이션을 할 수 있었습니다.
- ex The conference didn't go well as planned. 회의는 계획대로 잘 진행되지 않았습니다.

사과하면서 마무리하기

- I apologize for any inconvenience that this delay may cause you.
  이번 일을 미룸으로써 겪으실 불편에 사과 드립니다.
- I'm so/really/terribly sorry for this delay. It won't happen again. 정말 죄송합니다. 다시는 이런 일이 없을 거예요.
- I'm very sorry to bother you again, and I'll see you tomorrow. 다시 한 번 매우 죄송하고 내일 뵙겠습니다.
- I'm sorry to trouble you, and I'll meet you then. 귀찮게 해서 죄송하고 그 때 뵙겠습니다.

MAKE YOUR ANSWER

질문에 대한 여러분의 답변을 만들어보세요.

I'm sorry, but there is a problem you need to resolve. Your boss told you the new sample won't arrive until tonight, but you need to use it when you meet your business associate this afternoon. Call him or her and explain your situation including some alternatives to solve the problem.

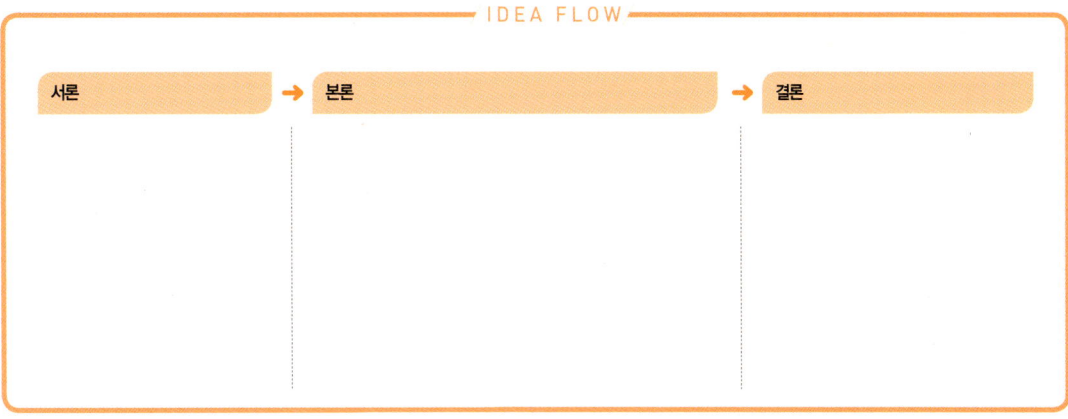

ANSWER

Q3 That's the end of the situation. Please tell me about the most unexpected or difficult incident you have had during your business trip. What was the incident about and how did you handle the situation? Tell me the whole story from the beginning to the end.

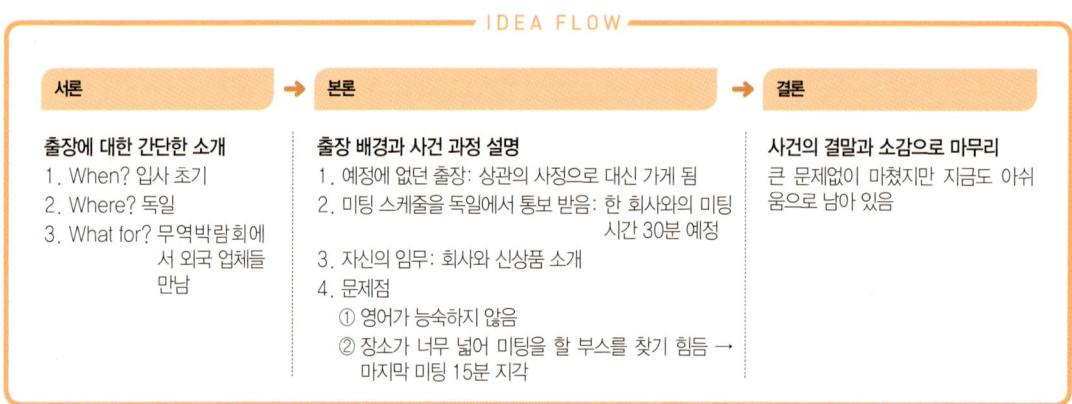

ANSWER

I went on a three-day business trip to Frankfurt in Germany when I just started working for my company. The purpose of the trip was to join the Frankfurt trade show and meet some foreign businessmen. That was actually an unscheduled trip to me. My boss was originally scheduled to take the trip by himself, but he had a family emergency. Therefore, I was urged to attend the trade show at the last minute, so I wasn't informed of the meeting schedule until I arrived in Germany. According to the schedule, I was given 30 minutes to complete a meeting for each company. During the meeting, I had to introduce my company and our new products briefly. The job might seem simple and easy, but it was challenging for me. Since my English was not that good, I often stuttered especially when I had to answer their questions. What's worse, the conference hall, where the trade show was held, was too huge to find the right location of the booth that I had to drop by. I ended up being 15 minutes late for the last meeting. Fortunately, I managed to finish my business trip without a serious problem, but I still wish I had completed my task better at that time.

[해석 p.304 참조]

IH 답변 파헤치기

문장 구조 응용하기

be scheduled to 부정사 ~할 예정이다 (=be supposed to 부정사)
- I was scheduled to start a meeting with my client today at 3 pm, but we pushed it back to another day. 고객과 3시에 미팅을 시작하려 했으나 다른 날로 연기했습니다.
- The assignment is scheduled to be completed by next week. 그 업무는 다음 주까지 완료될 예정입니다.

Word trade show/fair/exhibition 무역박람회
- 본문 The purpose of the trip was to join the Frankfurt trade show and meet some foreign businessmen.
- ex The London trade exhibition has been delayed until September 21.
  런던 무역박람회가 9월 21일로 연기되었습니다.
- ex We were not allowed to take pictures at the trade exhibition.
  그 무역박람회에서는 사진을 찍는 것이 허용되지 않았습니다.

Word family emergency 급한 집안일
- 본문 My boss was originally scheduled to take the trip by himself, but he had a family emergency.
- ex I couldn't help but get back home early from the business trip because of my family emergency.
  저는 급한 가정일 때문에 출장 중에 일찍 귀국할 수 밖에 없었습니다.

Word stutter 더듬거리다
- 본문 Since my English was not that good, I often stuttered especially when I had to answer their questions.
- ex Since I was very embarrassed at her abrupt questions, I stuttered more.
  그녀의 갑작스런 질문에 무척 당황했기 때문에 저는 더 더듬거렸습니다.

Idiom drop by (잠깐 동안)들르다, 방문하다 (=stop by, make a short visit)
- 본문 What's worse, the conference hall, where the trade show was held, was too huge to find the right location of the booth that I had to drop by.
- ex I dropped by the factory to check our manufacturing facilities.
  저는 생산 설비들을 둘러보기 위해 공장에 잠깐 들렀습니다.
- ex When I go to foreign countries, I try to stop by local bookstores.
  저는 외국에 가면 지역 서점에 들르려 노력합니다.

사건의 시기와 장소를 언급하면서 서두 열기

- I faced a difficult situation when I went on a business trip to Singapore last month.
  지난 달 싱가포르에 출장을 갔을 때 저는 어려운 상황에 부딪쳤습니다.
- I had a terrible experience during a business trip to Los Angeles in June.
  저는 6월에 로스앤젤레스로 간 출장 중에 지긋지긋한 경험을 했습니다.

출장 중에 벌어지는 예기치 않은 사건 아이디어

- Once we arrived at the trade fair, there was no booth assigned to us. Soon we found out that our company name was left out on the list of participants.
  막상 무역박람회장에 도착했더니, 우리 부스가 배정된 게 없는 거였습니다. 곧 우리 회사 이름이 참가자 명단에서 누락되었다는 것을 알았습니다.
- After eating out for dinner in Rome, I got lost on my way back to the hotel. I didn't even remember the name of the hotel. 로마에서 외식을 하고 호텔에 돌아가던 길에 길을 잃어버렸습니다. 저는 호텔의 이름조차 기억이 나지 않았습니다.

Lesson 19 | 해외출장   243

질문에 대한 여러분의 답변을 만들어보세요.

That's the end of the situation. Please tell me about the most unexpected or difficult incident you have had during your business trip. What was the incident about and how did you handle the situation? Tell me the whole story from the beginning to the end.

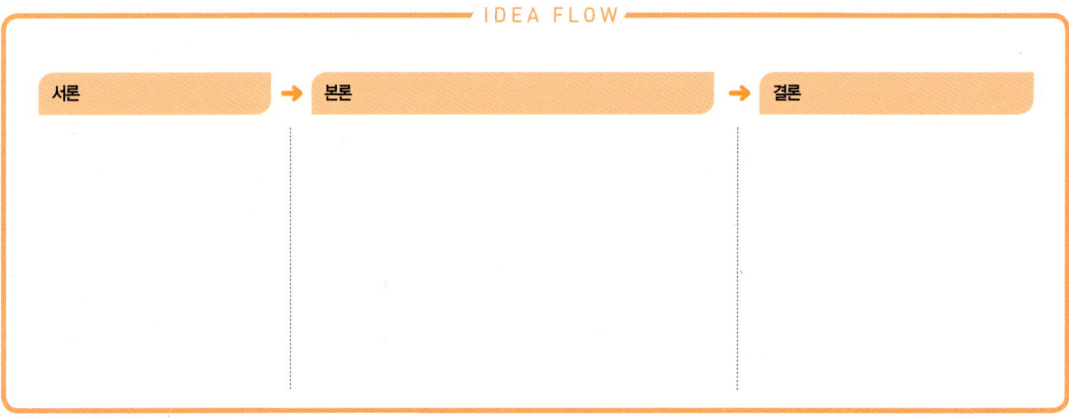

ANSWER

Memo

Lesson 20 해외여행

Oral Proficiency Interview-computer

INTRO

여행은 OPIc에서 워낙 비중 있게 다뤄지는 주제라서 그 범위도 국내여행과 해외여행으로 나뉘어 출제됩니다. 여행은 많은 사람들이 좋아하는 보편적인 주제인 만큼 다른 주제들에 비해 준비하기가 좀 수월하고 편안하다고 볼 수 있습니다. 또한 여행에 대한 답변을 준비하면, 그것이 출장과 휴가에 대한 답변에도 활용이 되기 때문에 여러모로 유익하고 즐거운 주제라고 할 수 있습니다. 먼저 해외여행은 국내여행에 비해 체류기간이 긴 만큼 실제로도 더 꼼꼼한 여행 준비가 필요하겠죠? 그래서 그런지 OPIc 해외여행에서도 여행지에 대한 정보를 문의하는 상황과 항공편과 관련된 예기치 않은 상황 등이 자주 출제되고 있으니 이번 과에서는 이를 대비한 Role-play를 준비해보겠습니다.

IH 답변 전략

① 전화로 여행 정보를 문의하거나 여행에 대해 의논하기

- 여행사에 전화를 걸어 문의를 하는 상황이나 친구에게 여행을 제안하는 상황 등 제시되는 상황은 다양할 수 있겠지만 답변에 들어가야 할 필수 여행 정보는 공통적입니다. 즉, 목적지, 여행 일정, 동행인 수 등의 기본적인 정보를 서론 부분에 포함시켜 줍니다.
- 기본 정보를 간단히 언급해 준 다음에는 여행과 관련한 구체적인 질문을 구성해야 합니다. 항공편의 가격, 가능한 여행수단, 여행지에서 할 수 있는 활동들 등 자신만의 질문을 준비해 봅시다.

② 예기치 않은 상황 설명하고 대안 제시하기

- 해외여행을 하다 보면 사소한 문제로도 당황할 수 있고, 여러 가지 예기치 않은 상황도 벌어지기 쉽겠죠. 항공편 취소나 소지품 분실, 급작스런 배앓이나 식중독 등 발생할 수 있는 상황들을 생각해서 정리해 봅니다.
- 문제에서 제시된 상황은 답변 초반에 간단하게만 설명해주고 대부분의 답변은 대안으로 구성되어야 합니다. 가능한 상황이나 사건들을 모두 적어놓고 각 상황마다 적합한 대안을 준비해두어야 하겠습니다.

③ 여행 관련 경험담 소개하기

- 위에서 제시된 상황들을 여행 관련 경험담의 소재로 활용할 수 있습니다.
- 사건 배경과 사건의 과정, 그리고 마지막으로 그 경험에 대한 짧은 소감으로 답변을 준비해 봅시다.

'해외여행'에서는 어떠한 질문들이 출제될까요? 다음의 예상 질문에 대해 여러분은 어떻게 답변할지 한 번 생각해 보세요.

1. You indicated in the survey that you travel abroad. Tell me your favorite overseas trip that you have taken. Where did you travel to and when did you leave? What made you like the trip so much?

2. How do you prepare for your overseas trip? What do you normally do before you leave for the destination? Give me all the details.

3. I'd like to know about your first overseas trip. Which country or city did you go to and where did you stay? What did you like about the destination and what did you not like about it?

✓ 4. I'll give you a situation and ask you to act it out. You are planning to go on an overseas trip. Call a travel agency and ask three or four questions about the trip.

✓ 5. I'm sorry, but there is a problem you need to resolve. When you arrived at the airport, you found that your flight has been canceled. Unfortunately, all the other flights are booked, too. Call your travel agency and explain your situation including three alternatives to solve the problem.

✓ 6. That's the end of the situation. You might have experienced unexpected, surprising, or funny incidents during your overseas trip. Where and when did you have the experience? What exactly happened then? What made you still remember the incident?

7. I'll give you a situation and ask you to act it out. You just checked in at the hotel and want to start traveling around the city. Ask the receptionist three or four questions about what you can do today.

8. I'm sorry, but there is a problem you need to resolve. The travel agency called you and told you that the tour package you and your friend had looked into was not available now. Call you friend and explain the situation including three alternatives to solve the problem.

9. Why do you think many people like to travel? What do you think they get from their trips? Explain in as much detail as possible.

Q1 I'll give you a situation and ask you to act it out. You are planning to go on an overseas trip. Call a travel agency and ask three or four questions about the trip.

IDEA FLOW

서론 →	본론 →	결론
자기소개와 용건 1. 이름: 김현민 2. 용건: 여행상품 문의 　① Where? 푸켓 　② When? 올 7월 　③ How long? 나흘 　④ With whom? 아내와	**질문하기** 1. 비행기표 가능한지? 가격은 얼마인지? 2. 비행기표와 호텔을 함께 묶는 것과 따로 예약하는 것의 가격 차이는 얼마인지? 3. 단체여행의 가격과 기간은? 4. 단체여행에서도 스쿠버 다이빙 배울 수 있는지? 5. 단체여행 일정표를 보내줄 수 있는지?	**정보 전달 방식의 언급과 감사 표시** 1. 이 메일 주소 알려줌 2. 감사함 표시

ANSWER

Hello, TBC Travel Agency? My name is Hyun Min Kim. I'm calling to ask you some questions about the travel products you have. My wife and I are planning a 4-day trip to Phuket in July this year. Is it possible to get plane tickets? If it is, could you tell me how much they are? I've heard that it's more economical to book my flight and hotel together than separately. What's the price difference? We're also thinking of going on a package tour. How much is it and how long is the tour for? I'm wondering if I can learn to scuba dive through the package tour as I can do through my independent tour. I'd also like you to send me the itinerary for the trip. My email address is HMK@credu.com. Thank you in advance!

[해석 p.305 참조]

IH 답변 파헤치기

문장 구조 응용하기

1. 간접의문문을 이용한 정보 요청

- What should I prepare for the group trip?
  = Could you tell me what I should prepare for the group trip?
  그 그룹 관광을 위해서는 제가 뭘 준비해야 하나요?

- How long does it take to get to Fukuoka by ship?
  = Do you know how long it takes to get to Fukuoka by ship?
  후쿠오카까지 배로 가는데 얼마나 걸리는지 아세요?

2. 평서문을 이용한 정보 요청

본문 I'm wondering if I can learn to scuba dive through the package tour as I can do through my independent tour.
  = Can I learn to scuba dive through the package tour as I can do through my independent tour?

ex I'm sorry, but I'm wondering if I can cancel my reservation.
  = I'm sorry, but can I cancel my reservation?
  죄송하지만, 제 예약을 취소할 수 있는지 궁금합니다.

본문 I'd also like you to send me the itinerary for the trip.
  = Could you send me the itinerary for the trip?

ex I'd like you to email me all the information.
  = Would you please email me all the information?
  모든 정보를 제게 이메일로 보내주시겠습니까?

여행사에 문의할 수 있는 사항들

- What is the minimum number of people on a tour? 관광의 최소 인원은 몇 사람입니까?
- When I arrive at the airport, can I rent a car to get around the city?
  공항에 도착하면 차를 빌려 도시를 다닐 수 있습니까?
- If I book the hotel and flight together, do I get special discounts?
  호텔과 항공편을 함께 예약하면 할인 혜택을 받을 수 있습니까?
- Can I get a discount if I travel with a family of five or more?
  다섯 명 이상의 가족여행을 간다면 할인을 받을 수 있습니까?
- Do you offer us adequate travel insurance? Or should I purchase personal travel insurance?
  우리한테 적절한 여행보험을 제공하는 건가요? 아니면 제가 개인적으로 여행보험을 구매해야 하나요?

Word 여행(준비) 관련 표현들

- **plan one's trip/itinerary** 여행일정을 짜다
- **go on a trip/take a trip/travel** 여행을 가다
- **go on vacation** 휴가를 가다
- **go on a honeymoon** 신혼여행을 가다
- **go on a day trip** 당일치기 여행을 가다
- **travel alone/with one's family** 혼자(가족과) 여행가다
- **package tour** 패키지 관광
- **reserve(book) a plane ticket** 항공권을 예약하다
- **change/confirm/cancel one's reservation** 예약을 변경/확인/취소하다
- **purchase a plane ticket** 항공권을 구매하다
- **apply for a visa** 비자를 신청하다
- **final destination** 최종 목적지
- **departure/arrival time** 출발/도착 시간
- **check in** 탑승 수속을 밟다
- **take off/land** 이륙하다/착륙하다

MAKE YOUR ANSWER

질문에 대한 여러분의 답변을 만들어보세요.

I'll give you a situation and ask you to act it out. You are planning to go on an overseas trip. Call a travel agency and ask three or four questions about the trip.

ANSWER

Q2 I'm sorry, but there is a problem you need to resolve. When you arrived at the airport, you found that your flight has been canceled. Unfortunately, all the other flights are booked, too. Call your travel agency and explain your situation including three alternatives to solve the problem.

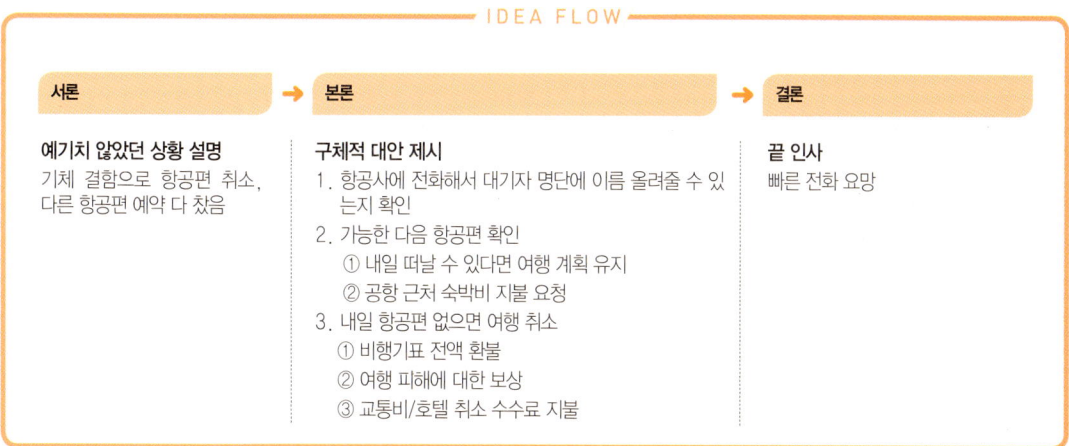

ANSWER

Hello, Mr. Yoon? This is Hyun Min Kim. I called to let you know about this unexpected, ridiculous situation. When we were about to check in at the airport, we found that our flight has been canceled due to mechanical troubles. What is worse, all the other flights have been booked today! We're now very frustrated, but I want to get our travel plans back in order if possible. Would you call the reservation hotline for more exact information? They could put us on the waiting list for the flight. If that's not possible, please check about the next available flight we can take. We don't have to give up this trip if we leave for our destination tomorrow. But even so, you need to pay for a hotel stay near the airport since we came from Cheongju to Incheon. If there is no available flight tomorrow, we will cancel our trip, so you need to give us a full refund for the tickets we bought. I'd also like you to provide compensation for our lost vacation. The transportation and hotel cancelation fees will be surely additional. Call me back as soon as possible.

[해석 p.305 참조]

IH 답변 파헤치기

문제 상황이 발생했음을 암시하면서 서두열기

- **본문** I called to let you know about this unexpected, ridiculous situation.
- **ex** I think I've got a serious problem here.
  아무래도 여기 심각한 문제가 생긴 것 같아요.
- **ex** You need to know about what happened here.
  여기 무슨 일이 발생했는지 알아야 합니다.

문제 상황을 정확히 전달하기

- I just arrived at the airport and saw the Word "Canceled" pop up on the departure screen. There aren't any flights available to take here either.
  방금 공항에 도착해서 출발 화면에 "취소"라는 글자가 올라온 걸 봤어요. 탈 수 있는 다른 항공편도 없고요.
- The airport personnel said my flight has been canceled because of its security issues. All other flights have already been booked, too!
  공항 직원이 그러는데 제 항공편이 보안상의 문제로 취소됐어요. 다른 항공편은 이미 다 예약이 찼고요!
  (※ 질문에는 항공편 취소 원인이 나오지 않았지만 답변에 이렇게 간단히 언급해줘도 좋습니다.)

Idiom what is worse = to top it all (off) = to make matters worse 설상가상으로, 엎친 데 덮친 격으로

- **본문** What is worse, all the other flights have been booked today!
- **ex** On the way to the airport, I had a car accident, my camera broke down, then to top it all, I left my passport at home.
  공항에 오는 길에 차 사고가 있었고, 카메라가 고장 났고, 엎친 데 덮친 격으로 제 여권을 집에 놓고 왔습니다.
- **ex** The phone arrived two days after the original estimated delivery date. To make matters worse, this isn't even what I ordered.
  전화기는 원래 예정된 배달 날짜에서 이틀 지나서야 도착했어요. 설상가상으로 이건 제가 골랐던 것도 아니에요.

Idiom give up 포기하다

- I can't give up this concert. You know how hard I've been practicing since last spring.
  저는 이 콘서트를 포기할 수 없어요. 작년 봄부터 제가 얼마나 열심히 연습을 해왔다는 걸 알잖아요.

Word leave for ~로 떠나다

- **본문** We don't have to give up this trip if we leave for our destination tomorrow.
- **ex** I'm planning to leave for London in the middle of October.
  10월 중순에 런던으로 떠날 계획입니다.
- **ex** The plane leaves for Philippines at 3:30 pm. 그 비행기는 오후 3시 30분에 필리핀으로 떠납니다.
  =The plane to Philippines departs at 3:30 pm. ※ depart는 사람이 떠난다고 할 때는 쓰지 않습니다.

예기치 않은 피해에 대한 불만 전달하기

- **본문** We're now very frustrated, but I want to get our travel plans back in order if possible.
- **ex** I've never been informed of this kind of situation before, so I'm quite confused now.
  이런 종류의 상황을 사전에 공지 받지 못해서 상당히 당황스럽군요.
- **ex** I am a little disappointed that you didn't even know about this cancelation until I called you. Don't you confirm the flights for your customers?
  제가 전화해서야 이 취소 사실을 알았다는 것이 좀 실망스럽네요. 당신들은 고객을 위해 비행 확인도 안 합니까?

질문에 대한 여러분의 답변을 만들어보세요.

I'm sorry, but there is a problem you need to resolve. When you arrived at the airport, you found that your flight has been canceled. Unfortunately, all the other flights are booked, too. Call your travel agency and explain your situation including three alternatives to solve the problem.

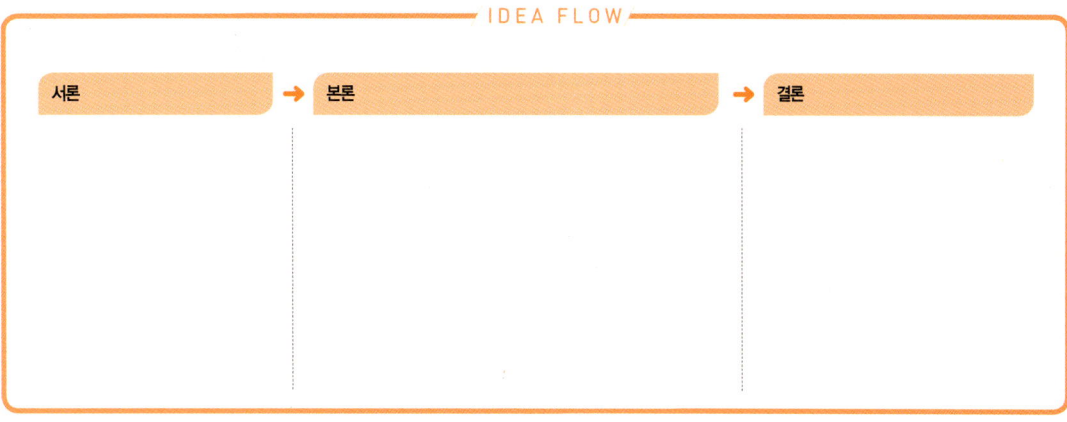

ANSWER

That's the end of the situation. You might have experienced unexpected, surprising, or funny incidents during your overseas trip. Where and when did you have the experience? What exactly happened then? What made you still remember the incident?

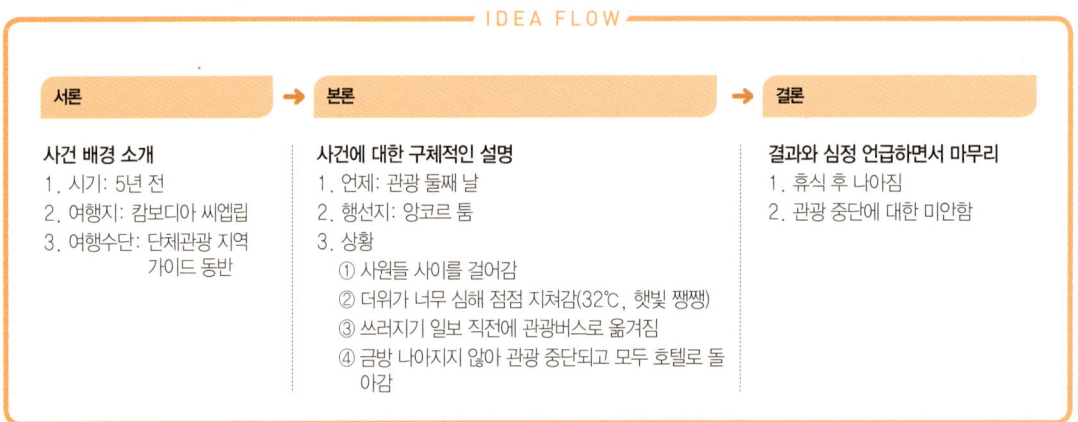

ANSWER

My friend and I took a package tour to Siem Reap in Cambodia five years ago. We had seven members all nice and gentle in our tour group. The tour was accompanied by an experienced local guide. The incident took place on the second day of the tour. It was a blazing hot day, and at around 2 pm, we arrived at Angkor Thom, which was a complex with several splendid temples. We got off the tour bus and walked from temples to temples to observe awesome ruins and Khmer art. But as times went by, I got more exhausted, sweating a lot from the heat. Although it was winter in Cambodia, the daytime temperature reached 32℃, and the sun was beating down. I felt dizzy and my arms and legs felt weak. I nearly fainted when my friend was surprised to see my pale face. He hurriedly told the guide about my condition, and I was carried to the tour bus. The guide and other tour members were so worried about me, but I didn't get better soon. We ended up stopping the tour and returned to the hotel. I felt better after resting in bed, but I felt so guilty about interrupting the tour.

[해석 p.305 참조]

IH 답변 파헤치기

Word blazing/burning/scorching 타는 듯한

- 본문 It was a blazing hot day, and at around 2 pm, we arrived at Angkor Thom, which was a complex with several splendid temples.
- ex As soon as we got to the island, we could sense the scorching heat of a midsummer day.
  우리는 그 섬에 도착하자마자 한 여름의 타는 듯한 더위를 느낄 수 있었습니다.
- ex We traveled around the city in the burning sun all day long.
  우리는 타는 듯한 태양 속에서 하루 종일 그 도시를 돌아다녔습니다.

Word end up ~ing 결국 ~하게 되다

- 본문 We ended up stopping the tour and returned to the hotel.
- ex After discussion with a travel agency, we ended up canceling our trip to Singapore.
  여행사와 상의 후 우리는 결국 싱가폴 여행을 취소하게 되었습니다.
- ex We ran toward the entrance as soon as we got out of the taxi but ended up missing the ferry.
  우리는 택시에서 내리자마자 입구로 뛰어갔지만 결국 여객선을 놓치고 말았습니다.
  (※예문에서 보여지듯이 end up~은 대부분의 경우 상황이 안 좋은 방향으로 귀결이 되었을 때 사용됩니다.)

Word be accompanied by ~을 동반하다, ~와 동행하다

- 본문 The tour was accompanied by an experienced local guide.
- ex Fortunately, we were accompanied by a Chinese-speaking travel agent.
  다행히도, 중국말을 할 수 있는 여행사 직원이 우리와 동행했습니다.
- ex Your application must be accompanied by supporting documents such as your transcripts and recommendation letters.
  당신의 지원서에는 성적표와 추천서와 같은 증빙서류들이 첨부되어야 합니다.

여행지에서 생길 수 있는 사건들에 관한 아이디어

- When I was traveling to Rome in Italy, I had my wallet stolen. Surprisingly, the pickpocket dressed as a police officer. I ran into him on the main street, and he said he had to check my passport. I didn't have any doubt of him because I believed he was a police officer. When I realized my wallet was missing, he had already disappeared.
  이태리 로마에 여행 갔을 때 지갑을 도둑맞았어요. 놀랍게도 소매치기는 경찰 복장을 하고 있었죠. 저는 그를 큰 길에서 만났는데 제 여권을 검사해야겠다고 하더라고요. 경찰이라고 믿어서 아무 의심도 하지 않았어요. 제 지갑이 없어진 걸 알았을 때 그는 이미 사라져버렸죠.

- I obviously booked a non-smoking room online, but once I got to the hotel, there were only smoking rooms left. I couldn't help accepting one of them, but I felt very unpleasant about the bad cigarette smell that had seeped in the room.
  저는 분명히 인터넷으로 금연실로 예약했는데 막상 호텔에 가보니 남아 있는 방은 흡연실뿐이었습니다. 어쩔 수 없이 그 방들 중의 하나에 들어갔지만 방에 밴 안 좋은 담배 냄새 때문에 굉장히 불쾌했습니다.

- The local food that I tried from some street vendors caused me big trouble. I suffered from a terrible stomachache and diarrhea from the third day of the trip. I took some medicine for food poisoning, but it didn't work well. I ended up returning home three days ahead of schedule. It was my worst overseas trip.
  길거리에서 먹은 지역 음식으로 저는 큰 불편을 겪었습니다. 여행 셋째 날부터 지독한 복통과 설사 때문에 힘들었어요. 식중독 약을 먹었는데도 잘 듣지를 않았습니다. 결국 일정을 사흘 앞당겨 집으로 돌아왔습니다. 최악의 해외여행이었습니다.

질문에 대한 여러분의 답변을 만들어보세요.

That's the end of the situation. You might have experienced unexpected, surprising, or funny incidents during your overseas trip. Where and when did you have the experience? What exactly happened then? What made you still remember the incident?

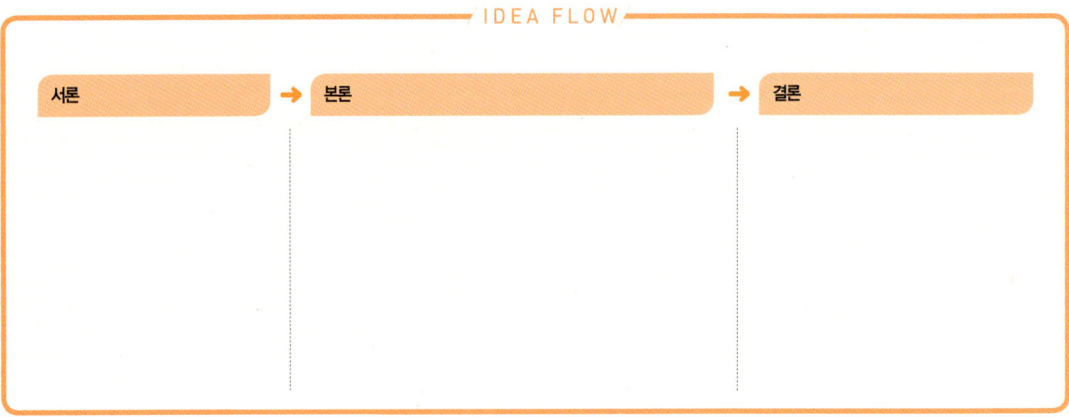

ANSWER

Actual Test 1

Oral Proficiency Interview-**computer**

자기소개

Let's start the interview. Please tell me a little about yourself.

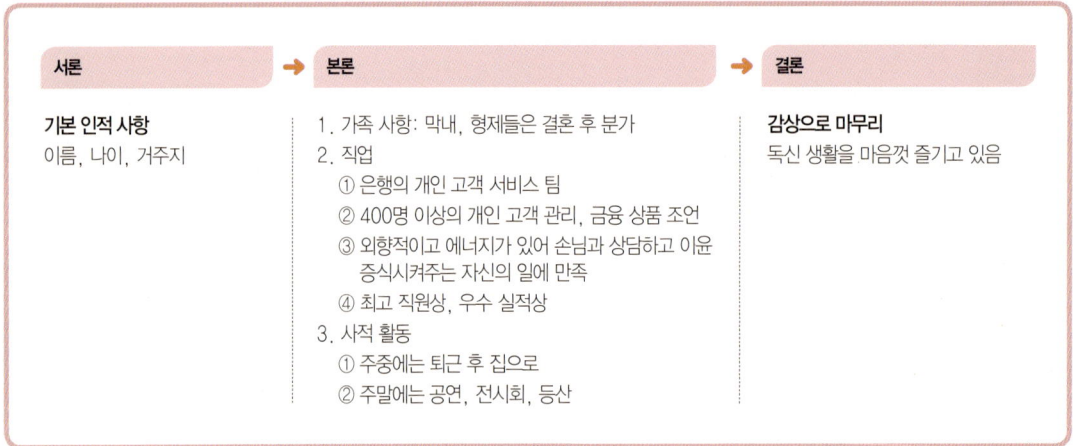

ANSWER

My name is Min Jung Kim. I am in my late 20s and living with my parents in the suburbs of Seoul. My sister and brother moved out after their marriage. I am the youngest daughter, and like many other last-born children, I am treated as the eternal baby of the family. I am currently employed in the Individual Customers Service Team of Nara Bank. My job is to manage over 400 individual customers, advising them on choosing banking products such as fixed deposits, MMF, or installment savings. Dealing with customers may seem difficult, but I like my job very much because I am outgoing and energetic. It's rewarding to consult with customers and try to increase their profits. I was selected as the best employee two years ago and have received a prize of excellent performance more than five times so far. On weekdays, I normally go straight home after work while enjoying a variety of activities on weekends. I go to see performances including musicals, plays, or rock concerts, and I never miss quality exhibitions. I also go hiking at least twice a month. I can say I fully enjoy my single life.

[해석 p.306 참조]

집 1

I'd like to know about your house. How do your house and its neighboring area look? Which room is your favorite in your home? What do you normally do there?

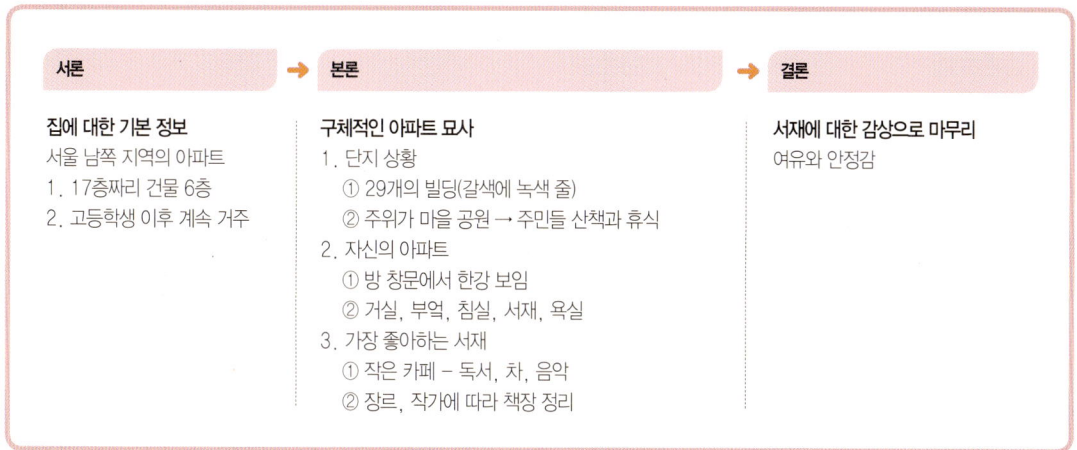

ANSWER

I live in an apartment in the southern part of Seoul. I live on the 6th floor of a 17-story-building. I've been living in this place since I began high school. My apartment complex has 29 buildings that are light brown colored with dark green stripes around them. My apartment is surrounded by local parks, which enables the residents to walk around them and use them for the resting places. The view from my place is amazing, too. I can look down on the Han River from the windows of my bedroom. There is a living room, a kitchen, two bedrooms, a study, and a bathroom in my home, but my favorite space is the study that has a cozy and comfortable atmosphere. It's like a small book-café for me, where I can have some coffee or tea and listen to music while reading books. I've arranged bookshelves based on genre and authors, which makes it possible for me to choose what I want to read easily. When sitting alone in my study, thumbing through the pages of a book, I feel relaxed and stable.

[해석 p.306 참조]

집 2

How do you keep the room clean and comfortable? What do you do for the room?

서론	본론	결론
서재를 깨끗하고 편안하게 유지하는 이유 마음 차분, 독서에 집중 잘됨	본격적인 서재 청결 유지 방법 1. 책상, 책장, 차 탁자 청소 ① 먼지떨이로 먼지를 털어냄 ② 윈덱스로 닦아냄 2. 책장 정돈: 책은 꺼낸 자리에 다시 꽂음 3. 책상과 서랍에서 불필요한 자료 치움 4. 음식물 반입 금지: 쿠키 부스러기, 음식 냄새	정리하면서 마무리 위와 같은 방법으로 서재 청결과 편안함 유지

ANSWER

I obviously try to keep my study clean and comfortable because a clean room helps me stay calm and concentrate better on reading. The first thing I regularly do is to keep the desk, bookshelves, and a tea table tidy. I wipe off the dust from them with a feather duster. Then I spray Windex to a rag and clean every nook and corner of them with it. I do these two things on a weekly basis. What I always care about is to keep my bookshelves organized. To do so, I take some books out of the shelves and keep them in the same place when I put them back in. Another thing I always do is to put away unnecessary materials from the desk and drawers. The messy desk distracts me from reading or thinking while I'm in the room. Here is one more thing left. I hardly bring food like chips and cookies to the study. I don't want cookie crumbs to fall and the room to be filled with the smell of food. This is how I keep my study clean and comfortable.

[해석 p.306 참조]

집 3

Tell me about the house you lived in when you were a child. How was it different from or similar to your current house?

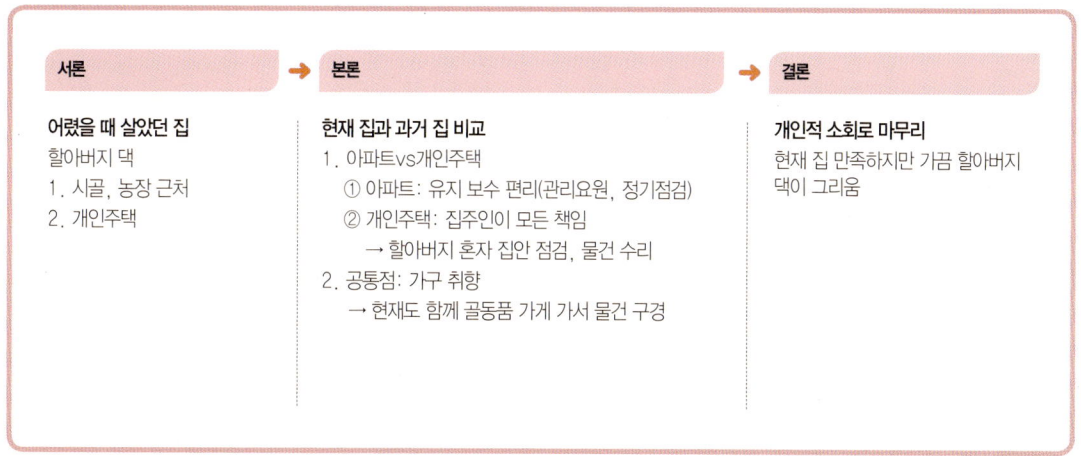

ANSWER

When I was young, I lived with my grandfather in the rural area, which was three hours away from my current house by car. He was living in a detached house near his farm. In terms of maintenance, living in an apartment is very convenient because a full-time maintenance staff is available to assist with repairs and check the apartments on the regular basis. On the contrary, living in the single home, especially in the country, requires a lot of maintenance works since the homeowner is wholly responsible for most repairs. I used to watch my grandfather check the roof, the floors, and all the sprinklers for himself, and try to fix things moving back and forth from upstairs to basement. My grandfather's house and my current house have only one thing in common, which is the furniture style. We are both deeply interested in antique furniture, and most pieces of furniture we have look very similar. We often go to antique shops together to see some carpets, chairs, tables, vases, etc. I'm satisfied with living in my current house, but I sometimes miss living in his house.

[해석 p.306 참조]

호텔 1

Tell me about hotels in your country. How do they look? What facilities do they have and which services do they provide? Please tell me in as much detail as possible.

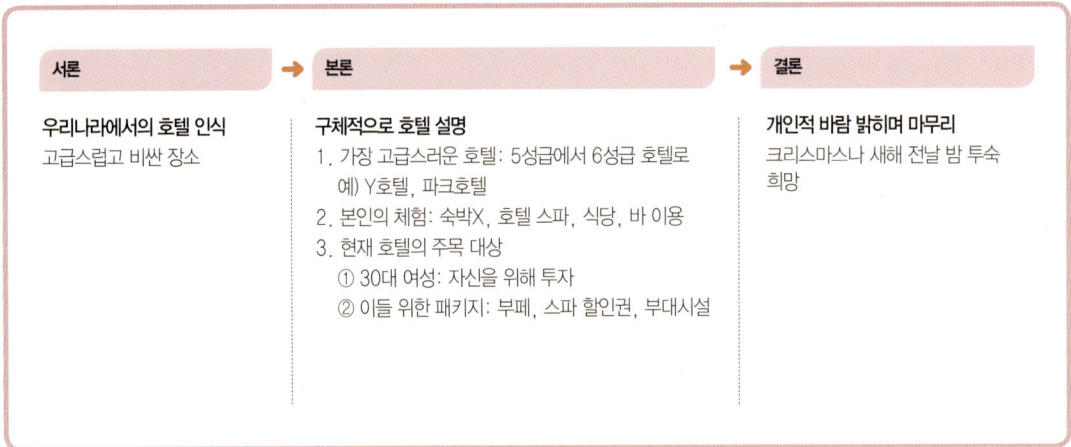

ANSWER

Hotels are generally considered very luxurious and expensive places to stay in my country. In fact, most hotels with over five stars are very high in room rate. About ten years ago, five-star hotels were most luxurious, but recently there are some six-star hotels such as Y Hotel, Park Hotel and so on. I've never stayed at those kinds of hotels, but I sometimes use their facilities like restaurants, spas, and bars. Especially, hotel spas are famous for their services. Recently, many hotels are paying attention to female guests. More women in their 30s are willing to spend their money taking care of themselves, so the hotels plan for some package services to draw their attention. The packages generally include breakfast buffet, spa discounts, and attractive amenities. Young women are interested in beauty, so the hotels have begun to upgrade their amenities into famous beauty or spa brands. I also want to experience 'a hotel stay' with my friends on a special day like Christmas or New Year's Eve.

[해석 p.307 참조]

호텔 2

Tell me about the best hotel that you have ever stayed in. Where was it and when did you go there? Why did you like the hotel so much? Give me all the details about the hotel.

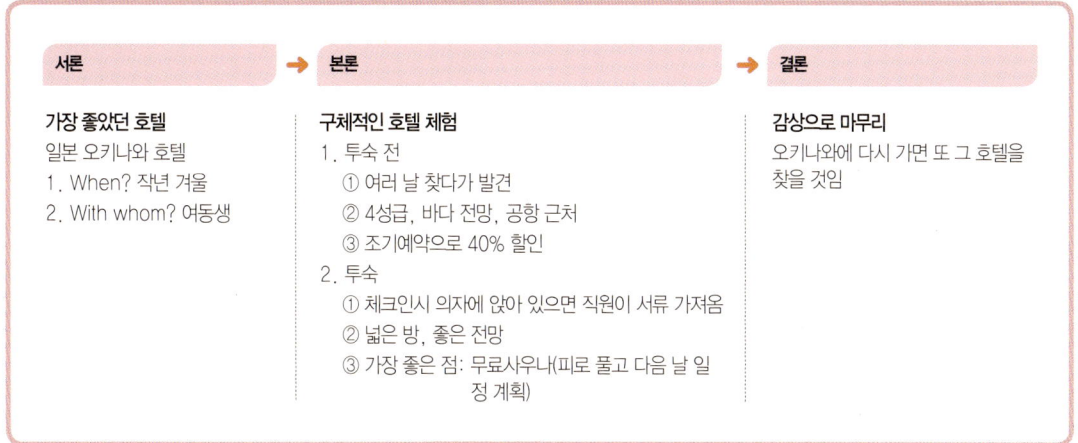

ANSWER

Last winter, I went to Okinawa, Japan with my sister. We planned an itinerary together and chose a hotel to stay. Most hotels we liked to stay were very expensive for our budget. After searching for many days, I found the perfect hotel for us. The four-star hotel was close to the airport and had a sea view. Moreover, I got a discount of 40% for early booking. The hotel was really great. When we were checking in, we didn't have to stand at the front desk. We just sat on the cozy sofa, drinking welcoming juice. Then, the staff member brought us some documents for the check-in. We were also surprised at the size of the room. It was very large and had a nice view. Among many free services they provided, we liked the hotel sauna the best. The sauna had an outdoor sauna pool as well. After the day-tour, we could relax ourselves in the sauna. At night, we discussed the next day's tour, looking at the stars in the sky in the warm water. We often talk about the tour and the hotel. We will choose that hotel if we go to Okinawa again.

[해석 p.307 참조]

호텔 3

Tell me about the hotel where you stayed most recently. When and why did you visit there? What did you like or dislike about it?

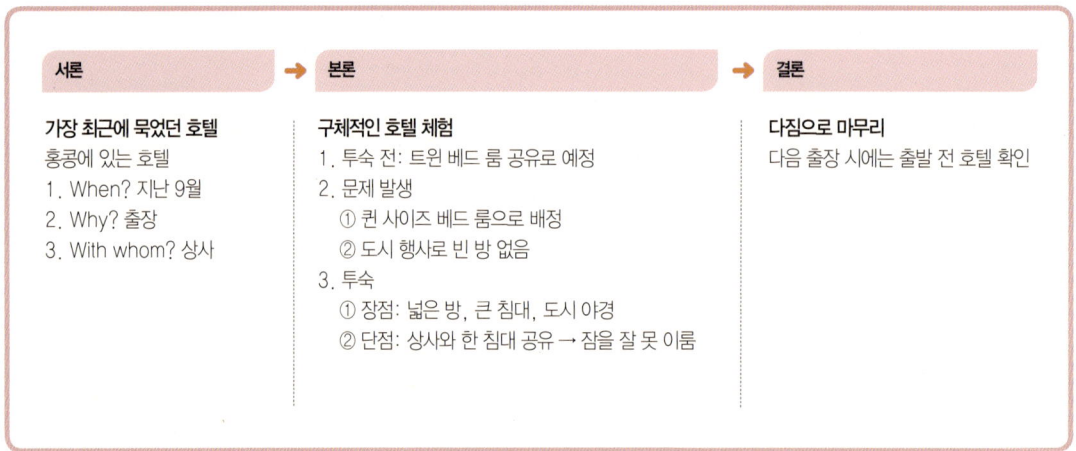

ANSWER

I went on a business trip to Hong Kong last September with my boss. A staff member in Human Resources Department made a reservation, and I didn't have any information about the hotel. I just knew I share a twin room with my boss through the voucher. Once we got there, however, we were given a room with a queen size bed. Indicating my voucher, I asked the receptionist to change the room into a twin room, but he said that all the rooms were fully occupied because of a certain event in the city. He politely apologized to us, so we couldn't complain anymore. The room itself was not that bad, though. It was spacious and the bed was larger than I expected. The night view of the city seen through the windows was also great. But still, you can imagine how uncomfortable it was to share a bed with my boss. I couldn't fall asleep easily because she tossed and turned all night. I'll certainly confirm the room of the hotel before traveling on business in the future.

[해석 p.307 참조]

명절 1

What is the biggest holiday in your country? What traditional activities do people do on that day? Give me a detailed description of the holiday.

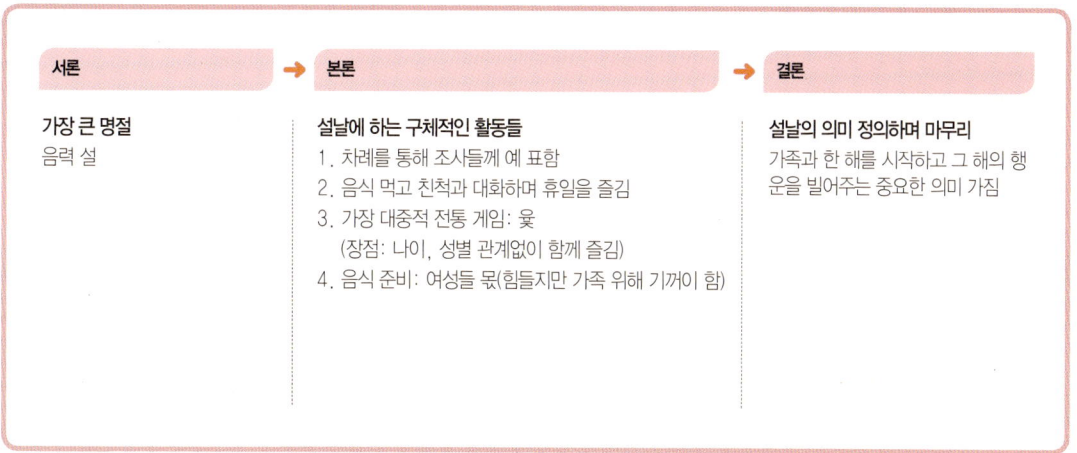

ANSWER

Lunar New Year's Day is the biggest holiday in my country. The holiday lasts for about three to four days since it is the day when family members who live apart from their parents visit their parents' home. When the entire family gathers, they pay tribute to their ancestors through a sincere memorial service. After that, they eat lots of food, spend time talking with their relatives, and enjoy the rest of the holiday. They also play some traditional games. Of these games, the most famous and popular traditional one is yut. One good aspect of this game is that many people can play it together regardless of their age and gender. The food preparation is mostly done by the women, and it requires lots of work since many people come together in one place. Even though the work is very demanding and challenging, the women are willing to do it for their families. Lunar New Year's Day is more than just a holiday. The holiday has a significant meaning to the people in my country in that they can start their new year safely with their family members and pray for good luck for the rest of the year for everyone.

[해석 p.307 참조]

명절 2

You may have some memorable holiday experiences when you were a child. What was it and what happened? Why is it so memorable to you? Tell me the story from the beginning to the end.

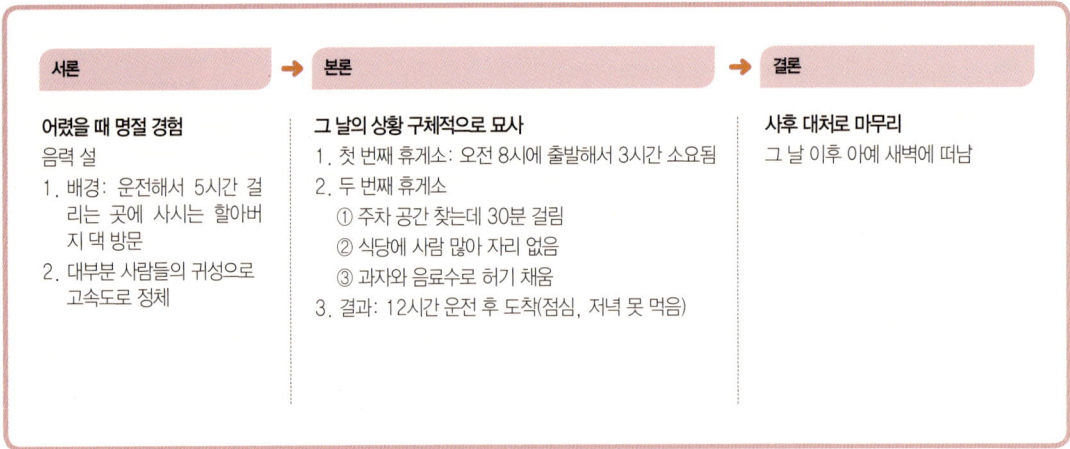

ANSWER

When I was young, I used to visit my grandparents' house with my parents on Lunar New Year's Day every year. My grandparents' house was quite far away from my house, so it took us five hours to drive there normally. Since most people had gone back to their hometown for Lunar New Year's Day, we always got stuck in traffic on the highway. One year, the traffic conditions were more terrible than ever, which made the trip an unforgettable experience for me. We left home at 8 a.m., but it took 3 hours to get to the first rest area. I suffered from motion sickness, and my father was so tired after driving for several hours. When we stopped at the second rest area to have a late lunch, we spent almost 30 minutes trying to find a parking space. Once we entered the restaurant, there were so many people that we couldn't even find a table to sit at. We gave up having lunch there and just bought some snacks and beverages to satisfy our hunger. We couldn't eat lunch or dinner until we got to my grandparents' house after a 12-hour drive. After that terrible experience, we started leaving home at dawn to visit my grandparents on holidays.

[해석 p.308 참조]

10

명절 3

I'd like to know the holiday that you recently had. What was it and what did you do on that day?

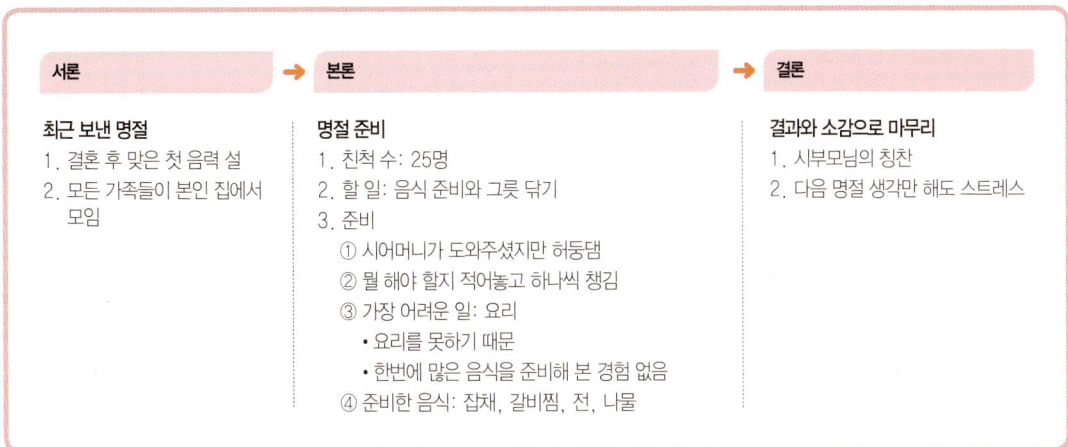

서론 → **본론** → **결론**

최근 보낸 명절
1. 결혼 후 맞은 첫 음력 설
2. 모든 가족들이 본인 집에서 모임

명절 준비
1. 친척 수: 25명
2. 할 일: 음식 준비와 그릇 닦기
3. 준비
   ① 시어머니가 도와주셨지만 허둥댐
   ② 뭘 해야 할지 적어놓고 하나씩 챙김
   ③ 가장 어려운 일: 요리
      • 요리를 못하기 때문
      • 한번에 많은 음식을 준비해 본 경험 없음
   ④ 준비한 음식: 잡채, 갈비찜, 전, 나물

결과와 소감으로 마무리
1. 시부모님의 칭찬
2. 다음 명절 생각만 해도 스트레스

ANSWER

I recently celebrated my first Lunar New Year's Day after I got married. My husband is the oldest son in his family, so all of his family members came to our place for the family reunion. I had to prepare for the holiday for a few days. I made a lot of holiday foods and cleaned all of the plates and bowls. I was almost panicking because 25 relatives were supposed to come. I didn't know where to start and what to do. My mother-in-law helped me prepare for the holiday, but it was not easy at all. I wrote down what I should buy, do, and cook and took care of everything one by one. Food preparation was the most challenging for me since I am not that good at cooking. Also, I had never cooked so much food for so many people at once. I managed to play my role as the eldest daughter-in-law, preparing japchae, galbi jjim, jeon, many kinds of vegetables, etc. My parents-in-law praised me for having a major event, but thinking of the next holiday I should prepare, I'm already stressed out.

[해석 p.308 참조]

직장 1

I'll give you a situation and ask you to act it out. You and your employees have been working on a project. Call one of your employees that you supervise and leave a message ordering some updates on the project.

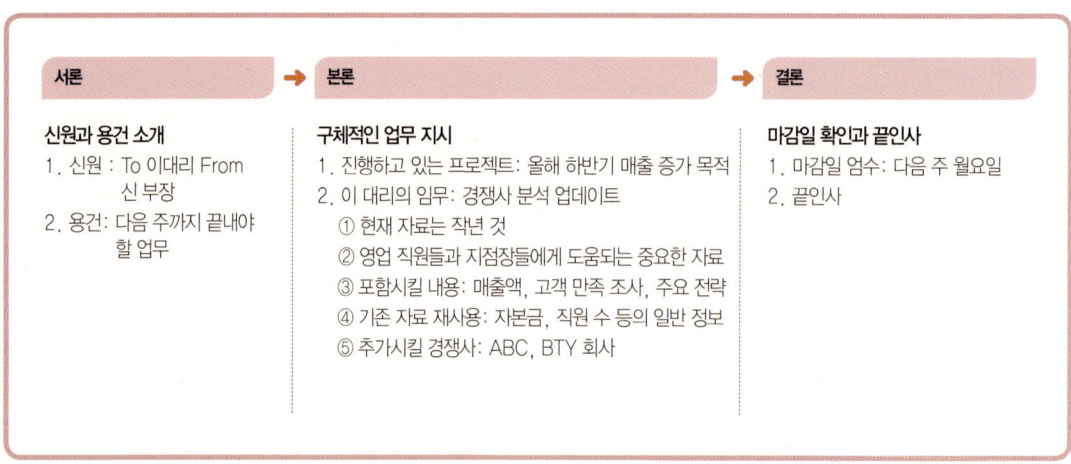

ANSWER

Hi Mr. Lee, this is Ms. Shin. There is something I need you to finish by next Monday. You know we've been working on the marketing project that aims at increase in sales of the second half of this year, don't you? I want you to be responsible for some updates on the competitor analysis. The data we're currently having were updated last year, and we need their recent status updates. The competitor analysis is one of the most important parts of the project, which are helpful for sales representatives and branch managers. You have to include their sales figures, customer satisfaction research, and major strategies in the analysis. But you can reuse the data that was made last year for general information such as their capital, the number of employees, etc. Oh, you need to add ABC Company and BTY Company as our new competitors in addition to our existing ones. They are both fast growing companies in our food business. It's too obvious to mention, but please keep the deadline. Again, it's due on Monday. Talk to you later.

[해석 p.308 참조]

12

직장 2

I'm sorry, but there is a problem you need to resolve. Your employee called you back and told you that he or she could not complete the task on time. Leave him a message including two or three suggestions to solve the problem.

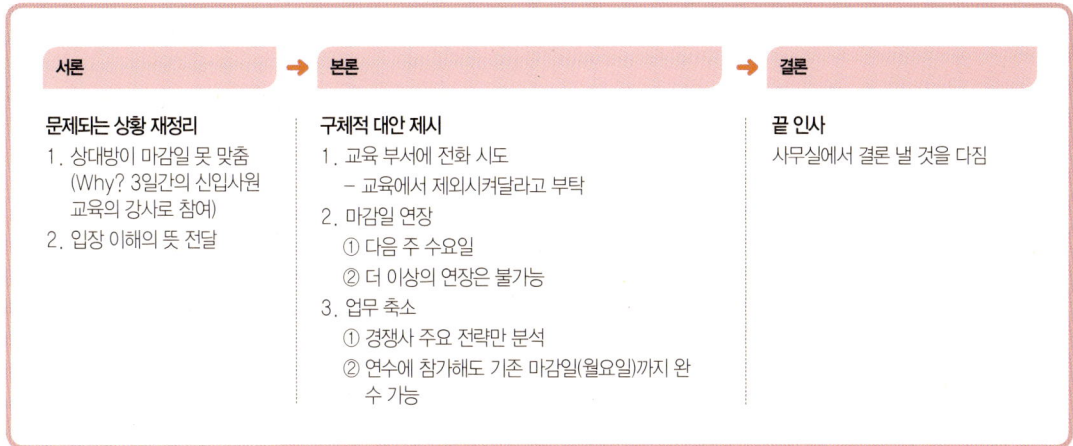

ANSWER

I'm sorry to hear that you won't be able to meet the deadline. As you have to participate in a 3-day orientation program for new employees as a trainer, you don't seem to have enough time to complete your task on time. The training won't be finished by this Thursday, right? Hmm, let me call the Training Department and ask them to leave you out of the orientation. They can find another staff to replace you with. If that's not accepted, I'll extend the deadline until next Wednesday, meaning you'll have 2 more days for the updates, but the submission deadline cannot be extended anymore though. It may cause the whole process of the project to be delayed. I can give you another option, too. I'll divide up the work so that you can work on analyzing major strategies of our competitors only, and I'll assign the rest to other staff members. Then, you can complete the task by next Monday as scheduled even if you participate in the orientation program, can't you? Let's conclude our discussion later at the office. See you soon.

[해석 p.308 참조]

13

직장 3

You may have had many good or bad experiences while you've been supervising employees. Tell me about one of your positive experiences.

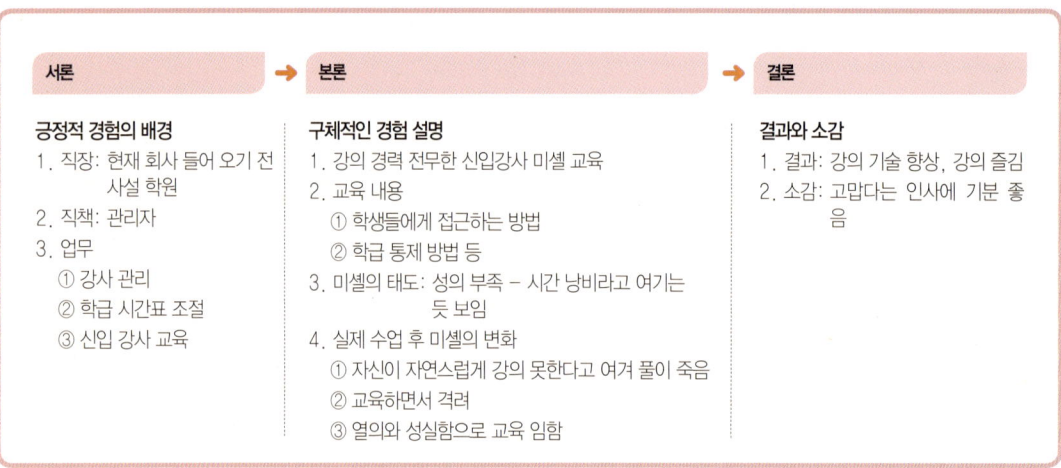

ANSWER

I used to work as a supervisor in a private institute long before I started working for my current company. My duty was to supervise instructors, manage the whole class schedules for them, and conduct a week-training sessions for new instructors. One day, I met a new teacher, Michelle, and she had no teaching experience before. I started giving her a training such as on how to approach her students, how to control them easily, etc. At first, she didn't like the training sessions and lacked sincerity during the training. She seemed to think the training sessions were a waste of time. However, after going through a few classes, she felt she was not really good at delivering her lessons to the students effectively and naturally. She got a bit frustrated, but I encouraged her to complement her disadvantages through the trainings. Since then, she took the training with enthusiasm and sincerity. Her teaching skills improved, and she started to enjoy teaching. When she thanked me for helping her, I felt very good.

[해석 p.309 참조]

수영 1

You indicated in the survey that you swim. What do you like about swimming? How is it different from other sports? Describe swimming in detail in comparison with other sports.

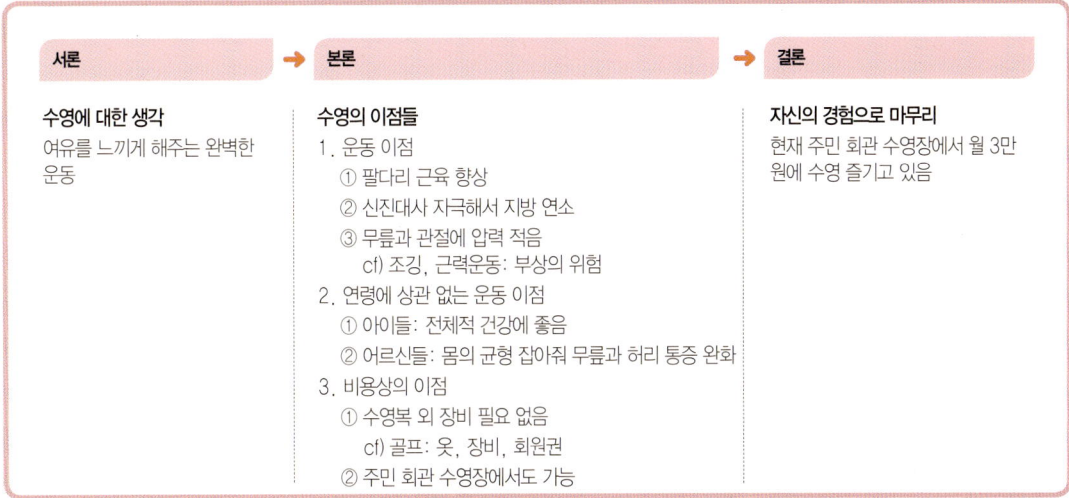

ANSWER

I think swimming is the perfect exercise that makes me feel so free. Swimming gives me clear exercise benefits. It improves the muscles of my arms and legs and allows me to burn fat by stimulating metabolism. Swimming doesn't give a lot of pressure to the joints and knees compared to other sports. When jogging or weight training, there's always a danger of injury. Under water, however, your body floats due to buoyancy in the water and your joints have by far less pressure. Anyone can have exercise benefits of swimming regardless of age. For children, swimming can be the best workout for their general fitness. For the elderly, it is just perfect to balance their body and alleviate their knees or back pains. Swimming is also cheaper to learn than any other sport. You don't have to be equipped with any gear except your swimsuit. If you play golf, you need to buy golf clothes, equipment, and a membership to use the course. There are also many swimming pools available in a local community center like YMCA. I actually pay 30,000 won per month for swimming at my local community center pool and enjoy it whenever I am free.

[해석 p.309 참조]

수영 2

When did you start swimming? How did you get interested in swimming? How has your interest changed over the years?

서론	본론	결론

수영 시작한 배경
1. 시기: 중학생
2. 장소: YMCA 센터
3. 동기: 어머니의 권유(나쁜 자세로 인한 허리 문제)
	본격적인 수영 강습
	1. 수업 전: 수영에 관심 없고 물을 무서워함
	2. 수업 중
	  ① 초반에 배운 내용 – 일반적인 자세, 호흡법
	  ② 선생님의 열성 – 지도를 따라가면서 자신감 얻음
	  ③ 6개월 동안 자유형, 배영 마스터
	3. 현재
	  ① 그 이후 10년 동안 수영함
	  ② 허리에 아무런 문제 없음
	  ③ 전체적인 몸 상태도 좋음
		감상으로 마무리
		수영 시작한 것에 대한 후회 전혀 없고 어머니께 감사

ANSWER

My mother took me to a YMCA swimming center when I was a middle school student. She wanted me to start exercising on a regular basis since I had a back problem due to my bad posture. In fact, I was not interested in swimming at all, and I was a bit afraid of water. It was the first time I had a swimming lesson since I was born. At the beginning, the coach taught me the basic forms and way to breathe while swimming. He was eager to teach me, and I became more and more confident while following his directions step by step. I went to the swimming lessons for 6 months, and I mastered freestyle and backstroke swimming. Since then, I have swum for 10 years, and I don't have any back problem now. Not only is my back improved but also my general fitness is much better than before. I have no regret about starting swimming as my regular exercise, and I really thank my mother, who led me to start swimming.

[해석 p.309 참조]

Actual Test 2

Oral Proficiency Interview-**computer**

자기소개

01 Let's start the interview. Please tell me a little about yourself.

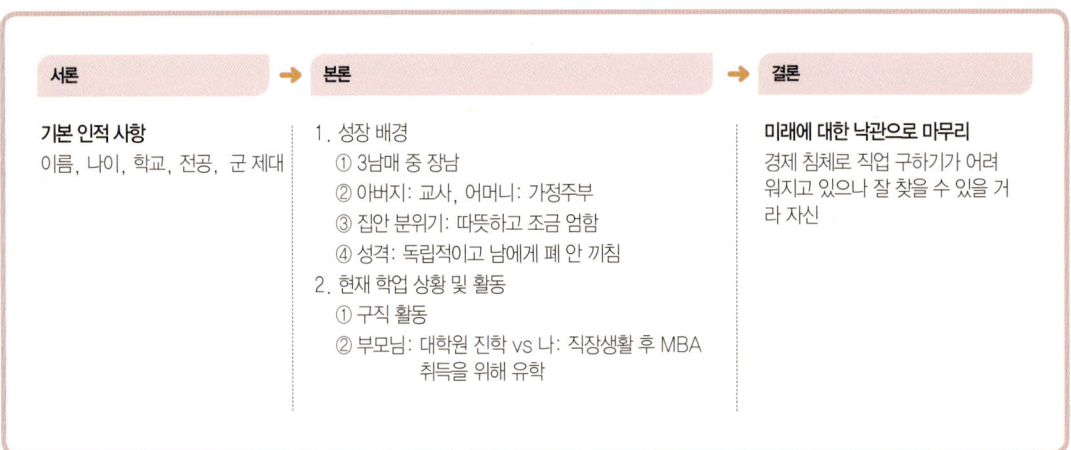

ANSWER

Hello, my name is Dong Hyun Lee. I am 25 years old and a senior at Han Il University majoring in economics. I went back to school last year after finishing my 25-month-military service. I am the oldest of three siblings and grew up in a warm, but a little strict family. My father has been teaching at a high school in Seoul, and my mother is a typical housewife. Thanks to their educational philosophy, I became a person who always tries to be independent and not to cause troubles to others. I've been spending most of the time seeking a job since this semester started. My parents want me to go to graduate school right after graduation, but I have a different idea. I am planning to pursue an MBA in the US after three or four years of building work experiences in my country. I want to involve myself in a social experience in the heyday of youth, which I believe would help me apply for better graduate schools in the future. It's been harder to get a job due to the economic recession, but I am quite confident that I'll find a job that suits me well.

[해석 p.310 참조]

공연 1

You indicated in the survey that you watch performances. Which theater do you usually go to? Where is it located? How does it look? Why do you like the theater?

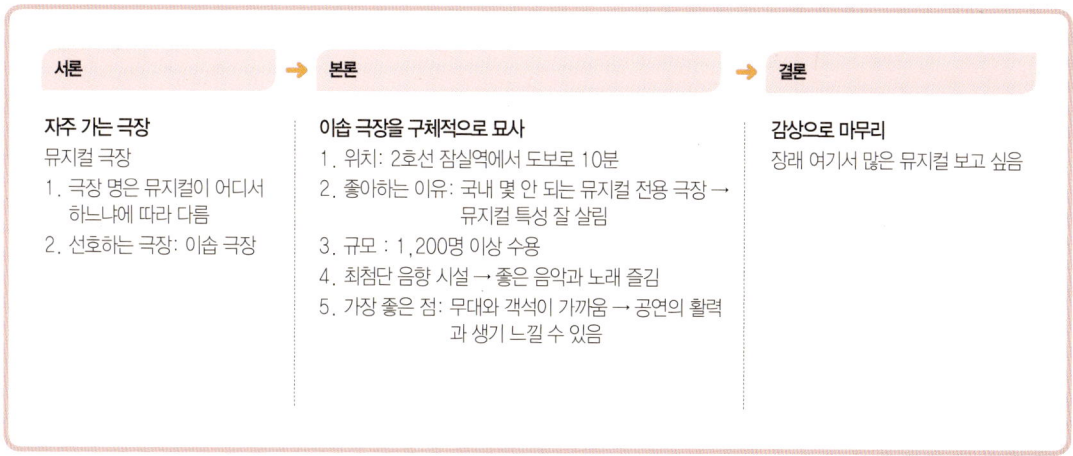

ANSWER

Since I like musicals a lot, I often go to the musical theaters. I go to different theaters depending on the musicals I choose to see. While the same movies are shown in many different cinemas, the same musical is played in the designated theater during the certain period. However, I do have a preferable theater, which is the Aesop Theater. It is located within a 10-minute walking distance from Jamsil Station on the Subway Line 2. I like the theater because it's one of the few theaters designed only for musicals in Korea, which emphasizes the nature of musicals. It's large enough to accommodate more than 1,200 people and has state-of-the-art sound systems so that audience can enjoy good music and songs. The best part of the theater is that the stage is very close to the seats, which enables audience to feel the energy and liveliness of the performances. I hope to watch more musicals in the Aesop Theater in the future.

[해석 p.310 참조]

03

공연 2

How did you first become interested in watching performances or shows? How has the interest changed over the years? Tell me about how your interest has been developed including the performances or shows you saw.

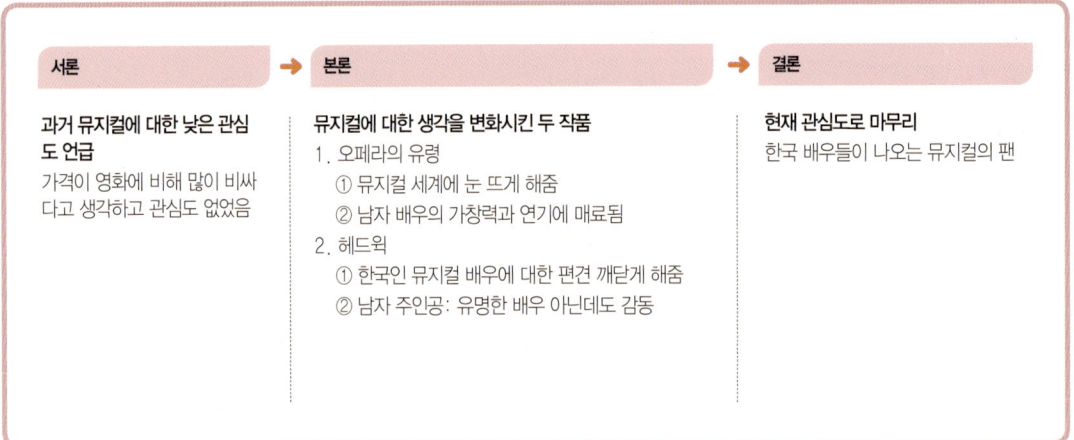

ANSWER

I wasn't actually interested in musicals several years ago. I used to think ticket prices for musicals were ridiculously expensive compared to those for movies. But the musical, The Phantom of the Opera, has opened my eyes to the world of musicals. I watched it in London when I went backpacking across Europe. I wasn't able to understand every lyric in the songs but became fully assimilated into the emotions of the characters. Especially, the actor playing the Phantom was so excellent at singing, and his fabulous voice and acting fascinated me. Since then, I have searched good musicals to watch in Korea. Frankly speaking, I had low expectations of musicals where Korean actors and actresses starred at first, so I tried to watch only western musicals played by their original team such as Notre-Dame de Paris. However, when I watched Hedwig in which Korean actors played last year, I realized that I had held a strong prejudice on Korean musical actors and actresses. Although the main actor wasn't a very famous actor, his appealing voice and singing ability were amazing enough to impress me. Now, I'm a huge fan of musicals where Korean actors and actresses appear.

[해석 p.310 참조]

공연 3

Which performance or show did you last watch? When did you watch it and which theater did you go to? What did you do before and after going to the theater?

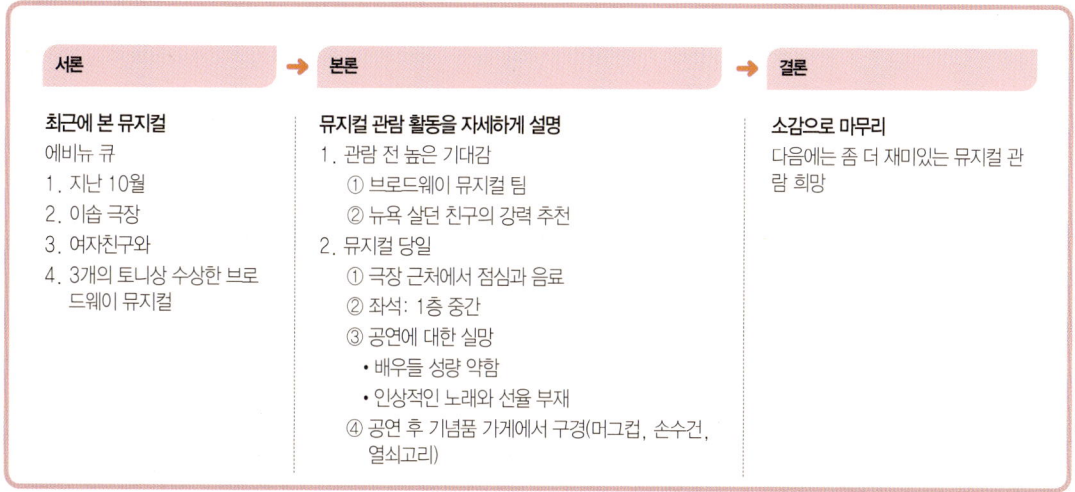

ANSWER

I watched the musical, Avenue Q, last October with my girlfriend. I watched it in the Aesop Theater I mentioned at the beginning. It was a famous Broadway musical that won three Tony Awards including the best musical. I had great expectations of the musical where the original Broadway cast members performed, and my friend who studied in New York strongly recommended me to check it out, too. It started at 3 p.m., so we had lunch and beverages near the theater before the musical started. We had seats in the middle of the ground level, which had a fairly nice view of the actors. However, I think I expected too much of the performance. Although the characters sang well, they seemed to have a weak voice, and more importantly, there were no impressive music and songs. Even right after getting out of the theater, I had no melodies ringing in my ears. We went to the gift shop in the lobby to browse. Since many musicals like Lion King, Cats, and Mamma Mia performed at the theater, I could see some famous characters painted or printed on the mugs, handkerchiefs, key holders, etc. I hope to watch a more interesting musical next time.

[해석 p.310 참조]

걷기 1

You indicated in the survey that you like walking. What is your favorite place for walking? What does it look like? What can you see there? What do you like about the place?

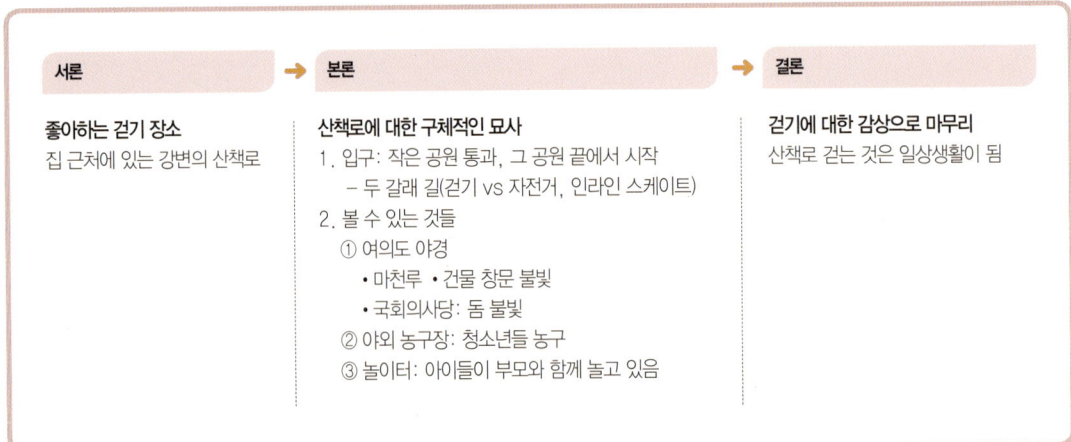

ANSWER

I'm living in a studio apartment near the Han River. There is a well-made walking path around the river, which is my favorite place to walk along. I usually start walking on the path at around 8 o'clock after dinner. To reach the path, I need to pass through a small park, and at the end of the park, the walking path begins. The path is divided into two; one is for walkers and the other is for bikers and inline skaters. Walking on the path, I can enjoy the night view of Yeoido, the center of finance with lots of skyscrapers in Korea. Looking at the light streaming through the windows of the buildings, I sometimes guess how many people are working overtime. I can see the National Assembly Hall walking along the path, too. The light from the dome of the building makes the night view more beautiful. There are an outdoor basketball court and a playground along the path, too. I see adolescents playing basketball and some kids playing with their parents. Walking along the path has already become my daily routine, and I haven't found better places than that for walking.

[해석 p.311 참조]

걷기 2

How did you first start walking? How has your interest in walking changed over the years?

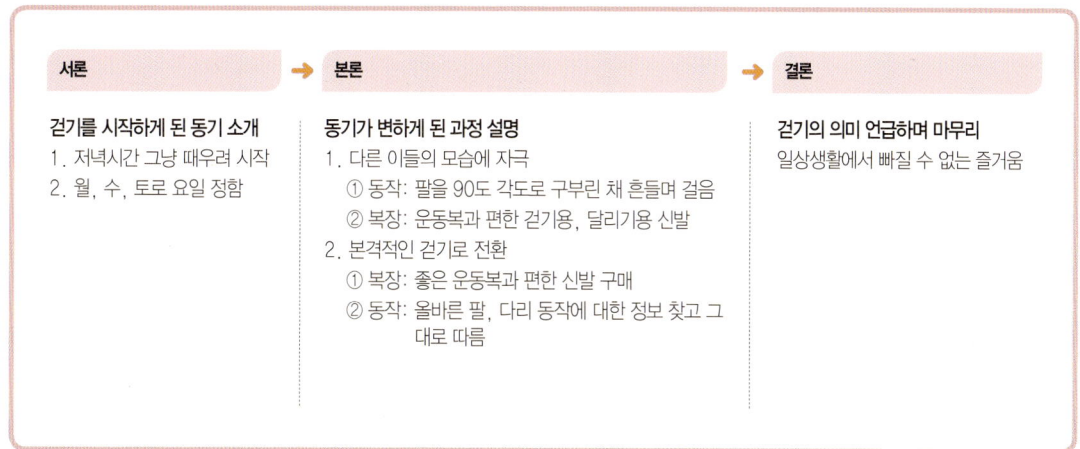

ANSWER

I just started walking to fill in time between dinner and bedtime. I didn't have any special things to do from 8 to 10 at night, so I decided to walk. I planned to walk three times a week after dinner in the beginning. It was not a hard exercise, and I set up the days roughly on Mondays, Wednesdays, and Saturdays. Once I started walking along the path that I mentioned before, I was a little surprised to see some women strenuously walking or running. They were swinging their arms back and forth as they walked folding their elbows almost 90 degrees while I just walked with my hands in my pockets. Their walking attire was quite different from mine, too. They wore training suits and comfortable walking or running shoes. It was sort of refreshing to see young, pretty women walking and running briskly. I soon bought a good training suit and a pair of comfortable walking shoes, and my walking began in earnest. I searched for tips for proper arm and foot movements in waking and followed the instructions. The more time and efforts I put the more active I became in walking. Now, walking is an unmissable delight in my daily life.

[해석 p.311 참조]

걷기 3

Please tell me about your interesting, unexpected, or surprising experience related to walking.

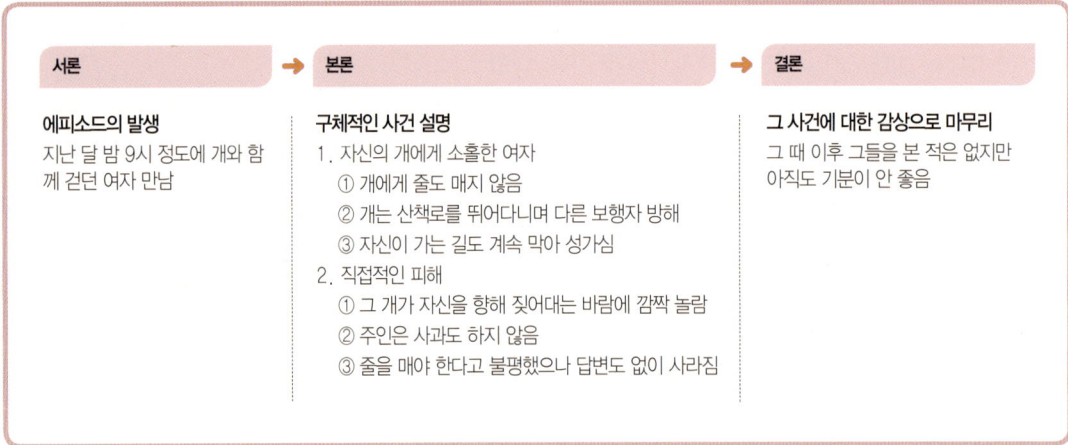

ANSWER

It was at around 9 p.m. last month when I saw a woman walking with her dog on the walking path. I don't mind seeing dogs or puppies on the path if their owners take a good care of them. The woman I saw, however, didn't seem to care for her dog. She didn't even keep her dog on a leash, and the dog was running around the track, blocking the way of other walkers. They had to stop walking whenever the dog appeared before them. I was trying to control my temper at first, but the dog that kept blocking my way really irritated me. When I was resting on the bench, the dog passed by me again. Then I was so surprised because the dog suddenly barked at me! Now the owner held the dog, but she didn't even say sorry to me. I finally complained to her about her dog, saying she should leash her dog outside, but she didn't give any answer and went away with her dog. I've never seen her and her dog again since then, but I still feel bad looking back on that night.

[해석 p.311 참조]

학원 수강 1

You indicated in the survey that you go to a language school. Which school do you go to? Which language do you study? Why do you study it? Please tell me about it in as much detail as possible.

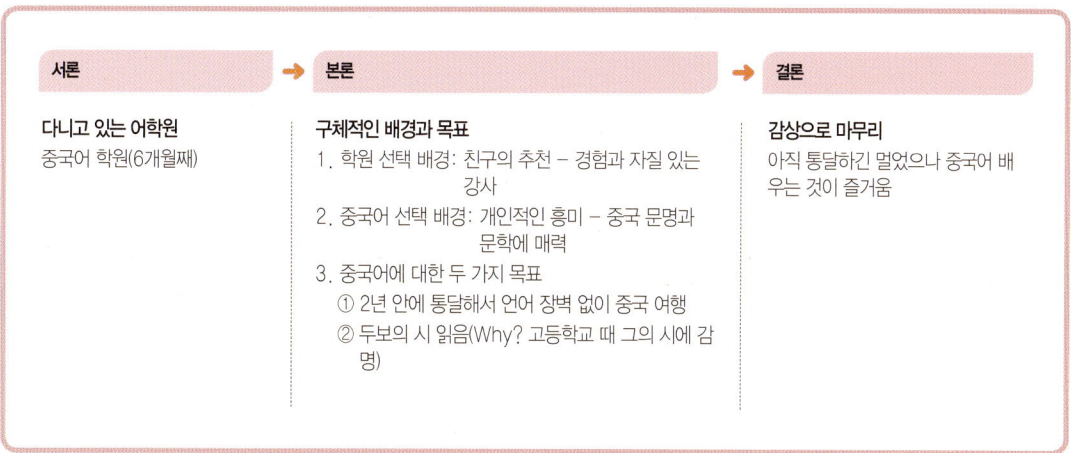

ANSWER

I've been attending a language institute to learn Chinese for six months. As I thought that large-scale institutes could pay little attention to their students, I chose a small-scale, but renowned one. A friend of mine, who is pretty good at Chinese, recommended me the institute. According to her, it has some experienced and qualified Chinese instructors. I started learning Chinese just for my own personal interest. I'd been attracted to Chinese civilization and literature. I set up two goals of learning Chinese when I decided to learn Chinese. First, I decided to master Chinese within two years so that I can travel around China without language barriers. Second, I wanted to read the poems written by Tu Fu, an outstanding Chinese poet of the Tang Dynasty after having reading ability in Chinese. I was deeply impressed by his poems during my high school years. Although I have a long way to go before mastering Chinese, I enjoy learning it very much.

[해석 p.311 참조]

학원 수강 2

Tell me about the first class you took in the language school. What was your first impression about the school, your teacher, and your classmates? Please describe them in detail.

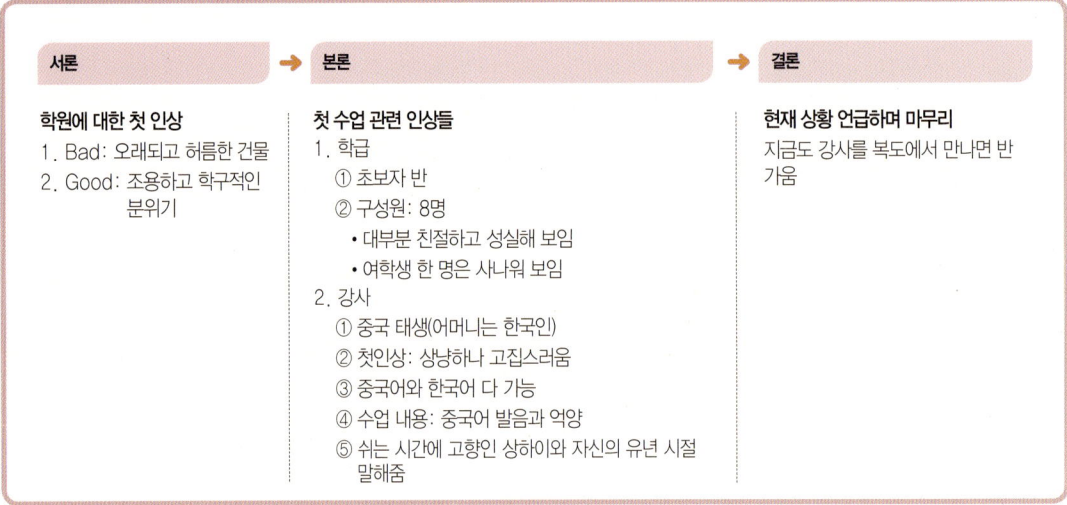

ANSWER

Well, I can't say I had a good first impression on the language institute. I was pretty much disappointed at the old, shabby building. I liked the quiet, academic atmosphere of the institute, though. I registered for the novice level, and my class consisted of eight students including myself. Most of them looked kind and honest, but one young female student looked a bit fierce. My teacher was born in China, but her mother is Korean. She looked nice but a little stubborn. Since she was bilingual in Chinese and Korean, she taught Chinese in Korean and, at the same time, could speak Chinese with the native speaker's pronunciation. She taught us basic pronunciation and intonation first. I knew the intonation of Chinese was critical for meaning distinction, but it was very strange to me. During the break, the teacher told us about her hometown, Shanghai, and her childhood. I'm now learning an intermediate level of Chinese from a different teacher, but I'm still glad to run into her in the hallway.

[해석 p.312 참조]

10

학원 수강 3

Tell me about an interesting, funny, or surprising experience you had in the language school.

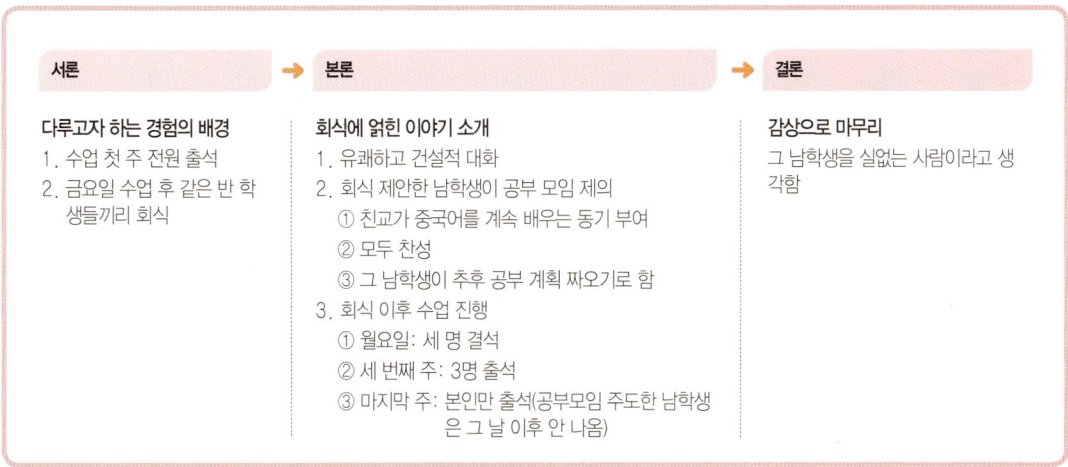

ANSWER

I've already told you that my first class was composed of eight students. For the first week, no one was absent from class. After the Friday class of the first week, one of the students suggested that we should go get some beer to get along well with each other. We were willing to join the unexpected, but enjoyable get-together. We had cheerful and constructive conversations over a glass of beer. We talked about why we started learning Chinese and what our ultimate goal would be. The man who arranged the gathering suggested that we have a study group. He said that close relationships between classmates could motivate him to keep learning Chinese. All of us agreed with his idea, and he said he would bring a further plan of the study. When the class started the following Monday, I was a bit surprised because three students including him were absent. I thought they might come the next day, but only one of them came. In the third week, the class size decreased to three students, and in the last week, I was the only one who left in the class. More strangely, the man who suggested a study group had never showed up since that night. I thought he was a real flake.

[해석 p.312 참조]

애완동물 1

11 I'll give you a situation and ask you to act it out. Your neighbors have told you that their cat is missing. You want to help them find the cat but do not have much information of the cat. Call them and ask three to four questions about the cat.

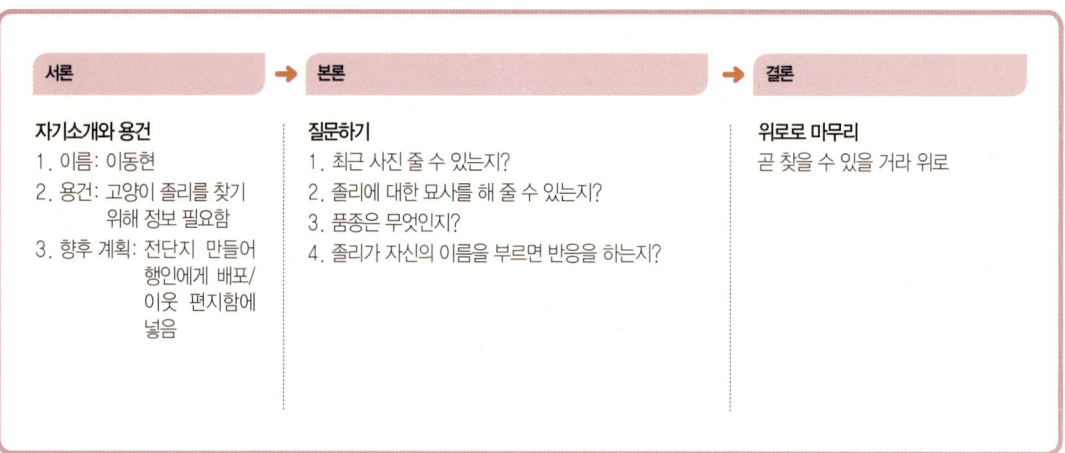

ANSWER

Hello, Mrs. Moon? This is Dong Hyun Lee, your neighbor. I have some ideas to help you find your cat and need some information about your cat. I know nothing but her name, Jolie. I want to make flyers and hand them out to passers-by or put them in the mailboxes of my neighbors. The first thing I need is her recent photo that I'll add to the flyer. Most cats looked similar, but if she has distinct features, it'll be easier for people to recognize her. If you don't have her photo, could you give me any other descriptions of her? What color is she? My brother told me that he had seen a cat spotted with white and brown near my house, but I'm not sure if it was your cat. I'm also going to include her breed on the flyer. The only cat breed I know is the Persian, but she may belong to a different breed. One more question, does she know her name? I'm just asking if she responds to her name being called. If she does, I'll write the information on the flyer. Don't worry too much about Jolie. You'll find her soon.

[해석 p.312 참조]

12 애완동물 2

I'm sorry, but there is a problem you need to resolve. You find out that the cat has climbed up a tree in your yard. Call your neighbors and explain the situation and where the cat is. Give two or three suggestions to solve the problem.

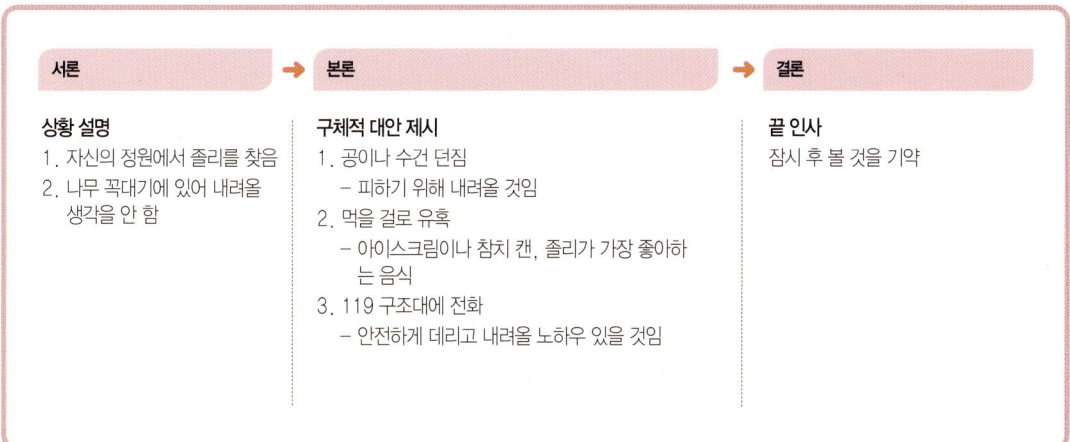

서론 → **본론** → **결론**

상황 설명
1. 자신의 정원에서 졸리를 찾음
2. 나무 꼭대기에 있어 내려올 생각을 안 함

구체적 대안 제시
1. 공이나 수건 던짐
   – 피하기 위해 내려올 것임
2. 먹을 걸로 유혹
   – 아이스크림이나 참치 캔, 졸리가 가장 좋아하는 음식
3. 119 구조대에 전화
   – 안전하게 데리고 내려올 노하우 있을 것임

끝 인사
잠시 후 볼 것을 기약

ANSWER

Hi, Mrs. Moon! I've got good news to tell you. I finally found your cat, Jolie! This might be hard to believe, but I found her here in my yard. I don't know for how long she's been here, but I'm so glad to find her so soon. But, Mrs. Moon, we've got a little problem. She's climbed to the treetop and can't come down. Do you think it'll be dangerous to throw a ball or a towel at her? She might come down to avoid it. If you don't want her to be frightened, I won't do that. I was thinking of tempting her with some food, too. I've learned that cats can eat some human food like ice cream or canned tuna fish. You can also bring her favorite food on the way here. If she never climbs down no matter what we do, I think you should call 119 rescue teams to ask them for help. They must have the know-how to take her safely from the tree. Then, see you in a few minutes!

[해석 p.313 참조]

13

애완동물 3

That's the end of the situation. Unexpected problems might have happened while you were raising pets. Tell me about an incident you had with your pet. What was the problem about and how did you handle the situation?

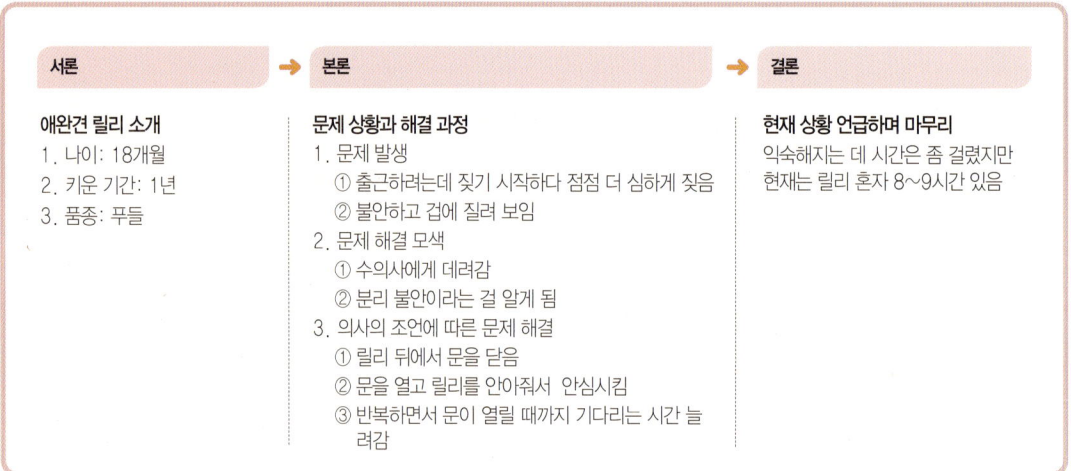

ANSWER

My wife and I have been raising an 18-month dog for a year. We call her Lily and she's a lovely white poodle. Since we brought her home during our summer vacation, we could spend all week together. After vacation, however, when we were about to leave home to go to work, she began to bark. We thought she would stop soon but barked harder and harder. She looked so nervous and frightened. Eventually, I had the morning off and brought her to a veterinarian to have her examined. The vet said she just showed separation anxiety, which is common in the young of many animals. Then he gave some tips to relieve her. I followed his pieces of advice, and they were really effective. For example, I closed the door behind her and waited two or three seconds, and then I opened the door and hugged her so that she could calm down. I repeated that exercise and gradually increased the time that she waited for me to open the door. It took a while for her to be ready to be alone, but now, my wife and I can leave the house for eight to nine hours without worry.

[해석 p.313 참조]

14 해변 1

You indicated in the survey that you go to the beach. Please tell me about the beach you often go to. Where is it and how do you go there? How often do you go there and who do you go with? What do you see and what do you do at the beach? Give me all the details.

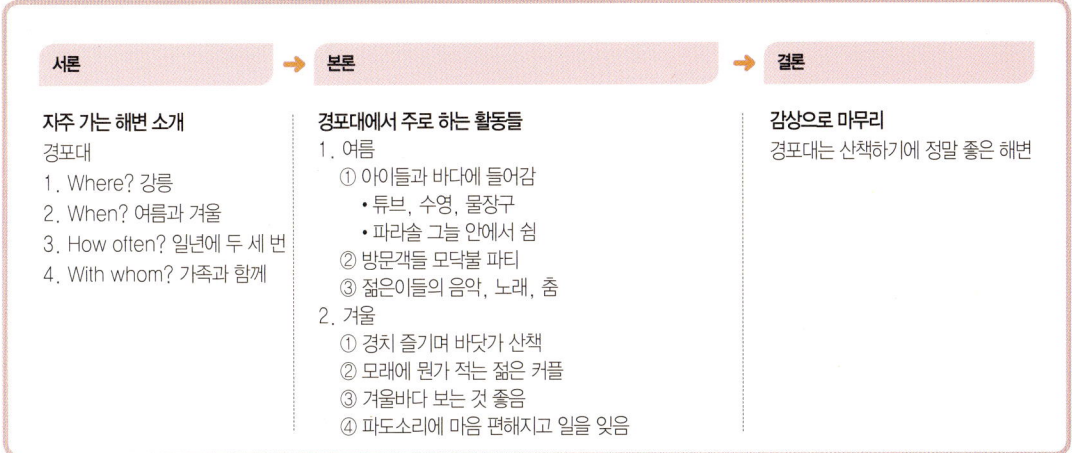

ANSWER

I go to Kyung Po Dae in Gangneung twice or three times a year both in summer and winter. I mostly drive there with my family. It is located a three-hour drive away from Seoul, but it takes four to five hours during the summer vacation season. In summer, I go in the water with my kids to check if they play safely in the water. They float on tubes, swim, and splash around in the water. They don't really like building sand castles as many other kids do. We bring a sunscreen tent to the beach so that we can rest in the shade. We can also see some people have bonfire parties at night. Some young people play music, sing songs, or dance, too. In winter, on the other hand, we walk along the beach while enjoying the view. I smile at some young couples writing messages on the sand. I like looking at the winter sea. It's very touching to see the sun setting above the horizon. The sound of the waves crashing against the shore makes me feel relaxed and forget everything about work. Kyung Po Dae is a really good beach to take a walk.

[해석 p.313 참조]

해변 2

I'd like to hear about the most memorable beach that you've been to. When and who did you go there with? How did the beach look? What did you see and what did you do?

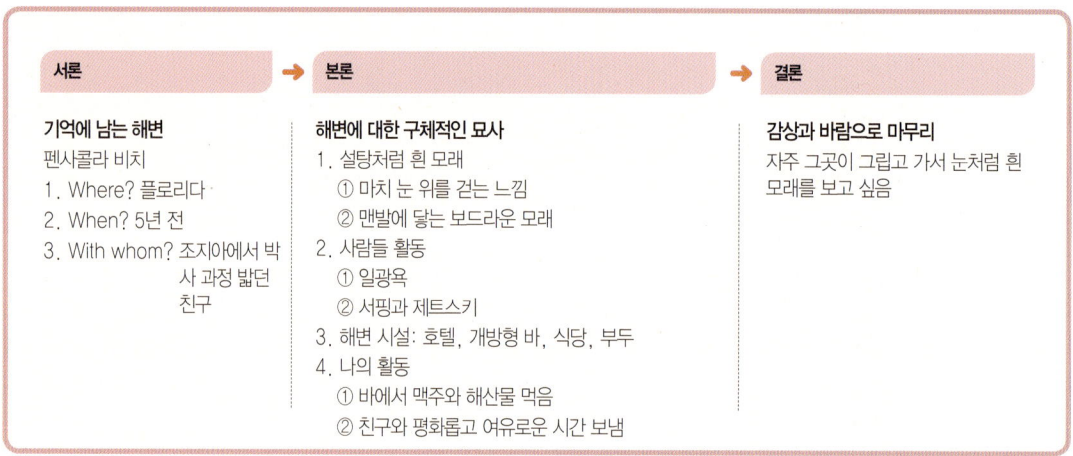

ANSWER

My most memorable beach is Pensacola Beach in Florida. I went to the beach five years ago when I visited my friend who was in the doctoral program in Georgia. He told me that I would see one of the most beautiful beaches in the world, and when arriving at the beach, I realized he was not exaggerating at all. Its sugar-white sand looked like snow to me, and I felt like I was stepping on the snow while walking along the beach. I took off sandals and felt the soft sand against my bare feet. Some people were enjoying sunbathing under the warm sun while others were occupied themselves with water sports such as surfing and jet skiing. The beach was well developed with many facilities like hotels, open-air bars, restaurants, and piers. I remember we had some fresh seafood with cold beer in a bar. It was pleasant and happy to have peaceful, relaxing time with my close friend in such a wonderful place. I often miss Pensacola Beach and want to let go of worries and stress, looking at the snow-white sand.

[해석 p.313 참조]

해석

Oral Proficiency Interview-computer

본문 해석

직장 1-회사 소개

Question 1   p.20

[질문]
사전조사에서 일을 한다고 하셨습니다. 일하고 있는 회사에 대해 말해주세요. 어디에 있나요? 어떤 서비스나 제품을 제공하고 있죠? 당신은 무슨 일을 하나요?

[모범답변]
제가 일하는 회사는 충남 아산에 있는 중소회사입니다. 우리 회사는 TV보드, 변환기, LCD 패널 등의 LCD 제품의 부품을 개발하고 만듭니다. 우리는 이러한 부품을 불스, CS 또는 외국회사들과 같은 대기업에게 공급합니다. 우리 회사는 좋은 품질의 부품, 경쟁력 있는 가격, 그리고 정확한 배달로 주 거래처들과 10년 이상 동안 굳건한 신뢰를 쌓아왔습니다. 매해 부품 생산량은 증가하고 있고 매출 수익도 마찬가지로 증가하고 있습니다. 직원 수는 170명 가까이 되고 공장과 사무실은 국내와 중국 여러 곳에 있습니다. 본사는 여기 아산에 있고 직원 수는 90명 정도인데 이 직률은 연간 약 10프로 정도 됩니다. 저는 대리로서 영업사원들을 고용하고 관리하는 역할을 맡고 있습니다. 기존 사원과 신입사원이 우리 품질 좋은 부품들에 대해 잘 알게 해주고 매출목표를 달성하는 것을 독려하고 있지요. 저는 제 일과 회사를 무척 좋아하고 2년 안에 팀장으로 승진될 것을 기대하고 있습니다.

Question 2   p.23

[질문]
당신 회사의 역사에 대해 말해주세요. 언제 설립되었고 누가 창시자인가요? 창립 이후 어떻게 발전되었나요? 가능한 자세하게 말해주세요.

[모범답변]
우리 회사는 2003년 두 명의 기술자에 의해 아산에서 창립되었어요. 그들은 대기업 전자 회사에서 함께 일했었고 업무는 전자 부품을 개발하는 것이었죠. 일하는 동안 그들은 LCD 제품들에 대해 몇 개의 특허를 땄고 자신들의 사업을 하기로 결심했어요. 외부에서 투자를 좀 받고 본인들의 돈을 다 투자해서 두 명의 다른 기술자와 함께 아산에 조그만 회사를 차렸습니다. 두 창립자는 부품을 개발하고 고객을 확보하는 일에서부터 기술자들을 관리하는 것까지 여러 일들을 했어요. 초기 몇 년 동안은 겨우 회사 운영만 했습니다. 그들의 아이디어를 잠재 거래처에서는 번번이 거절했지만 그들은 LCD 부품에 대한 열정을 가지고 꾸준히 주 거래처를 찾아 다녔어요. 2년 후 두 곳의 대기업의 주 공급업체가 되는데, 이로 인해 직원을 더 채용하면서 사업을 안정적으로 유지할 수 있었죠. 2008년 LCD가 큰 인기를 끌게 되면서, 많은 회사들이 LCD TV, LCD 화면이 달린 냉장고 등과 같은 LCD 제품들을 만들었죠. 이 추세는 그들이 만든 부품의 매출이 호황을 이루게 해줬고 그들은 사업도 확장시켰어요. 한국과 중국에 공장을 짓고 사업도 점점 좋아졌죠. 저는 그들이 능력 있는 기술자라는 걸 믿지만, 또 한편으로는 사업적으로 운이 좋았다고 생각합니다.

Question 3   p.26

[질문]
회사에서 일하는 동안 특별하거나 재미있거나 또는 어려웠던 경험에 대해 말해보세요.

[모범답변]
저는 제 동료들과 다양한 에피소드들을 경험해왔는데 그들 중에서 제 속을 정말 썩인 동료에 대해 말을 하려 합니다. 제가 그를 처음 만났을 때 그는 우리 부서에 발령받은 신입사원이었어요. 제 임무는 그가 자신의 일을 하기 위해 필요한 기술을 갖추도록 도와주는 것이었는데, 그는 너무 산만했어요. 제 말을 듣지도 않았고 업무시간에도 자주 멍하니 앉아 있었어요. 저는 그가 제대로 된 길을 가도록 많은 시간을 들여 그에게 말을 했지만 그의 태도는 좋아지지 않았죠. 사실 저도 그 동료보다 고작 2년 선배였기 때문에 누군가를 가르치는 경험과 자질이 없었어요. 결국 저는 상관에게 도움을 요청했는데 그분은 이미 그의 나태함을 알고 있었어요. 제 상관은 우리 부서에서 좀 독재자인 편이었는데 동시에 능력 있는 상관이었죠. 그분은 그 신입사원을 직접 가르치기 시작했고 그는 곧 상관의 카리스마에 압도되었어요. 그는 거의 매일 야근을 해야 했고 상관에게 일일 근무일지를 제출했어야 했어요. 몇 주 지나지 않아 그는 완전 새 사람이 되었고 저는 그가 일할 때 산만한 걸 거의 보지 못했답니다. 그를 위해서는 잘된 일이지만 그를 가르치는 걸 포기해버린 제 자신에게는 좀 좌절감을 느꼈답니다.

직장 2-사내 업무 및 연수

Question 1   p.32

[질문]
당신의 회사가 직원들에게 제공하는 연수에 대해 말해보죠. 강사

가 있나요? 기술을 사용하나요? 연수에서 무엇을 배우나요? 연수과정에 대해 어떻게 생각하죠?

[모범답변]
우리 회사는 분기별로 고객 서비스에 대한 정규 연수를 제공하고 있습니다. 처음 두 연수는 고객 서비스 부서의 감독관들이 시행하고 다른 두 개는 외부 강사들에 의해 실시되고 있죠. 연수는 대개 회의장에서 열리고 모든 강사들은 컴퓨터, 비디오 클립, 영사기와 같은 기술을 사용합니다. 작년에 제가 받은 네 번의 교육을 예로 말해보겠습니다. 처음 두 훈련 과정에서 우리는 고객 불만을 처리하는 필수 규범과 실례를 배웠는데, 그건 현장에서 까다롭고 변덕스러운 고객들을 감당하는데 실제적인 도움이 되었습니다. 나머지 두 연수는 협동과 활발한 토론을 필요로 하는 활동들을 통해 팀워크를 강화하는 것을 목표로 하고 있었어요. 이 연수 과정을 통해서 저는 동료와 힘을 모으는 것이 우리의 매출 목표를 달성하는데 얼마나 중요한 것인지를 배웠습니다. 그리고 그들과 협동하는 것의 기쁨도 경험했고요. 저는 이제까지 회사에서 받은 연수들이 제 직장생활에 유용했다고 생각해요.

Question 2   p.35

[질문]
당신이 처음 일을 시작할 때 받았던 연수과정에 대해 알고 싶군요. 요즘 받고 있는 것들과는 상당히 다를 수 있겠죠. 연수과정들은 해가 지나면서 어떻게 변했나요?

[모범답변]
저는 회사에 입사하자마자 신입사원 연수에 참가했었어요. 3일 동안의 연수 프로그램이 경기도에 있는 회사 연수원에서 실시되었는데, 저를 비롯한 모든 신입직원들이 그 연수를 받기 위해 그곳에서 먹고 자야 했죠. 연수 내용은 대부분 회사 소개에 관련된 것이었는데, 예를 들면 회사 역사, 전망, 향후 목표, 인사구성 등이었죠. 연수 목적은 신입직원들로 하여금 회사에 대한 필수 정보들을 알게 하고 회사에 대한 자부심을 갖게 하는 것이라 말할 수 있어요. 이후에 받은 연수는 보다 구체적인 직무 방향을 다루는 것으로 바뀌었죠. 그런 직무관련 연수 과정들은 제가 제 필수 업무들에 더 빨리 숙달되고 준비되게 해줬습니다. 그 중 어떤 것들은 제 의사소통과 발표 기술을 발전시키는 기회도 줬는데요. 그런 것들은 새로운 고객들을 확보하는데 매우 유용했답니다. 관리직으로 승진한 후에는 리더십에 관련된 연수도 받았습니다. 제 직위와 직무가 변하면서 연수의 내용도 변해온 것입니다.

Question 3   p.38

[질문]
당신이 경험한 가장 기억나는 연수에 대해 알고 싶군요. 그 연수를 언제 받았고 무엇에 관한 것이었나요? 왜 그것이 기억에 남죠? 자세하게 말해주세요.

[모범답변]
입사 2년째 받았던 교육이 생각나네요. 발표 기술에 관한 교육이었는데요, 우리 상품을 주요 고객들에게 소개하는 저로서는 꼭 필요한 자질이었죠. 좋은 발표 기술로 훌륭한 판매 실적을 거뒀던 일부 영업부장님들에게 받은 연수였어요. 그 교육은 이전에 받았던 다른 발표 기술 교육에서 경험하지 못했던 한 가지 두드러진 특징이 있었어요. 발표 기술에 관한 대부분의 교육들은 좋은 발표가 무엇인지 알려주고 그 좋은 예들을 보여주는 것이었어요. 하지만 그 교육 과정에서는 참가자들이 주어지는 아무 주제에 대해 사람들 앞에서 발표를 해야 했고, 또 그 발표들은 녹음이 되었지요. 그리고 나서 부장님들이 우리의 동작, 눈맞춤, 그리고 말하는 스타일에 대해 보완을 해줬습니다. 목청과 목소리 톤을 어떻게 조절해야 하는가도 가르쳐주셨죠. 처음에는 비디오를 통해 제 발표를 보는 것과 제 연설체에 대해 지적을 당하는 것이 창피했지만 결국은 제 문제점을 찾아냈고 고칠 수 있었어요. 그 교육 후에 사람들 앞에 서는 것에도 자신이 생겼고요. 거기서 배운 기술들은 아직도 사용하고 있답니다.

Lesson 3 학생 생활 소개하기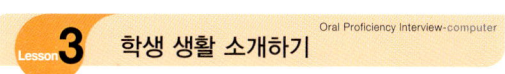

Question 1   p.44

[질문]
사전조사에서 학생이라고 표시하셨습니다. 학교 캠퍼스에 대해 묘사해주세요. 어떤 모습인가요? 가능한 자세히 설명해보세요.

[모범답변]
저는 서울에 있는 용신대학교에 다니고 있는데, 아름다운 교정으로 유명한 곳이죠. 꽃과 나무, 녹색 잔디로 가득 찬, 잘 손질된 정원들이 있습니다. 특히 봄이 되면, 교정 주위에 200그루가 넘는 벚꽃나무들이 무성하게 피어납니다. 그림 같은 풍경들을 감상하면서 학교를 거니는 것은 즐거운 경험입니다. 그래서 우리 학교가 어른들이 휴식을 취하는 장소일 뿐 아니라 초등학교와 중학교 학생들의 소풍 장소로 유명한 것이랍니다. 우리 학교는 40여 채나 되는 건물들이 있는 꽤 큰 학교입니다. 처음 교정에 들어서면 의대와 법대 건물이 있습니다. 그 두 건물은 큰 분수를 중심으로 서로 마주보고 있는데요, 그 분수는 우리 대학 학생들의 만남의 장소로 잘 알려져 있지요. 교정에는 꽤 오래된 건물들이 있는데요, 본관과 도서관이 그 예가 되는 건물입니다. 그 건물들은 우아하고 고풍스러운 외관을 지닌 석조건물이에요. 대강당 같은 다른 건물들은 새로 건축된, 세련되고 현대적인 스타일을 가진 건물입니다. 저는 우리 학교의 고전적이면서 현대적인 건축 스타일의 조합이 마음에 들어요. 이런 멋진 곳에서 공부를 하며 재미있게 보낼 수 있어 운이 좋다고 생각합니다.

Question 2
p.47

[질문]
학교에서 무엇을 공부하나요? 전공이 무엇에 관한 것이죠? 자신의 전공을 좋아하나요? 전공에 대해 자세히 말해주세요.

[모범답변]
저는 현재 영어 언어학을 전공하고 있습니다. 언어학이란 소위 인간 언어의 과학적 연구이죠. 다른 과학과 마찬가지로, 언어학은 언어의 본질을 이해하기 위해 자료를 모으고, 가설을 시험하며, 신뢰할만한 이론들을 제안합니다. 그리고 영어 언어학은 물론 영어에 초점을 맞추는 것이고요. 저는 인간이 어떻게 언어를 습득하느냐 하는 것에 흥미를 가져왔거든요. 뭐 그 질문에 쉽고 간단하게 대답할 수는 없겠지만 제 과목들을 통해 명쾌한 아이디어를 갖고 싶습니다. 정직하게 말해 영어 언어학을 전공한다는 것이 즐겁다고는 말할 수 없어요. 어떤 과목들은, 특히 음성학과 음운론은 따라가기 상당히 어렵습니다. 소리에 대한 학문인데요, 더 구체적으로 말하자면 각각의 소리가 어떻게 다른가와 그 소리들이 어떻게 체계와 패턴을 이루는가에 관한 것이에요. 저는 각각의 소리나 소리 모음을 구별하는 것이 매우 어려워서 가끔씩 그것들을 이해하지 못하는 제 자신에 좌절하기도 합니다. 하지만 그렇다고 제가 그 과목들을 싫어한다거나 제 전공을 선택한 것을 후회한다는 의미는 아닙니다. 아주 분명한 것은, 모든 과정들이 언어에 대한 지식에 필수적인 것이고 부담을 느끼는 것은 제가 인간 언어에 보다 깊게 접근하기 위해 넘어야 할 산임에 분명하니까요.

Question 3
p.51

[질문]
학교에서 수행했던 프로젝트에 대해 알고 싶네요. 무엇에 관한 프로젝트였나요? 혼자 일했나요 아니면 그룹으로 일했나요? 그 일을 완수하기 위해 당신은 무엇을 했죠?

[모범답변]
흥미로운 프로젝트가 있었는데요, 제가 2학년 첫 학기 때 했던 것입니다. 이 프로젝트는 심리적이고 사회적인 요소들이 성공적인 언어 습득에 어떻게 기여하는가에 관한 것이었어요. 그룹 프로젝트여서 배정된 다른 네 명과 함께 작업을 해야 했습니다. 저는 그룹으로 일하는 것보다 혼자 일하는 것을 더 선호하는 종류의 사람이긴 하지만 그 프로젝트를 성공적으로 완수하기 위해 그들과 협력하려고 애썼습니다. 운 좋게도, 모든 멤버들이 부지런하고 일에 대한 열의가 대단했어요. 우리는 금새 친해졌고 프로젝트가 본격적으로 시작되기 앞서 몇 번 만났죠. 우리가 필요한 업무가 무엇인지 의논하고 각자에게 업무를 배정하고, 각 업무에 대한 마감일을 정했어요. 저는 성공적인 언어 습득의 이론적인 배경을 정리하는 업무를 맡았어요. 저는 이를 위해 책과 저널, 그리고 연구자료들로부터 많은 자료들을 수집했습니다. 그리고 요점들을 정리하고 다른 멤버들과 공유했어요. 방대한 양의 자료를 몇 페이지로 압축시키는 일은 상당히 어려웠지만 보람 있었지요. 프로젝트는 순조롭게 진행되었고 결과적으로 우리의 노력은 보상을 받았죠. 뛰어난 점수를 받았을 뿐 아니라 학급에서 최고의 팀으로 선정되었으니까요.

Lesson 4 뉴스를 보거나 듣기

Question 1
p.56

[질문]
뉴스를 시청하거나 청취하기 위해서 어떤 기기를 사용하나요? 뉴스를 TV로 보나요? 라디오를 통해 뉴스를 듣나요? 어떻게 뉴스를 보거나 듣는지 자세하게 말해보세요.

[모범답변]
저는 대개 뉴스를 보는데 스마트폰을 사용해요. 연결 상태가 좋은 한, 실시간 TV 뉴스를 스마트폰으로 볼 수도 있거든요. 스마트폰에는 무료로 다운로드 받을 수 있는 애플리케이션들 역시 많아요. 저는 그 중에 몇 개를 다운로드 받아서 제가 가장 좋아하는 시청 목록에 추가시켜놓고 뉴스를 보고 싶을 때마다 체크해봐요. 뉴스 애플리케이션은 중요한 뉴스들의 표제를 보여주는데, 그건 계속 업데이트된답니다. 그럼 저는 표제들 중 한 개를 눌러서 관련 뉴스를 보기 시작하는 거예요. 스마트폰 애플리케이션이 제공하는 뉴스를 보는 게 좋은 이유 중 하나는 TV에서는 제가 관심 있는 뉴스들이 나올 때까지 기다려야 하는 반면, 거기서는 그것들을 바로 볼 수 있기 때문이에요. 게다가 어떤 뉴스 애플리케이션은 새로운 정보나 사건들을 제 인 박스 안에 보내주고 제게 그것들이 도착했다는 것을 알려주기까지 해요. 그런 서비스로 중요한 뉴스들을 신속하게 알 수 있어요. 그렇다고 제가 TV로 뉴스를 전혀 보지 않는다는 건 아니에요. 우리 부모님과 밤에 함께 있을 때는 함께 TV로 뉴스를 보려고 하거든요.

Question 2
p.59

[질문]
뉴스를 시청하거나 청취할 때 어떤 주제에 가장 관심이 가죠? 그 뉴스를 시청하거나 청취하기 위해서 무엇을 하죠?

[모범답변]
저는 확실히 스포츠에 관한 뉴스를 좋아합니다. 뉴스 애플리케이션에 있는 표제어들을 검색할 때도, 저는 스포츠와 관련된 것을 가장 먼저 고릅니다. TV로 뉴스를 볼 때도 역시 스포츠 뉴스가 시작할 때까지 기다립니다. 모든 종류의 스포츠를 다 좋아하지

만, 그래도 가장 좋아하는 건 야구죠. 야구 시즌 동안에는 그 날의 하이라이트를 보여주는 스포츠 뉴스를 거의 놓치는 법이 없어요. 정규 TV 뉴스는 스포츠 뉴스에 시간을 많이 할애하지 않기 때문에 저는 주로 밤에 몇 개의 스포츠 채널을 봅니다. 스포츠 애플리케이션을 다운로드 받아서 제가 가장 좋아하는 팀의 점수나 뉴스를 따라잡기도 하고요. 최근에는 추신수와 류현진 등의 한국 야구 선수들이 메이저리그에서 좋은 활약을 펼치고 있어서 그들에 관한 뉴스를 수시로 찾아 보고 있죠. 부디 더 많은 스포츠 채널이 생겨나고 더 좋은 스포츠 애플리케이션들이 있으면 좋겠어요.

Question 3 p.62

[질문]
당신이 어렸을 때는 어떻게 뉴스를 접했나요? 지금 뉴스를 접하는 방법과 다를 수 있었겠죠. 어떻게 변했나요?

[모범답변]
제가 어렸을 때는 사람들이 세 가지 방법으로만 뉴스를 접할 수 있었어요. TV 뉴스를 보거나 라디오 뉴스를 듣거나 신문을 보는 것이었죠. 사람들은 TV나 라디오가 뉴스를 중계해주거나 신문이 배달되기 전에는 어떤 사건이 발생했는지 알지 못했어요. TV와 신문이 다루지 않는 뉴스는 알지도 못했고요. 주요 사건과 사고들이 실시간으로 검색되는 인터넷 환경에서 자라난 사람들에게는 어처구니 없고 말도 안 되게 보일지도 모르겠네요. 오늘날은 컴퓨터와 스마트폰에서 뉴스를 볼 수 있고 뉴스들도 무척 빠르게 업데이트됩니다. 케이블 TV가 생긴 이후로는, 심지어 일부 뉴스 채널에서는 하루 종일 뉴스를 볼 수도 있어요. 저는 다른 커다란 변화, 즉 시청자들과 청취자들의 뉴스 프로그램에 보이는 적극적인 참여를 언급하고 싶어요. 그들은 아나운서나 제작자들의 이 메일에 직접 의견을 보냅니다. 또한 프로그램 홈페이지의 게시판에 격려나 불만이 담긴 의견을 남겨놓기도 하지요. 이런 일들은 제가 어렸을 때는 생각조차 못한 일들이죠.

Lesson 5 콘서트보기

Oral Proficiency Interview-computer

Question 1 p.68

[질문]
당신은 사전조사에서 콘서트에 간다고 했습니다. 어떤 종류의 콘서트를 보러 가길 좋아하고 누구와 자주 가나요? 콘서트에 가는 주된 목적은 무엇인가요? 가능한 자세히 말해보세요.

[모범답변]
저는 록, 고전음악, 팝 등 어떤 종류의 콘서트라도 보러 가는 걸 좋아합니다. 하지만 가장 좋아하는 것을 고르라고 한다면 한국 팝 콘서트라고 말하겠습니다. 저는 많은 한국 가요들을 좋아하는데, 콘서트장에서는 그 음악의 열기와 열정을 느낄 수 있습니다. 저는 대개 친구와 함께 K팝 콘서트를 보러 갑니다. 우리는 음악에 있어 취향이 비슷하기 때문에, K팝 스타들의 노래와 콘서트 같은 정보들을 공유하죠. 콘서트는 스트레스와 긴장으로 가득 찬 제 일상생활의 탈출구와 같습니다. 특히 록 콘서트와 K팝 콘서트에서 다른 관중들과 함께 노래를 따라 부르고 소리를 지르면서 카타르시스를 느낍니다. 고전음악 콘서트는 저를 편안하게 해주고 치유해주기도 하고요. 그런 감정적 해방감이나 정화를 통해 제 인생에 대해 좀 더 긍정적인 태도를 갖게 됩니다. 어떤 사람들은 콘서트 표 값이 너무 비싸다고들 하지만, 저는 좋은 콘서트는 그렇게 돈을 쓸 가치가 충분히 있다고 생각해요.

Question 2 p.71

[질문]
가장 최근에 간 콘서트는 무엇인가요? 언제, 어디서 열렸나요? 콘서트홀이 좋았나요? 그 콘서트홀을 자세히 묘사해보세요.

[모범답변]
저는 지난 12월에 두 명의 촉망 받는 한국 음악가인 손여름과 강클라라 주미가 공연하는 피아노와 바이올린 듀오 콘서트를 보러 갔어요. 서울 양재동에 있는 예술의 전당에 있는 콘서트 홀에서 열렸었지요. 저는 예술의 전당에 가는 걸 좋아하는데, 그 곳이 산으로 둘러싸여 있고 음악당 외에도 미술관들과 다른 시설들이 잘 갖춰져 있기 때문이죠. 콘서트홀은 3층으로 되어있는데 상당히 넓었어요. 정확한 좌석 수는 잘 모르겠지만 2천 석이 넘는다고 봐요. 저는 1층 뒤에 앉았는데, 자리가 2시간 반 동안의 콘서트를 끝까지 보고 앉아있기에 충분히 편안했어요. 앞에 있는 큰 무대를 보았고, 그 무대 위에는 연주자들에게 스포트라이트를 줄 수 있는 소냉시설이 있었어요. 그 홀의 음향시설도 좋았던 걸로 기억이 됩니다. 결론적으로 그 콘서트홀은 관객에게 쾌적하고 편안한 분위기를 줬어요.

Question 3 p.74

[질문]
당신이 콘서트를 보면서 겪었던 가장 인상적인 경험은 무엇인가요? 왜 그 콘서트가 당신에게 기억할만한 것이 되었나요? 모든 이야기를 해주세요.

[모범답변]
저는 몇 년 전에 싸이의 콘서트를 다녀왔는데, 그가 강남스타일이라는 노래로 세계적인 유명 가수가 되기 얼마 전이었죠. 12월 마지막 날에, 남자친구와 새해 전날 밤을 기념하기 위해 그 콘서트를 봤어요. 그의 콘서트를 보러 간 건 그 때가 처음이었지만 사실 기대를 그렇게 많이 하지는 않았어요. 저에게 그는 가수라

기보다는 노래가 아닌 현란한 공연으로 관중을 흥분시키는 예능인이었거든요. 하지만 공연이 진행되면서 저는 제가 틀렸다는 걸 깨달았죠. 그는 제가 생각했던 것보다 노래를 훨씬 잘했고 역동적인 춤으로 제 눈과 마음을 사로잡았어요. 저는 점점 신나서 그의 빠른 음악에 맞춰 다른 관객들과 노래를 따라 부르고 춤을 추지 않을 수가 없었죠. 그는 시각적으로 인상적인 무대를 만들기 위해 공연에 교묘한 무대장치들을 혼합했는데, 그것이 우리들을 더 신나게 했어요. 그는 콘서트 내내 그의 과거와 현재 노래를 모두 불렀고 미국 팝송도 불렀습니다. 8시에 시작했던 콘서트가 자정이 거의 다 되어서야 끝났답니다. 정말 즐거운 콘서트였고 저는 그가 눈부신 무대매너만이 아니라 가창력까지 가진 좋은 가수라는 걸 알게 되었습니다.

Question 1　　　　　　　　　　　　　　　　　　　　p.80

[질문]
당신은 사전조사에서 체스를 둔다고 했습니다. 체스는 어떤 것이고 어떻게 두는 거죠? 언제 어디서 주로 체스를 두나요? 왜 체스를 좋아하죠? 체스에 대해 가능한 자세하게 말해보세요.

[모범답변]
체스는 64개의 사각무늬가 있는 체스판에서 두 명의 대결자가 겨루는 게임입니다. 왕 1개, 여왕 2개, 루크 2개, 비숍 2개, 기사 2개, 졸 8개로 한 명당 16개의 말을 갖게 됩니다. 체스에서 이기려면 상대편의 왕을 불러야 합니다. 그건 제가 그 말을 도망가지 못하는 장소에 놓아야 한다는 걸 의미해요. 저는 우리 아버지와 집에서 자주 체스를 두는데 주로 저녁 먹고 둡니다. 저에게 체스 두는 걸 가르쳐주신 아버지께선 저의 가장 좋은 체스 상대시죠. 저는 체스가 재미있어서 좋습니다. 체스를 두다 보면 시간 가는 줄 몰라요. 체스를 두면 두뇌에도 좋습니다. 많은 연구들이 체스는 뇌의 양 쪽을 운동시킨다고 하고, 그 운동이 기억력을 향상시키고 문제해결 능력을 증가시켜준다고 합니다. 그들은 또한 체스가 어르신들이 알츠하이머를 예방하는 것에도 도움이 된다고 해요. 사실 제가 우리 아버지와 자주 체스를 두는 가장 큰 이유 중의 하나가 그것이기도 합니다.

Question 2　　　　　　　　　　　　　　　　　　　　p.83

[질문]
에바도 체스 두는 걸 좋아합니다. 그녀에게 체스에 관해 알고 싶은 서너 가지 질문들을 해보세요.

[모범답변]
당신이 체스를 즐겨 둔다고 들었어요. 우리 나라에서는 대중적인 게임이 아니라서 어떻게 둬야 하는지 아는 사람이 거의 없어요. 체스의 기본적인 규칙에 대해 설명해주실 수 있나요? 누가 먼저 움직이나요, 흰 말을 가진 사람인가요 아니면 검정 말을 가진 사람인가요? 각각의 다른 말들은 어떻게 움직여야 하죠? 모든 말들이 위, 아래, 옆, 대각선으로 움직일 수 있나요? 저는 체스의 역사에 대해서도 알고 싶어요. 어떤 사람들은 6세기 전에 인도에서 체스의 초기 형태의 게임에서 유래되었다고 해요. 다른 사람들은 최초의 보드 게임이었던 장기가 중국의 매우 초기 문학작품에 등장했다고도 하고요. 그리고 마지막 질문이 있어요. 체스 두는 것을 왜 좋아하세요? 단순히 시간을 보내기 위해 두나요? 아니면 체스가 두뇌를 훈련시켜줘서 좋아하나요? 저도 체스를 무척 좋아하는데 가까운 장래에 당신과 체스를 뒀으면 해요, 에바.

Question 3　　　　　　　　　　　　　　　　　　　　p.86

[질문]
체스를 두면서 겪었던 인상적인 경험에 관해 듣고 싶군요. 어떤 것이었고 언제 일어났나요? 자세히 말해보세요.

[모범답변]
대학교 때 제 후배와 함께 둔 체스 게임이 생각나네요. 우리는 그 애의 집에서 2년 전쯤 체스를 뒀어요. 우리는 누가 이길지 내기를 했어요. 진 사람이 이긴 사람한테 점심을 사기로 했죠. 그 애는 저한테 체스를 배웠고 전에 한 번도 저를 이겨본 적이 없었으니까 좀 불공정한 것 같기도 했어요. 하지만 그냥 재미를 위해 비싸지 않은 식당에서 점심을 먹는 것으로 협의했어요. 놀랍게도 그 애의 체스 실력은 제 예상과 달리 많이 향상됐었어요. 저는 그 애의 말을 몇 개 잡았지만 그 애는 제 말을 더 잡고 게임 내내 중앙을 지배했어요. 나중에 안 것이지만 그 애는 혼자 계속 연습을 해서 그렇게 잘하게 된 것이었죠. 결국 그 애가 이겼고 저는 점심을 샀어요. 저는 청출어람이라며 기쁜 척 했지만 사실 게임에 진 것이 너무 화가 났어요. 저는 지는 걸 싫어하는 경쟁적인 사람이거든요. 제 얼굴이 벌게지게 되었기 때문에 그 애도 제가 기분이 안 좋은 걸 눈치챘을 거예요. 아, 그 기억 때문에 기분이 나빠지려고 하네요. 아무래도 제 자존심이 상했던 그 날을 잊을 수가 없나 봅니다.

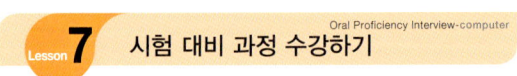

Question 1　　　　　　　　　　　　　　　　　　　　p.92

[질문]

사전조사에서 시험 준비 과정을 수강한 적이 있다고 했습니다. 언제 어디서 그 과정들을 수강했나요? 그 과정을 왜 수강했고 왜 그 기관을 선택했나요? 그 과정이 당신의 시험 준비에 도움이 되었나요? 자세하게 말해보세요.

[모범답변]
대학교 3학년 때, 저는 공인중개사 자격시험을 준비했습니다. 그 자격증은 부동산업계에 취직하고 싶어하는 사람들에게는 필수적인 것이었죠. 많은 대학생들이 취직하기 힘들어했기 때문에 이력서에 추가할 자격증을 가능한 많이 가지고 있으려고 노력했거든요. 저도 예외는 아니라서 다른 두 명의 친구들과 함께 그 시험을 준비했어요. 우리는 3개월짜리 온라인 과정을 등록했는데요. 우리가 그 과정을 선택한 이유는 수업료가 다른 오프라인 과정들의 절반 정도였기 때문이죠. 우리는 일주일에 세 번 만나서 강의를 듣고 함께 공부했어요. 시험은 1차, 2차가 있었는데, 두 시험 모두 같은 날 봐야 했죠. 두 개 다 객관식 문제로 되어 있었지만 저는 2차 시험이 더 까다롭고 어려웠어요. 저는 그 온라인 과정을 통해 배웠던 것을 기반으로 열심히 공부했고, 그 과정을 마친 3개월 후 마침내 두 시험 모두 통과했어요. 하지만 다른 두 친구들이 2차 시험에 떨어졌기 때문에 대놓고 좋아할 수는 없었답니다.

Question 2   p.95

[질문]
어떤 과목들을 수강했나요? 시험 준비에 대해 무엇을 배웠나요? 시험 준비는 어떻게 했나요?

[모범답변]
제가 수강했던 온라인 과정은 다섯 개의 수업으로 구성되어있었어요. 두 개의 수업은 부동산 이론과 규제를 가르쳤고, 두 개는 세금 제도와 부동산공법을 다뤘으며, 나머지 한 개는 공인중개사 실무를 가르쳤지요. 선생님은 첫 달 동안 부동산의 기본적인 법령과 이론에 대한 강의를 하셨는데 우리가 모두 외워야 할 것들이었어요. 그리고 나서 좀 더 구체적인 내용으로 넘어갔고 그 내용의 실제적인 적용을 위한 예들을 보여주셨어요. 마지막 단계로 10세트의 모의고사를 주셨는데, 그것들은 제가 배운 것들을 복습하고 실제 시험에 잘 준비하는데 도움이 되었죠. 저는 그 온라인 과정의 수업을 충실히 따랐어요. 주어진 과제들은 모두 완수했고 수업 후에 복습도 했죠. 일부 어려운 문제들이나 개념들은 친구들과 논의했고 온라인 기관에서 운영했던 질문게시판에 남기기도 했어요. 한 번에 시험을 통과하면서 제 노력이 보상을 받았으니 저는 운이 좋은 셈이죠.

Question 3   p.98

[질문]
시험 준비를 하면서 일어났던 흥미롭거나 놀랍거나 예측하지 못했던 일들에 대해 알고 싶군요. 무슨 일이었고 언제 일어났나요? 모두 이야기해보세요.

[모범답변]
제 자격증 시험 며칠 전, 차 사고가 났어요. 운전을 하며 집에 가는 중이었는데 차 한대가 속도도 줄이지 않고 갑자기 골목에서 튀어나왔던 거예요. 저는 부딪치는 걸 피하기 위해 급하게 핸들을 왼쪽으로 꺾을 수 밖에 없었는데, 그로 인해 제 차가 연석을 박게 되었죠. 반대 차선에서 차가 한 대도 오지 않았던 건 정말 행운이었지만 제 차의 앞 부분이 그 충격으로 좀 찌그러졌어요. 비록 외상은 없었지만 저는 교통사고로 인해 생길 수 있는 후유증이 걱정되었어요. 차가 연석에 부딪쳤을 때 제 왼쪽 어깨에 충격을 받았거든요. 제가 생각했던 가장 끔찍한 건 통증이 커져서 시험을 볼 수 없게 되는 것이었어요. 저는 곧장 근처에 있는 정형외과에 가서 엑스레이를 찍어봤어요. 결과가 나오길 기다리는데 정말 불안했습니다. 다행히 어깨 골절과 같은 심각한 문제는 없었습니다. 가벼운 타박상을 입긴 했지만 시험을 치는 데는 아무 문제가 없었지요. 지금 생각해도 참 예기치 않은 사고였습니다.

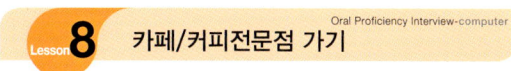

Lesson 8 카페/커피전문점 가기

Question 1   p.104

[질문]
사전조사에서 카페에 간다고 했습니다. 당신 동네에는 어떤 카페나 커피숍이 있나요? 어떤 모습이죠? 어떤 카페를 좋아하나요? 왜 그곳을 좋아하죠? 가능한 자세히 말해보세요.

[모범답변]
우리 동네에는 10개 이상의 카페가 있어요. 대부분이 스타카페나 빈커피 같은 커피 체인점이죠. 그런 커피 체인점들이 어느 지역에서나 생기는 것이 일종의 트렌드 같아요. 비슷한 내부 디자인과 다양한 종류의 커피를 팔죠. 목조 가구, 밝은 조명, 그리고 직원들이 뒤에서 커피를 만드는 조리대가 있습니다. 스타카페만이 가지고 있는 두드러진 특징은 각이 있는 커다란 책상이 있어서 여덟 명에서 열 명의 사람들이 둘러 앉아있을 수 있다는 거죠. 하지만 제가 가장 좋아하는 카페는 도도카페라고, 우리 집에서 몇 블록 떨어진 곳에 있는 작은 카페입니다. 작긴 하지만 분위기가 무척 따뜻하고 아늑해요. 공원 바로 건너편에 있는 건물 2층에 있거든요. 그래서 창가 쪽에 자리를 잡은 후에 공원과 거리의 멋진 경치를 즐기곤 하죠. 오래된 커피제조기와 커피분쇄기가 있고, 두세 개의 아름다운 유화들이 벽에 걸려있어요. 아무래

도 카페 주인은 커피 볶는 비결이 있는 것 같은데, 향이 너무 좋고 맛도 환상적이기 때문입니다. 그 카페에 있는 모든 것이 저를 편안하고 여유 있게 해줍니다.

지는 않아요.

Lesson 9 악기 연주하기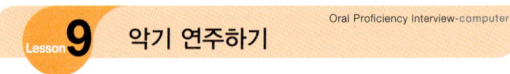

Question 2   p.107

[질문]
당신 나라에서는 사람들이 카페나 커피숍에서 무엇을 하나요?

[모범답변]
10년 전만 해도, 대부분의 사람들은 카페나 커피숍을 단순히 만남의 장소라고 여겼습니다. 혼자 카페에 가거나 노트북으로 일을 하는 사람들도 거의 없었죠. 하지만 스타카페와 같은 커피 체인점들이 점점 더 많이 개장을 함에 따라 사람들은 카페나 커피숍에 대해 완전히 다른 개념을 갖게 되었습니다. 그곳은 사람들을 만나는 장소일 뿐 아니라 공부하고 책을 읽고 일하는 장소가 되었습니다. 이제는 사람들이 커피숍에 혼자 앉아 있는 걸 보는 일이 흔합니다. 아침에는 출근하면서 샌드위치와 커피를 가져가는 사람들을 자주 봅니다. 최근에는 많은 커피숍들이 합리적인 가격으로 브런치를 제공해서 젊은 부부들이 주말마다 먹기도 합니다. 프리랜서와 학생들도 카페에서 컴퓨터로 일을 하면서 긴 시간 동안 앉아 있기도 하죠. 저도 가끔 책을 읽거나 컴퓨터 작업을 하기 위해 스타카페를 갑니다. 제 생각에는 우리 나라에 있는 커피숍의 숫자가 당분간은 계속 늘어날 것 같습니다.

Question 3   p.110

[질문]
카페나 커피숍에서 겪었던 가장 기억에 남는 경험에 대해 말해보세요.

[모범답변]
대학생일 때 저는 카페에서 시간제 근무를 한 적이 있었습니다. 12월 1일 그 카페에서 저는 크리스마스 트리 장식을 하고 있었어요. 손님들이 크리스마스 분위기를 느끼실 수 있도록 저는 작고 귀여운 뿔이 있는 루돌프 모자를 쓰고 있었죠. 제가 막 나무 장식을 끝마쳤을 때 엄마와 브런치를 먹고 있던 한 어린 소년이 저에게 다가왔어요. 저는 그 애가 제 모자에 달린 뿔에 관심이 있다고 생각을 했어요. 그 뿔을 만져봐도 좋다고 말하니까 제 이름이 루돌프냐고 물었어요. 그 애가 너무 진지해 보여서 저는 그렇다고 말했죠. 그랬더니 그 애는 크리스마스 이브에 산타와 함께 자기에게 올 거냐고 묻더군요. 저는 부모님하고 친구에게 친절하게 굴면 제가 그 애를 찾아갈 거라고 말했어요. 좀 오그리는 것 같긴 했지만 그 아이를 실망시키고 싶지 않았기 때문이에요. 신나고 즐거워했던 걸 보아 제 말을 믿었던 것 같습니다. 그 애가 너무 귀여워서 저는 그 애의 부모님이 그 애가 자는 사이에 머리맡에 멋진 선물을 놓아두길 바랬습니다. 지금 생각해보면 제가 좀 촌스럽고 유치했던 것도 같지만 그런 말을 한 것을 후회하지는 않아요.

Question 1   p.116

[질문]
사전조사에서 악기를 연주한다고 했습니다. 어떤 악기를 연주하나요? 그 악기는 어떻게 연주하는 거지요? 연주하기 위해 뭘 해야 하나요? 연습은 주로 어디서 합니까?

[모범답변]
저는 바이올린을 켤 줄 압니다. 바이올린은 네 개의 현이 있고 그 위로 활을 켜면서 소리가 나는 것이죠. 바이올린을 켜기 전에 저는 제 바이올린에 대해 두 가지를 꼭 체크합니다. 첫째, 활에 로진을 바르는데 그건 현 위로 활이 부드럽게 움직이게 하기 위해서입니다. 그렇지 않으면 소리가 잘 나지 않아요. 둘째, 전자 튜너로 바이올린을 조율합니다. 이미 줄을 조율해놓았다 해도, 그 조율한 것이 공기나 날씨에 따라 변할 수가 있거든요. 바이올린은 습기에 매우 예민해서 연주를 할 때마다 새로 조율해야 합니다. 저는 주로 퇴근 후 제 바이올린으로 집에서 연습을 합니다. 주말에는 더 많은 시간을 연습에 할애하고 있고요. 이웃에게 소음이 될 수도 있어서 소리를 작게 해주는 기구를 사용합니다. 처음 바이올린을 켰을 때는 소리가 아주 거칠고 제 팔 근육도 쑤셨지만 이제는 좋고 깨끗한 소리를 낼 줄 압니다.

Question 2   p.119

[질문]
그 악기를 누구에게 배웠나요? 얼마나 오래 그 악기를 연주해왔나요? 정기적으로 얼마나 연습을 하나요?

[모범답변]
저는 8년간 스타 피아노 학원에서 바이올린을 배웠어요. 제 집 근처의 학원들을 몇 군데 찾아보고 성인 수강생이 가장 많은 한 곳을 골랐어요. 우리 선생님은 대학에서 바이올린을 전공했고 5년 이상 학생들을 가르친 경력이 있었죠. 3년 동안 저는 매주 토요일 20분씩 개인 교습을 받았어요. 선생님은 리듬을 맞추거나 악보를 읽는 법과 같이 기본적인 규칙들을 가르쳐주었어요. 얼마 후 저는 바이올린과 활을 잡는 법을 배웠어요. 선생님은 항상 활을 켜는 연습의 중요성을 강조했죠. 5년 전부터는 그룹으로 수업을 배우기 시작했어요. 개인 수업에서만큼 많은 관심을 받을 수는 없지만 다른 사람들과 함께 배우는 것도 재미있다는 것을 알았어요. 다른 사람들 앞에서 바이올린을 켜는 것이 부끄럽긴 하지만 동시에 다른 사람들이 연주하는 것을 듣는 것도 상당히 설레고 흥미롭더라고요. 저는 바이올린 켜는 걸 아주 좋아해서 수

업 후에도 학원에서 30분 혹은 그 이상 연습을 합니다.

Question 3   p.122

[질문]
어떻게 처음 그 악기에 관심을 갖게 된 거죠? 그 악기로 결정한 이유는 뭔가요? 당신의 관심은 수년간 어떻게 변했나요?

[모범답변]
바이올린에 대한 제 관심은 수년 동안 분명히 변했습니다. 8년 전 저는 단지 취미로 뭔가 새로운 것을 배우고 싶었어요. 악기를 연주하는 것은 재미있고 보람 있는 취미일 수 있겠다 싶었죠. 사실 처음에는 피아노를 칠까 생각했어요. 하지만 아시다시피 피아노는 너무 비싸 살 수가 없고 가지고 다닐 수도 없잖아요. 좀 속물적일 수도 있는 거겠지만 그 당시에 저는 악기케이스를 들고 다니는 사람들이 부러웠거든요. 첫 수업을 들을 때까지만 해도 저는 이렇게 오래 바이올린을 배울 생각을 전혀 안 했어요. 바이올린을 웬만큼 켜게 되면 그만 배울 생각이었거든요. 하지만 일단 시작하고 나니 저는 바이올린에 깊게 빠져들게 되었어요. 저는 바이올린의 소리가 너무 좋습니다. 아직도 저는 새로운 악보를 읽고 박자를 세는 것이 어렵게 느껴지긴 해요. 가끔은 한 곡을 끝내는데 1년 이상이 걸려요. 하지만 그것이 또한 바이올린의 매력이죠. 매우 어려운 곡들을 끝내고 제가 연주하는 음악을 들을 때 성취감이 느껴져요. 이제 바이올린은 제게 취미 훨씬 그 이상이에요. 저는 언젠가 작은 콘서트를 여는 꿈을 가지고 있습니다.

Question 1   p.128

[질문]
당신의 나라에서 사람들은 어떻게 신문을 읽나요? 신문을 구독하나요 아니면 읽고 싶을 때 구매를 하나요? 집이나 사무실에서는 어떤 신문을 읽나요? 그들은 왜 신문을 읽나요?

[모범답변]
우리나라에서는 사람들이 일반적으로 일간신문을 구독합니다. 배달 받는 것이 밖에서 사는 것보다 더 편리하니까요. 하지만 아침에 신문을 읽을 시간이 잘 없는 사람은 읽을 시간이 날 때 뉴스가판대에서 사기도 하죠. 사람들이 어떤 신문을 보느냐는 그들의 성향과 관심에 따라 다릅니다. 어떤 사람들은 주요 신문사들을 선호하고 또 다른 사람들은 지역 신문을 선호하죠. 어떤 사람들은 자신들의 목적에 맞춰 경제신문이나 영자신문을 고를 수도 있을 테고요. 저는 대부분의 사람들이 정치, 사회 사건, 사람과 경제 등의 다양한 영역에서 정보를 얻기 위해 신문을 읽는다고 생각해요. 신문은 그날의 복잡한 주제에 대해 심층보도를 통해 사람들이 사건들에 대해 더 잘 알게 해주니까요. 어떤 사람들은 논리적이고 좋은 글을 읽으면서 즐거움을 찾기 위해 신문을 읽기도 합니다. 저도 사실은 신문에서 인상적인 문장들을 보면 제 노트에 적어놓습니다. 그리고는 제가 글을 쓰면서 저만의 문장을 만들 때 본보기로 사용한답니다.

Question 2   p.131

[질문]
신문은 수년간 어떻게 변해왔나요? 신문의 미래를 어떻게 보나요? 왜 그렇게 생각하죠?

[모범답변]
신문은 시간이 지나면서 많은 점에 있어 변해 왔습니다. 첫째, 레이아웃이 더 나은 시각적인 효과를 위해 변했어요. 우리 가족이 구독하는 신문을 생각해보면, 글자와 사진, 광고들이 페이지에 배열되는 방식이 과거보다 훨씬 더 보기 좋습니다. 신문의 내용도 변했어요. 신문들은 과거에 그랬던 것보다 문화와 예술에 대한 보도에 더 많은 지면을 할애하고 있죠. 가장 큰 변화들 중의 하나는 온라인 뉴스의 출현이라고 생각해요. 인터넷과 스마트폰이 발달되면서 사람들은 온라인으로 거의 모든 종류의 신문들을 볼 수 있습니다. 그러한 변화로 종이 신문들의 구독률이, 특히 젊은 사람들 사이에서 떨어졌죠. 어떤 사람들은 머지 않아 온라인 신문이 모든 종이 신문들을 대신할 거라고 예측합니다. 하지만 저는 그 생각에 동의하지 않는데요, 왜냐하면 사람들은 그렇게 오랫동안 해오던 그들의 방식을 쉽게 포기하지 않기 때문입니다. 게다가, 온라인 뉴스를 보는 것은 종이 신문을 보는 것보다 시간과 노력이 더 필요합니다. 온라인 뉴스에서 보여지는 많은 제목들을 계속 클릭해서 어떤 정보들이 그 안에 있는지 확인해야 하잖아요. 허지민 종이 신문의 경우는 그냥 페이지를 넘기면서 어떤 정보든 쉽게 찾을 수가 있죠.

Question 3   p.134

[질문]
당신이 기대하는 신문의 역할은 무엇인가요? 신문은 어떤 역할을 해야 한다고 생각하죠? 신문을 읽음으로써 얻는 혜택은 무엇인가요?

[모범답변]
저는 신문이 우리 사회의 효과적인 의사소통 도구로서의 역할을 하길 기대합니다. 우리는 신문을 통해 우리 주위나 전 세계 다른 지역에서 무슨 일이 일어나고 있는지 알 수 있습니다. 모든 종류의 뉴스를 전달하면서, 신문은 독자들로부터 이해와 선의를 끌어낼 수도 있고 적개심과 분노를 유발할 수 있습니다. 저는 좋은 신문은 독자들에게 정확한 사실에 근거한 공정한 보도를 하는

신문이라고 믿습니다. 그러려면 균형잡힌 관점으로 어떤 주제에 대해서도 건설적인 의견을 제시해야 하겠죠. 신문을 읽는 것의 이점 중 하나는 다양한 주제에 관해 믿을만한 정보를 얻을 수 있다는 것입니다. 신문은 다른 어떤 출처의 정보보다 믿을 만 합니다. 웹 포탈은 자주 사실 확인도 없이 어떤 이야기나 사건을 급하게 보도하지만 신문은 전문 기자들이 사건에 대한 심층보도를 근거로 기사를 씁니다. 그런 신용도 말고도 신문은 우리에게 매우 구체적인 지식과 정보를 제공합니다. 대부분의 경우 뉴스 포탈이나 TV 뉴스는 신문만큼 자세한 분석을 제공하지 않습니다. 저는 자주 정보력이 좋고 아는 게 많다는 말을 듣는데요, 그건 부지런히 신문을 읽는 제 습관 덕이라고 할 수 있습니다.

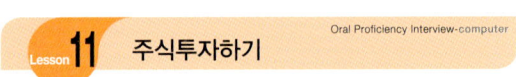

Question 1　　　　　　　　　　　　　　　　　　p.140

[질문]
당신의 나라에서는 사람들이 어떻게 주식을 매매합니까? 거래를 하러 증권회사에 가나요 아니면 온라인으로 하나요? 주식 매매를 위해서는 뭘 해야 합니까?

[모범답변]
우리 나라에서는 사람들이 주로 인터넷으로 주식을 거래해요. 어떤 사람들은 주식을 거래하러 증권회사로 직접 가기도 하지만, 온라인으로 거래하는 것이 훨씬 흔합니다. 온라인 주식거래를 위해서 가장 먼저 해야 하는 일은 매매 거래를 위해 증권회사와 제휴한 은행을 선택하는 것입니다. 그런 다음 계좌를 개설하러 그 은행을 한 번은 방문해야 합니다. 방문할 때는 주민등록증을 포함한 일부 서류들을 제출해야 하죠. 일단 계좌개설을 하면 가상 계좌에 입금을 해서 매매를 시작할 수 있어요. 휴대폰, 컴퓨터, 홈 매매 시스템으로 거래를 하면 됩니다. 인터넷에서는 투자하고 싶은 회사를 검색하거나 선택할 수 있고 그 회사 주가가 어떻게 상승하고 하락하는지 볼 수 있어요. 그리고 실시간으로 주식을 사고 팔 수도 있고요. 저는 사람들이 주식동향에 관해 잘 안다면 주식투자로 돈을 벌 수 있는 기회를 얻을 수 있다고 생각합니다.

Question 2　　　　　　　　　　　　　　　　　　p.143

[질문]
언제 처음 주식에 투자를 했나요? 얼마를 투자했죠? 어느 주식을 샀나요? 처음부터 끝까지 전부 말해보세요.

[모범답변]
저는 대학교를 졸업하고 바로 첫 번째 직장을 가졌을 때 주식에 백 만원을 투자했습니다. 그 당시에는 어디서 주식을 사야 하는

지도 몰랐고, 주식차트를 어떻게 보는지도 몰랐죠. 증권회사에 다니던 제 친구의 도움으로 저는 그 친구의 증권회사와 제휴된 은행에서 계좌를 개설했어요. 그리고 나서는 주식시장의 경향을 관찰하기 시작했고 일부 기업들에 관한 뉴스, 예를 들면 그들이 만든 신상품과 경제 상황이 그 회사들한테 어떻게 영향을 미치는가에 대한 것들을 들었죠. 한 달 뒤에 저는 한 자동차 회사 주식을 샀습니다. 그 회사는 하이브리드 승용차 신 모델을 개발 중이었고, 저는 그 차가 곧 출시될 거라고 전망했어요. 그래서 한 주당 만원에 주식을 샀죠. 두 달 후에 주가는 한 주에 4만원으로 치솟았고, 저는 제 투자액의 4배를 벌었어요. 그때 이후로 저는 주식을 더 열심히 하고 있습니다. 회사의 주가가 어떻게 오르고 떨어지는지를 보여주는 주식차트를 점검하죠. 물론 제가 매번 주식거래로 돈을 버는 건 아니지만 돈을 벌기 위해 저는 계속 주식에 투자할 거예요.

Question 3　　　　　　　　　　　　　　　　　　p.146

[질문]
주식시장과 관련된 가장 기억에 남는 사건에 대해 말해보세요.

[모범답변]
저는 천 만원 이상 주식에 투자해본 적이 없어요. 저는 더 많은 돈을 투자할수록 위험이 더 커진다고 생각했거든요. 하지만 저로 하여금 마음을 바꾸게 만든 사건이 작년에 있었어요. 아마 북한이 남한을 핵무기로 공격한다고 위협했던 것을 기억하실 거예요. 이 일이 일어났을 때 주식시장은 굉장히 심하게 영향을 받았고 많은 주식의 가격이 폭락했었죠. 저는 본능적으로 돈을 많이 벌 수 있는 기회라는 느낌이 들었어요. 제가 가진 대부분의 돈을 인출해서 주식시장이 정상적일 때는 빈번히 높은 가격으로 거래되다가 주가가 심하게 떨어져버린 주식을 샀어요. 그리고는 북한과 남한 사이의 관계에 대한 뉴스를 주시하면서 주가가 오르길 기다렸어요. 저는 대담한 결정을 하는 것만큼 인내심도 중요하다는 걸 알고 있었어요. 1년이 지나고 저는 그 주식을 제가 산 가격의 세 배 가격에 팔았고, 돈을 많이 벌었죠. 아주 좋은 순간에 투자를 했고 그건 제가 한 최고의 결정이었어요. 이런 기회가 다시 또 올 거라는 생각은 하지 않습니다. 운이 좋았던 거죠.

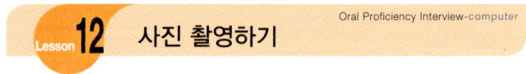

Question 1　　　　　　　　　　　　　　　　　　p.152

[질문]
사전조사에서 사진을 찍는다고 했습니다. 현재 어떤 카메라를 가지고 있나요? 어디서 난 건가요? 기능은 어떤가요? 카메라에 만

족하나요? 당신의 카메라에 대해 모든 걸 이야기해보세요.

[모범답변]
저는 작년 아버지께 생일선물로 받은 캠코 제품 D700 디지털 카메라를 갖고 있어요. 셔터, 3인치 컬러 모니터, 자동 초점 버튼, 그리고 다양한 기능 모드가 갖춰져 있죠. 소형 디지털 카메라보다 좀 무겁고 부피가 있긴 하지만 저는 이 카메라가 좋아요. 활동적이고 움직이는 이미지를 찍을 때 장점이 드러나는데요. 이 사진기는 특별 기능이 있어 1초에 8장까지 연속으로 찍힌답니다. 이 기능 덕분에 대상이 움직이는 동안에도 모든 움직임을 잡을 수 있어요. 또 초음파 센서는 카메라 렌즈에 묻은 먼지 입자를 제거해 주는데, 이건 제가 깨끗하고 자연스러운 사진을 찍는데 도움이 돼요. 이 카메라의 가장 좋은 기능은 빛이 자동 조정 된다는 거예요. 어두운 곳에서 사진 찍을 때 그림자가 생기거나 어둡게 나올 수 있는데요. 이런 경우 자동 활성 조명 모드가 어둠 속에 있는 세밀한 것들을 저장하고 포착해줍니다. 이 카메라로 비디오를 더 오래 찍을 수 있으면 더 좋겠지만 전반적으로 저는 제 카메라에 만족해서 항상 가지고 다닌답니다.

Question 2 p.155

[질문]
카메라는 수년에 걸쳐 크게 변해왔습니다. 당신이 처음 사진을 찍기 시작했을 때를 기억하나요? 그 카메라들은 현재의 카메라와 어떻게 달랐나요? 그러한 변화가 사진 찍는 방법에 어떻게 영향을 미쳤나요?

[모범답변]
기능에 있어서 카메라는 수년간 급진적인 변화를 겪었어요. 아날로그 시대에는 대부분의 카메라들이 손으로 작동되었고 카메라가 찍는 사진들도 흑백이었죠. 하지만 요즘은 수많은 디지털 카메라가 있고 대부분의 기능이 자동이에요. 제가 필름 카메라로 사진을 찍었을 때가 17살이었어요. 그 카메라는 우리 할아버지 때부터 내려온 것이었는데 사진 찍을 때마다 필름을 손으로 돌리고 뭘 찍느냐에 따라 렌즈 초점을 다르게 조정했어요. 플래시는 매우 컸고 거기서 나오는 빛이 상당히 셌어요. 현대의 카메라는 더 작고 다기능이죠. 빛도 자동으로 조정되고 줌 기능은 사진을 찍을 때마다 렌즈를 건드리지 않아도 되게 해 줍니다. 디지털 카메라는 많은 것들을 편하게 해줍니다. 예를 들어, 사진을 찍자마자 바로 카메라에 부착된 모니터를 통해 확인할 수 있어서 사진이 잘 안 나왔을 때 삭제하고 다시 찍기가 쉽습니다. 저는 디지털 카메라에 익숙해져서 이제는 아날로그 카메라는 못 쓸 것 같아요.

Question 3 p.158

[질문]
사진 찍는 것과 관련된 예상치 못했거나 놀라웠던 경험에 대해 말해주세요.

[모범답변]
저는 작년에 친구들과 함께 일본 오사카로 여행을 갔어요. 친구들과 가능한 많은 사진을 찍으려고 디지털 카메라와 메모리카드 두 개, 그리고 삼각대 한 개를 가져갔어요. 하지만 여행 첫 날 저는 삼각대를 잃어버리고 말았어요. 어디 뒀는지 기억도 안 나서 그냥 다른 걸 샀죠. 근데 그 다음날은 또 호텔에서 메모리카드를 갖고 나가는 걸 잊어버려서 사진도 많이 못 찍었어요. 가장 최악은 여행 마지막 날이었어요. 호텔에서 제 짐을 다 싸고 공항에서 탑승수속을 했어요. 비행기를 타려고 기다리는데 그만 카메라 가방이 없다는 걸 안 거예요. 공항에 오면서 공항버스에 두고 내린 게 분명했어요. 저는 공항 직원의 도움으로 그 셔틀버스 운전기사에게 연락을 해봤지만 제 카메라는 없어져버렸어요. 너무 속이 상했지만 카메라 없이 그냥 돌아올 수 밖에 없었죠. 친구들이 제가 나온 사진들을 저에게 보내줬지만 제가 찍은 오사카 사진은 하나도 없게 되고 말았어요. 그때 이후로는 소지품을 다시 확인하는 습관을 갖게 되었어요.

Lesson 13 재활용

Question 1 p.164

[질문]
당신의 나라에서 쓰레기 재활용은 어떻게 관리되고 있나요? 구체적인 재활용 정책들이 있습니까? 당신 나라에선 사람들이 어떻게 재활용을 하는지 가능한 자세하게 말해주세요.

[모범답변]
우리나라에서 재활용은 의무입니다. 재활용 쓰레기들은 플라스틱, 종이, 유리, 금속 등으로 분리된 쓰레기통에 넣어야 합니다. 한국 사람들이 지정된 장소 또는 아파트나 집 밖에서 쓰레기를 분리해서 버리는 걸 보는 것은 흔한 일이지요. 그렇게 분리된 쓰레기는 그 후 재활용 수거 날에 거둬가는데, 그날은 구역에 따라 좀 다를 수 있습니다. 우리 동네를 예로 들자면 재활용 쓰레기가 매주 화요일과 목요일에 수거됩니다. 우리는 또 음식물과 일반 쓰레기를 철저하게 분리합니다. 일반 쓰레기들은 종량제봉투라는 특별한 쓰레기봉투에 넣어야 합니다. 이 봉투는 동네 슈퍼에서 살 수 있고요. 쓰레기 수거원들은 종량제 봉투에 넣지 않은 쓰레기는 거둬가지 않죠. 그리고 음식물 쓰레기 또한 다른 색깔 봉투에 넣어야 하거나 또는 주거 건물 외부에서 따로 폐기해야 해요. 봉투 색깔과 가격 등과 같은 구체적인 절차는 구역에 따라 다르지만 모든 구역들이 재활용 원칙에 대해서는 엄격합니다. 한국의 재활용 제도가 복잡하거나 성가시게 보일 수도 있겠지만, 환경을 보호하고 음식물 쓰레기 양을 줄이는데 도움이 되어왔다고 생각합니다.

Question 2 p.167

[질문]

가정 내 재활용은 시간과 노력을 요구하지요. 집에서 하는 재활용에 시간과 노력을 줄일 수 있는 당신만의 방법에 관해 말해주세요.

[모범답변]

쓰레기처리의 양을 줄이려고 애쓰는 것이 집에서 재활용을 하는 시간과 노력을 절약하는 데 가장 중요하겠죠. 저는 종이컵이나 종이접시를 전혀 사용하지 않고 페트병과 유리병은 재사용하려고 합니다. 그 병들을 물로 씻고 음식이나 양념들을 저장하는 것으로 사용해요. 저는 포장음식도 거의 집으로 가져오지 않는데, 플라스틱과 스티로폼 쓰레기를 야기시키기 때문이죠. 저에게는 재활용 쓰레기들과 재활용이 되지 않는 쓰레기들을 분리하는 시간과 노력을 절감하는 저만의 방법이 있습니다. 저는 예전에 모든 쓰레기들을 밖으로 가지고 나가서 분류하곤 했어요. 재활용 쓰레기통 앞에서 재활용 쓰레기와 그냥 쓰레기들을 분리하는 것은 상당히 귀찮고 시간이 가는 일이죠. 겨울에 밖에 있는 건 너무 춥기까지 하고요. 그래서 저는 쓰레기를 집에서 분리하는 생각을 해봤어요. 저는 플라스틱, 종이, 금속 등의 이름표를 붙인 재활용 주머니를 몇 개 만들었어요. 그리고는 각각의 쓰레기를 해당하는 주머니에 넣을 수 있도록 테라스에 두었어요. 분리된 쓰레기 주머니들을 들고 나가 비우는 데는 5분 밖에 걸리지 않더라고요. 시간을 절약할 수 있는 더 좋은 아이디어를 찾기 전까지는 저는 이런 식으로 재활용 쓰레기를 분리하려고 합니다.

Question 3 p.170

[질문]

당신이 어렸을 때는 쓰레기가 어떻게 재활용 되었나요? 동네에 가정 재활용 처리 구역이 있었나요? 재활용과 관련된 어렸을 때의 경험에 대해 말해보세요.

[모범답변]

제가 아이였을 때는 쓰레기 재활용에 관심을 많이 쏟는 사람이 많지 않았어요. 제 기억으로는 정부에서조차 재활용에 대한 구체적인 정책이 없었거든요. 하지만 우리 동네는 쓰레기를 재활용하는 노력을 했어요. 저는 초등학교 다닐 때 대전에 살았는데 학생들이 종이와 유리병을 모아서 매주 수요일마다 학교에 가져갔어요. 자발적인 재활용 날이었는데 저 또한 그 활동에 참여했죠. 모든 학급에서 수거된 재활용 쓰레기들은 몇 개의 마대에 합쳐지고, 그러고 나면 우리 동네에 있던 재활용 센터에서 나온 쓰레기 수거인들이 가져갔어요. 제 친구들과 저는 빈 병들을 우리 동네 슈퍼마켓에 가져가서 돈을 받기도 했어요. 그 당시는 슈퍼마켓에 빈 병을 돌려주면 한 병당 10원 또는 20원을 받곤 했어요. 그 때 제가 환경을 보존하는 중요성에 대해 진지하게 생각했던 것 같지는 않아요. 하지만 그런 재활용 경험들이 우리나라의 현재 재활용 제도를 기꺼이 준수하도록 하게 해주었습니다.

Lesson 14 전화 통화

Oral Proficiency Interview-computer

Question 1 p.176

[질문]

친구와 자주 통화를 하나요? 보통 언제, 그리고 무엇에 관해 통화를 하나요? 전화 통화에 대해 자세히 말해보세요.

[모범답변]

저는 친구와 꽤 자주 통화를 합니다. 저에게 전화로 수다를 떠는 것은 스트레스를 푸는 데 가장 좋은 방법들 중 하나거든요. 가깝게 지내는 동료가 거의 없기 때문에 제가 주로 통화를 하는 대상은 대학 친구들입니다. 보통 저녁 식사 후 밤 9시경에 통화를 하죠. 통화 내용은 우리가 얼마나 친하냐에 따라 다릅니다. 친구이긴 하지만 그렇게 친한 친구가 아닐 경우 그냥 서로의 안부를 묻고 어떻게 지내는지에 대해 말을 합니다. 연예인, 영화, 스포츠 등 그렇게 진지하지 않은 것들이 우리의 대화에 등장하죠. 그렇게 일상적인 주제에 관해 정보를 교환하고 농담을 주고 받는 것은 재미있고 즐거워요. 반면 아주 친한 친구들과는 제 개인적인 일에 대해 자주 이야기하고 고민도 털어놓습니다. 제 남자친구와의 문제점, 제 상사와의 갈등, 제 미래에 대한 불안함 같은 것들을 말하죠. 그들도 답답하고 우울할 때 또는 힘든 결정을 해야 할 때 저에게 전화를 하고요. 우리는 항상 서로를 북돋아주고 조언을 해 줍니다. 친구와 전화 통화할 때가 하루 중 가장 편안한 시간이랍니다.

Question 2 p.179

[질문]

전화 통화가 당신의 생활에 중요한가요? 왜 중요하죠? 당신의 생활에 어떻게 영향을 미치나요?

[모범답변]

네, 전화 통화는 물론 제 삶에 중요합니다. 저는 제 친구들과 거의 전화로 연락을 유지하고 있습니다. 너무 바빠서 자주 얼굴을 볼 수 없기 때문에, 전화 통화를 자주 함으로써 우정을 돈독하게 해야 합니다. 멀리 떨어진 시골에 살고 있는 친구들의 경우 전화를 하지 않으면 연락이 끊기기 쉽거든요. 저는 개인적으로 친구들과 연락을 할 때 문자를 보내는 것보다 전화를 하는 것이 더 좋아요. 전화 통화는 제가 일을 하는 데도 중요합니다. 매우 심각한 사안에 대해 의논해야 하는 것이 아닌 한 저는 거래처 사람들과 만나서 대화를 할 기회가 거의 없어요. 우리는 대부분의 일을, 가끔은 주말에조차 전화로 해결합니다. 우리는 파일을 첨부할 때를 제외하고는 이메일도 거의 주고 받지 않는데, 서로 즉각적인 피드백을 주고 받아야 하기 때문이죠. 전화 통화는 크고 작은 일들을 효율적이고 신속하게 처리하는 것을 가능하게 해 줍니다.

Question 3　　p.182

[질문]
기억에 남는 전화 통화가 있나요? 누구와 한 통화였고 무엇에 관한 것이었나요? 왜 당신에게 그 통화가 기억에 남나요? 그 대화에 대해 자세하게 말해보세요.

[모범답변]
제가 미국에서 공부할 때 매주 토요일 서울 시간으로 오후 3시에 어머니께 전화를 드렸습니다. 어머니는 항상 전화벨이 울리자마자 전화를 받으셨어요. 그런데 어느 날은, 제가 계속 전화를 해도 받지를 않으시는 거예요. 그래서 언니에게 전화를 걸었더니 언니가 힘 없는 목소리로 전화를 받았습니다. 뭔가 불길한 생각이 들었고 저는 엄마와 왜 연락이 되지 않느냐고 물었어요. 언니는 잠시 대답하기를 주저하더니 제게 "내 말에 너무 놀라지 마라"라고 말했어요. 짧은 순간이지만 머릿속에 별의별 생각이 다 지나가더군요. 언니는 어머니께서 지난 밤에 넘어지셔서 고관절이 부러졌다고 했습니다. 구급차로 병원에 실려가셨고 수술 중이시라고요. 그리고선 수술이 예상시간보다 길어지고 있다는 말을 덧붙였습니다. 언니는 저에게 그렇게 걱정할 필요는 없다고 했지만 저는 슬픔과 두려움으로 울 수 밖에 없었어요. 어머니와 너무 멀리 떨어져 있다는게 저를 더 슬프고 죄송하게 했습니다. 다행히 수술은 성공적으로 끝났고 어머니도 곧 회복하셨어요. 하지만 전 아직도 그 통화로 얼마나 놀랐던가를 기억합니다.

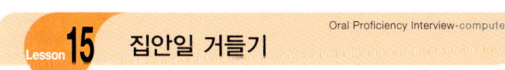

Lesson 15 집안일 거들기
Oral Proficiency Interview-computer

Question 1　　p.188

[질문]
당신과 당신의 가족이 집에서 하는 역할에 대해 알고 싶군요. 당신의 역할은 무엇인가요? 누가 무슨 역할을 하고 있나요? 가능한 자세하게 말해보세요.

[모범답변]
저와 아내는 모두 일을 하기 때문에 가사 책임을 분담하기로 합의했어요. 다섯 살짜리 아들을 키우는 것에 있어서는 각자의 책임을 엄격하게 나누지는 않았습니다. 번갈아 아이를 목욕시키고 옷을 갈아 입혀요. 누구든 빨리 퇴근하는 사람이 유아원에서 아이를 데려오고 저녁을 챙겨주죠. 제 업무시간이 아내보다 더 유연해서 아이 예방접종을 시켜야 할 때는 제가 주로 아이를 병원에 데려갑니다. 하지만 집안일은 균등하게 나눈답니다. 제 아내는 음식을 만드는 반면 저는 설거지를 하고 쓰레기를 버려요. 우리는 대부분의 집안일을 토요일 오전에 합니다. 저는 진공청소기로 집을 치우고 화장실 청소를 하고, 제 아내는 세탁과 다림질을 합니다. 토요일 오후에는 대개 아들과 계속 놀아주죠. 책을 읽어주고, 로봇과 놀기도 하고, 공원에 데려가기도 합니다. 우리는 한 달에 한 번 식료품을 사러 가요. 한 달치 음식을 한 번에 사기 위해 케이마트와 홈마트와 같은 대형 마트에 가죠. 우리 부부 모두 공정하게 가사분담을 했다고 생각합니다.

Question 2　　p.191

[질문]
당신이 어렸을 때 어떤 집안일을 했나요? 그것들을 어떻게 다뤘죠? 성장하면서 집안에서의 책임이 어떻게 바뀌었나요?

[모범답변]
우리 부모님께서는 제가 학교에 들어가기 전까지는 특정 집안일을 시키지 않으셨습니다. 그저 장난감을 치우라거나 냉장고 문을 꼭 닫으라는 말씀을 하셨죠. 하지만 초등학교에 입학한 후에는 자리를 개고 저녁 식탁을 차리는 등의 작은 일들을 주셨지요. 학년이 올라가면서 제 집안일은 더 복잡해지고 많아졌어요. 제 방을 청소하고, 저녁 식탁을 깨끗이 치우고 세탁물을 접기도 했어요. 제 옷과 양말을 옷장 서랍에 넣기도 했습니다. 중고등학교 기간에는 일주일에 두 세 번 마당을 쓸었고 매주 일요일마다 청소기를 돌렸어요. 가끔씩 설거지도 하고 제 교복도 다림질 했어요. 저는 지금도 다리미로 바지에 주름 잡는 것은 정말 잘한답니다. 집안일을 하는 것이 저에겐 귀찮은 일이 아니었어요. 저는 엄마를 도와드리고 싶었기 때문에 그 모든 일들을 기꺼이 했답니다.

Question 3　　p.194

[질문]
어떤 집안일은 당신에게 어렵고 또 다른 일은 쉽겠지요. 그 일들에 대해 말해주세요.

[모범답변]
제가 어렸을 때 맡았던 집안일에 대해서는 어렵다고 느끼지 않았어요. 휴지와 식기류들을 탁자 위에 놓거나 옷을 개는 일은 전혀 어려운 일이 아니니까요. 우리 부모님께서 제가 자라면서 다른 수준의 일들을 맡기셨기 때문에 저는 제가 아이들이나 10대가 하기에 너무 어려운 집안일을 했다고는 생각하지 않아요. 하지만 제가 좋아하지 않았던 어려운 책임이 하나 있었어요. 그건 제 남동생을 돌보고 공부를 도와주는 일이었어요. 저는 제 동생을 사랑하지만 제 동생은 산만하고 고집이 세서 저는 자주 힘들어했어요. 대부분의 맏이들이 동생들을 보살핀다는 건 알고 있지만 전 부모님이 맏이도 어린아이라는 것과 그 애들이 그런 책임

에 스트레스와 부담을 가질 수 있다는 걸 알아야 한다고 생각해요. 지금 제가 하고 있는 가사일에 대해서는 설거지와 집 청소 다 개의치 않아요. 하지만 솔직히 말해서 화장실 청소하는 건 안 좋아합니다. 힘든 편이에요. 바닥을 닦고, 벽과 큰 거울을 닦고 솔로 변기의 세균들을 제거하는 일은 끝도 없어요. 가끔씩 화장실 청소를 한 주 거르고도 싶지만 제 아내가 결코 용납을 안 한답니다.

Lesson 16 테크놀로지

Question 1 p.200

[질문]
회사에서 어떤 종류의 테크놀로지를 주로 사용하나요? 어떤 임무에 그것을 사용하죠?

[모범답변]
저는 회사에서 컴퓨터, 복사기, 팩스, 프로젝터 등 여러 종류의 기기를 사용합니다. 제가 가장 많이 사용하고 있는 기기는 단연 컴퓨터입니다. 컴퓨터를 켜는 것으로 하루를 시작하고 끝날 때까지 사용합니다. 컴퓨터의 유용한 소프트웨어로 제 일을 체계적으로 정리할 수 있습니다. 저는 제 고객에 대한 모든 자료를 엑셀파일에 저장하고 파워포인트 발표 자료도 만듭니다. 저는 또한 이 메일로 제 고객들 및 거래처에게 연락을 합니다. 컴퓨터가 없었다면 저는 그들을 직접 만나고 전화하느라 많은 시간을 썼겠지요. 우리 회사는 최근에 인트라넷을 시행했는데, 그걸로 모든 직원들이 온라인 상에서 서로 의사소통을 할 수 있습니다. 직원들은 그 인트라넷을 통해서 상관에게 보고서를 제출하거나 휴가 결재를 받습니다. 이처럼 컴퓨터는 제 일의 속도를 높여주고 의사소통 과정을 크게 향상시켜줬습니다.

Question 2 p.203

[질문]
직장생활에서의 테크놀로지는 수 년 동안 어떻게 변했나요? 그 변화가 당신의 업무에 어떻게 영향을 끼쳤나요?

[모범답변]
테크놀로지의 발전이 제 직장생활에 많은 변화를 가져왔습니다. 이런 변화들 중에서는 저는 다른 사람들과 정보를 공유하는 방식에 대해 이야기하고 싶습니다. 10년 전쯤에는 회의에 참가해야 할 때와 다른 직원들과 문서를 공유해야 할 때, 회의 배포 자료들과 그 문서들을 인쇄하거나 원본을 복사했어요. 하지만 수년간 유용한 온라인 저장 서비스가 생겨나면서 우리는 온라인 상에서 대부분의 업무를 공유합니다. 예를 들면, 우리는 웹스토어를 적극적으로 사용하는데, 아이디와 비밀번호를 공유하고 있는 한 문서들을 다른 사람들과 공유할 수 있도록 해줍니다. 한 사람이 웹스토어에 파일을 업로드 시키면, 다른 사람들이 그 파일을 검토하기 위해 언제든지 파일에 접속해서 다운로드를 받을 수 있습니다. 우리는 더 이상 배포 자료와 서류들을 전달하기 위해 복사하지 않습니다. 그건 시간을 절약시켜줄 뿐 아니라 종이 낭비와 비용을 줄여주죠. 저는 제가 오늘날 사용하고 있는 테크놀로지에 아주 만족하긴 하는데, 제가 예측하기에는 기술은 더 발전해서 우리가 일을 처리하는 방식을 계속 바꿀 것입니다.

Question 3 p.206

[질문]
테크놀로지가 작동을 잘 안 한 경험이 있을 겁니다. 그 경험에 대해 가능한 자세히 말해보세요.

[모범답변]
지난 가을에 일어났던 사건에 대해 말하고 싶군요. 저는 호주에서 온 고객들 앞에서 프레젠테이션을 하기로 되어있었습니다. 저는 그 업무를 맡은 후 한달 동안 철저하게 준비를 했어요. 저는 프레젠테이션 15분 전에 파일을 열기 위해 컴퓨터를 켰습니다. 하지만 컴퓨터 어디에도 그 파일을 찾을 수 없었어요. 저는 왜 그런 일이 벌어졌는지 몰랐지만 파일이 날라간 것은 분명합니다. 지워진 건지 아니면 저장이 안되었던 건지조차 알지 못했어요. 백업을 해놓지 않은 것이 후회되었지만 이미 늦었었죠. 고객은 회의실 밖에서 기다리고 있고, 제 상관은 화가 나서 저에게 소리를 질렀습니다. 저는 사직서를 내야겠다고 생각하면서 패닉상태에 빠졌습니다. 갑자기 클라우드 서버 생각이 났습니다. 제 컴퓨터는 제가 작업한 파일을 실시간 자동으로 클라우드에 저장시키거든요. 저는 클라우드 계정으로 접속을 했는데, 고맙게도 파일의 내용이 다 그곳에 저장되어 있었어요. 저는 제 시간에 프레젠테이션을 했고 고객들은 매우 만족해했어요. 다시는 절대로 겪고 싶지 않은 끔찍한 경험이었습니다.

Lesson 17 지역 행사

Question 1 p.212

[질문]
당신의 지역에는 어떤 특별 행사들이 있나요? 그 행사에서 사람들은 무엇을 하나요? 어떻게 참여합니까?

[모범답변]
제 지역은 고양인데 1997년 이후로 꽃 박람회를 개최하고 있습니다. 연례행사는 아니지만 전국 규모의 꽤 유명한 행사이죠. 지

난 4월에 일곱 번째 박람회가 16일 동안 열렸는데 대단한 성공을 거뒀습니다. 그 행사에는 세 개의 각기 다른 전시회장이 있었는데, 세계 꽃 전시장, 한국 꽃 전시장, 고양시 꽃 전시장입니다. 세계 꽃 전시장에서는 네덜란드, 독일, 말레이시아 등 35개국의 많은 종류의 꽃들을 볼 수 있었습니다. 한국과 고양 꽃 전시장은 아름답고 눈부신 꽃꽂이와 장식들을 보여줘서 우리의 관심을 충분히 자아냈습니다. 시민들은 꽃꽂이 대회, 꽃 그리기 행사 등 다양한 활동에 참여할 수 있었습니다. 다른 매력적인 행사로는 전시회 개막식과 폐막식 때 있었던 라이브 공연들과 한 밤의 불꽃놀이였습니다. 저는 다음에 이 전시회가 열릴 때도 참가할 것이고, 이 행사가 단순히 우리 지역 사람들을 위해서만이 아니라 세계인들을 위한 고유하고 특별한 행사가 되길 희망합니다.

Question 2 p.215

[질문]
당신 지역에서 가장 인상 깊었던 행사는 무엇이었나요? 언제, 어디서 열렸나요? 왜 그 행사가 기억에 남나요?

[모범답변]
제가 흥미로운 모금 행사를 알게 된 건 2011년이었어요. 그 해에 저는 석사학위 공부를 위해 미국 버지니아에 있었어요. 그 행사의 목적은 그 해 지진과 해일로 피해를 입은 일본인들을 도와주는 것이었습니다. 지역센터는 그 지역 초등학교들과 협력해서 모금 행사 공지를 학교 게시판에 올렸습니다. 행사 이름은 "페니 전쟁"이라고 불렸는데 학급간 경쟁의 틀을 따 온 것입니다. 모든 학생들이 그 행사에 참여할 수 있었고 각 학급은 한 달 동안 학생들에게서 페니 동전들을 모집했습니다. 그럼 학교들은 그 돈을 지역센터에 제출하고, 지역센터는 다시 그 경쟁의 우승자를 발표하는 것이었습니다. 어린 아이들은 적극적으로 행사에 참여해서 가능한 많은 페니를 모으려고 애썼습니다. 지역센터는 그들의 목적을 성공적으로 달성했고 또한 학생들에게 도움이 필요한 다른 사람들 돕는 법도 가르쳐 주었습니다. 그 지역이 우리나라에 속한 것은 아니었지만 저는 그 행사를 마음 속에 간직해왔습니다. 장래에 그런 비슷한 행사를, 아마도 다른 이름과 다른 목적이겠지만, 주관해 보고 싶습니다.

Question 3 p.218

[질문]
당신이 최근에 참여한 지역 행사에 대해 알고 싶군요. 언제 참여했고 무엇에 관한 행사였나요? 무엇이 좋고 무엇이 좋지 않았나요?

[모범답변]
몇 달 전 저는 교회에서 주관한 자선기금 모집에 참여했습니다. 일종의 바자회였는데 저는 아이들 옷을 파는 일을 맡았죠. 모든 수익금은 캄보디아에 있는 아이들을 위한 의약품과 응급용품들을 구매하는 데 쓰였습니다. 그 바자회를 위해서 교회는 신자들과 다른 교회에게 기부를 부탁했고 석 달 동안 옷과 책에서부터 일용 생필품에 이르기까지 많은 품목들을 받았습니다. 자선 행사는 오전 11시에 교회 앞마당에서 열렸는데 많은 사람들이 자발적으로 일을 했습니다. 제가 팔았던 제품들의 품질이 제법 좋았기 때문에 구매자들은 만족스러워했지요. 하지만 행사 장소가 좀 좁은데 사람들은 잔뜩 모여있었습니다. 거기다 주차 공간도 제한적이어서 앞마당과 뒷마당이 사람들과 차로 가득 찼었죠. 장소는 비록 많은 사람들을 수용하기에 충분하지 않았지만 행사 자체는 성공적으로 끝났습니다. 대부분의 물건이 팔렸고 우리는 상당한 금액의 돈을 모았습니다. 결과적으로 그 행사는 저에게 기억에 남을 귀중한 경험을 선사해줬습니다.

Lesson 18 국내여행

Question 1 p.224

[질문]
당신이 가장 좋아하는 국내여행지에 대해 말해보세요. 언제 가고 누구와 가나요? 그곳을 왜 좋아하나요?

[모범답변]
제가 가장 좋아하는 곳은 제주도인데 우리나라 남쪽에 있는 섬이지요. 시간이 날 때마다 저는 가족과 함께 혹은 혼자 제주도에 가서 며칠씩 머뭅니다. 제주도에는 즐길 거리가 많습니다. 풍경이 숨이 멎을 듯 아름답기 때문에 특히 봄과 가을에는 어디를 보든 다 멋집니다. 올레라고 불리는 섬을 따라 나 있는 산책로는 제가 가장 좋아하는 장소예요. 바다와 자연이 형성한 놀라운 모양의 바위들과 같은 여러 자연 풍경들을 감상하면서 걸을 수가 있답니다. 그 길 말고 제가 좋아하는 또 다른 걷는 장소로는 한라산이 있는데요, 국립공원 안에 있는 우리나라에서 가장 높은 산이에요. 한라산은 꼭대기에 큰 화구호가 있는 휴화산인데 산을 올라가면서 많은 고산 식물들과 다른 식물들을 볼 수 있어요. 제주 특산품들은 제가 그곳에 방문하는 또 다른 이유입니다. 신선한 해산물도 그렇고 제주 흑돼지 바비큐는 정말 육즙이 풍부하고 맛있어요. 저는 제주도가 정말 좋고 다가오는 겨울에 또 갈 것입니다.

Question 2 p.227

[질문]
국내여행은 어떻게 준비하나요? 여행가기 전에 무엇을 합니까?

[모범답변]
여행 가기 전에 생각해야 할 것들은 참 많죠. 제가 가장 먼저 하

는 일은 여행 가서 처음부터 끝까지 뭘 할지 완전한 일정표를 짜는 것이에요. 여행지 결정에 따라 예산과 여행에 가져갈 준비물을 정합니다. 일단 출발 날짜를 정하면 예약을 합니다. 제주도 여행을 예로 말씀 드리자면 많은 여행사와 항공사에서 좋은 가격의 항공운임을 제시하기 때문에 가격을 비교하면서 가장 합리적인 운임을 선택할 수 있어요. 비행 일정을 잡은 후에는 호텔과 렌터카를 예약합니다. 호텔 위치가 가장 중요해요. 제가 가려는 관광지와 가까워야 하죠. 저는 보통 공항에서 차를 렌트 해서 호텔로 운전해 가요. 교통과 숙박이 정해진 후에 짐을 싸기 시작합니다. 제주도에서는 등산을 많이 하기 때문에 등산복, 등산화, 그리고 다른 필요 장비들을 넣습니다. 운전할 때 필수적이고 유용한 GPS와 지역 지도도 챙깁니다. 이상이 제가 여행가기 전에 기본적으로 하는 것들입니다.

Question 3
p.230

[질문]
여행에 대해 사람들은 무엇을 염려하고 고려하나요? 이런 염려와 고려들은 그들의 여행에 대한 수고와 비용에 어떤 영향을 미치나요?

[모범답변]
사람들이 여행을 갈 때는 안전과 비용 등의 여러 가지를 고려합니다. 가장 큰 염려거리는 여행하는 동안의 안전성이겠죠. 안전한 여행을 위해 대개 여행 하면서 생기는 부상과 비상 상황을 커버해주는 여행자보험을 삽니다. 비행기 사고는 곧잘 대형참사로 이어지기도 하니까 비행기로 여행을 가는 사람들의 경우에는 보험이 아주 중요하게 여겨집니다. 운전을 해서 가는 경우에는 교통상황이 아주 중요한 사안입니다. 저는 대개, 특히 휴일에는 운전해서 갈 때 교통체증을 피하기 위해 아침 일찍 집을 떠납니다. 사람들은 여행 기간 동안 빈 집에 도둑이 들지 몰라 걱정을 하기도 합니다. 우리 가족도 예외는 아니라서 여행 가는 동안에는 옆집 사람에게 쌓여 있는 신문들을 좀 치워달라고 부탁합니다. 대문 앞에 쌓여 있는 신문들은 현재 집에 아무도 없다는 걸 암시하니까요. 전기를 끄고 수도꼭지를 잠그는 것도 집을 나서기 전 여행자들에게는 필수적인 일이고요. 이런 모든 일들은 몇 분만 신경 쓰고 수고하면 되는 일이며, 이걸로 여행을 편하게 다녀올 수 있는 것입니다.

Lesson 19 해외출장
Oral Proficiency Interview-computer

Question 1
p.236

[질문]
상황을 드릴 테니 연기를 해보세요. 당신은 지금 출장 중인데 당신이 가져간 샘플에 문제가 있습니다. 상관에게 전화를 걸어서 상황을 설명하고 새로운 샘플을 요청하는 메시지를 남겨보세요.

[모범답변]
여보세요, 저 김민우에요. 제가 여기 가져왔던 전자책 단말기 샘플에 문제가 생겼어요. 그게 계속 켜졌다 꺼졌다 해요. 충전도 다시 해보고 건전지도 갈아봤지만 같은 일이 계속 일어나네요. 서울에서 시험해봤을 때 작동상에 아무 문제도 없었으니 제가 불량품을 가져온 것 같지는 않은데 말이죠. 아무래도 제가 여기서 고칠 수 없을 것 같으니 새로운 샘플 하나 보내주시겠어요? 제가 Nobo PTR3 가져온 것 아시죠? 아, 샘플을 몇 개 더 보내주시는 게 만약을 대비해서 더 안전할 것 같네요. 배달해주실 주소를 남길게요. 일리노이 주 시카고 220 웨스트 마트 드라이브, 다이아몬드 호텔이에요. 내일 오후에 프레젠테이션을 할 때 그 기기를 소개해야 하니까 늦어도 내일 아침까지는 받아야 해요. 감사하고 나중에 또 말씀 나눠요!

Question 2
p.239

[질문]
미안하지만 당신이 해결해야 할 문제가 있습니다. 당신의 상관이 새로운 샘플이 오늘 밤에야 도착한다고 합니다. 하지만 당신은 오늘 오후 거래처를 만날 때 그걸 사용해야 해요. 거래처에 전화를 해서 문제를 해결할 수 있는 몇 가지 대안과 함께 상황을 설명해보세요.

[모범답변]
여보세요, 톰슨 씨? 저는 제일전자의 김민우에요. 오늘 오후에 당신에게 프레젠테이션을 하기로 되어 있어요. 프레젠테이션 때 다음 달 시판될 Nobo PTR을 소개하려고 하는데요. 그런데 안타깝게도, 제가 가져온 기기가 작동을 잘 하지 않아서 당신에게 오늘 그 기기를 보여줄 수 없어요. 프레젠테이션을 내일로 미루면 안될까요? 다른 기기가 지금 배달 중이고 오늘 밤에 도착할 거예요. 저는 내일 아무 때나 찾아 뵐 수 있어요. 만일 오늘만 시간이 되는 거라면, 제가 예정대로 오늘 찾아 뵙고 그 제품의 일반적인 설명을 해 드릴게요. 내일 그 제품을 사무실에 갖다 놓을테니 시간이 날 때 그 기기를 살펴보면 되고요. 정말 이런 불편을 끼쳐드려 죄송하고 제 상황을 이해해주시길 바랍니다. 이 메시지 받으시면 전화 부탁 드려요. 감사합니다.

Question 3
p.242

[질문]
앞의 상황은 종료 되었습니다. 출장 중에 있었던 가장 예상치 못했거나 어려웠던 사건에 대해 말해주세요. 무슨 사건이었고 어떻게 그 일을 해결했나요? 처음부터 끝까지 전체 이야기를 해보세요.

[모범답변]
제가 막 입사했을 때 독일에 사흘 동안 출장을 갔습니다. 출장의 목적은 프랑크푸르트 무역박람회에 참가해서 외국 업체사람들을 만나는 것이었어요. 사실 그건 저에게 예정에 없던 출장이었어요. 원래는 제 상관 혼자서 그 출장을 가려고 했는데 집에 급한 일이 생겨서 제가 급하게 참가하게 된 것이었죠. 저는 미팅 스케줄을 독일에 도착해서 통보 받았어요. 그 스케줄에 따르면 한 회사와의 미팅을 끝내는 데 제게 주어진 시간이 30분이었어요. 미팅 중에 저는 우리 회사와 제품을 간단하게 소개해야 했습니다. 일은 단순하고 쉬워 보일 수 있겠지만 저에게는 힘들었답니다. 제가 영어를 잘 못했기 때문에 특히 그들의 질문에 대답을 할 때는 자주 더듬거렸어요. 한술 더 떠서, 박람회장이 너무 넓어서 제가 방문해야 하는 부스의 위치를 찾지 못했어요. 결국 마지막 미팅에는 15분 늦었죠. 다행히 심각한 문제 없이 겨우 출장을 마치긴 했지만 아직도 그 당시 일을 좀 더 잘 완수했더라면 하고 생각합니다.

Lesson 20 해외여행

Oral Proficiency Interview-computer

Question 1
p.248

[질문]
상황을 드릴 테니 연기를 해보세요. 당신은 외국여행을 가려고 합니다. 여행사에 전화를 걸어서 여행에 대해 서너 가지 질문을 해보세요.

[모범답변]
여보세요, TBC 여행사인가요? 제 이름은 김현민이라고 합니다. 여행상품에 대해 몇 가지 질문을 하고 싶어 전화했어요. 제 아내와 제가 올해 7월 나흘 동안의 푸껫 여행을 계획하고 있어요. 비행기표를 구하는 게 가능한가요? 가능하다면 얼마죠? 비행기표와 호텔을 함께 묶는 것이 각각 예약하는 것보다 경제적이라고 들었어요. 가격 차이가 얼마나 되나요? 우리는 단체여행도 생각하고 있어요. 가격이 얼마고 기간은 어떻게 되나요? 단체여행에서도 단독 여행처럼 스쿠버 다이빙을 배울 수 있을지 궁금합니다. 그 여행에 대한 일정표를 보내주실 수 있나요? 제 이 메일 주소는 HMK@credu.com이에요. 미리 감사 드립니다!

Question 2
p.251

[질문]
미안하지만 당신이 해결해야 할 문제가 있습니다. 당신은 공항에 도착해서 당신의 비행편이 취소되었다는 걸 알았습니다. 유감스럽게도 다른 모든 비행기표의 예약도 이미 다 찼습니다. 여행사에 전화를 해서 문제를 해결할 수 있는 세 가지 대안과 함께 상황을 설명해보세요.

[모범답변]
안녕하세요, 윤선생님? 저는 김현민이에요. 저 예상치 않은 황당한 상황을 알리려 전화했어요. 우리가 탑승수속을 하려고 하니 우리 항공편이 기체 결함으로 취소되었다는 걸 알았어요. 설상가상으로 다른 비행편도 오늘 모두 다 찼다는 거예요! 우리는 지금 굉장히 불만스러워하고 있지만 가능하면 우리 여행을 원래대로 돌려놓고 싶어요. 항공사 직통전화를 이용해서 더 정확한 정보를 알아보시겠어요? 대기자 명단에 우리를 올려줄 수도 있잖아요. 만약 불가능하다면 우리가 탈 수 있는 다음 항공편을 알아봐 주세요. 우리가 목적지로 내일 떠날 수 있다면 이 여행을 포기하지 않을 거거든요. 하지만 설사 그렇더라도, 우리는 청주에서 인천까지 왔기 때문에 공항 근처 호텔에서의 숙박비는 여행사에서 지불해야 해요. 내일도 가능한 항공편이 없다면 우리는 여행을 취소하겠습니다. 그러니 우리가 구매한 비행기표를 전액 환불해주세요. 또한 우리가 여행을 하지 못한 것에 대한 보상액도 제공해주시길 바랍니다. 교통비와 호텔 취소 수수료는 당연히 추가해줘야 하고요. 가능한 빨리 전화해주세요.

Question 3
p.254

[질문]
앞의 상황은 종료 되었습니다. 당신은 해외여행 도중 예상치 못했거나 놀랐거나 또는 재미있었던 사건을 겪어봤을 거예요. 어디서 그리고 언제 그런 경험을 했나요? 그 때 정확히 무슨 일이 일어난 건가요? 왜 지금까지 그 사건을 기억하는 건가요?

[모범답변]
친구와 저는 5년 전 캄보디아 씨엠립에 단체관광을 갔어요. 우리 그룹에는 모두 친절하고 예의 바른 일곱 명의 회원이 있었죠. 그 관광에는 그 지역의 경험 있는 가이드가 동반했어요. 사건은 관광 두 번째 날에 일어났어요. 타는 듯이 더운 날이었는데, 오후 두 시경에 우리는 멋진 사원들이 있는 단지인 앙코르 톰에 도착했어요. 우리는 관광버스에서 내려서 경이로운 유적들과 크메르 예술을 보기 위해 사원들 사이를 걸었어요. 하지만 시간이 지나고 저는 더위 때문에 땀을 흘리면서 점점 지쳐갔죠. 캄보디아에서는 겨울이었지만 낮 기온이 섭씨 32도까지 올라갔고 햇볕이 쨍쨍 내리쬐고 있었거든요. 저는 어지러움을 느꼈고 팔다리에는 힘이 없었어요. 제 친구가 제 창백한 얼굴을 보고 깜짝 놀랐을 때 저는 쓰러지기 일보 직전이었죠. 그는 다급하게 제 상태를 가이드에게 알렸고 저는 관광버스로 옮겨졌어요. 가이드와 다른 관광 멤버들은 저를 무척 걱정했지만 빨리 좋아지지 않았어요. 우리는 결국 관광을 중단하고 호텔로 돌아갔어요. 쉬고 난 후 좋아졌지만 관광을 방해하게 되어서 너무 미안했어요.

Actual Test 1 해석

01 자기소개

[질문] p.258
인터뷰를 시작하겠습니다. 당신에 대해 말해주세요.

[모범답변]
제 이름은 김민정입니다. 20대 후반이고 서울 외곽에서 부모님과 함께 살고 있어요. 저희 언니와 오빠는 결혼 후 분가를 했고요. 저는 막내 딸이고, 다른 많은 막내가 그렇듯이, 가족에게는 영원한 막내로 여겨지고 있어요. 저는 현재 나라 은행에서 개인 고객 서비스 팀에서 근무하고 있어요. 저는 400분이 넘는 개인 고객께 정기예금, MMF, 또는 적금 등과 같은 금융상품 선택을 조언해드리며 그분들을 관리하고 있어요. 고객들을 상대하는 것은 어려워 보일 수도 있지만 저는 외향적이고 에너지가 넘쳐 제 일을 무척 좋아한답니다. 고객과 상담하고 그분들의 수익을 올려드리는 건 보람 있는 일이에요. 저는 2년 전에 최우수 직원으로 뽑혔고 이제까지 우수 실적상을 다섯 번도 넘게 받았답니다. 주중에는 대개 퇴근 후 바로 집으로 가지만 주말에는 다양한 활동을 즐겨요. 뮤지컬, 연극, 또는 록 콘서트 같은 공연을 가고 좋은 전시회는 꼭 챙겨봅니다. 한 달에 적어도 두 번은 등산을 가기도 하고요. 독신 생활을 마음껏 즐긴다고 말할 수 있습니다.

02 집 1

[질문] p.259
당신의 집에 대해 알고 싶군요. 당신의 집과 인근 지역은 어떤 모습입니까? 어떤 방을 가장 좋아하나요? 거기선 주로 무엇을 합니까?

[모범답변]
저는 서울의 남쪽 지역에 있는 아파트에서 살고 있습니다. 17층짜리 건물의 6층에서 살아요. 저는 이 집에서 고등학교에 입학한 이후부터 계속 살고 있어요. 저희 아파트 단지는 옅은 갈색 빛에 어두운 녹색 줄이 둘러져 있는 29개의 빌딩으로 이루어져 있습니다. 저희 아파트는 마을 공원에 둘러싸여 있어서 주민들이 그 근처를 산책하고 휴식의 장소로 사용할 수 있답니다. 저희 집에서 보이는 전망도 좋아요. 제 방 창문에서 한강을 볼 수 있죠. 저희 집에는 거실, 부엌, 침실 두 개, 서재, 그리고 화장실이 있는데 제가 가장 좋아하는 공간은 분위기가 아늑하고 편안한 서재예요. 거긴 제게 작은 북카페 같은데, 거기서 책을 읽으면서 커피나 차를 마시고 음악도 듣습니다. 저는 장르와 작가에 근거해 책장을 정리하는데, 그렇게 하면 제가 읽고 싶은 책을 쉽게 찾을 수 있게 돼요. 책장을 넘기면서 서재에 앉아 있으면 여유와 안정감을 느끼게 됩니다.

03 집 2

[질문] p.260
그 방을 어떻게 깨끗하고 편안하게 유지하나요? 그 방을 위해 무엇을 하나요?

[모범답변]
저는 물론 제 서재를 깨끗하고 편안하게 유지하는데요. 그건 깨끗한 방은 마음을 차분하게 해주고 독서에 집중이 더 잘 되게 해주기 때문이죠. 제가 정기적으로 하는 첫 번째 일은 책상, 책장, 그리고 차 탁자를 깔끔하게 정돈하는 것입니다. 먼지떨이로 먼지를 털어내는 거죠. 그리고 나서는 윈덱스를 뿌린 걸레로 구석구석 닦아요. 저는 이 두 가지 일은 매 주 한답니다. 제가 늘 신경 쓰는 것은 책장을 정돈된 상태로 유지하는 것입니다. 그렇게 하기 위해서 저는 책들을 책장에서 꺼내고 그 책들을 다시 넣을 때는 같은 자리에 넣습니다. 제가 항상 하는 다른 한 가지 일은 책상과 서랍에서 불필요한 자료들을 치우는 것이에요. 지저분한 책상은 제가 서재에 있을 때 책을 읽거나 뭔가를 생각할 때 방해가 되거든요. 하나가 더 남았네요. 저는 과자와 쿠키 같은 음식물을 서재에 가지고 들어가지 않아요. 쿠키 부스러기가 떨어지거나 방이 음식 냄새로 가득 차게 되는 걸 원치 않거든요. 저는 이렇게 제 서재를 깨끗하고 편안하게 유지하고 있습니다.

04 집 3

[질문] p.261
당신이 어렸을 때 살았던 집에 대해 말해보세요. 현재의 집과 어떻게 다르거나 비슷한가요?

[모범답변]
저는 어렸을 때 지금 있는 집에서 차로 세 시간 거리에 있는 시골에 살았어요. 저희 할아버지께서는 농장 근처에 있는 개인주택에 사셨어요. 유지보수 면에서는 아파트에 사는 것이 무척 편리한데, 그건 보수를 해주는 관리요원들이 아파트를 정기적으로 점검해주기 때문이죠. 반대로, 주택에 사는 건, 특히 시골에 있는 주택이라면 집주인이 모든 수리에 책임이 있기 때문에 굉장히 많은 유지보수 일들이 필요해요. 저는 할아버지께서 지붕, 바닥, 살수장치를 혼자서 점검하시고 위층과 지하실을 오르내리시면서

물건들을 고치시는 걸 보곤 했어요. 저희 할아버지 댁과 지금 현재의 제 집의 공통점이 딱 한 개 있는데, 그건 가구 스타일이에요. 저희 둘 다 골동품 가구에 관심이 많아서 우리가 가진 대부분의 가구는 무척 비슷해 보입니다. 우리는 자주 골동품 상점에 함께 가서 카펫, 의자, 탁자, 꽃병 등을 구경합니다. 저는 지금 제 집에 사는 게 만족스럽긴 하지만 가끔씩은 할아버지 댁에서 살았던 때가 그립기도 합니다.

05 호텔 1

[질문] p.262
당신 나라의 호텔에 관해 말해보세요. 어떤 모습인가요? 어떤 시설들이 있고 어떤 서비스를 제공하나요? 최대한 자세하게 말해주세요.

[모범답변]
우리나라에서 호텔은 숙박하기에 무척 고급스럽고 비싼 장소로 여겨져요. 사실상 별 다섯 개의 대부분 호텔들은 숙박료가 무척 고가죠. 10년 전쯤에는 5성급 호텔이 가장 고급스러운 것이었는데 최근에는 Y호텔과 파크호텔 등의 6성급 호텔도 있어요. 저야 그런 종류의 호텔에는 한 번도 묵어보지 못했지만 그래도 거기 있는 식당, 스파, 바 같은 시설은 가끔 이용합니다. 특히, 호텔 스파 서비스가 유명하죠. 최근에는 많은 호텔들이 여성고객들에게 주목하고 있어요. 점점 더 많은 30대 여성들이 스스로에게 돈을 투자하는 것을 개의치 않기 때문에, 호텔들도 그들을 유치하기 위해 패키지 서비스들을 기획하고 있죠. 그런 패키지들은 일반적으로 아침 부페, 스파 할인권, 멋진 부대시설 등이 포함되어 있어요. 젊은 여성들은 미에 관심이 많아서 호텔들은 그들의 편의시설을 유명한 미용 혹은 스파 브랜드로 격상시키기 시작했어요. 저도 친구들과 함께 크리스마스나 새해 전날 밤 호텔 숙박을 체험해보고 싶어요.

06 호텔 2

[질문] p.263
당신이 묵었던 최고의 호텔에 대해 말해보세요. 어디였고 언제 갔나요? 그 호텔을 왜 그렇게 좋아하는 거죠? 그 호텔에 대해 자세히 말해보세요.

[모범답변]
작년 겨울 저는 여동생과 함께 일본 오키나와에 갔습니다. 우리는 함께 일정을 짰고 묵을 호텔을 정했어요. 우리가 묵고 싶었던 대부분의 호텔은 우리 예산으로 많이 비쌌어요. 며칠을 조사해본 후 저는 우리에게 완벽한 호텔을 찾아냈죠. 공항과 가까운 4성급 호텔인데 바다가 보이는 전망이었어요. 더군다나 일찍 예약을 한 덕에 40%할인까지 받아냈답니다. 그 호텔은 정말 굉장했어요. 우리가 체크인을 하려고 할 때도 안내 데스크에 서있을 필요가 없었어요. 우리는 그냥 환영 주스를 마시면서 편안한 소파에 앉아 있었어요. 그럼 직원이 와서 체크인을 위한 서류들을 가져왔어요. 우리는 또 방의 크기에 깜짝 놀랐는데요. 굉장히 넓고 전망도 좋답니다. 호텔에서 제공했던 많은 무료 서비스 중에서 우리는 호텔 사우나가 가장 좋았어요. 그 사우나는 야외 사우나장도 있었어요. 하루 동안의 관광을 끝내고 나서 그 사우나에서 쉴 수가 있었던 거죠. 밤에는 따뜻한 물 속에서 밤 하늘의 별을 보면서 다음 날 관광에 대해 의논했고요. 우리는 자주 그 여행과 호텔에 대해 이야기해요. 오키나와에 또 가게 되면 그 호텔을 또 고를 겁니다.

07 호텔 3

[질문] p.264
당신이 가장 최근에 묵었던 호텔에 대해 말해보세요. 언제, 왜 그곳을 방문했나요? 어떤 점이 좋았고 어떤 점이 싫었나요?

[모범답변]
저는 지난 9월 제 상사와 함께 홍콩에 출장을 갔어요. 인사과 직원이 예약을 했는데 저는 그 호텔에 대한 아무 정보도 알지 못했어요. 바우처를 통해 상관과 함께 트윈 베드 룸에 함께 묵는다는 것만 알았어요. 하지만 막상 그곳에 도착하니까 우리에게 퀸 사이즈 침대가 한 개 있는 방이 배정된 거였어요. 제 바우처를 가리키면서 저는 안내데스크 직원에게 트윈 베드 룸으로 바꿔 달라고 요청했어요. 하지만 그는 도시 내에 행사가 있어서 모든 방이 다 찼다고 하는 거였어요. 우리에게 정중하게 사과를 했기 때문에 더 이상 불평도 할 수 없었죠. 방 자체는 그래도 나쁘지 않았어요. 방도 넓었고 침대도 제가 예상했던 것 보다는 컸거든요. 창문을 통해 보이는 도시의 야경도 좋았고요. 하지만 역시 상관과 함께 한 침대에서 잔다는 것이 얼마나 불편한 일일지 상상하실 수 있잖아요. 상관이 밤새도록 뒤척이는 바람에 저는 쉽게 잠에 들 수 없었어요. 앞으로는 출장 가기 전에 호텔 방을 꼭 확인해야겠어요.

08 명절 1

[질문] p.265
당신 나라에서 가장 큰 명절은 무엇인가요? 그날에 하는 전통적인 활동은 무엇인가요? 그 명절에 대해 자세하게 묘사해보세요.

[모범답변]
우리나라에서는 음력 설이 가장 큰 명절이에요. 부모님과 떨어져

살던 가족들이 부모님 댁을 방문하는지라 사나흘의 휴일이 지속됩니다. 모든 가족이 모이면 정성스런 차례를 통해 조상들께 예를 표합니다. 그 후에는 많은 음식을 먹고 친척들과 대화를 나누며 남은 휴일을 즐기죠. 사람들은 전통 게임을 하기도 합니다. 그 게임들 중에 가장 유명하고 대중적인 전통 게임은 윷이라는 것인데요. 이 게임의 좋은 점은 많은 사람들이 나이와 성별에 상관없이 함께 즐길 수 있다는 것입니다. 음식 준비는 대부분 여성들의 몫인데, 많은 사람들이 한 장소로 모이는 것이기 때문에 많은 일들을 해야 해요. 고되고 힘들긴 하지만 여성들은 가족을 위해 기꺼이 음식 준비를 합니다. 음력 설은 단순한 휴일 그 이상이에요. 우리나라에서는 사람들이 가족과 함께 한 해를 무사히 시작할 수 있고, 모든 사람을 위해 그 해의 행운을 빌어주는 중요한 의미를 가진 휴일입니다.

09 명절 2

[질문] p.266
어렸을 때 기억에 남는 명절 경험이 있을 거예요. 어떤 것이고 어떤 일이 일어났나요? 처음부터 끝까지 이야기해주세요.

[모범답변]
저는 어렸을 때 매 해 음력 설이 되면 저희 부모님과 할아버지 댁을 방문했어요. 저희 할아버지께서는 저희 집에서 상당히 먼 곳에 사셨는데 운전해서 가면 보통 다섯 시간이 걸렸어요. 하지만 음력 설에는 고향으로 가는 사람들이 대부분이기 때문에 고속도로에서 항상 차가 정체되었죠. 어느 해인가 교통 상황이 그 어느 해보다 최악이어서 저에게는 그 여행이 잊지 못할 경험이 되었어요. 저희는 아침 8시에 떠났는데 첫 번째 휴게소에 도착하기까지 3시간이 걸렸어요. 저는 멀미로 힘들어했고 저희 아버지께서는 운전을 몇 시간 동안 하셔서 피곤해하셨죠. 저희가 늦은 점심을 먹으려 두 번째 휴게소에서 멈췄을 때도 주차 공간을 찾는데만 거의 30분이 걸렸어요. 막상 식당에 들어가보니 사람들이 너무 많아서 앉아 있을 자리조차 찾을 수 없었죠. 거기서 점심을 먹는 건 포기하고 그냥 과자와 음료수를 사서 허기를 달랬어요. 12시간 운전 후 할아버지 댁에 도착했을 때까지 저희는 점심이건 저녁이건 먹지도 못했죠. 그 끔찍했던 경험 후 설날 할아버지 댁에 갈 때는 아예 새벽에 출발한답니다.

10 명절 3

[질문] p.267
당신이 최근 지낸 명절에 대해 알고 싶군요. 어떤 명절이었고 그날에 무엇을 했나요?

[모범답변]
저는 최근에 결혼 후 첫 음력 설을 지냈어요. 저희 남편이 장남이기 때문에 모든 가족들이 저희 집에 왔습니다. 저는 며칠 동안 명절 준비를 해야 했어요. 많은 명절 음식을 만들고 접시와 그릇들을 닦아야 했죠. 25명의 친척들이 올 예정이어서 저는 정말 허둥댔어요. 어디서부터 시작해야 할지, 뭘 해야 할지도 몰랐어요. 저희 시어머니께서 명절 음식 준비를 도와주시긴 했지만 전혀 쉽지 않았어요. 저는 뭘 사야 할지 뭘 해야 할지 적어놓고 요리도 하고 모든 것들을 하나하나 챙겼어요. 전 요리를 못하기 때문에 음식 준비가 가장 어려웠어요. 게다가 한 번에 많은 사람들을 위해 필요한 음식을 준비해 본 적이 없었거든요. 저는 잡채, 갈비찜, 전, 여러 종류의 나물들을 준비하며 겨우 맏며느리로서의 역할을 수행했습니다. 저희 시부모님께서는 큰 일을 치렀다고 저를 칭찬해주셨지만, 제가 준비해야 할 다음 명절을 생각을 하면 벌써 스트레스를 받습니다.

11 직장 1

[질문] p.268
상황을 드릴 테니 연기를 해보세요. 당신과 당신의 직원들은 프로젝트를 준비 중에 있습니다. 직원들 중 한 명에게 전화를 걸어 프로젝트 업데이트를 요청하는 메시지를 남겨보세요.

[모범답변]
안녕하세요, 이 대리. 나 신 부장이에요. 다음 주 월요일까지 당신이 끝내야 할 일이 있어요. 우리가 올해 하반기 매출 증가를 목표로 하는 전략 프로젝트를 준비하고 있다는 것 알고 있을 거예요. 그렇죠? 당신이 경쟁사 분석을 책임지고 업데이트해줬으면 해요. 우리가 지금 가지고 있는 자료는 작년에 업데이트 된 거라 최근 상황 업데이트가 필요해요. 경쟁사 분석은 프로젝트의 가장 중요한 부분 중 하나로 영업 직원들과 지점장들에게 도움이 되는 거잖아요. 경쟁사들의 매출액, 고객 만족 조사, 그리고 주요 전략을 포함시켜야 해요. 하지만 자본금, 직원 수 같은 일반적인 자료는 작년에 만들었던 자료를 재사용해도 좋습니다. 아, 기존 경쟁사들과 더불어 ABC와 BTY 회사도 우리 경쟁사로 추가하세요. 두 회사 모두 식품업계에서는 빠르게 성장하고 있는 회사니까요. 너무나 당연한 말이지만, 마감일을 지켜주세요. 다음 주 월요일이에요. 나중에 또 이야기합시다.

12 직장 2

[질문] p.269
미안하지만 당신이 해결해야 할 문제가 있습니다. 당신의 직원이

전화를 해서 임무를 제 때에 완성하지 못할 거라고 합니다. 문제를 해결할 수 있는 두 세 가지 대안을 포함한 메시지를 남겨보세요.

[모범답변]
마감일을 못 맞출 것 같다니 유감이네요. 하지만 3일 간의 신입사원 교육에서 강사로 참여해야 한다고 하니 제 시간에 임무를 맞추기에는 시간이 충분치 않아 보이기도 하네요. 교육은 이번 주 목요일에 끝난다고 했죠? 음, 내가 교육 부서에 전화를 걸어 그 교육에서 제외시켜달라고 부탁해볼게요. 그쪽에서도 당신을 대체할 사람을 찾을 수 있을 거예요. 만일 받아들여지지 않는다면 마감일을 다음 주 수요일까지 연장해줄게요. 즉, 이틀을 더 사용할 수 있다는 거죠. 하지만 제출 마감일을 더 이상 연장할 수는 없어요. 그렇게 되면 프로젝트의 전 과정이 연기될 거니까요. 다른 선택 사항을 하나 더 줄게요. 당신이 경쟁사의 주요 전략만 분석할 수 있도록 업무를 분담시켜볼게요. 나머지 부분은 다른 직원들에게 주는 거죠. 그럼 당신은 신입사원 연수에 참여해도 다음 주 월요일까지는 그 일을 끝낼 수 있을 거예요. 그렇지 않은가요? 이따 사무실에서 결론을 냅시다. 곧 봅시다.

13 직장 3 Oral Proficiency Interview-computer

[질문]
이제까지 직원들을 감독하면서 좋거나 나쁜 경험들이 있었을 겁니다. 긍정적인 경험 중 하나를 말해보세요.

[모범답변]
저는 지금 회사에 들어오기 한참 전에 개인 학원에서 관리자로 일했던 적이 있어요. 제 업무는 강사들을 관리하고, 그들의 학급 시간표를 조절하며, 신입 강사들에게 일주일 교육을 시행하는 것이었어요. 어느 날 미셸이라는 새로운 강사를 만났는데 강의 경험이 전혀 없었던 강사였어요. 저는 어떻게 학생들에게 접근하고 그들을 어떻게 통제해야 하는가 등의 교육을 하기 시작했어요. 처음에는 그 교육을 싫어하는 눈치였고 교육하는 동안에도 성의가 부족했어요. 그녀는 그런 교육이 시간 낭비라고 여기는 것 같았어요. 하지만 수업을 몇 개 해보더니 자신이 학생들에게 효과적이고 자연스럽게 강의 전달을 잘 못한다고 느꼈죠. 좀 풀이 죽어 있어서 저는 교육하면서 그녀의 단점을 보완하도록 용기를 북돋아줬어요. 그 후 그녀는 열의와 성실함을 가지고 교육에 임했죠. 강의 기술이 향상되고 그녀는 가르치는 걸 즐기기 시작했어요. 그녀가 나에게 도와줘서 고맙다고 했을 때 기분이 참 좋았습니다.

14 수영 1 Oral Proficiency Interview-computer

[질문] p.271

사전조사에서 당신은 수영을 한다고 표시했습니다. 수영의 어떤 점을 좋아하나요? 수영은 다른 운동과 어떻게 다른가요? 수영을 다른 운동과 비교해서 자세히 묘사해보세요.

[모범답변]
저는 수영이 저로 하여금 여유를 느끼게 해주는 완벽한 운동이라고 생각해요. 수영은 확실한 이점이 많죠. 팔다리 근육을 향상시켜주고 신진대사를 자극해서 지방을 연소시켜주죠. 수영은 다른 운동들에 비해 무릎과 관절에 큰 압력을 주지 않아요. 조깅이나 근력 운동을 할 때는 항상 부상의 위험이 도사리고 있죠. 하지만 물 속에서는 부력에 힘입어 몸이 떠서 관절에 가해지는 부담이 훨씬 적어요. 누구든 연령에 상관 없이 수영의 이점을 누릴 수 있어요. 아이들에게 수영은 전체적으로 건강에 좋은 최고의 운동이 될 수 있어요. 연세 드신 분들에게는 몸의 균형을 잡아줘서 무릎 통증과 허리 통증을 감소시켜주는데 안성맞춤이죠. 수영은 다른 운동에 비해 배우는 비용이 가장 저렴해요. 수영복 외에는 어떤 장비도 갖출 필요가 없어요. 골프를 치게 되면 골프 복, 장비, 그리고 코스 이용을 위한 회원권도 사야 하잖아요. 수영은 YMCA같은 지역 주민 회관에서도 할 수 있어요. 저도 사실은 저희 동네 주민 회관이 운영하는 수영장에서 한 달에 3만 원을 내고 시간 날 때마다 수영을 즐긴답니다.

15 수영 2 Oral Proficiency Interview-computer

[질문] p.272

언제 수영을 시작했나요? 어떻게 수영에 관심을 갖게 되었죠? 그 관심은 시간이 지나면서 어떻게 변했나요?

[모범답변]
제가 중학생일 때 어머니께서 저를 YMCA 수영센터에 데리고 가셨어요. 제가 나쁜 자세 때문에 허리에 문제가 좀 있었기 때문에 어머니께서는 제가 정기적으로 운동을 하길 바라셨어요. 사실 저는 수영에 전혀 관심이 없었고 물이 좀 무서웠어요. 제가 수영 수업을 받아본 건 태어나서 그 때가 처음이었거든요. 초반에 선생님은 일반적인 자세와 수영할 때 호흡하는 방법을 가르쳐줬어요. 그는 저를 가르치는 데 무척 열성적이었고 저는 단계별로 선생님의 지도를 따라가면서 점점 자신감이 생겼어요. 6개월 동안 수영 강습을 다녔고, 자유형과 배영을 마스터했어요. 그때 이후로 저는 10년 동안 수영을 했고 지금까지 허리에 아무런 문제가 없답니다. 허리만 좋아진 것이 아니라 전체적인 몸 상태도 이전보다 훨씬 좋아졌어요. 수영을 정규 운동으로 시작한 것에 어떤 후회도 없고 수영을 시작하도록 이끌어주신 어머니께 정말 감사드려요.

Actual Test 2 해석

01 자기소개

[질문] p.274
인터뷰를 시작하겠습니다. 당신에 대해 말해주세요.

[모범답변]
안녕하세요, 제 이름은 이동현이라고 합니다. 저는 25세이고 한일 대학교에서 경제학을 전공하고 있는 4학년 학생이에요. 저는 25달의 군복무를 마치고 작년에 복학했습니다. 저는 3남매 중 맏아들이고, 따뜻하지만 약간은 엄격한 집안에서 자랐어요. 저희 아버지께서는 서울에 있는 고등학교 교사로 계시고 저희 어머니께서는 주부세요. 두 분의 교육철학 덕분에 저는 항상 독립적이려고 노력하고 다른 사람들에게 폐를 끼치지 않는 사람이 되었죠. 저는 이번 학기가 시작된 이후로 대부분의 시간을 구직에 쏟고 있어요. 저희 부모님께서는 졸업 후 바로 대학원에 가길 원하시지만 저는 다른 생각이 있어요. 우리나라에서 3~4년 간의 직장 경험을 쌓은 후 미국에서 MBA를 취득하려 계획하고 있거든요. 저는 한참 젊을 때에 사회 경험을 가져보고 싶고, 또 그 경험이 제가 장래에 더 좋은 대학원에 지망하는 데 도움이 될 거라고 믿고 있어요. 경제 침체 때문에 직장을 구하기 힘들어지고 있긴 하지만 저에게 맞는 직업을 잘 찾으리라 확신합니다.

02 공연 1

[질문] p.275
당신은 사전조사에서 공연을 본다고 했습니다. 어떤 극장에 주로 가나요? 그 극장은 어디에 있죠? 어떤 모습인가요? 그 극장을 왜 좋아하나요?

[모범답변]
저는 뮤지컬을 무척 좋아하기 때문에 뮤지컬 극장에 자주 가요. 제가 고른 뮤지컬이 어디서 공연되는가에 따라 가는 공연장이 다르죠. 같은 영화들이 다른 여러 개의 극장에서 상영되는 것과 달리 같은 뮤지컬이라도 특정 기간 동안은 지정된 한 극장에서만 공연되니까요. 하지만 제가 선호하는 극장이 있긴 한데, 바로 이솝 극장이에요. 2호선 잠실역에서 도보로 10분 거리에 있어요. 저는 그 극장이 한국에서 몇 안 되는 뮤지컬 전용극장이라 뮤지컬의 특성을 잘 살려줘서 좋아요. 1,200명 이상을 수용할 만큼 넓고 최첨단 음향시설이 있어서 관객들이 좋은 음악과 노래를 즐길 수 있어요. 가장 좋은 점은 무대가 좌석에서 아주 가까워 관객들이 공연의 활력과 생기를 느낄 수 있다는 거예요. 저는 장래에도 그 극장에서 보다 많은 뮤지컬을 보고 싶어요.

03 공연 2

[질문] p.276
처음에 어떻게 공연 관람에 관심을 갖게 되었나요? 그 관심은 시간이 지나면서 어떻게 바뀌었나요? 당신의 관심이 어떻게 변했는지 당신이 보았던 공연을 포함해서 말해보세요.

[모범답변]
저는 사실 몇 년 전만 해도 뮤지컬에 관심이 없었어요. 뮤지컬 가격은 영화에 비해 턱없이 비싸다고 생각했죠. 하지만 오페라의 유령이라는 뮤지컬이 제 눈을 뜨게 해줬어요. 제가 유럽 배낭여행을 갔을 때 봤는데요. 노래에 나오는 모든 가사를 알아들을 수는 없었지만 저는 인물들의 감정에 완전히 동화됐어요. 특히 유령으로 나왔던 남자 배우는 노래를 너무 잘했고 그의 가창력과 연기는 저를 매료시켰죠. 그 때 이후로는 한국에서도 좋은 뮤지컬을 찾아 다니고 있어요. 하지만 솔직히 말해서 처음에는 한국 배우들이 나오는 뮤지컬에 대한 기대는 낮았어요. 그래서 원래의 팀들이 나오는 뮤지컬, 예를 들면 노트르담 드 파리 같은 뮤지컬만 보려고 했죠. 하지만 작년에 한국 배우들이 나오는 헤드윅을 보고서야 제가 한국 뮤지컬 배우들에게 강한 편견을 지녀왔음을 깨달았죠. 주인공이 그렇게 유명한 배우가 아니었는데도 그의 호소력 있는 목소리와 노래 실력은 저를 감동시키기 충분했어요. 이제 저는 한국 배우들이 출연하는 뮤지컬을 아주 좋아한답니다.

04 공연 3

[질문] p.277
가장 최근에 본 공연은 무엇인가요? 언제 봤고 어느 극장에 갔나요? 극장에 가기 전과 후에는 뭘 했나요?

[모범답변]
저는 지난 10월에 제 여자친구와 함께 에비뉴 큐라는 뮤지컬을 봤어요. 초반에 제가 언급했던 이솝 극장에서 봤는데요. 최우수 뮤지컬 상을 포함해 3개의 토니상을 수상했다는 유명한 브로드웨이 뮤지컬이었어요. 저는 원래의 브로드웨이 출연진들이 나온다고 하고, 뉴욕에서 공부했던 제 친구가 저보고 꼭 보라고 강력히 추천도 하고 해서 기대를 아주 많이 했어요. 오후 3시에 시작해서 뮤지컬 시작 전에 극장 근처에서 점심과 음료를 먹었죠. 1층 가운데 자리에 앉았는데 배우들이 상당히 잘 보이는 자리였어요.

하지만 공연에 대한 기대가 너무 컸나 봐요. 인물들이 노래는 잘 부르는데도 성량이 약한 것 같았고, 더 중요한 건 인상적인 음악과 노래가 하나도 없었다는 거예요. 극장 문을 나선 직후에도 귀에 맴도는 선율이 전혀 없었다니까요. 저희는 로비에 있는 기념품 가게에 가서 이것 저것 둘러봤어요. 라이온 킹, 캣츠, 맘마미아와 같은 많은 뮤지컬들이 그 극장에서 열렸기 때문에, 여러 유명 주인공들이 그려진 머그컵, 손수건, 열쇠고리 등을 볼 수 있었죠. 다음 번에는 좀 더 재미있는 뮤지컬을 보고 싶네요.

05　걷기 1

[질문]　　　　　　　　　　　　　　　　　　　　p.278
사전조사에서 걷는 걸 좋아한다고 했습니다. 가장 좋아하는 걷기 장소가 어디인가요? 어떤 모습이죠? 거기서 무엇을 볼 수 있나요? 어떤 점을 좋아하나요?

[모범답변]
저는 한강 근처에 있는 원룸에서 살고 있습니다. 강 주위에 잘 만들어진 산책로가 있는데, 그곳이 바로 제가 가장 좋아하는 걷기 장소예요. 저녁을 먹고 밤 8시쯤 산책을 시작하죠. 산책로에 가기 위해서는 작은 공원 하나를 통과해야 하는데, 그 공원 끝에서 산책로가 시작됩니다. 산책로는 두 길로 나뉘어져 있어요. 하나는 걷는 사람들을 위한 길이고 다른 하나는 자전거 타는 사람들과 인라인 스케이트를 타는 사람들을 위한 길이에요. 길을 걸으면서 저는 한국에서 마천루들이 굉장히 많은 금융중심지인 여의도의 야경을 즐길 수 있답니다. 건물 창문들을 통해 흘러나오는 불빛들을 보면서 저는 가끔씩 몇 명이나 야근을 하고 있을까라고 추측해보곤 해요. 산책로를 걸으면 국회의사당도 보여요. 돔에서 나오는 불빛들은 야경을 더욱 아름답게 해주죠. 산책로 주변에는 농구장과 놀이터가 있습니다. 청소년들이 농구를 하고 아이들이 부모님과 함께 놀고 있는 걸 보죠. 그 산책로를 걷는 것은 이미 제 일상생활 중의 하나가 되었고, 이곳보다 더 좋은 걷기 장소는 없어요.

06　걷기 2

[질문]　　　　　　　　　　　　　　　　　　　　p.279
어떻게 처음 걷기를 시작했나요? 걷기에 대한 관심이 수년간 어떻게 변해왔나요?

[모범답변]
저는 저녁 식사 후 잘 때까지의 시간을 때우고자 걷기를 시작했어요. 밤 8시에서 10시 사이에 특별히 할 일이 없어서 걷기로 한 거죠. 처음에는 일주일에 세 번 저녁 식사 후 걸을 계획이었어요. 그렇게 힘든 운동도 아니고 해서 대략 월, 수, 토요일로 정했습니다. 하지만 막상 제가 앞에서 언급했던 산책로를 따라 거닐어보고 저는 사람들이 열심히 걷거나 뛰는 모습을 보고 좀 놀랐습니다. 저는 호주머니에 손을 넣고 그냥 걷는 반면 그들은 팔을 90도 각도로 구부린 채 걸으면서 팔을 흔들더군요. 운동 복장 또한 저와 무척 달랐습니다. 그들은 운동복과 편안한 걷기용 또는 달리기용 신발을 신고 있었어요. 젊고 예쁜 여성들이 활기차게 걷고 뛰는 모습을 보는 것이 신선했다고나 할까요. 저는 곧 좋은 운동복과 편한 걷기용 신발을 샀고 제 걷기는 본격적으로 시작되었죠. 저는 걷기의 올바른 팔, 다리 동작에 대한 정보를 찾아봤고 그 설명을 따랐어요. 많은 시간과 노력을 쏟을수록 걷기에 더욱 적극적으로 되었죠. 지금은 걷기가 제 일상생활에서 빠질 수 없는 즐거움이 되었습니다.

07　걷기 3

[질문]　　　　　　　　　　　　　　　　　　　　p.280
걷기에 관련된 재미있거나 예기치 않았거나 놀라웠던 경험에 대해 말해주세요.

[모범답변]
제가 개를 데리고 산책로를 걷고 있던 여자를 본건 지난달 밤 9시 정도였어요. 저는 주인이 잘 관리만 해준다면 산책로에서 개나 강아지를 보는 걸 개의치 않아해요. 하지만 제가 본 그 여자는 자기 개한테 관심도 없어 보였어요. 개에게 줄도 묶어놓지 않아서 그 개는 산책로를 뛰어다니면서 다른 보행자들이 다니는 걸 방해했어요. 그 보행자들은 개가 앞에 나타날 때마다 멈춰서야 했죠. 저도 처음에는 화나는 걸 참으려 했는데, 제 길을 계속 가로 막는 그 개가 정말 성가셨어요. 제가 의자에 앉아 쉬고 있는데 그 개가 제 앞을 또 지나갔어요. 그런데 그 개가 저를 향해 갑자기 싶는 바람에 너무 깜짝 놀란 거예요! 그제서야 그 주인은 개를 붙잡았지만 저에게 사과도 하지 않았어요. 저는 그 여자에게 밖에서는 개에게 줄을 매야 한다고 말하면서 결국 그 개에 대해 불만을 표시했습니다. 하지만 그녀는 아무런 대답도 안하고 자기 개와 함께 가버렸어요. 그 때 이후로 그 여자와 개를 본 적은 없지만 그날 밤을 생각하면 아직도 기분이 나빠요.

08　학원 수강 1

[질문]　　　　　　　　　　　　　　　　　　　　p.281
당신은 어학원에 다닌다고 했습니다. 어떤 어학원에 다니나요? 무슨 언어를 공부하나요? 왜 하는 거죠? 가능한 자세하게 말해 보세요.

[모범답변]

저는 중국어를 배우러 6개월째 어학원에 다니고 있어요. 큰 규모의 학원들은 학생들에게 신경을 거의 안 쓴다고 생각해서 작지만 이름 있는 곳을 골랐어요. 중국어를 꽤 잘하는 친구가 그 학원을 추천해줬죠. 친구가 그러는데 그 학원에 경험도 많고 자질도 좋은 중국어 강사들이 있다고 하더라고요. 저는 순전히 제 개인적인 흥미로 중국어를 배우기 시작했어요. 저는 중국 문명과 문학에 매력을 느끼고 있었거든요. 중국어를 배우기로 했을 때 저는 두 가지 목표를 세웠어요. 첫째, 중국을 언어 장벽 없이 여행할 수 있도록 2년 안에 중국어를 통달하리라 결심했어요. 둘째, 중국어를 읽을 줄 알게 된 다음에는 당나라 때 유명한 중국 시인인 두보의 시를 읽고 싶었어요. 고등학생 시절에 그의 시에 깊게 감명받았거든요. 비록 제가 중국어를 통달하기까지는 갈 길이 멀지만 중국어를 배우는 건 정말 즐겁습니다.

09 학원 수강 2

[질문] p.282
그 어학원에서 받은 첫 수업에 대해 말해보세요. 학원, 선생님, 그리고 같은 반 학생들에 대한 첫 인상은 어땠나요? 자세하게 묘사해주세요.

[모범답변]
글쎄요, 학원에 대한 첫 인상이 좋았다고는 말 못하겠어요. 오래되고 허름한 건물에 상당히 실망했으니까요. 하지만 조용하고 학구적인 학원 분위기는 좋았어요. 저는 초보자 반에 등록을 했고, 저희 반은 저를 포함해 여덟 명의 수강생이 있었어요. 대부분 친절하고 성실해 보였지만 한 젊은 여학생은 좀 사나워 보였어요. 저희 선생님은 중국에서 태어났지만 어머니는 한국 분이었어요. 상냥해 보였지만 좀 고집스러워 보이기도 했죠. 중국어와 한국어를 다 할 줄 알았기 때문에 중국어를 한국어로 가르치는 동시에 원어민의 발음으로 중국어를 말할 수 있었죠. 선생님은 기본적인 발음과 억양을 먼저 가르쳐줬어요. 중국어 억양이 의미를 구별하는데 결정적이라는 건 저도 알고 있었지만, 저에게는 무척 생소했었죠. 쉬는 시간에 선생님은 자신의 고향인 상하이와 어린 시절에 대해 말해줬어요. 저는 지금 다른 선생님으로부터 중급자 수준의 중국어를 배우고 있긴 하지만 복도에서 그 선생님을 보면 지금도 반가워요.

10 학원 수강 3

[질문] p.283
당신이 그 학원에서 겪었던 흥미롭거나, 재미있었거나, 혹은 놀라웠던 경험에 대해 말해보세요.

[모범답변]
저의 첫 반이 여덟 명의 학생들로 구성됐다는 말은 이미 했는데요. 첫째 주에는 아무도 결석하지 않았어요. 첫 주의 금요일 수업이 끝나고 학생들 중 한 명이 서로 친하게 지내자는 의미로 맥주를 한 잔 하자고 제안했어요. 우리는 예기치 않았지만, 즐거운 회식에 기꺼이 참가했어요. 맥주를 마시며 유쾌하고 건설적인 대화를 나눴죠. 중국어를 왜 공부하는지 최종 목표는 무엇인지에 대해 이야기를 나눴죠. 그 회식을 주선했던 남자가 이번에는 공부 모임을 갖자고 제안했어요. 그는 같은 반 사람들끼리 친한 것이 중국어를 계속 배우는 동기 부여가 될 수 있다고 하더라고요. 우리 모두는 그 생각에 동의했고 그 남자는 공부 계획을 짜겠다고 했어요. 다음주 월요일에 저는 그 남자를 포함해 세 명이 결석해서 좀 실망했어요. 다음날 나올 거라고 생각했는데 그들 중 한 명만 나왔어요. 세 번째 주에는 3명으로 줄더니 마지막 주에는 반에 남은 사람이 저 혼자였어요. 더 이상한 건, 그 공부 모임을 제안한 남자는 그날 밤 이후로 한 번도 안 나왔다는 거예요. 정말 실없는 사람이라고 생각했습니다.

11 애완동물 1

[질문] p.284
상황을 드릴 테니 연기를 해보세요. 당신 이웃이 당신에게 그들의 고양이가 없어졌다고 했습니다. 당신은 그들이 고양이를 찾게 도와주고 싶지만 고양이에 대한 정보가 없습니다. 이웃에게 전화를 걸어서 고양이에 대해 서너 가지 질문을 해보세요.

[모범답변]
여보세요, 문여사님? 저 이웃에 사는 이동현이에요. 고양이 찾으시는데 도움이 될 아이디어가 좀 있는데 고양이에 대한 정보가 필요해요. 전 졸리라는 이름 밖에 모르거든요. 전단지를 만들어서 행인들에게 나눠주거나 제 이웃들의 편지함에 넣어놓고 싶어요. 제가 알아야 할 첫 번째는 전단지에 붙일 졸리의 최근 사진이에요. 대부분 고양이들은 비슷하게 생겼지만 두드러진 특징이 있다면 사람들이 졸리를 알아보기 쉬울 거예요. 사진이 없다면 졸리에 대한 묘사를 좀 해주시겠어요? 무슨 색깔을 지녔나요? 제 남동생이 집 근처에서 흰색과 갈색의 얼룩 고양이를 봤다고 하는데 그 고양이가 여사님네 건지는 잘 모르겠네요. 저는 전단지에 졸리의 품종도 포함시키고 싶어요. 제가 아는 유일한 품종은 페르시안 고양이인데, 다른 품종일 수도 있겠죠. 한 가지 더요, 졸리가 자신의 이름을 알고 있나요? 이름을 누가 부르면 반응을 하는지 알고 싶은 거예요. 만약 반응을 하면 그 정보를 전단지에 적어놓을게요. 걱정 마세요. 곧 찾을 수 있을 거예요.

12 애완동물 2

[질문] p.285
미안하지만 당신이 해결해야 할 문제가 있습니다. 당신은 그 고양이가 당신의 집 정원에 있는 나무 위에 올라가 있는 걸 발견했습니다. 이웃에게 전화해서 문제를 해결할 수 있는 두 세 가지 대안을 제시하세요.

[모범답변]
문여사님, 안녕하세요! 좋은 소식이 있어요. 드디어 여사님 고양이 졸리를 찾았어요! 믿기 어려우실지 모르겠지만 글쎄 저희 집 정원에 있지 뭐예요. 얼마나 오래 여기 있었는지는 잘 모르겠지만 빨리 찾아서 참 다행이에요. 그런데 문여사님, 문제가 좀 있어요. 졸리가 나무 꼭대기에 올라가서 좀처럼 내려올 것 같지 않아요. 제가 공이나 수건 같은 걸 던지면 위험할까요? 그걸 피하기 위해서 내려올 것 같은데요. 하지만 졸리가 놀라는 걸 원치 않으신다면 하지 않을게요. 먹을 걸로 유혹을 해보는 건 어떨까도 생각해봤어요. 고양이가 아이스크림이나 참치 캔 같이 사람이 먹는 음식도 먹을 수 있다는 걸 배운 적이 있거든요. 문여사님이 여기 올 때 졸리가 가장 좋아하는 음식을 가져와도 되고요. 만일 우리가 뭘 해도 졸리가 안 내려온다면 119 구조대에 전화를 걸어 도움을 요청해야 할 것 같아요. 그분들에게는 나무에서 졸리를 무사히 데리고 내려올 노하우가 틀림없이 있을 거예요. 그럼 잠시 후에 봐요!

13 애완동물 3

[질문] p.286
앞의 상황은 종료 되었습니다. 애완동물을 키우는 동안 예기치 않은 문제들이 일어났을 겁니다 당신의 애완동물과 있었던 사건에 대해 말해보세요. 어떤 문제였고 그 상황을 어떻게 해결했나요?

[모범답변]
제 아내와 저는 18개월 된 강아지를 1년 째 키우고 있어요. 이름은 릴리인데 사랑스러운 하얀 푸들이에요. 저희가 여름 휴가 때 릴리를 데려왔기 때문에 일주일 내내 함께 있을 수 있었는데요. 휴가가 끝나고 저희가 회사에 가려고 집을 나서려고 하는데, 릴리가 짖기 시작하는 거예요. 저희는 곧 짖기를 멈출 거라 생각했지만 점점 더 심하게 짖어댔어요. 릴리는 너무나 불안하고 겁에 질려 보였죠. 결국 제가 반차를 내고 수의사에게 데려가서 검진을 받았어요. 의사선생님은 릴리가 분리 불안을 보이는 것인데, 많은 어린 동물들에게 흔하게 나타나는 것이라고 했죠. 그러면서 릴리를 안심시킬 방법을 주셨습니다. 저는 그분의 조언을 따랐는데 정말 효과적이었어요. 예를 들어 릴리 뒤에서 문을 닫고 2~3초 기다리는 거예요. 그리고 나서 문을 열어 릴리가 진정할 수 있도록 안아줘요. 저는 그 훈련을 반복하면서 점차 제가 문을 열기를 기다리는 시간을 늘려나갔죠. 릴리가 혼자 있을 준비가 되는데 시간이 좀 걸렸지만 지금은 아내와 제가 걱정 없이 8~9시간 동안은 집을 비울 수 있답니다.

14 해변 1

[질문] p.287
당신은 사전조사에서 해변에 간다고 표시했습니다. 당신이 자주 가는 해변에 대해 말해 주세요. 어디 있고 어떻게 그곳에 가나요? 얼마나 자주 가고 누구와 가나요? 해변에서 누구를 보고 무엇을 하죠? 자세히 말해보세요.

[모범답변]
저는 강릉에 있는 경포대에 일 년에 두 세 번, 여름과 겨울에 갑니다. 저는 주로 가족과 그곳에 가죠. 서울에서 세 시간 운전하면 갈 수 있는데 있지만 여름 휴가 기간에는 네다섯 시간 걸립니다. 여름에는 아이들이 물 속에서 안전하게 노는지 확인을 하러 저도 바다로 들어갑니다. 아이들은 튜브를 타고 놀고, 수영도 하고, 물장구도 치죠. 우리 애들은 다른 애들처럼 모래성 쌓는 걸 별로 좋아하지 않더라고요. 우리는 그늘 안에서 쉬려고 파라솔을 해변으로 가져갑니다. 밤에는 방문객들이 모닥불 파티를 하는 것도 볼 수 있죠. 일부 젊은 사람들은 음악을 켜고, 노래를 부르고 춤도 추고 말이에요. 하지만 겨울에 가면, 저희는 경치를 즐기면서 바닷가를 거닐어요. 모래사장에 메시지를 적는 젊은 연인들을 보면 미소가 지어집니다. 저는 겨울 바다를 보는 게 좋아요. 태양이 수평선 위로 지는 걸 보는 건 참 감동적이에요. 해안에 부딪치는 파도소리는 저를 편하게 해주고 일에 대한 모든 것을 잊게 해 줍니다 경포대는 산책하기에 정말 좋은 해변입니다.

15 해변 2

[질문] p.288
당신이 갔던 가장 기억에 남는 해변에 대해 알고 싶군요. 언제, 그리고 누구와 거길 갔나요? 해변은 어떤 모습이었나요? 당신은 무엇을 봤고 무엇을 했나요?

[모범답변]
저의 가장 기억에 남는 해변은 플로리다에 있는 펜사콜라 해변입니다. 저는 그곳에 5년 전, 조지아에서 박사 과정을 밟고 있던 친구를 방문했을 때 갔습니다. 그는 나에게 세상에서 가장 아름다운 해변 중 한 곳을 보게 될 거라고 말했는데요. 해변에 도착해 보니 그 말이 과장이 아니었다는 걸 알았습니다. 설탕처럼 하얀

모래는 저에게 눈처럼 보여서 해변을 따라 걸을 때 마치 제가 눈 위를 걷는 것처럼 느껴졌어요. 저는 샌달을 벗고 맨발에 닿는 보드라운 모래를 느꼈죠. 어떤 사람들은 서핑과 제트 스키 같은 해양 스포츠에 몰두하는 반면 또 어떤 사람들은 따뜻한 햇살 아래 일광욕을 즐기고 있었어요. 해변은 호텔, 개방형 바, 식당과 부두 등의 많은 시설들로 잘 갖춰져 있었습니다. 바에 앉아 시원한 맥주와 신선한 해산물을 먹었던 기억이 나는군요. 그런 멋진 곳에서 친한 친구와 평화롭고 여유로운 시간을 보낸다는 게 즐겁고 행복했어요. 저는 자주 펜사콜라 해변이 그립고, 눈처럼 흰 모래를 바라보며 걱정과 스트레스를 떠나 보내고 싶습니다.

Supplementary Materials

Oral Proficiency Interview-**computer**

Supplementary Materials

Lesson 1 직장 1–회사 소개

Activity 1 Write the correct word, phrase or sentence in English.

H1 Key expressions

1. ~에 위치하다
2. 지역
3. 생산하다
4. 부품
5. 주 거래처
6. 매출 수익
7. 본사
8. 이직률
9. 영업사원
10. ~를 맡고 있다

H1 Answers

1. located in
2. province
3. manufacture
4. component
5. major accounts
6. sales profits
7. headquarters
8. the turnover rate
9. sales representative
10. be in charge of

(p.20 참조)

Activity 2 Fill in the blanks with appropriate words or clauses in the brackets to answer the question.

Q. Please tell me about the history of your company. When was it established and who was the founder? How has it developed since its foundation? Give me as many details as possible.

H2 Fill in blanks

My company _____ by two engineers back in 2003 in Asan. They were _____ a large electronics company together, and their jobs were to develop electronic parts. During the period of working, they obtained several _____ on LCD products and decided to _____ their own business. After getting some _____ from outside sources and investing all their money, they _____ a small company in Asan with two more engineers. The two founders did _____ from developing parts and _____ customers to managing the engineers. For the first few years, they _____ operate their company. Their ideas were frequently _____ their potential associates, but they persistently _____ find major accounts with enthusiasm for their LCD components. Two years later, they became _____ for two large companies, which enabled them _____ their business stable with more employees. As LCDs had a huge popularity in 2008, more companies made LCD products such as LCD TVs and refrigerators with LCD screens. This trend _____ the sales of their components, and they expanded their business. They _____ some factories both in Korea and China, and their business _____ better. I believe they were capable engineers, but also, were lucky _____.

H2 Answers

1. was founded
2. working for
3. patents
4. start
5. investment
6. established
7. multiple-jobs
8. gaining
9. managed to
10. rejected by
11. sought to
12. a major supplier
13. to keep
14. boosted
15. have built
16. has gotten
17. in business

(p.23 참조)

Activity 3 Come up with one sentence for each question. And then make a story combining the answers.

H3 Write your answers

Q1 Have you had a coworker who you had trouble with?
_____

Q2 What was your duty?
_____

Q3 What was the problem?
_____

Q4 What did you do to set him on the right track, and how did he react?
_____

Q5 How did you deal with the situation? How did it end eventually?
_____

Your Own Answer

H3 Model Answers

A1 I've gone through various episodes with my coworkers, and I'd like to talk about one of them, who was a real pain in the neck.

A2 My duty was to help him have the necessary skills for his job, but he was so unfocused.

A3 He didn't concentrate on listening to me and was often sitting absent-mindedly during working hours.

A4 I spent lots of time talking to him to set him on the right track, but his attitude didn't get better.

A5 I eventually asked my boss for help, and my boss had already been aware of his indolence. My boss was sort of a tyrant in our department but also a competent supervisor. He started training the new employee himself, and he was soon overwhelmed by his boss's charisma. He had to work overtime almost every day and submit his daily work report to his boss.

(p.26 참조)

Lesson 2 직장 2-사내 업무 및 연수

Activity 1 Write the correct word, phrase or sentence in English.

H1 Key expressions

1. 제공하다
2. 분기별로
3. ~에 의해 실시되다
4. 고객 서비스 부서
5. ~에서 열리다
6. 기술적 장치
7. 고객 불만
8. 까다로운
9. ~와 협업하다
10. 목표를 달성하다

H1 Answers

1. offer
2. quarterly basis
3. be administered by
4. customer service department
5. be held in
6. technological device
7. customers' complaints
8. fastidious
9. cooperate with
10. achieve goals

(p.32 참조)

Activity 2 Fill in the blanks with appropriate words or clauses in the brackets to answer the question.

Q. I'd like to know about the training sessions that you took when you first started working. They may have been quite different from the ones that you're receiving nowadays. How have the training sessions changed over the years?

H2 Fill in blanks

I attended an orientation for new employees as soon as I _____ my company. The three-day orientation program _____ in the company training center in Gyeonggi-do, and all the new employees including myself _____ there _____ it. The contents of the program were mostly _____ the introduction of the company such as its history, vision, future goals, and personnel policies. I can say that its objective was _____ the new employees to get the essential information and _____ their company. In contrast, the trainings that I received after the orientation were related to more specific _____ of the job. Those job-related training sessions _____ me to become skilled and _____ my required tasks more quickly. Some of them also gave me some opportunities _____ communication and presentation skills, which were very useful for me _____ new clients. After my _____ to the managerial position, I got the training _____ leadership, too. As my position and job duties _____, the contents of _____ have been changed.

H2 Answers

1. joined
2. was given
3. had to stay
4. to receive
5. related to
6. to motivate
7. take pride in
8. directions
9. enabled
10. qualified for
11. to develop
12. to secure
13. promotion
14. regarding
15. have been changed
16. trainings

(p.35 참조)

Activity 3 Come up with one sentence for each question. And then make a story combining the answers.

H3 Write your answers

Q1 What was the most memorable training you received at your work?
_____

Q2 Who gave the training, and what was he/she good at?
_____

Q3 What was special about the training?
_____

Q4 How did you feel about the training?
_____

Q5 How did it affect your presentation skills at the end?
_____

Your Own Answer

H3 Model Answers

A1 I remember receiving a training program during my second year of working. It was about the presentation skills training, which was a necessary qualification for me to introduce our products to major clients.

A2 It was given by some sales managers who had excellent sales performances with good presentation skills.

A3 During that training session, the participants were asked to make a presentation about any topics given in public and the presentations were videotaped.

A4 It was embarrassing to see my speech through video tapes and also have them point out my speech style at first, but I could eventually find out my problems and correct them.

A5 I became more confident of standing in public after the training. I'm still using the skills that I learned from the training.

(p.38 참조)

Lesson 3 학생 생활 소개하기

Activity 1 Write the correct word, phrase or sentence in English.

H1 Key expressions

1. ~에 다니다
2. 꽃을 피우다, 꽃
3. 마주보다
4. 잘 손질된
5. 거닐다
6. 그림 같은
7. 건물
8. 세련된
9. ~의 혼합
10. 잔디

H1 Answers

1. attend
2. blossom
3. face each other
4. well-groomed
5. stroll
6. picturesque
7. architecture
8. refined
9. mixture of
10. lawn

(p.44 참조)

Activity 2 Fill in the blanks with appropriate words or clauses in the brackets to answer the question.

Q. What do you study in school? What is your major about? Do you like studying that major? Please tell me about your major in as much detail as possible.

H2 Fill in blanks

I'm currently _____ English Language and Linguistics. Linguistics is the _____ scientific study of human language. Like other sciences, it _____ data, tests _____, and suggests _____ theories to understand _____. Therefore, English Language and Linguistics, of course _____ the study of English. I _____ how humans _____ language. It's not a question that I can't answer easily and simply, but I want to have a clear idea of this issues through my courses. I honestly can't say that _____ English Language and Linguistics is enjoyable. Some subjects, especially phonetics and phonology, are quite difficult to _____. They're the study of the sound, and more specifically, how each sound _____ others and how they _____ systems and patterns. It's very hard for me _____ each sound or group of sounds, and sometimes, I _____ myself for not understanding them. However, I don't mean that I hate learning those subjects or regret choosing my major. _____, all the courses are essential for knowledge of language, and _____ must be one of the mountains I need to climb over to deeply understand the human language.

H2 Answers

1. majoring in
2. so-called
3. collects
4. hypotheses
5. reliable
6. the nature of language
7. focuses on
8. have been interested in
9. acquire
10. majoring in
11. keep up with
12. differs from
13. form
14. to identify
15. feel discouraged with
16. As it is quite clear
17. feeling pressure

(p.47 참조)

Activity 3 Come up with one sentence for each question. And then make a story combining the answers.

H3 Write your answers

Q1 Have you worked on any interesting projects at school?

Q2 What was the project about?

Q3 How were your group members?

Q4 What did you do with your group members?

Q5 How did your project go at the end?

Your Own Answer

H3 Model Answers

A1 I had worked on an interesting project, which was given to me in the first semester of my sophomore year.
A2 The project was about how psychological and social factors contribute to successful language learning.
A3 All of my group members were industrious and enthusiastic for our work.
A4 We discussed which tasks we need, assigned each member each task, and set the deadline for each task.
A5 The project was running on all cylinders, and consequently, our efforts paid off. We not only got an excellent grade but were selected as the best team in my class.

(p.51 참조)

Lesson 4 뉴스를 보거나 듣기

Activity 1 Write the correct word, phrase or sentence in English.

H1 Key expressions

1. A에게 B를 알리다
2. 주로
3. 무료로
4. 표제
5. 관련된
6. 제공하다
7. 즉시
8. 방송하다
9. 사건
10. 정확히 제 시간에

H1 Answers

1. inform A of B
2. primarily
3. for free
4. headline
5. relevant
6. provide
7. instantly
8. broadcast
9. incident
10. promptly

(p.56 참조)

Activity 2 Fill in the blanks with appropriate words or clauses in the brackets to answer the question.

Q. Which topics are you most interested in when you watch or listen to the news? What do you do to watch or listen to the news?

H2 Fill in blanks

I definitely like the news about sports. Whenever I _____ headlines on my news applications, I _____ the one about sports first. When I watch the news on TV, I also _____ the sports news to start. I _____ all kinds of sports, but my favorite is baseball. During the baseball season, I hardly _____ the sports news _____ the highlights of the games of the day. You know that I can't see all the baseball games played _____. Since regular TV news doesn't usually _____ much time to sports-related news, I watch it on _____ sports channels on TV mostly at night. I also download some sports applications and _____ scores or news of my favorite teams. Some Korean baseball players like Choo Shin Soo and Ryu Hyun Jin are recently _____ very well in Major League, so I _____ check the news about them. I hope we _____ more sports channels and better sports applications _____.

H2 Answers

1. search
2. choose
3. wait for
4. am interested in
5. miss
6. showing
7. in different regions
8. devote
9. several
10. keep track of
11. playing
12. frequently
13. get
14. available

(p.59 참조)

Activity 3   Come up with one sentence for each question. And then make a story combining the answers.

H3 Write your answers

Q1   How did people get news when you were a child?
_____

Q2   What were the shortcomings?
_____

Q3   How can we get news these days?
_____

Q4   How has the role of the viewer changed?
_____

Q5   How do people interact with the news?
_____

Your Own Answer

H3 Model Answers

A1   They watched the TV news, listened to the radio news, or read a newspaper.
A2   People didn't know which events had taken place until the TV or radio broadcast the news or the newspaper was delivered, and they didn't know the news that wasn't covered.
A3   Today, we can also get the news from computers and smartphones, and the news is updated very quickly. Since the cable TV became available, we can even watch the news all day long on several news channels.
A4   I also want to mention another big change, which is viewers' and listeners' active participation in the news programs.
A5   They send their opinions of the news directly to the anchors' or producers' emails without hesitation. They also post comments with encouragement or complaint on the bulletin board of the program homepage.

(p.62 참조)

Lesson 5 콘서트보기

Activity 1 Write the correct word, phrase or sentence in English.

H1 Key expressions

1. 취향
2. 고전적인
3. 열정
4. 공유하다
5. 탈출구
6. 일상
7. 긴장
8. 카타르시스
9. 정화
10. 충분히 가치가 있는

H1 Answers

1. taste
2. classical
3. passion
4. share
5. escape
6. daily life
7. tension
8. catharsis
9. purification
10. worth

(p.68 참조)

Activity 2 Fill in the blanks with appropriate words or clauses in the brackets to answer the question.

Q. Which concert have you been to most recently? When and where was the concert held? Did you like the concert hall? Please describe the concert hall in as much detail as you can.

H2 Fill in blanks

Last December, I went to the piano and violin duo concert _____ the two _____ Korean musicians, Son Yeol-eum and Clara-Jumi Kang. The concert _____ at the Concert Hall of Seoul Arts Center, which _____ Yangjae-dong in Seoul. I like to go to Seoul Arts Center because it _____ mountains and is well _____ some art museums and other facilities _____ music halls. The concert hall was pretty large with three _____. I'm not sure about the _____ number of seats, but I guess it has more than 2,000 seats. I sat in the back of the first floor and the seat was _____ for me to sit through the two-and-a-half-hour concert. I saw a large stage in the front, and above the stage, there was _____ to give a spotlight on the performers. I remember _____ of the hall was also good. _____, the concert hall provided a _____ and comfortable _____ for its _____.

H2 Answers

1. played by
2. promising
3. was performed
4. is located in
5. is surrounded by
6. equipped with
7. as well as
8. stories
9. exact
10. comfortable enough
11. lighting equipment
12. the acoustics
13. To conclude
14. pleasant
15. atmosphere
16. audience

(p.71 참조)

Activity 3 Come up with one sentence for each question. And then make a story combining the answers.

H3 Write your answers

Q1 What was your most memorable concert experience?

Q2 What expectations did you have about the concert?

Q3 Was the concert experience the same as what you expected?

Q4 How did you feel during the concert?

Q5 What was your overall impression of the concert?

Your Own Answer

H3 Model Answers

A1 I went to Psy's concert a few years ago, not long before he has become a world-famous singer through his song, Gangnam Style.
A2 It was my first time to attend his concert, but honestly, I didn't expect much about it.
A3 As the show went by, however, I found I was totally wrong. He sang much better than I'd expected, and his energetic dances captured my eyes and mind.
A4 I was getting excited and couldn't help but sing along and dance to his fast beat songs with other audience.
A5 It was a really enjoyable concert, and I found him a good singer with singing ability as well as dazzling stage presence.

(p.74 참조)

Lesson 6 체스하기

Activity 1 Write the correct word, phrase or sentence in English.

H1 Key expressions

1. 시간 가는 줄 모르다
2. 대결자
3. 기사
4. 탈출하다
5. 포로로 잡다
6. 유익하다
7. 연구
8. 문제해결 능력
9. 노인
10. 앞으로 움직이다

H1 Answers

1. lose track of time
2. opponent
3. knight
4. escape
5. capture
6. benefit
7. study
8. problem-solving skills
9. the elderly
10. move forward

(p.80 참조)

Activity 2 Fill in the blanks with appropriate words or clauses in the brackets to answer the question.

Q. Eva also likes playing chess. Ask her three or four questions that you want to know about chess.

H2 Fill in blanks

I _____ that you _____ chess. It isn't a _____ game in my country, and few people know how to play it. Could you explain some basic _____ of chess? Who should _____ first, the player _____ the white pieces or the one with the black pieces? How should _____ the different _____ pieces move? Can all of them move up, down, sideways, and _____? I'd also like to _____ the history of chess. Some people say it _____ the earlier chess-like game _____ India before the 6th century AD. Others suggest Xianggi, which is the world's oldest board game, _____ the very early Chinese literature. And here is my last question. Why do you like playing chess? Do you play it to simply _____? Or do you like it because chess _____ your brain? I also like playing chess a lot, so I hope that we'll play it _____, Eva.

H2 Answers

1. heard
2. enjoy playing
3. popular
4. rules
5. move
6. with
7. each of
8. kinds of
9. diagnally
10. know about
11. evolved from
12. played in
13. appeared in
14. spend your time
15. trains
16. in the near future

(p.83 참조)

Activity 3 Come up with one sentence for each question. And then make a story combining the answers.

H3 Write your answers

Q1 What was the most memorable chess game you had?
_____

Q2 Did you have any special rules, and how did you feel?
_____

Q3 How did you expect the game to be?
_____

Q4 How did the game actually go?
_____

Q5 How did you feel about the result of the game?
_____

Your Own Answer

H3 Model Answers

A1 I remember the game of chess that I played with my junior in college. We played it at his place about two years ago.
A2 The loser was supposed to buy lunch for the winner.
A3 It seemed a bit unfair because he learned how to play chess from me and had never beaten me before.
A4 Surprisingly, his chess had improved a lot against my expectations. I captured some of his pieces, and he captured more of mine and controlled the center of the board throughout the game.
A5 I pretended to be glad that he surpassed his teacher, but I was actually so upset about losing the game. I don't think I can forget the day when my pride was hurt.

(p.86 참조)

Lesson 7 시험 대비 과정 수강하기

Activity 1 Write the correct word, phrase or sentence in English.

H1 Key expressions

1. 마음 놓고 ~하다
2. ~에 근거하여
3. 직장을 구하다
4. 공인중개사 자격시험
5. ~을 필요로 하는
6. 업계
7. ~하는데 어려운 시간을 보내다
8. 자격증
9. ~에 등록하다
10. 어려운, 힘든

H1 Answers

1. feel free to
2. based on
3. find a job
4. real estate license examination
5. necessary for
6. industry
7. have hard time ~ing
8. certificate
9. register for
10. demanding

(p.92 참조)

Activity 2 Fill in the blanks with appropriate words or clauses in the brackets to answer the question.

Q. Which classes did you take? What did you learn about test preparation? How did you prepare for the tests?

H2 Fill in blanks

The online course I took _____ five classes. Two classes were _____ real estate principles and regulations, two _____ tax systems and real estate public law, and _____ was about real estate practices. _____ the first month, the instructor gave us lectures _____ basic laws and principles on real estate, and we had to _____ all of them. Then he moved to more specific contents and _____ some examples _____ the practical application of the contents. _____ the final step, he gave us 10 sets of practice tests _____. Particularly, the practice tests helped me _____ what I had learned and _____ for the real examination. I _____ his instructions faithfully. I completed all the assignments _____ the instructors and had a review after class. I discussed some difficult questions or concepts with my friends and also _____ the message board that the online institute operated. I'm lucky that my efforts _____ by enabling me to pass the tests on the first try.

H2 Answers

1. consisted of
2. about
3. covered
4. the other
5. During
6. on
7. memorize
8. showed
9. for
10. At
11. to answer
12. review
13. get well prepared
14. followed
15. given from
16. posted on
17. paid off

(p.95 참조)

Activity 3 Come up with one sentence for each question. And then make a story combining the answers.

H3 Write your answers

Q1 Have any unexpected things happened to you while preparing for a test?

Q2 What was the situation?

Q3 How did you react?

Q4 What did you feel?

Q5 How was the result, and did it cause any problems for you to take the exam?

Your Own Answer

H3 Model Answers

A1 A few days before my licensing examination day, I had a car accident.
A2 I was driving home, and a car came suddenly around the corner without slowing down. I had no choice but to swerve quickly to the left to avoid hitting the car, which caused my car to hit the curb.
A3 Although I didn't have any external injuries, I was worried about possible after effects from the traffic accident. My left shoulder was hurt because it hit the window when my car bumped into the curb. I immediately went to a nearby orthopedic hospital, and the doctor got my shoulder X-rayed.
A4 I was really nervous while I was waiting for the result to come out.
A5 Fortunately, there were no serious problems like fractures with my shoulder. I was slightly bruised but didn't have any trouble taking the exam.

(p.98 참조)

Lesson 8 카페/커피전문점 가기

Activity 1 Write the correct word, phrase or sentence in English.

H1 Key expressions

1. 독특한
2. 아늑한
3. 유행
4. 이웃
5. 특징
6. 수용하다
7. 위치하다
8. 분위기
9. 고풍식의
10. 맛을 보다

H1 Answers

1. distinctive
2. cozy
3. trend
4. neighborhood
5. feature
6. accommodate
7. be located
8. atmosphere
9. antique
10. taste

(p.104 참조)

Activity 2 Fill in the blanks with appropriate words or clauses in the brackets to answer the question.

Q. What do people in your country do in the café or coffee shop?

H2 Fill in blanks

Ten years ago, most people _____ a café or a coffee shop _____ a meeting place. Few people _____ the café alone or _____ their laptops. As more coffee chains _____ Star Café _____, however, people have a totally different _____ a café or a coffee shop. It became a place where they study, read books, and work as well as meet people. Now _____ people sitting alone in a coffee shop. In the morning, we can often see some commuters _____ some sandwiches and coffee _____ their breakfast in the coffee shop. Recently, many coffee shops _____ brunch _____, so young couples have it on weekends. Some freelancers and students spend long hours _____ their laptops in the café, too. I sometimes go to Star Café to read a book or _____ some computer work. I think _____ coffee shops in my country will continuously increase _____.

H2 Answers

1. considered
2. simply
3. came in
4. worked on
5. like
6. have opened
7. conception of
8. it is very common to see
9. take out
10. for
11. offer
12. at a reasonable price
13. working on
14. do
15. the number of
16. for the time being

(p.107 참조)

Activity 3 Come up with one sentence for each question. And then make a story combining the answers.

H3 Write your answers

Q1 Have you ever worked at a coffee shop?

Q2 Did you have any memorable customers?

Q3 How did you react to the customer?

Q4 How did the customer react to you?

Q5 What do you think of the incident now?

Your Own Answer

H3 Model Answers

A1 When I was a university student, I worked part time at a café. I was decorating a Christmas tree in the café on December 1st.
A2 When I just finished trimming the tree, a little boy who had brunch with his mom approached me. I thought that he was interested in the antlers on my hat. I told him to touch the antlers on my hat, and he asked if my name was Rudolph.
A3 He looked so serious that I told him yes. Then he asked if I would visit him with Santa on Christmas Eve. I told him Santa and I would visit him if he was good to his parents and friends.
A4 He seemed to trust me since he looked excited and happy. He was adorable, and I hoped that his parents would leave a nice present on his pillow while he was sleeping.
A5 As I don't know if was childish, now I come to think of it, but I don't regret saying so to him.

(p.110 참조)

Lesson 9 악기 연주하기

Activity 1 Write the correct word, phrase or sentence in English.

H1 Key expressions

1. 활을 켜다
2. 잘 되다
3. 부드럽게
4. 조율하다
5. ~에게 달려있다
6. 습도
7. ~에 민감한
8. 거친
9. 아프다
10. 현

H1 Answers

1. draw a bow
2. come out right
3. smoothly
4. tune
5. depend on
6. humidity
7. sensitive to
8. rough
9. ache
10. string

(p.116 참조)

Activity 2 Fill in the blanks with appropriate words or clauses in the brackets to answer the question.

Q. Who did you learn to play the instrument from? How long have you played the instrument? How regularly do you practice?

H2 Fill in blanks

I've been _____ to play the violin in an academy called Star Piano _____ eight years. I _____ some academies near my house and _____ this academy that had more adult students _____ academy. My teacher _____ violin at university and had over five _____ students. For three years, I took a _____ lesson every Saturday for 20 minutes. She taught me basic rules _____ how to _____ the rhythm and how to read music and _____. _____, I learned how to grip the violin and the bow. She always emphasized the _____ bowing practice. I began joining group lessons five years ago. I can't get as much attention as I could in the private lesson, but I _____ to learn with others. I'm shy to play the violin _____ others, but at the same time, it's quite exciting and interesting to _____ others playing. I like playing the violin a lot, and even after class, I _____ 30 minutes or more in the academy.

H2 Answers

1. learning	2. for	3. searched	4. chose	5. than any other
6. majored in	7. years of experience teaching		8. one-on-one	9. such as
10. follow	11. so on	12. After a while	13. importance of	
14. found it enjoyable		15. in front of	16. hear	17. practice for

(p.119 참조)

Activity 3 Come up with one sentence for each question. And then make a story combining the answers.

H3 Write your answers

Q1 How did you start learning a musical instrument?

Q2 What was your intention when you started learning the instrument?

Q3 Why did you change your mind during the course of learning?

Q4 Do you think it is easy to play it?

Q5 How do you feel about playing the musical instrument these days?

Your Own Answer

H3 Model Answers

A1 Eight years ago, I just wanted to learn something new as a hobby. Playing a musical instrument would be a fun and rewarding hobby.
A2 When I took my first lesson, I never intended to learn it for so long. I planned to quit learning if I could play the violin fairly well enough.
A3 But once I started it, I became deeply into violin. I like its sound so much.
A4 Still, I feel it's hard to read new music and count rhythm. Sometimes, it takes over one year to finish just one piece.
A5 I can feel a sense of accomplishment when I finish very hard pieces and listen to the music that I'm playing. Now playing the violin is much more than a hobby for me.

(p.122 참조)

Lesson 10 신문 읽기

Activity 1 Write the correct word, phrase or sentence in English.

H1 Key expressions

1. ~을 구독하다
2. 인상적인
3. ~보다 편리한
4. 심층보도
5. 성향
6. 정치
7. 이해하다
8. 사건
9. 배달
10. 뉴스가판대

H1 Answers

1. subscribe to
2. impressive
3. more convenient than
4. in-depth coverage
5. inclination
6. politics
7. comprehend
8. incident
9. deliver
10. newsstand

(p.128 참조)

Activity 2 Fill in the blanks with appropriate words or clauses in the brackets to answer the question.

Q. How have newspapers changed over the past years? How do you see the future of the newspapers? Why do you think so?

H2 Fill in blanks

The newspapers _____ over time in many _____. _____, the layout has changed for better visual effects. Thinking of the newspaper my family _____, the way the texts, photos, and advertisements _____ on the pages _____ much better than _____ the past. The contents of newspapers have also changed. Newspapers are devoting more space to the articles on culture and art than they did _____. I think one of the greatest changes is the _____ online newspapers. As the Internet and smartphones _____, people can read almost all types of newspapers online. The change _____ the readership for printed newspapers to decline, especially among young people. Some people _____ online newspapers replace all printed newspapers in the near future, but I don't _____ this idea because people do not _____ their old ways easily for a long time to come. _____, reading online news requires us more time and effort than reading the printed version. We have to keep clicking many news headlines _____ online to find what information is in them. In the printed edition, however, we can find any information easily, just _____ the pages.

H2 Answers

1. have changed
2. aspects
3. First
4. subscribes to
5. are arranged
6. looks
7. that of
8. in the past
9. advent of
10. have developed
11. has led
12. predict
13. agree with
14. give up
15. Besides
16. displayed
17. flipping through

(p.131 참조)

Activity 3 Come up with one sentence for each question. And then make a story combining the answers.

H3 Write your answers

Q1 What role do you think newspapers should play?

_____

Q2 What feature should the newspapers have?

_____

Q3 What is the benefit of reading newspapers?

_____

Q4 What are the shortcomings of other sources of information such as web portals?

_____

Q5 How has reading the newspaper helped you?

_____

Your Own Answer

H3 Model Answers

A1 I expect newspapers to play a role of effective communication tools of our society. They enable us to know what is happening around us or in different parts worldwide.

A2 I believe that good newspapers should give their readers impartial reporting based on actual facts; therefore, they should present constructive opinions of any issues with a balanced view.

A3 We can get reliable information on various subjects. Newspapers are more trustworthy than any other source of information. Also, newspapers offer us very specific knowledge and information.

A4 Web portals often rush to report some stories or cases without ascertaining the truth. In terms of reliability, news portals or TV news do not provide as detailed analysis as newspapers do, in most cases.

A5 I am often told that I am informative and knowledgeable, and the credit should go to my habits of reading newspapers diligently.

(p.134 참조)

Lesson 11 주식투자하기

Activity 1 Write the correct word, phrase or sentence in English.

H1 Key expressions

1. 증권회사
2. 주식 거래하다
3. 가장 먼저 해야 하는 일
4. ~와 제휴한
5. 매매하다, 거래하다
6. 계좌를 개설하다
7. 주가가 어떻게 상승하고 하락하는지 보다
8. 실시간으로
9. 사람들에게 ~할 기회를 주다
10. ~에 투자하다

H1 Answers

1. securities firms
2. trade stocks
3. the very first thing to do
4. affiliated with
5. make transactions
6. open an account
7. see how their stocks have gone up and down in value
8. in real time
9. give people a chance to
10. invest in

(p.140 참조)

Activity 2 Fill in the blanks with appropriate words or clauses in the brackets to answer the question.

Q. When was the first time you invested in stocks? How much did you invest? Which stocks did you buy? Tell me the whole story from the beginning to the end.

H2 Fill in blanks

I invested a million won _____ when I got my first job right after _____ university. At that time, I didn't know where to buy stocks and how to read flow charts about stocks. _____ my friend who was working at the securities company, I opened a bank account _____ his company. Then, I started to observe the trends in stock market and tried to get news about some companies _____ their new products and how the economic situation affected those companies. A month later, I bought some shares of an automobile company. The company was _____ developing a new model of hybrid cars, and I predicted that the car would be released soon. Thus, I bought stocks of that company for 10,000 won a share. In two months, the stock price _____ 40,000 won a share, so I earned 4 _____ my initial investment. Since then, I've been more actively _____ trading stocks. I check the stock charts that show how the value of companies' stocks has _____ every day. Of course, I don't get _____ from trading stocks all the time, but I will continue investing in stocks to try to make money.

H2 Answers

1. in stocks
2. graduating from
3. With the help of
4. affiliated with
5. such as
6. in the middle of
7. soared to
8. times of
9. involved in
10. risen and fallen
11. a good return

(p.143 참조)

Activity 3 Come up with one sentence for each question. And then make a story combining the answers.

H3 Write your answers

Q1 What is your opinion about investing in stock?
_____

Q2 What made you change your view towards the stock market?
_____

Q3 So, what did you do? Did you invest in the stock market?
_____

Q4 What was the result? Did you earn or lose money?
_____

Q5 What do you feel about that experience?
_____

Your Own Answer

H3 Model Answers

A1 I had never invested more than ten million won in stocks. I thought that the more money I invest, the riskier it becomes.

A2 North Korea threatened to attack South Korea with nuclear weapons. When this happened, the stock market was greatly affected, and the prices of many stocks plummeted deeply. This, I felt instinctively, was a chance to make lots of money.

A3 I withdrew most of the money that I had and bought stocks that had greatly declined in value, but which had frequently traded at high prices when the market was better.

A4 After one year, I sold all of my stocks for three times the price I had bought it at, so I made a lot of money.

A5 I had the great timing when I invested, and that was the best decision I have ever made. I don't think this kind of opportunity will ever come again. I was so lucky to have that opportunity.

(p.146 참조)

Lesson 12 사진 촬영하기

Activity 1 Write the correct word, phrase or sentence in English.

H1 Key expressions

1. ~로 구성되다
2. ~때 장점이 드러나다
3. 모든 움직임을 잡을 수 있다
4. 이 카메라의 가장 좋은 기능
5. 빛이 자동 조정되다
6. 문제를 발생시키다
7. 이런 경우
8. 전반적으로
9. 셔터를 누르다
10. 현상하다

H1 Answers

1. be equipped with
2. it shows its charm when
3. can capture every motion
4. the most amazing feature of this camera
5. automatically adjust the lighting
6. cause problems
7. in cases like this
8. overall
9. click/press the shutter
10. develop

(p.152 참조)

Activity 2 Fill in the blanks with appropriate words or clauses in the brackets to answer the question.

Q. Cameras have changed greatly over the years. Do you remember when you first started taking pictures? How were they different from present-day cameras? How has the change affected the way you take pictures?

H2 Fill in blanks

_____ their functions, cameras have _____ radical changes over the years. In the analogue age, most cameras _____ manually, and the images they shot were _____. However, nowadays, so many digital cameras are available, and most of their functions are automatic. I was seventeen years old when I used a film camera to _____. It had been _____ me from my grandfather, and whenever I took a picture, I had to wind the film manually and adjust the focus of the lens _____ the picture I was taking. The flash was very big, and the light coming from it was quite strong. Present-day cameras are more compact and multifunctional. They adjust the light automatically, and the zoom function helps me not touch the lens every time I take a picture. Digital cameras make many things convenient. _____, images on digital cameras _____ right after taking a picture by _____ the monitor _____ the camera, so it is very _____ delete or retake photos when the pictures don't _____. Since I got _____ digital cameras, I don't think I can operate the analogue cameras _____.

H2 Answers

1. In terms of
2. gone through
3. were operated
4. black and white
5. take pictures
6. handed down to
7. depending on
8. For instance
9. can be checked
10. looking at
11. attached to
12. easy to
13. look nice
14. used to
15. anymore

(p.155 참조)

Activity 3   Come up with one sentence for each question. And then make a story combining the answers.

H3 Write your answers

Q1 Tell me about a recent trip that you brought a camera with you.
_____

Q2 What kind of troubles did you experience?
_____

Q3 What did you do to resolve the situation?
_____

Q4 How did you react towards the situation?
_____

Q5 How has the experience affected you?
_____

Your Own Answer

H3 Model Answers

A1 I traveled to Osaka, Japan, with my friends last year. I brought my digital camera with two memory cards and a tripod to take as many photos with my friends as possible.

A2 On the first day of the trip, however, I lost my tripod. Then, the next day, I forgot to bring my memory card from my hotel room, so I was not able to take many pictures. I packed all of my stuff at the hotel and checked in at the airport. While waiting to board the plane, I realized that I didn't have my camera bag.

A3 I contacted the bus driver with the help of the airport staff, but my camera was missing.

A4 I was very frustrated but had no choice but to come back home without it.

A5 Since then, I have made a habit of double-checking my belongings.

(p.158 참조)

Lesson 13 재활용

Activity 1 Write the correct word, phrase or sentence in English.

H1 Key expressions

1. 의무적인
2. 지정된, 정해진
3. A에서 B까지 다양하다
4. 재활용 쓰레기
5. 버리다
6. 재활용 쓰레기는 매주 화요일에 수거된다.
7. 꽤 엄격하게 지키다
8. 분리하다
9. 복잡하게 보이다
10. 환경을 보호하고 음식물 쓰레기 양을 줄이다

H1 Answers

1. mandatory
2. designated
3. vary from A to B
4. recyclable waste
5. dispose of
6. Recyclable waste is collected every Tuesday.
7. be fairly strict with
8. separate
9. seem complicated
10. preserve our environment and reduce the amount of food wastes

(p.164 참조)

Activity 2 Fill in the blanks with appropriate words or clauses in the brackets to answer the question.

Q. Home recycling may require some time and effort. Tell me about your own ways to save time and effort while recycling at home.

H2 Fill in blanks

I try to reduce the amount of waste I _____, which can save me time and effort when I am separating recyclable items from non-recyclable garbage. I never use paper cups or plates and try to _____ PET and glass bottles. I _____ the bottles and use them to store some food or seasonings. I hardly bring takeout food home either, which definitely causes plastic and Styrofoam waste. I also _____ spend less time and effort _____ my recyclables. I _____ all of my trash outside and started to _____ it there. It was pretty _____ and _____ to separate the recyclables from the trash in front of the recycling bins. It was also freezing outside in winter. So I _____ the idea to separate them at home. I made several recycling bags _____ Plastic, Paper, Metal, etc. Then, I _____ them _____ the terrace _____ I could _____ the items _____ each suitable bag. It _____ me only five minutes to take the separate recycling bags outside and to empty them. I'll use this way to separate my recyclables until I find a better time-saving idea.

H2 Answers

1. dispose of
2. reuse
3. rinse out
4. have my own way to
5. separating
6. used to take
7. sort
8. annoying
9. time consuming
10. came up with
11. labeled
12. put
13. on
14. so that
15. place
16. into
17. took

(p.167 참조)

Activity 3 Come up with one sentence for each question. And then make a story combining the answers.

H3 Write your answers

Q1 What did people think of recycling when you were young?

Q2 Have you participated in recycling at school?

Q3 What else did you do for recycling?

Q4 What did you think of recycling? Did you think it was important?

Q5 How did the childhood experience affect your current recycling habit?

Your Own Answer

H3 Model Answers

A1 When I was a child, not many people were very interested in recycling.
A2 I lived in Daejeon when I was in elementary school, and some students brought paper and glass bottles that were collected in school every Wednesday.
A3 My friends and I also took empty glass bottles to our local supermarkets to get refunds.
A4 I don't think I was seriously aware of the importance of saving our environment back then.
A5 But I think that those recycling experiences have led me to readily follow the current recycling system in my country.

(p.170 참조)

Lesson 14 전화 통화

Activity 1 Write the correct word, phrase or sentence in English.

H1 Key expressions

1. 전화 통화 하다
2. 스트레스를 풀다
3. 대학 친구
4. 친한, 친근한
5. 정보를 교환하다
6. 농담하다
7. 반면에
8. 고민을 털어놓다
9. 답답하고 우울할 때
10. 우리는 항상 서로를 북돋아주고 조언을 해줍니다.

H1 Answers

1. talk on the phone
2. reduce stress
3. friends from college
4. intimate
5. exchange information
6. joke around
7. on the other hand
8. get something off one's chest
9. when feeling dull and gloomy
10. We always cheer each other up and give advice to one another.

(p.176 참조)

Activity 2 Fill in the blanks with appropriate words or clauses in the brackets to answer the question.

Q. Are phone calls important for your life? Why do you think they are important? How do they affect your life?

H2 Fill in blanks

Yes, phone calls are _____ important for my life. I've been _____ my friends mostly _____ phone. Since we are _____ each other often, we need to promote our friendship by having frequent phone conversations. _____ some friends who are living in the remote country, it'd be easy to _____ them without phone calls. I personally _____ talking on the phone _____ texting when contacting my friends. Phone calls are also essential for me to work. I have few chances to have conversations with my business associates _____ _____ we have to discuss a very serious issue. We _____ most work _____ on the phone, sometimes even on weekends. We _____ exchange emails except attaching some files because we have to give and receive immediate feedback from each other. Phone calls _____ for me to _____ large and small incidents efficiently and promptly.

H2 Answers

1. surely	2. keeping in touch with	3. by	4. too busy to see
5. In case of	6. lose touch with	7. prefer	8. to
9. in person	10. unless	11. sort	12. out
13. hardly	14. make it possible	15. deal with	

(p.179 참조)

Activity 3 Come up with one sentence for each question. And then make a story combining the answers.

H3 Write your answers

Q1 Who did you frequently call when you were young?
___

Q2 What happened to the person you used to call?
___

Q3 How did you feel?
___

Q4 How did the situation turn out?
___

Q5 What do you remember about the incident?
___

Your Own Answer

H3 Model Answers

A1 When I studied in the US, I used to call my mother at 3 p.m. Seoul time every Saturday.
A2 Mom fell down last night and broke her hip joint. She was taken to the hospital by ambulance and was under operation.
A3 I couldn't help but cry in sadness and fear.
A4 Fortunately, the operation was successfully finished, and my mother was recovered soon.
A5 I still remember how astonished I was from the phone call.

(p.182 참조)

Lesson 15 집안일 거들기

Activity 1 Write the correct word, phrase or sentence in English.

H1 Key expressions

1. 가사책임을 분담하다
2. 교대로 하다
3. 누구든지
4. 아내가 음식을 만드는 반면 저는 설거지를 하고 쓰레기를 버려요.

5. 진공청소기로 집을 청소하다
6. 식료품을 사다
7. 한꺼번에
8. 이불을 개다
9. 공과금을 납부하다
10. 가사분담이 공정하다

H1 Answers

1. share/divide up household responsibilities   2. take turns   3. whoever
4. I do the dishes and take out the garbage while my wife cooks.
5. vacuum the house   6. go grocery shopping
7. at one time   8. make the bed
9. pay one's utility bills   10. The division of our housework is fair.

(p.188 참조)

Activity 2 Fill in the blanks with appropriate words or clauses in the brackets to answer the question.

Q. What were your housework responsibilities at home when you were a child? How did you handle them? How have your responsibilities at home changed as you grew up?

H2 Fill in blanks

My parents didn't have me do _____ housework or chores during my preschool years. They just told me to _____ my toys or close the refrigerator door all the way. But after I became an elementary school student, they gave me small tasks to _____ like _____ and _____. As I moved up to higher grades, my housework tasks increased and became more complex. I cleaned my room, cleared the dinner table, and folded _____. I took my clothes and socks to my dresser drawers too. During my middle and high school years, I _____ clean twice or three times a week and _____ the floor every Sunday. I sometimes _____ dishes and _____ my school uniforms too. I'm still very good at putting a _____ in my trousers with an iron. Doing housework chores was not a big _____ to me. I wanted to help my mom, so I was willing to do all the chores.

H2 Answers

1. specific
2. put away
3. handle
4. making the bed
5. setting the dining table
6. a load of laundry
7. swept the garden
8. vacuumed
9. washed
10. ironed
11. crease
12. hassle

(p.191 참조)

Activity 3 Come up with one sentence for each question. And then make a story combining the answers.

H3 Write your answers

Q1 What did you think of household responsibilities when you were young?

Q2 What kind of household work did you do and how did it make you feel?

Q3 What task was difficult for you?

Q4 What kind of household work do you do nowadays?

Q5 What do you feel about the responsibilities?

Your Own Answer

H3 Model Answers

A1 As for my household responsibilities that I had during my childhood, I didn't feel them that challenging.

A2 Putting a napkin and silverware on the table or folding some clothes was not a difficult task at all.

A3 I had a responsibility that was tough for me. It was to take care of my little brother and help him with study.

A4 When it comes to my housework that I'm currently doing, I don't mind washing dishes and vacuuming the house.

A5 I don't like cleaning the bathroom. It is kind of hard work. Mopping the floor, cleaning the walls and a big mirror, and getting rid of germs in the toilet with a brush are just endless work.

(p.194 참조)

Lesson 16 테크놀로지

Activity 1 Write the correct word, phrase or sentence in English.

H1 Key expressions

1. 기술적인 기기 _____
2. ~함으로써 하루를 시작한다 _____
3. ~을 가능하게 하다 _____
4. 이 메일로 고객들 및 거래처에게 연락한다 _____
5. ~가 아니었다면(없다면) _____
6. 직접 _____
7. 온라인 상에서 의사소통을 할 수 있게 하다 _____
8. 휴가 결재를 받다 _____
9. 시행하다 _____
10. 최첨단 테크놀로지 _____

H1 Answers

1. technological equipment
2. start the day by
3. enable
4. contact with clients and associates by email
5. if it were not for
6. in person
7. make it possible to communicate with each other online
8. get approval to take leave
9. implement
10. up-to-date technology

(p.200 참조)

Activity 2
Fill in the blanks with appropriate words or clauses in the brackets to answer the question.

Q. How has technology changed at work over the years? How has the change affected your life at work?

H2 Fill in blanks

There are many changes that the development of technology _____ in my work life. Among these changes, I'd like to talk about _____ we share information with _____. About 10 years ago, when I had to attend a meeting and share documents with other staff members, I printed meeting handouts and the documents or photocopied the original documents. But as useful online storage services have _____ over the years, we share most of our work online. _____, we actively use Webstore, which _____ us to share documents with others _____ we share the ID and password. When one person uploads a file onto Webstore, the others can _____ the file anytime and download it to _____ it. _____, we _____ print the handouts and documents to give the others. That reduces paper waste and expenses _____ saves time. I'm pretty much _____ the technology I use today, but I predict it'll be further developed, which will keep changing the way we do our jobs.

H2 Answers

1. has caused
2. the way
3. one another
4. sprung up
5. For example
6. allows
7. as long as
8. access
9. look through
10. As a result
11. no longer
12. as well as
13. satisfied with

(p.203 참조)

Activity 3 Come up with one sentence for each question. And then make a story combining the answers.

H3 Write your answers

Q1 Was there any time that your technology did not work properly?
___

Q2 What were you supposed to do with the technology?
___

Q3 What happened? What was the problem?
___

Q4 How did you feel?
___

Q5 How did the incident end?
___

Your Own Answer

H3 Model Answers

A1 I'd like to talk about an incident that took place last fall.
A2 I was supposed to make a presentation in front of some clients who came from Australia.
A3 I turned on my computer to open the files about 15 minutes before the presentation, but I couldn't find the files anywhere on the computer.
A4 The clients were waiting outside the conference room, and my boss shouted at me in anger. I got into a panic, thinking that I should submit my resignation.
A5 All of sudden, it occurred to me that I had a cloud server. I logged in with my cloud account, and, thankfully, all of the texts in the file were saved there. Fortunately, I made my presentation on time, and my clients were satisfied with it. It was a terrible experience that I never want to go through again.

(p.206 참조)

Lesson 17 지역 행사

Activity 1 Write the correct word, phrase or sentence in English.

H1 Key expressions

1. 전국적으로
2. 열리다, 개최되다
3. 대단한 성공을 거뒀다.
4. 장관인, 극적인
5. 주의를 끌다
6. 참여하다
7. 벼룩시장
8. 기금을 모으다
9. 지역사회를 홍보하다
10. 나는 다음에 이 전시회가 열릴 때도 참가할 것이다.

H1 Answers

1. on a national scale
2. take place
3. It was a great success.
4. spectacular
5. catch one's attention well
6. take part in
7. flea market
8. raise funds
9. promote community networking
10. I will attend the exhibition the next time it takes place.

(p.212 참조)

Activity 2 Fill in the blanks with appropriate words or clauses in the brackets to answer the question.

Q. What was the most memorable event in your community? When was it held and where did it happen? What made you think it's memorable?

H2 Fill in blanks

It was in 2011 _____ I found an interesting fundraising event. That year I was staying in Virginia in the US to _____ my master's degree. The event _____ help the Japanese recover from the damage _____ an earthquake and tsunami of the year. _____ local elementary schools, the community center put the notice of the fundraising event on their bulletin boards. The event was called "Penny War," which took the format of a competition among classes. All students could _____ this event, and each class collected pennies from the students for a month. Then the schools submitted it to the community center, which _____, announced the winner of the contest. Young children actively _____ this event and tried to collect _____ many pennies _____ they could. The community center successfully _____ and also taught their students how they could help others _____. Even though that community did not _____ my country, I've kept that event _____. I want to organize such a fundraiser, maybe under a different name and purpose, in the future.

H2 Answers

1. when
2. study for
3. aimed to
4. caused by
5. Cooperating with
6. take part in
7. in turn
8. participated in
9. as
10. as
11. achieved its goals
12. in need
13. belong to
14. in mind

(p.215 참조)

Activity 3 Come up with one sentence for each question. And then make a story combining the answers.

H3 Write your answers

Q1 What kind of event was held in your community?

Q2 What did you do at the event?

Q3 What was the community event for? What was the purpose?

Q4 When and where did the event take place?

Q5 How did the event go? Did it go well?

Your Own Answer

H3 Model Answers

A1 A few months ago, I participated in the charity fundraiser held by my church.

A2 It was a type of bazaar, and I took a task of selling children's clothing.

A3 All profits from this bazaar went to purchasing some medicine and first aid supplies for children in Cambodia.

A4 The charity event was started at 11 a.m. in the front yard of the church, and many people voluntarily worked for it.

A5 Even though the place was not spacious enough to accommodate many people, the charity itself was successfully finished. Most items were sold, and we got a substantial amount of money. As a result, that event gave me a memorable and valuable experience.

(p.218 참조)

Lesson 18 국내여행

Activity 1 Write the correct word, phrase or sentence in English.

H1 Key expressions

1. 시간이 날 때마다
2. 숨이 멎을 듯한
3. ~에 더해서, 더불어서
4. 국립공원
5. 꼭대기에
6. ~가 많은
7. ~로 올라가는 길에
8. 특산품
9. 충전이 되다
10. 내가 좋아하는 또 다른 걷는 장소는

H1 Answers

1. whenever I have some time off
2. breathtaking
3. in addition to
4. national park
5. at the top
6. plenty of
7. on the way up
8. specialties
9. refresh one's mind
10. another favorite hiking place of mine is

(p.224 참조)

Activity 2 Fill in the blanks with appropriate words or clauses in the brackets to answer the question.

Q. How do you prepare for a trip in your country? What do you do before you go on the trip?

H2 Fill in blanks

There are many things to _____ before _____ a trip. Making a complete itinerary _____ is the first thing that I do. Determining which places I want to go makes me _____ and know what to bring on the trip. Once I _____, I make my travel reservations. _____ my trip to Jeju Island as an example, many travel agencies and airlines offer good _____ on airfare, so I can compare the prices to find the most reasonable one. After _____ my flight _____, I _____ a hotel and rental car next. The location of the hotel is crucial. It should be _____ I am going to visit. I normally rent a car at the airport and drive to the hotel. After deciding on my transportation and accommodations, I start _____. Since I spend most of my time there hiking on Jeju Island, I pack climbing clothes, hiking boots, and other necessary equipment. I also always bring my GPS and a local map since they are essential and useful when _____. This is what I basically do before _____.

H2 Answers

1. consider
2. going on
3. from the beginning to the end
4. plan my budget
5. set the departure date
6. To mention
7. deals
8. making
9. arrangements
10. book
11. close to the attractions
12. packing
13. driving around
14. going on a trip

(p.227 참조)

Activity 3 Come up with one sentence for each question. And then make a story combining the answers.

H3 Write your answers

Q1 What do people worry about most when traveling?

Q2 What do people do to feel better?

Q3 What else do people worry about when going on a trip?

Q4 Have you ever done something to feel more secure before leaving for a trip?

Q5 What do you think of such efforts people take to feel more secure?

Your Own Answer

H3 Model Answers

A1 When people go on a trip, they are considering many things, including safety and expenses. The biggest concerns they have may be their safety while on their trip.
A2 For a safe and secure trip, they normally buy travel insurance, which can cover injuries and emergency situations for the duration of the trip.
A3 People can also be concerned that burglars may break into their empty house during their trip.
A4 My family is no exception, so we ask our next-door neighbor to pick up our newspapers while we are away.
A5 All of these activities can be done with just a few minutes' care and effort, and they will make you feel comfortable during your trip.

(p.230 참조)

Lesson 19 해외출장

Activity 1 Write the correct word, phrase or sentence in English.

H1 Key expressions

1. ~인 것 같다
2. ~에 문제가 생기다
3. 불량품
4. 만약을 대비해서
5. 발표를 하다
6. 늦어도
7. 큰 문제가 생겼어요.
8. 우리 오후 5시에 만나기로 되어 있죠, 그렇죠?
9. 계속 켜지고 꺼지는 것을 반복한다
10. 내 전화기가 작동하지 않을 걸 대비해서

H1 Answers

1. it appears that
2. have trouble with
3. a defective device
4. just in case
5. make a presentation
6. at latest
7. I'm in big trouble here.
8. We are supposed to meet at 5 pm, aren't we?
9. keep turning on and off
10. in case my phone is not working

(p.236 참조)

Activity 2 Fill in the blanks with appropriate words or clauses in the brackets to answer the question.

Q. I'm sorry, but there is a problem you need to resolve. Your boss told you the new sample won't arrive until tonight, but you need to use it when you meet your business associate this afternoon. Call him or her and explain your situation including some alternatives to solve the problem.

H2 Fill in blanks

Hello, Mr. Thomson? _____ Min Woo Kim from Jaeil Electronics Corporation. I'm supposed to _____ to you this afternoon. I _____ introduce the Nobo PTR3 that will _____ next month during the presentation. But unfortunately, the device that I brought is not _____, which makes it impossible to present it to you today. Could we _____ the presentation _____ tomorrow? Another device is _____ and will arrive here tonight, so I can visit your office anytime tomorrow. If you are only _____ today, then I'll visit you today _____ and give you the general instruction of the product. Then, I'll just leave the sample device at your office tomorrow. You can review it whenever you're _____. I really apologize to you _____ and hope you will understand my situation. Please call me back if you get this message. Thank you.

H2 Answers

1. This is
2. make a presentation
3. am expecting to
4. come into the market
5. functioning properly
6. push back
7. until
8. in the mail
9. available
10. as scheduled
11. free
12. for the inconvenience

(p.239 참조)

Activity 3 Come up with one sentence for each question. And then make a story combining the answers.

H3 Write your answers

Q1 Have you ever been on a business trip?
___

Q2 What was the purpose of the trip?
___

Q3 What were you expected to do during the meeting?
___

Q4 Did you have any difficulty during your business trip?
___

Q5 How did it end? Do you have any regrets?
___

Your Own Answer

H3 Model Answers

A1 I went on a three-day business trip to Frankfurt in Germany when I just started working for my company.
A2 The purpose of the trip was to join the Frankfurt trade show and meet some foreign businessmen.
A3 During the meeting, I had to introduce my company and our new products briefly.
A4 Since my English was not that good, I often stuttered especially when I had to answer their questions. What's worse, the conference hall, where the trade show was held, was too huge to find the right location of the booth that I had to drop by. I ended up being 15 minutes late for the last meeting.
A5 Fortunately, I managed to finish my business trip without a serious problem, but I still wish I had completed my task better at that time.

(p.242 참조)

Lesson 20 해외여행

Activity 1 Write the correct word, phrase or sentence in English.

H1 Key expressions

1. 4일간의 여행
2. ~가 가능한가?
3. 그렇다면
4. 경제적인
5. 가격 차이가 얼마나 되나요?
6. 단체여행을 가다
7. 나는 ~인지가 궁금하다
8. 미리 감사 드린다.
9. 여행 일정을 짜다
10. 관광의 최소 인원은 몇 사람입니까?

H1 Answers

1. a 4-day trip
2. is it possible to
3. if it is
4. economical
5. What's the price difference?
6. go on a package tour
7. I'm wondering if
8. Thank you in advance.
9. plan one's trip/itinerary
10. What is the minimum number of people on a tour?

(p.248 참조)

Activity 2 Fill in the blanks with appropriate words or clauses in the brackets to answer the question.

Q. I'm sorry, but there is a problem you need to resolve. When you arrived at the airport, you found that your flight has been canceled. Unfortunately, all the other flights are booked, too. Call your travel agency and explain your situation including three alternatives to solve the problem.

H2 Fill in blanks

Hello, Mr. Yoon? This is Hyun Min Kim. I called to let you _____ this unexpected, ridiculous situation. When we _____ at the airport, we found that our flight has been canceled _____ mechanical troubles. _____, all the other flights have been booked today! We're now very frustrated, but I want to get our travel plans _____ if possible. Would you call the reservation hotline for more exact information? They could _____ us _____ the waiting list for the flight. If that's not possible, please check about the next available flight we can take. We don't have to _____ this trip if we _____ our destination tomorrow. But _____, you need to pay for a hotel stay near the airport since we came from Cheongju to Incheon. If there is no available flight tomorrow, we will cancel our trip, so you need to _____ us a full _____ for the tickets we bought. I'd also like you to _____ for our lost vacation. The transportation and hotel cancelation fees will be surely additional. Call me back _____.

H2 Answers

1. know about
2. were about to check in
3. due to
4. What is worse
5. back in order
6. put
7. on
8. give up
9. leave for
10. even so
11. give
12. refund
13. provide compensation
14. as soon as possible

(p.251 참조)

Activity 3 Come up with one sentence for each question. And then make a story combining the answers.

H3 Write your answers

Q1 Which overseas trip do you remember most?

Q2 Who did you go on the trip with?

Q3 When did an unexpected, surprising incident happen?

Q4 Tell me about the incident in as much detail as possible.

Q5 How did it end?

Your Own Answer

H3 Model Answers

A1 My friend and I took a package tour to Siem Reap in Cambodia five years ago.
A2 We had seven members all nice and gentle in our tour group. The tour was accompanied by an experienced local guide.
A3 The incident took place on the second day of the tour.
A4 We got off the tour bus and walked from temples to temples to observe awesome ruins and Khmer art. But as times went by, I got more exhausted, sweating a lot from the heat. I felt dizzy and my arms and legs felt weak. I nearly fainted when my friend was surprised to see my pale face.
A5 We ended up stopping the tour and returned to the hotel. I felt better after resting in bed, but I felt so guilty about interrupting the tour.

(p.254 참조)

Memo

Memo

Memo

OPIc 대비 멀티캠퍼스 Best 온라인 과정

OPIc 전략과정
美ACTFL과의 공동연구 기반의 OPIc 전략 과정

한국인의 말하기 특징 분석 IL공략	한국인의 말하기 특징 분석 IM공략	한국인의 말하기 특징 분석 IH공략	한국인의 말하기 특징 분석 AL공략

OPIc 등급공략과정
OPIc 주관사 멀티캠퍼스에서 제시하는 레벨별 맞춤 공략 과정

New OPIc 첫걸음	New OPIc SOS Start	New OPIc SOS IM공략	New OPIc의 정석! IH공략

OPIc 실전과정
OPIc 최고 강사진이 전하는 최신 경향의 실전 대비 과정

OPIc IL Master	OPIc IM Master	OPIc IH Master
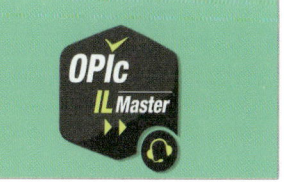		

OPIc 특화과정
니즈에 따라 선택 가능한 맞춤 특화 과정

막판뒤집기 2주 완성 학생편/직장인편	OPIc 모의테스트	Talklish OPIc IL/IM/IH

중국어 대비 멀티캠퍼스 Best 온라인 과정

新BCT 대비 멀티캠퍼스 Best 온라인 과정

과정 특징
- BCT 평가 주관사 멀티캠퍼스에서 제시하는 고득점 전략
- 새롭게 바뀐 BCT(Business Chinese Test) 문제 유형 완벽 분석
- 엄선된 빈출 문제 풀이를 통한 실전 감각 UP
- 비즈니스 핵심 어휘 및 표현 학습을 통한 비즈니스 중국어 회화 능력 향상

| 초단기 新BCT Speaking 공략 | 초단기 新BCT Speaking 실전테스트 | 新BCT 첫걸음 A형 공략 | 新BCT 첫걸음 B형 공략 |

OPIc 중국어 대비 멀티캠퍼스 Best 온라인 과정

과정 특징
- OPIc 평가 주관사 멀티캠퍼스에서 개발한 국내 유일무이한 OPIc 중국어 대비 과정
- 최신 경향을 반영한 빈출 문제 및 OPIc 중국어 전문가가 제시하는 고득점 전략
- 시험장에서 바로 활용할 수 있는 핵심 패턴 및 어휘 제공
- OPIc 레벨 달성과 중국어 회화 실력 향상을 동시에 만족시켜 주는 과정

| New OPIc 중국어 첫걸음 | OPIc 중국어의 정석! IM공략 | OPIc 중국어의 정석! IH공략 |

TSC 대비 멀티캠퍼스 Best 온라인 과정

과정 특징
- 최신 시험 경향을 반영한 국내 최고의 TSC 대비 과정
- 단기간에 레벨 UP! 하기 위한 핵심 전략과 유형별 공략법 제시
- 실제 시험과 유사한 실전테스트 제공
- 다양한 표현과 문장 확장 연습을 통한 중국어 회화 실력 향상

| 한달에 끝내는 TSC 첫걸음 3급공략 | 한달에 끝내는 TSC 실전테스트 | 초단기 TSC 4급공략 | 초단기 TSC 4급공략 실전테스트 |

온라인 교육과정 문의 TEL 1544-9001 | Website www.opic.co.kr